The One Year Book of Devotions for Boys

The ONE YEAR® BOOK OF

Devotions for Boys

TYNDALE KIDS

Tyndale House Publishers, Inc., Wheaton, Illinois

Visit Tyndale's exciting Web site at www.tyndale.com

Edited by Debbie Bible and Betty Free

Designed by Jackie Noe

Stories written by Katherine R. Adams, Hope L. Aderman, Susan S. Arcand, Elzena A. Arguello, Esther M. Bailey, Melissa M. Bamberg, Trula H. Bensinger, Judith K. Boogaart, Carol J. Brookman, Jean A. Burns, Linda E. Champagne, Dorothy T. Clemmens, Janet W. Cobb, Karen E. Cogan, Lisa D. Cowman, V. Louise Cunningham, Linda J. Dahlin, Tracy J. Ellifrits, M. Tanya Ferdinandusz, Patricia L. Fitch, Rose Goble, Jorlyn A. Grasser, D. Anne Gross, Veronica R. Guerriero, Jan L. Hansen, Lynn Hansen, Cindy Huff, Ruth I. Jay, Gail L. Jenner, Dean Kelley, Beverly Kenniston, Nance E. Keyes, Phyllis I. Klomparens, Sherry L. Kuyt, VaDonna J. Leaf, Jacqueline J. Leaycraft, Kathy Lehey, Linda L. Leonard, Agnes G. Livezey, H. Lee Mack, Richard S. Maffeo, Deborah S. Marett, Hazel W. Marett, Eunice C. Matchett, Della D. May, Beverly McClain, Ruth McQuilken, Gloria D. Morrison, Gordon Muscott, Sara L. Nelson, Violet E. Nesdoly, Mary Rose Pearson, Carolyn A. Penner, Raelene E. Phillips, Connie I. Rainbolt, Victoria L. Reinhardt, L. Gail Rhodes, Barbara Riegier, Phyllis Robinson, Deana L. Rogers, Lucinda J. Rollings, Catherine Runyon, Doris L. Seger, Rhonda S. Sherrill, Marie Shropshire, Georgia L. Smelser, Steven R. Smith, Linda R. Stai, Lynn Stamm-Rex, Heather M. Tekavec, Gayle J. Thorn, Elizabeth L. Toner, Jennifer Townsend, Harry C. Trover, Tom VandenBerg, Charles VanderMeer, Sandra K. Vaughn, Elisient M. Vernon, Geri Walcott, Linda M. Weddle, Barbara J. Westberg, Jane Weverink, Deborah L. Whitsitt, Carolyn E. Yost, Susan I. Zampich, Rose R. Zediker

Authors' initials appear at the end of each story.

All stories are taken from issues of *Keys for Kids*, published bimonthly by the Children's Bible Hour, P. O. Box 1, Grand Rapids, Michigan 49501.

Library of Congress Cataloging-in-Publication Data

One year book of devotions for boys.
    p. cm.
    Includes index.
    Summary: Presents stories for meditation, memory verses from Scripture, and questions to internalize the messages for each day of the year.
    ISBN 0-8423-3620-6
    1. Boys—Religious life—Juvenile literature.   2. Devotional calendars—Juvenile literature. [1. Devotional calendars. 2. Christian life.] I. Title: Devotions for boys. II. Tyndale House Publishers.
BV4541.2 .O54 2000
242'.62—dc21
                                          00-028667

Printed in the United States of America.

07 06 05 04 03 02 01 00
7   6   5   4   3   2   1

Table of Contents

Introduction

For many years Children's Bible Hour has published *Keys for Kids,* a bimonthly devotional magazine for kids. Parents and children have appreciated their fine ministry over the years, and Tyndale House is proud to present this new collection of stories from *Keys for Kids.*

The One Year Book of Devotions for Boys has a full year's worth of stories that boys will find especially interesting. Each story illustrates a Scripture reading for the day, and following each one is a "How about You?" section. This asks boys to apply the story to their lives.

There is also a memory verse for each day, often taken from the Scripture reading. Unless otherwise noted, memory verses are quoted from the *New Living Translation.* Verses marked NIV are from the *New International Version,* while those marked NKJV are from the *New King James Version.* You may want to encourage your boys to memorize each verse as it appears, or you can have them use the Bible translation your family prefers.

Each devotion ends with a key phrase. This three- to five-word phrase summarizes the lesson and helps boys know how to respond to it.

The stories in this devotional are geared toward boys between the ages of six and ten. Your sons can enjoy these stories by themselves as they develop their own daily quiet time. (You can supervise that time as much or as little as you wish.) Or the stories can be used as part of your family devotions. Like stories from the Bible, the stories here speak not only to children, but also to adults. They are simple, direct, and concrete. And they speak to everyone in understandable terms, just as Jesus' parables do.

This book contains Scripture indexes of daily readings and of memory verses, as well as a topical index. The Scripture indexes are helpful for locating a story or verse related to a passage that you want to discuss. The topical index is useful for dealing with concerns that arise in any family, such as health, relationships, telling the truth, and trusting God.

We hope you'll use this book every day, but don't feel locked into any one format. Please use any story any time you feel it relates to a special situation in your family.

Wonderfully Made

(Read Genesis 1:26-28)

Lee reached for a book, opened it curiously, then muttered, "Brett gave me this book to read, but I didn't know it was like this! It makes fun of God and people who believe in him. I need to talk to Brett."

The next evening Brett came to see Lee's new pups. While they were outside, the boys talked about the billions of stars and how God knows each one by name. "But these aren't his greatest works of creation," said Dad as he stepped out onto the porch. "Come inside. I want to show you something." They went into the house, and Dad showed them a picture.

"It's just a person," said Lee.

"Yes," agreed Dad, "but people are the greatest of all creation. Think about your bodies. Did you know your spine can support five hundred pounds?"

"And look at the heart," Lee put in. "We learned in school that it's no larger than a fist, yet it pumps blood at the rate of around four thousand gallons a day."

Dad grinned. "Right! Now look at your hands. Do you notice that the palms are sort of skid proof so you can get a grip on things? And think of all your fingers can do. God and his works are nothing to make fun of."

Brett was surprised. "What do you mean?"

Lee explained. "The book you gave me to read the other day makes fun of God and people who believe in him. I don't think it's a good book to read."

Brett answered, "I agree. I hadn't read it myself yet. But all the other kids are reading it. If you give it to me, I'll return it to the library. I don't want to be making fun of God."

"Me either," said Lee. "Let's go to the library together." *AGL*

HOW ABOUT YOU?

Are you ever tempted to make fun of God because your friends do? Think about how wonderfully he made your body and how much he loves you. Then ask him to help you stand up for him.

Never Make Fun of God or His Works

2

A "Life Puzzle"

(Read Isaiah 55:8-11)

Grandma looked at the puzzle Rebecca was working. "I like horses," she said.

"So do I," said Rebecca. "I'm excited about moving right next to a horse ranch!"

Grandma nodded and then looked at Rebecca's brother, Aaron, who was reading a sports magazine. "How about you, Aaron?" she asked. "Have you met any boys your age?"

"No," replied Aaron. "And I'm not excited about moving. I'll miss all my friends here . . . and I'll miss you and Grandpa, too."

Grandma put an arm around Aaron's shoulder. "I'll miss you, too," said Grandma, "but I know God has great things planned for you in your new place."

Rebecca suddenly stomped her foot. "Oh-h-h!" she exclaimed. "I know this piece goes here. It's the right color and everything." She tried again to make the piece fit.

Grandma looked at the piece Rebecca was holding. "It does look right," she said, "but you better look for a different piece." She pointed. "Try that piece over there, Rebecca."

"This one?" asked Rebecca, picking up another puzzle piece. She tried it in the space. "This one doesn't fit, either," she said.

"Turn it the other way," said Aaron, who was watching.

Rebecca turned the puzzle piece. "Hey! It *does* fit," she cried.

Grandma smiled. "In some ways, life is like a puzzle," she said, looking at Aaron. "Sometimes, it's hard for us to understand what God is doing, but slowly the pieces begin to fit into place."

"But why can't staying here be a piece of my life puzzle?" asked Aaron.

Grandma shook her head. "I don't know," she said. "But I do know that sometimes we try to force a piece into the puzzle that doesn't fit."

"And staying here may be one of those pieces?" asked Aaron slowly.

Grandma nodded. "Sometimes God's way seems painful," she said. "But there's one thing that I have learned: God is faithful, and he will work everything out." *GDM*

HOW ABOUT YOU?

Do you wonder why God allows certain things to happen in your life? Talk to him about it. Let him know how you feel. Even if you are angry, God wants to hear from you. And remember, you don't always need to understand what is happening in your life. But as you come to accept what he allows, he will take the pieces of your life and fit them together to make something beautiful.

MEMORIZE:

"Trust in the Lord with all your heart; do not depend on your own understanding." Proverbs 3:5

Trust God with Everything

Three Little Kittens

(Read Psalm 32:6-11)

Scott came into the living room carrying his white kitten, Snowflake, who purred and snuggled comfortably in his arms. "I'm so glad you let me keep this kitten, even though we already had two cats," he told his parents. "Snowflake is the only one that will let me pick her up and carry her anywhere I go." He sat down on the sofa, and Snowflake curled beside him. "See, she'll just peacefully rest here beside me."

Mom smiled at them. "Well, Scott, you've been so gentle with her ever since she was tiny," she said.

"I know," answered Scott, "but I'm just the same with Inkspot, and she howls and cries the whole time I hold her. She's so nervous and jittery. She just waits for a chance to run off."

Dad nodded. "She's that way with all of us," he said.

"Maybe that's because she had a rough 'kittenhood' before we got her," suggested Mother. "We've taken good care of her for all these years, and yet she's never learned to trust us completely."

"And that Tangerine!" added Scott. "I never even try to pick him up, because I don't want to be scratched!"

Dad put his newspaper down. "These three cats remind me of the ways people react to God's 'picking them up' and placing them where he wants them," he said slowly. "Think about it—which one do you think you're like?"

Scott looked at Snowflake, still lying peacefully beside him, and grinned. "I hope I'm like Snowflake," he decided, "content to be wherever God puts me."

Mother nodded. "But I'm afraid that once in a while we're more like Inkspot—nervous about everything that happens, or like Tangerine—too full of our own plans."

"We can all pray for grace to be content where God has placed us," said Dad with a smile. "We're happy as we trust him." *RSS*

HOW ABOUT YOU?

Has God placed you in a difficult spot—such as a broken home, a new school, or a class you don't enjoy? Don't be nervous and jittery about your circumstances, waiting for a chance to go a different way. And don't be so full of your own plans that you can't trust God and be content in his plan. God loves you, and he knows best. Trust him.

Trust God

MEMORIZE:

"The Sovereign Lord, the Holy One of Israel, says, "Only in returning to me and waiting for me will you be saved. In quietness and confidence is your strength." Isaiah 30:15

Log on the Fire

(Read Ecclesiastes 4:9-12)

"I don't think I'll go to church tomorrow," said Rodney. He was lying on the floor in front of the fireplace, watching the flames shooting toward the chimney.

Dad put down his newspaper. "Why is that?" he asked. "We let you stay home last Sunday because you had a sore throat. What is it this time?"

Rodney rolled over on his back. "Dad, I've gone to church all my life," he said. "Why do I have to listen to the same things over and over again?" As he saw Dad frown, he quickly added, "I can read my Sunday school lesson and do my workbook here at home just as well, can't I? I'll be glad when I'm old enough to do what I want to do," Rodney mumbled to himself. The fire crackled cheerfully for a while, but then it died down to a few embers. "There's one log left, Dad. Shall I put it on the fire?" Rodney asked.

Dad shook his head. "Just let it burn there in the wood carrier by itself."

Rodney stared. "You're kidding, aren't you?" he asked. "That log won't burn unless it's put in the fireplace," he said. He sat up and gave Dad a quizzical look. "Oh . . . you're trying to tell me something, aren't you?" he asked, a bit puzzled.

Dad chuckled. "Yep," he admitted. "Just like that log needs to be placed with the other logs in the fireplace, a Christian needs to be with other Christians. God tells us in his Word not to neglect getting together with them. We can grow by studying the Bible by ourselves, but God knows we also need to fellowship with other believers."

Rodney stood up. "All right," he said with a sigh. "I get the point. I'll be ready for church tomorrow." *BK*

HOW ABOUT YOU?

Do you grumble about going to church? Or do you go cheerfully because you love God and want to learn more about him? Thank God for the opportunity he has given you to fellowship and grow with other Christians.

MEMORIZE:

"Think of ways to encourage one another to outbursts of love and good deeds. And let us not neglect our meeting together. . . ."
Hebrews 10:24-25

Attend Church Faithfully

A Bad Day

(Read Matthew 6:6-13)

When Jared slammed his bedroom door, Mother knew something was wrong. She found him sitting on the edge of his bed crying. "What's the trouble, Son?" she asked gently as she sat down beside him.

Jared sniffed. "Well . . . I had a rotten day," he told her. "I got a D on my English test—the one I spent an hour studying for. And now it's raining, and I've got to bag all my papers before I deliver them!"

"Well, honey, I'm sorry you've had a tough time," said Mother putting her hand on his shoulder. "Tell you what . . . I'll help you study for your next test. English was my favorite subject, so we'll see if we can bring that grade up. As for your paper route, I can help you bag your papers tonight . . . and I'll even drive you."

As Mother helped Jared with his papers, he told her about other problems he was having at school, especially in gym class. "I'm just not good at that stuff," he said. Mother encouraged him to do his best, and he felt better after talking with her.

Before climbing into bed, Jared began to say the little rhyme prayer he had learned when he was small, but it seemed so empty—he was too big for that. *What should I say instead?* he wondered. As he thought over the events of the day, he remembered his mother's concern for him. She really loved him and was interested in what went on, and she had reminded him that God cared for him, too. *I guess I can talk to God just like I talk to Mom!* thought Jared.

Before he knew it, Jared was talking to God—telling him about the day. He told God about his bad grade and the guys in gym. He asked God to help him do better in basketball and with his schoolwork. He thanked God for parents to love and care for him, and he thanked God for his care, too. After Jared finished praying, he felt much better. He decided to talk with God more often! *KL*

HOW ABOUT YOU?

Are there times when you're not sure what to pray about? Do you ever feel as though praying won't help? Just remember that God cares for you, and you can talk to him as you would to your parents or to your closest friend. God has the power to help you in all areas of your life.

MEMORIZE:

"O my people, trust in him at all times. Pour out your heart to him, for God is our refuge." Psalm 62:8

Pray—God Cares

The Guest Book

(Read Revelation 21:22-27)

Megan was excited because she was in charge of the guest book at her Aunt Sally's wedding. As the guests filed past, she very politely asked each one, "Will you sign the guest book, please?"

Suddenly a big, deep voice boomed out, "Well, here's my little niece, nearly all grown up." It was Megan's Uncle Joe, who was in the army. He was her favorite relative, and today he looked more handsome than ever in his uniform. "I see they have you on guest book duty today," said Uncle Joe with a smile. "That's a mighty important job. Here's a riddle for you: Where is the most important 'guest book' of all?" He tweaked her chin. "You have until after you get off duty to think about it."

After the wedding, Megan looked for her uncle and sat down beside him. "I've got the answer," she said. "The most important guest book is in the White House."

Uncle Joe laughed and shook his head. "Good try," he said, "but wrong. The most important guest book is in heaven."

"In heaven?" asked Megan. "There's a guest book there?"

"The Bible tells us of a Book of Life," replied Uncle Joe. "It says that to enter heaven, our names must be written in that book."

"Do we write them in when we get there?" Megan asked.

"Oh, no," said Uncle Joe. "Your name has to be there so you can get into heaven."

"Well, how do we get it written there?" asked Megan.

"By believing in the Lord Jesus Christ," replied Uncle Joe. "Have you asked Jesus to be your Savior?" Megan nodded and Uncle Joe smiled. "Then your name's there," he said, "in the most important guest book of all!" *CEY*

HOW ABOUT YOU?

Have you asked Jesus to forgive your sin and be your Savior? He wants to write your name in the Book of Life so that you may some day join him in heaven and be happy forever.

MEMORIZE:

"But don't rejoice just because evil spirits obey you; rejoice because your names are registered as citizens of heaven." Luke 10:20

Accept Jesus as Savior

Weapons and Words

(Read James 3:8-10)

"Oh, how I love Jesus," sang Rame. "Oh, how I love . . . Stop it! Leave him alone. He's my pet, not yours!" Rame stopped singing to yell at his little sister. She was wiggling her fingers around in the chameleon's terrarium home. Rame reached over to pull Nisha's hand from the bowl. "Don't ever play with my chameleon again, you hear?" Then . . . CRASH! The terrarium plunged to the floor. "Now look what you've done!" yelled Rame hatefully. "Nisha, you are so clumsy!" He began to pick up the twigs and leaves that had spilled onto the floor. Dad, who saw and heard what happened, spoke sternly to Rame, but Nisha ran toward her bedroom, sobbing.

That afternoon, Rame's friend Josef came to play. Rame proudly showed Josef his new chameleon. "He eats bugs," said Rame, dropping a few into the terrarium.

Josef watched. "Hey!" he said after a few minutes. "Where did those bugs go? One minute I saw them, and the next . . . they're gone!"

"He's probably eaten them," said Rame.

"Really? I didn't see him," Josef replied. "I was watching, too."

"A chameleon's tongue is as fast as lightning," explained Rame. "God made their tongues like weapons so they could easily lash out and capture their prey."

"Sounds like some people I know," said Josef. "They like to use their tongues like weapons to hurt others."

Rame nodded. Then he thought about how he had yelled at his sister earlier. "Josef, you stay here a minute," Rame said. "I need to go do something." Rame walked to Nisha's room and knocked on the door.

When Nisha answered, Rame went in and apologized for his hurtful words. *LJR*

HOW ABOUT YOU?

Do you say hurtful things to others? Do you call your brothers and sisters names? The old saying, "Sticks and stones can break my bones, but words will never hurt me," is not true. What we say does hurt others—sometimes for a long time. Be careful with your words.

Don't Wound with Words

MEMORIZE:
"Some people make cutting remarks, but the words of the wise bring healing." Proverbs 12:18

What a Bird!

(Read Psalm 28)

Kent and Jessie were having a great time on a weeklong visit to their grandparents' home. The ground was covered with snow, and they stayed outside for hours, building snow forts, walking on the ice-covered lake, and tramping through the woods. Then they would come in and sip hot chocolate in front of the fire.

One afternoon they persuaded Grandpa to go for a walk with them. They took off down the road, laughing and talking and occasionally even throwing snowballs at each other. Suddenly Grandpa whispered, "Stop, children! Don't move. Look over there!" Kent and Jessie looked where Grandpa was pointing. A huge bird sat on the branch of a tree. "It's an eagle," whispered Grandpa. The children were amazed. They had never seen such a big bird out in the wild. Suddenly, with a powerful flap of its wings, the eagle took off over the treetops.

"Wow!" Kent said. "That's one strong bird!"

"You're exactly right," agreed Grandpa. With a twinkle in his eye, he added, "You can be strong like that, too."

"How?" Kent asked.

"The Bible says, 'Those who wait on the Lord shall renew their strength. They shall mount up with wings as eagles'," replied Grandpa.

"I've heard that verse, Grandpa," said Jessie, "but I never thought about what it meant before."

"It's a picture," said Grandpa, "a magnificent picture of the strength we have when we put our trust in God." *LMW*

HOW ABOUT YOU?

Do you have problems at school? Do you live in a rough home situation? Is it hard for you to make friends? Trust the Lord to help you. He doesn't promise to take problems away, but he does promise to give the strength needed to handle them. The next time you see a picture of an eagle, think of God's promise.

MEMORIZE:

"But those who wait on the Lord will find new strength. They will fly high on wings like eagles. They will run and not grow weary. They will walk and not faint." Isaiah 40:31

God Gives Strength

Christopher's Friend

(Read Psalm 145:8-9, 14-18)

Christopher buried his face deep into his pillow and cried softly. He did not hear someone slip quietly into his room, but a gentle touch caused him to look up from his bed. His mom was looking down at him. "What's the matter, Christopher?" she asked as she sat down beside him. "Is there some problem I can help you with?"

Christopher felt a warm blush color his face. He didn't really want to tell his mother what was bothering him. "Something happened at school," he stammered finally. "I . . . lied to Aaron, and now he won't talk to me. He knows I lied."

"Why did you do that?" Mom asked gently.

"I . . . I don't know," mumbled Christopher. He sniffed. "I told him I was sorry, but I don't think he believes me. I don't blame him."

"Are you really sorry?" asked Mom. Christopher nodded. "Then give your friend time to learn to trust you again," advised Mom.

"I don't think he'll ever believe me again," said Christopher sadly.

"Christopher, do you remember when your Dad and I used to give you piggyback rides?" asked Mom. Christopher nodded, wondering why Mom had brought that up. "You thought it was so much fun until you slipped off one day and hit your head on a chair," said Mom. "After that it took you awhile to trust us enough to try it again."

"But I finally did!" Christopher said eagerly. He thought he knew what Mom was getting at.

"Yes, and I'm sure Aaron will trust you again, too," said Mom. She patted Christopher's back. "It takes time for people to trust one another again," she said, "but let me tell you something wonderful." She smiled. "When you're truly sorry for the wrong you've done and confess it to God, *he* forgives you *right away*. There may still be sad consequences for what you've done—like a friend who won't speak to you for a while. But you can believe God when he says he forgives you. And he will help you to be a good friend to Aaron again." *VRG*

HOW ABOUT YOU?

Have you ever done anything that made you feel you might never be forgiven? If your heart is right, God knows you are really sorry. He will forgive you right away and help you to make things right with others, too. Trust him.

God Lifts the Fallen

MEMORIZE:
"The Lord helps the fallen and lifts up those bent beneath their loads."
Psalm 145:14

The Virus

(Read 1 Peter 5:8-11)

"Oh no!" Joey gazed at his computer screen in dismay. "A virus! My file is ruined."

Dad looked up from his newspaper. "How did that happen?" he asked. "Don't you virus-check your diskettes?"

Joey shrugged. "Yeah, but Brian had this neat space game yesterday and I was in such a hurry to play it, I forgot," he admitted. "I guess the virus came from that. Sorry, Dad!"

Dad sighed. "How much damage has it done?"

"I don't know yet," replied Joey gloomily.

"What's a virus? Is it what gives you the flu?" asked Rachel.

"That's right," said Dad, smiling. "When a virus gets into your body, it multiplies and spreads and makes you sick. And a computer virus, once it gets into the computer, can spread and ruin all the items you have stored there."

"I'll borrow Mr. Simpson's antivirus program and clean up the hard drive before the virus destroys all my files," said Joey.

Dad nodded. "Good idea," he said. "We need to get rid of viruses on the computer and in our lives."

"Yeah. We have to take medicine," said Rachel.

"That, too," agreed Dad, "but I was thinking of our spiritual lives. Sin is like a virus. If we don't pay attention to the Holy Spirit and check what we see and hear and do, sin creeps in quietly, then spreads and grows, and ultimately corrupts our hearts."

"Can we get cleaned up like Joey's computer?" asked Rachel anxiously.

Dad laughed and nodded. "We have something like an antivirus program," he said. "We can tell God the wrong things we've done and ask him to help us stop doing wrong things. Then God forgives us, which makes us clean again." *MTF*

HOW ABOUT YOU?

A small lie, a neglected chore, an unkind word, a forbidden movie . . . these might seem like little things, but when you allow them in your life, they can become habits. Remember that Satan is on the lookout, waiting to cause some sin to creep into your heart and corrupt you like a virus. But remember, too, that the Holy Spirit dwells in your heart. If you check out everything with him, and obey him, you can prevent the virus of sin from spreading in your life.

MEMORIZE:

"Be careful! Watch out for attacks from the Devil, your great enemy. He prowls around like a roaring lion, looking for some victim to devour."

1 Peter 5:8

Don't Give
Satan a Chance

Bad Breath

(Read Philippians 4:4-9)

The big garbage truck slowed down as it approached the stoplight. Brent strained forward against his seat belt so he could read the bumper sticker on the back of the truck. "This truck has bad breath," he read. Brent laughed.

The lights changed, and the truck went straight. So did Brent and his mother, and she passed the truck when it stopped at a house. Brent looked back just as the truck opened its huge jaws, and he watched as a man dumped bags of garbage into its big mouth. "No wonder that truck has bad breath," observed Brent. "It swallows garbage."

Mother nodded. "Yes," she agreed, "and I'm reminded of a conversation we had just last night." She glanced sideways at Brent.

"That wasn't a conversation, Mom," said Brent. "That was a lecture. You said I would become like a garbage truck if I filled my mind with junky stuff like that movie all the kids are going to see."

Mother smiled. "Well, those weren't my exact words, but I see that you do understand," she said. "And you wouldn't want your life to have bad breath like that truck, would you?"

Brent wrinkled his nose. "No way," he said. "In fact, I told the guys today that I wouldn't be going to see that movie." *EMV*

HOW ABOUT YOU?

Do friends encourage you to watch R-rated or X-rated movies or bad TV shows or to read dirty books? The temptation to follow the crowd may be strong, but God wants you to keep your mind and body pure. Fill your mind with good thoughts. Memorize the passage below, and use it whenever you are faced with temptation.

MEMORIZE:

"And now, dear friends, let me say one more thing as I close this letter. Fix your thoughts on what is true and honorable and right. Think about things that are pure and lovely and admirable. Think about things that are excellent and worthy of praise."

Philippians 4:8

Keep Your Mind Pure

An Old Piece of Wood

(Read Jeremiah 18:1-6)

Jason was helping his dad pile firewood in the backyard when their neighbor, Mr. Stevens, walked by.

"Looks like you got some walnut here," remarked Mr. Stevens as he stooped down and picked up a piece that Jason's dad had trimmed from a tree in the woods. "Mind if I borrow this for a week?"

"Sure, go ahead," said Dad. Jason wondered why Mr. Stevens would want to borrow the chunk of wood. He could see that Dad was as puzzled as he was.

They found out why exactly one week later. Mr. Stevens stopped by and returned the piece of walnut, except now it wasn't a chunk of firewood—it was a beautifully whittled bufflehead duck! "Wow!" Jason whistled. "Look what you did with just an old piece of wood!"

"We'll put this on our fireplace mantel instead of in the fire," Jason's dad said. "Thanks so much, Mr. Stevens."

The older man smiled. "Come over sometime and see my collection of ducks," he said. "I enjoy carving them. When I work on them and see the old piece of wood change into something beautiful, I like to think of what the Lord did for me. I was living a life of pride and selfishness, yet the Lord took me and made me a new person!"

"Hmmmm. I never thought of it like that," Jason said, "but every time I look at the duck made out of firewood, I'll think of how the Lord made me into a new person, too!" *LMW*

HOW ABOUT YOU?

Have you ever thought that the Lord couldn't love you because you are "so bad"? He tells you in his Word that he loved the whole world (that includes you) so much that he gave his life. He does love you. And if you accept him as your personal Savior, he will change you into a new person!

MEMORIZE:

"But now is the time to get . . . clothed . . . with a brand-new nature that is continually being renewed as you learn more and more about Christ, who created this new nature within you." Colossians 3:8, 10

Become a New Person

Help Available

(Read Psalm 46:1-5, 10-11)

"You're home early," said Mom when Blake came in after school. "I thought you were going to stay after school today and try out for your class play."

Blake set his books on the kitchen table. "I changed my mind," he said. "I've tried so hard to get along with all the kids in my grade, but a couple of them just don't like me. They make fun of everything I do and say. They're trying out for the play, and I just don't feel like being in a play with them."

Mom looked sympathetic. "Have you been praying about the problem?" she asked.

"Praying?" Blake shook his head. "Not really. How could that help?"

Before Mom could answer, Blake saw his cat rolling on the floor, tugging at her collar. "I think something's wrong with Molly," Blake said. Mom and Blake bent down to examine the fluffy white cat.

"Her claw is stuck in a slit on her bell," said Mom. She reached down to help the cat, but Molly rolled out of her reach.

Blake moved toward the cat. "Come on, Molly," he coaxed. "We only want to help. Please be still."

But Molly would not be still. She jerked her caught claw pitifully and scooted away on three legs every time Mom or Blake came close.

"I think we'll have to wait until she gets tired," said Mom.

After a while Molly settled down. This time when they tried to help, Molly allowed Blake to pick her up. Blake held the cat while Mom lifted Molly's paw and carefully slid the claw out of the slit in the bell.

"Wow!" said Blake as he cuddled the tired cat. "I'm glad she finally let us help."

Mom nodded. "Molly reminds me of you and your problem at school," she said.

"You mean, I'm trying to get 'unstuck' from a problem without asking for God's help?"

"That's right!" answered Mom. *KEC*

HOW ABOUT YOU?

Do you think you have to struggle with problems on your own? Problems such as a brother or sister who doesn't do his or her share of the work? A bully at school or in the neighborhood? A teacher who you think picks on you? Start by talking to God about these or any other problems. Then trust him to help you.

Let God Help You

MEMORIZE:
"God is our refuge and strength, always ready to help in times of trouble." Psalm 46:1

January

14

Answers from God

(Read Deuteronomy 30:11-16)

Richard slammed the screen door as he bolted into the kitchen. "Did I get any mail?" he asked anxiously.

"No," replied Mom. "Are you expecting something important?"

"A letter from the newspaper," Richard answered.

"What kind of letter?" asked Mom.

"Well, some of the guys in my class are starting a new club. They're calling it 'The Cycle Club,' and you can't be in it unless you've ridden on a motorcycle. But I haven't." Richard sighed. "So, I wrote to the kid's columnist at the newspaper asking if it was OK to join anyway. You know . . . just tell the guys that I've ridden. It's not like they'd ever know."

Mom put her hand on Richard's shoulder. "You don't need to write to the newspaper to know what God wants you to do," she told him. "Most of the answers to life's questions are in the Bible. Do you know what it says about lying?"

"Yeah." Richard nodded. "It says not to lie."

"That's right. When God set the Scriptures to paper, he knew that you were going to ask this question one day," said Mom. "What you read there is his answer for you."

Richard sighed. "Well, if he's been planning that answer for thousands of years, he's probably not going to change his mind," he said, "so I guess I won't get in."

"I guess not," said Mom. She handed him the Bible. "Here . . . why don't you go read the answers to some of tomorrow's questions." *HMT*

HOW ABOUT YOU?

Your future is full of big choices and decisions—about friends, school, and right or wrong. God knows about these struggles, and he has answers prepared for you. Sometimes he gives specific answers and sometimes he gives principles he wants you to follow. If you want to know God's answers, look for them in your Bible or talk with a trusted friend.

MEMORIZE:

"But be doers of the word, and not hearers only, deceiving yourselves."
James 1:22, NKJV

The Bible Has Answers

Beauty or Ashes

(Read Isaiah 1:16-18; 43:25)

Eight-year-old Jay bounced into the kitchen from the back porch where he had been talking to his friends. "Mom, can I go sliding with Tommy and Austin?" he asked.

"Empty the ashes first, and then you can go." Mother smiled at his eagerness. "Dress warmly now; it's colder than it looks."

Jay quickly filled a bucket with ashes from the fireplace. Then he slipped into his snowmobile suit and boots. Grabbing his mittens and the ash bucket, he hurried out the back door and trudged through the deep snow to the garden. The bright winter sun shining on the new fallen snow nearly blinded him at first. It made him squint until his eyes were almost closed.

Standing at the edge of the garden, he tossed the ashes from the bucket and watched as the wind scattered the dark soot across the white snow, covering the sparkles and destroying the beauty.

"Those ashes are sure messing up the beautiful snow, aren't they, Jay?" Jay's father had come to stand beside him. They quietly watched as the wind continued to scatter the ashes all across the garden. "It reminds me of what sin does to our life," added Dad. "When we sin, it leaves dirty marks, too. The only way we can have our life clean again is to confess our sin to God."

Jay looked up at the sky. "It's starting to snow," he said. "Maybe the new snow will cover up those old ashes." He paused. "But we'll still know they're there, won't we, Dad?"

Dad nodded. "Yes. That often happens in our life, too. God promises that when we're sorry for our sins and ask him to forgive us, he does. And he 'remembers our sin no more.' However, even after God forgives our sin, we often remember it."

"So it's best if we try not to sin in the first place, isn't it, Dad?"

"That's true, Jay," agreed Dad. "That's definitely true." *THB*

HOW ABOUT YOU?

Have your sins been washed away by the blood of Jesus? Then thank him for making you "white as snow." Ask him to help you keep your life free from the mess sin makes. If you do sin, quickly go to him for forgiveness. He promises to give it.

Jesus Makes You Clean

The Oil Man

(Read Isaiah 61:1-3, 10)

"Dad, I need some oil." Derek's father looked up at his eager young son. "I want to 'unsqueak' the cupboard doors for Mom. She says the hinges need a little oil and that I can be the 'oil man.' She says if they don't get it soon, they're going to drive her wild with their squeaking."

Dad laughed as he took the oil from the workbench and handed it to Derek.

When Derek returned the oil a little later, Dad was still at his workbench. "I oiled the hinges all over the house," Derek reported. Then he went out to play with his friends.

At dinner that evening Derek shared the neighborhood news. "Matt and David are mad at each other again," he said. "Did you know Mrs. Gentry broke her arm? She fell down the basement stairs. Mr. Snell—that old man at the corner—stood at his window for half an hour and watched us sliding. He's probably got nothing better to do." Derek paused to nibble at his salad.

"I guess the people in our neighborhood could use some oil," observed Dad.

"Oil?" asked Derek. "What do you mean?"

"The Bible speaks of the 'oil of gladness,' and it sounds to me like some of our neighbors could use a little gladness," said Dad.

"And maybe I could be their 'oil man' today, too. Only this time I could spread some joy oil! I know what I can do," he said, eyeing the dessert on the cupboard. "I can take a piece of pie to Mr. Snell. And I can offer to run errands for Mrs. Gentry. What can I do about Matt and David?"

"I don't know," said Mom. "But you're off to a good start. I'm sure you'll think of something." *HWM*

HOW ABOUT YOU?

Do you spread gladness? God's Word says Jesus was anointed with the "oil of gladness," and if you belong to him, there should be gladness in your heart, too. Will you share that with others? Offer a cheerful smile to help someone feel better. Take time to chat a few minutes with a lonely person. Lend a helping hand.

MEMORIZE:

"You love what is right and hate what is wrong. Therefore God, your God, has anointed you, pouring out the oil of joy on you more than on anyone else." Hebrews 1:9

Spread Gladness

A Heavy Burden

(Read Matthew 11:28-30; Philippians 4:6-7)

"Mom, I wish Dad still lived here," said Kyle as he finished getting ready for school. "If I had just behaved better, maybe he wouldn't have left."

"Honey, Dad's leaving had nothing to do with you. He loves you as much as ever," Mom said patiently, putting an arm around Kyle. She and Dad had told Kyle this many times. He wanted to believe them, but there was an ache in his heart that wouldn't go away. He was sure if he hadn't whined so much, or if he had minded more often, Dad wouldn't have moved out.

At school, thoughts of his dad often popped up between the sentences Kyle was reading. He finally got his mind off his problems when his teacher showed the class an interesting book. And he was thrilled when she said he could take it home for the evening.

Kyle tucked the heavy book under his arm and began walking home. As he walked, the book seemed to grow heavier and heavier. By the time he reached home, his arm ached.

Mother met him at the end of the driveway. "That book was a heavy burden, wasn't it?" she said. She reached down and took it. "Did you know, Kyle, that feelings can also be like a heavy burden?" She continued quietly as she carried the book to the house. "The sense that Dad's leaving is your fault is too heavy of a burden for you to carry."

"I wish I didn't feel guilty," Kyle said. "It hurts."

"Yes, just like your arm hurts from carrying the book." Mother gently rubbed his aching arm. "There is nothing for you to feel guilty about. But since you do, wouldn't you like Jesus to carry that burden of guilty feelings for you?" Kyle nodded, and together they asked Jesus to carry Kyle's heavy burden. "Now," said Mom, "every time you feel Dad's leaving is your fault, remember that Jesus is carrying that burden for you. Will you do that?"

Kyle nodded. His arm still hurt, but the ache in his heart felt better. *KRA*

HOW ABOUT YOU?

Do you have a burden too heavy for you? If your parents are separated, do you wonder if it's your fault? Or perhaps worries about school or friends constantly fill your mind. It's important to talk about heavy burdens with an adult who can help you turn them over to Jesus. Jesus loves you and wants you to be free of heavy burdens.

Give Your Burdens to Jesus

MEMORIZE:
"Give all your worries and cares to God, for he cares about what happens to you." 1 Peter 5:7

January

18

Discipline

(Read Hebrews 12:5-11)

"Brandon, go to your room!" ordered Mother.

"Oh, Mom, please! I won't do it again," pleaded Brandon.

Mother was firm. "I told you that the next time you pinched Stephanie, you'd get a time-out. The longer it takes you to get to your room, the longer the time-out will last," she warned.

As he went to his room, Brandon started crying. Before the time-out was over, he had figured out a plan that would guarantee no more time-outs. "I'm going to run away and never come back!" he exclaimed. "I don't want any more time-outs."

Now Mother's voice was gentle. "We give you time-outs because we love you, Brandon, and we don't want you to grow up doing things that are wrong," she said. She paused, then added, "Did you know that, in a way, Dad and I still get time-outs?"

Brandon stared in surprise. "Who gives you time-outs?" he asked.

"God does," replied Mother. "Just as your father and I give you a time-out, so God disciplines us when we do things that are wrong."

"How can God discipline people?" asked Brandon, puzzled.

Mother smiled. "He doesn't use time-outs, of course," she said. "But he has other ways. Sometimes he uses other people, or he may use problems that we get into. But usually he uses the Bible."

"The Bible?" interrupted Brandon.

Mother nodded. "That's right. When we do wrong, God often reminds us of Bible verses that tell us we have sinned. Because we love him, it hurts us to know that we have done something wrong. Each time God disciplines us, it helps us learn how to do what is right." She smiled at Brandon. "And he disciplines us only when we need it, just like Dad and I do with you and Stephanie."

"Well . . . " Brandon sighed. "I guess I'll stick around. I don't really know where else I would go. And I will try not to pinch Stephanie again. Then you won't have to give me time-outs so much." *HCT*

HOW ABOUT YOU?

Do you hate time-outs? Don't run away from them. Try to think of time-outs as something to help you learn to do what is right.

MEMORIZE:

"For the Lord corrects those he loves, just as a father corrects a child in whom he delights." Proverbs 3:12

Learn from Discipline

The Boss's Boss

(Read Colossians 3:22-25)

"Someone's always bossing me around," griped Tim. "My teacher said I had to quit talking in class. My dad said I had to clean the garage. My mom said I had to make my bed each morning. My Sunday school teacher said that I have to learn my Bible verses. My pastor said . . ."

"That's quite a list of bosses," Grandpa Hill teased.

"My pastor said that I have to obey all these people!" added Tim.

"And you do," Grandpa agreed.

"I'll be glad when I grow up. Then I'll be my own boss," sighed Tim.

Grandpa chuckled. "That's just what I thought when I was eleven, but now I have more bosses than ever."

"You do?" asked Tim. "Who's your boss?"

It was Grandpa's turn to count. "First, there is God. Second, your pastor is my pastor, too. Remember?"

"But does Pastor Green tell you what to do?"

"He certainly does! Oh, he doesn't say, 'Sweep the floor,' 'Pay your tithes,' 'Visit the nursing home.' But lots of times he has preached sermons that told me what I needed to do. God placed him in the church to lead me."

"Who else tells you what to do?" Tim questioned.

"My employer gives me orders at work. The city council tells me if I can build a new house and if I can keep chickens. The police tell me where I can park my car."

Tim sighed. "I guess you're right. There is no getting away from bosses!" *BJW*

HOW ABOUT YOU?

Do you get tired of being bossed around? Everyone does. But remember, God has placed people in authority over you to help you. You will never be sorry for being obedient.

Obey Those in Charge

MEMORIZE:
"Obey those who rule over you, and be submissive, for they watch out for your souls." Hebrews 13:17, NKJV

January
20

A Home for Greg (Part 1)

(Read James 3:2-10)

Ben scowled in the direction of Greg, one of the other boys who lived in the Hillsdale Children's Home. Greg had just learned that some people might be interested in adopting him. In fact, he had met the Johnsons just that morning, and he was going home with them for a visit the very next day! "Some people get all the breaks," grumbled Ben under his breath. "Why couldn't that happen to me?"

That evening as Greg was happily packing his clothes for the visit, he turned to see Ben watching him from the doorway. "Do you really think the Johnsons will want to adopt you?" sneered Ben. "Your hair is all scraggly, and you're so skinny your bones stick out. And those feet! Just look at those big clodhoppers!"

"Well . . . I . . . I guess I'm not much to look at, am I?" stammered Greg.

"You can say that again!" mocked Ben. "I'll bet those people will send you packing in a hurry." Ben turned and went to his own room to get ready for bed. "I sure cut him down to size," he muttered to himself.

But criticizing Greg didn't make Ben any happier. He felt jealous, guilty, and more miserable than ever. As he tossed and turned, unable to sleep, he could not rid his mind of a recent Sunday school lesson about how he should use his tongue. He knew that in the morning he must apologize to Greg. Meanwhile, he asked God to forgive him, and he thanked God for the good home he already had. Then, with a contented sigh, he turned over and fell asleep. *SLK*

HOW ABOUT YOU?

Do you try to make yourself feel better by criticizing others? People who are dissatisfied with themselves often try to make other people miserable, too. Today's Scripture tells you to watch what you say to others.

MEMORIZE:

"For the Scriptures say, 'If you want a happy life and good days, keep your tongue from speaking evil, and keep your lips from telling lies.'"

1 Peter 3:10

Don't "Put Down" Others

A Home for Greg (Part 2)

(Read Luke 5:27-31)

Greg lay awake, remembering the critical things Ben had said to him. Was he really so ugly the Johnsons wouldn't want to adopt him? He guessed he probably was, and he just couldn't bear to have everybody feel sorry for him when they returned him to the Children's Home. He didn't know what to do about it. *I'll run away, that's what I'll do,* he decided.

When the other boys were asleep, Greg took a scissors and cut two sheets into strips. He quickly tied the strips together, making a rope. He tied one end of his homemade rope to the leg of his bed and let the other end out the second-story window. After taking one last look around, he began to climb down. Suddenly, the rope broke, and he plunged down into the bushes below!

Some time later, Greg opened his eyes. He saw his housemother and . . . the Johnsons! "Are you all right?" Mr. Johnson asked.

"I . . . I think so," said Greg as he sat up weakly. "I'm all right, just a bump on my head."

"Why did you try to run away?" asked his housemother.

"B-because I knew the Johnsons wouldn't really want me after all," explained Greg, wiping away a tear. "I'm just not good enough to be adopted."

Mrs. Johnson smiled warmly. "You look good enough to me," she declared. "We like you just the way you are." *SLK*

HOW ABOUT YOU?

Did you know that God wants to adopt you into his family just like the Johnsons wanted to adopt Greg? Come to Jesus just as you are.

Come to Jesus as You Are

MEMORIZE:
"But God showed his great love for us by sending Christ to die for us while we were still sinners." Romans 5:8

January
22

Pass Out the Food

(Read Matthew 14:15-21)

Doug wanted to be a pastor someday, so he persuaded his father, who was a pastor, to let him go along on some of his hospital calls. But one evening when Dad was ready to go, Doug hesitated. "Dad, I really do want to be a pastor like you," he said, "but making hospital calls is kind of depressing sometimes, and it seems so useless."

"You don't have to go unless you want to," said Dad, "but what do you mean when you say it seems useless?"

"Well, the people have so many problems," explained Doug, "and we can't really help them. There's Mrs. Paul, with her broken hip and no family left to take care of her. And Mrs. Stewart, who just lost her baby. And what about Mr. Franklin, who has cancer and probably won't live very long? We can't fix any of their problems."

Doug's father nodded. "That's certainly true," he said. "These people are sad and hurt and suffering, and there's no way on earth that you or I can meet their needs. But we can go and simply pass out the food to them."

Doug stared in surprise. "But, Dad!" he protested. "They have nurses to do that!"

Dad smiled. "I'm thinking of a different kind of food," he said. "Remember the story about Jesus feeding the crowd of 5,000 people? When the disciples told him that the people were hungry, Jesus said, 'Give them something to eat.' The disciples didn't have that much food, but they simply told the Lord about the need, gave him what little they had, and obeyed his command to pass out the food. Jesus miraculously multiplied that bread and fish to feed the crowd."

Doug was silent a moment. "I still don't get it," he said.

"Well," said Dad, "we can't solve the problems of the people we visit, and it's not our responsibility to do so. All we can do is 'pass out the food.' In other words, we can bring their needs to Jesus in prayer. And we can offer ourselves for his use. He may want to use our lips to speak to them, or our hands to help them, or our money to meet their needs. You're a good helper when you go with me—so how about it?"

"OK," agreed Doug. "I guess I'll go." *SLK*

HOW ABOUT YOU?

Do you sometimes feel bad because people have problems that you can't solve? Do you feel helpless? God still says to you, "Give them something to eat." Do this through prayer and through helpful actions toward others. Turn their needs over to Jesus and encourage them to do the same.

MEMORIZE:

"You feed them." Matthew 14:16

Help Others

Too Much Visiting

(Read Job 16:1-7)

"Hey, Josh, can you play today?" asked Kyle.

Josh hesitated. "Well, I don't know. I have quite a few things to do."

"Aw, come on," begged Kyle. "What do you have to do? I could help you."

Josh shook his head. "Not really. I have to practice the piano, and you can't help me do that."

"I could just come in and listen," persisted Kyle.

"Kyle," said Josh, "we were together last night after school and Monday night, too. And we spent a lot of time together over the weekend. I like playing with you, but I really will be busy."

"Well, OK," agreed Kyle glumly.

Josh breathed a sigh of relief as he walked up the steps to the house. He found his mother in the kitchen starting supper. "Kyle wanted to play again today, but I told him I had a lot of things to do. I hope he's not mad."

"Why would he be mad?" asked Mother. "You've been spending most afternoons with him lately."

"I know," sighed Josh. "I'm glad he's my friend, but sometimes I like being alone. I like to read and draw and write letters. It's hard to do those things with a friend."

Mother nodded. "Did you know there's a verse in the Bible about this very situation?"

"In the Bible? What verse?" asked Josh in surprise.

"Proverbs 25:17 says, 'Don't visit your neighbors too often, or you will wear out your welcome,'" quoted Mother. "See, Josh, the Lord who created friendship understands your problem. Friends do need to give each other time to develop different interests."

"Thanks, Mom!" exclaimed Josh. "I feel better about it now! I wish Kyle could understand that verse, too." *LMW*

HOW ABOUT YOU?

Do you spend lots of time with only one friend? Reach out to other people and make new friends, too. Spend time alone and do a creative project or read a book. Often arguments start between two people because they spend too much time together. Listen to the Lord's advice concerning friendship!

Don't Become a Pest

MEMORIZE:
"Don't visit your neighbors too often, or you will wear out your welcome."
Proverbs 25:17

January
24

Dominoes

(Read Ephesians 4:29-31)

"Molly!" hollered Jeff. "Don't!" He had carefully stood all his dominoes up with just a little space between each one. "Molly, no!" It was too late. Molly pushed the first domino and the rest of them tumbled against one another, row after row. What had taken Jeff a long time to set up tumbled over in just a few seconds. Molly giggled, clapping her little hands. "You are such a pest, Molly," Jeff said angrily. "I wish you'd go away!" Molly's happy face crumpled with disappointment and then tears. She ran off sobbing.

Out of the corner of his eye, Jeff saw their dog, Rags, wander over to Molly, her tail wagging. She licked Molly's face. Molly kicked the dog. "Pest! Go away!" Molly said.

Then Jeff heard his mother's voice. "Time out, Molly!" said Mom.

Jeff pushed the dominoes into a pile and started to set them up again. As he worked, his anger died away. He began to feel really bad about what he had said to Molly.

When Jeff was finished, he had an idea. "Molly," Jeff called. "Come here!"

Molly slowly came into the room. "Did you build another one, Jeff?" she asked.

Jeff nodded. "Yep," he said. "It's for you. Go ahead, Molly—you can start it."

"Really?" asked Molly as Mom came to watch. Jeff nodded. Delighted, Molly pushed over the first domino. The rapid click of dominoes filled the room as they toppled against each other.

"You know, people are like those dominoes," Mom said thoughtfully.

Jeff stared at the rows of fallen dominoes, puzzled. "What do you mean?" he asked.

"Molly told me what happened before she kicked Rags," said Mother. "When we get angry, words come quickly, and sometimes our reactions affect more than one person." Mom patted the dog. "Or dog," she added.

"Oh, I get it!" said Jeff. "Like . . ." He looked embarrassed. "When I got mad and said mean things to Molly, I made her angry, too, so she took it out on Rags. It was like the dominoes—me to Molly to the dog."

"Yes," said Mom with a smile. "The Bible tells us to be careful about what we say." *ELT*

HOW ABOUT YOU?

Are you careful about what you say? The things you say to one person may affect the way he treats other people, too. The Bible says we should build each other up with our words, not knock each other down.

MEMORIZE:

"Don't use foul or abusive language. Let everything you say be good and helpful, so that your words will be an encouragement to those who hear them." Ephesians 4:29

Use Words to Build Others Up

The Braggers

(Read Jeremiah 9:23-24)

LaTorrance was the smartest boy in his class. It annoyed the other kids because he bragged so much. "Didn't you get all the answers to the questions in the lesson?" he sneered at one of the boys just as Mr. Townsend entered the classroom. "It was so easy I could do it in my sleep."

But LaTorrance wasn't the only one who bragged. After Mr. Townsend finished the lesson about Samson, he asked for a volunteer to take up the offering.

"May I take the offering?" asked Chris. "My dad is so rich he gave me a five dollar bill for the offering today!"

"Peter, will you take the offering?" asked Mr. Townsend. When Peter was finished, Mr. Townsend set his lesson book aside. "Turn in your Bibles to Jeremiah 9:23 and 24," he said. (See today's Scripture.) "Read these verses silently. Ask the Lord to speak to you if you have an attitude that doesn't please him."

The classroom was quiet for a while. "Does anybody want to comment on these verses?" asked Mr. Townsend.

"I shouldn't make others feel bad by talking about my family being rich," said Chris.

LaTorrance added, "And I shouldn't put other people down because I can learn fast."

Then Peter spoke. "I'm glad I don't brag like that."

"Whoa! Watch it!" warned Mr. Townsend. "Be sure you're not proud about not being proud!" The boys laughed.

"Oops!" said Peter with a grin. "Sorry."

Mr. Townsend smiled. Then he led the boys in prayer. *REP*

HOW ABOUT YOU?

Is it OK to feel proud of something that you have worked hard to accomplish? (Yes) But if you brag about yourself to make other people feel bad, then you are doing wrong. Ask God to forgive you and help you to remember to boast in him and the things that he does.

Don't Brag about Yourself

January
26

Till He Comes

(Read John 14:1-6)

"How long will you be gone?" Ian asked his father. Dad's firm was opening a branch office in South America, and he was to go and work there.

"I'm not sure," Dad replied. "I need to find a place for us to live and get it ready, and then I'll come back for you."

Ian was excited at the idea of seeing South America, but he missed Dad after he left. Dad was no longer available to help him with his math. Dad wasn't there when he hit a home run. Dad also missed the Christmas program when Ian played a trumpet solo. It seemed that Dad was gone a very, very long time!

"Don't get discouraged," Mother told Ian. "Let's just get ready for the time when Dad does come back to take us to live with him in South America."

"But how can we do that?" Ian asked.

"Well, we can study and learn about the country where we're going to live," suggested Mother. "We could even try to learn the language. Let's work at this and not feel sorry for ourselves." And so they did.

A short time later, Ian was feeling lonely again. "It shouldn't be too much longer," Mother comforted him. "You know, Ian, I've been thinking a lot about how Jesus has promised to come back for us, too, just like Daddy has."

"And we don't know when Jesus is coming, either, do we, Mom?" asked Ian.

Mother shook her head. "No, we don't," she replied. "But he will come! He promised that he would. We need to prepare and watch for his return, too."

How happy they all were when Dad finally did return for them. As they thanked God that day for Dad's safe return, they also thanked him for the reminder that Jesus would be coming for them someday, too! *AGL*

HOW ABOUT YOU?

Does it seem real to you that Jesus is coming again? Or does it seem as though he never really will? He has promised to prepare a wonderful place for his children and then, when the time is right, to come back for them. He always keeps his promises. Get ready for his return. Learn all you can about him. Do the things that please him. He is coming. Remember—it could be today!

MEMORIZE:

"When everything is ready, I will come and get you, so that you will always be with me where I am."
John 14:3

Jesus Is Coming

The Right Choice

(Read Joshua 24:14-15, 23-24)

Dirk's Sunday school teacher, Mr. Jackson, talked about how we each have an important choice in life, to follow Jesus or not to follow Jesus. Mr. Jackson went on to explain that the reward for following Jesus was heaven.

A few days later, Dirk and his friend Tim went to a museum. While they were looking at fossils, the fire alarm rang. Immediately a security guard yelled, "There's a fire! Come this way—follow me!" He headed for a nearby door.

The people hurried after the guard, but Dirk saw another door that was closer. "Let's go this way. We can get out faster!" he called to Tim.

"No!" yelled Tim. "The guard knows the way to the fire escape. Let's follow him." Reluctantly, Dirk decided to follow the guard, too.

That night as he watched the TV news report about the fire, Dirk learned that the door he had wanted to go through led right to the fire. He realized that by following the guard, he had made a good choice and his reward was safety. This got him to thinking about following Jesus and being rewarded with heaven. Before he went to bed that night, he made a list of questions to ask Mr. Jackson, his teacher. They were questions about how a person can choose to follow Jesus. *AGL*

HOW ABOUT YOU?

Have you chosen to follow Jesus yet? If not, talk to a trusted friend or adult about questions you might have.

Choose Jesus

MEMORIZE:
"Anyone who isn't helping me opposes me, and anyone who isn't working with me is actually working against me." Matthew 12:30

January
28

Not Good Enough

(Read Psalm 103:8-14)

Charlie came in from school and plopped his books onto the kitchen counter. "Mom, I don't think I can be a Christian," he said, sounding very discouraged.

"What happened?" Mom asked.

"Everything went wrong," mumbled Charlie. "Ted said something mean to me at recess, and I lost my temper. I said something just as mean. Then everybody was teasing Melissa about her new haircut, so I did, too. She started to cry, and Mr. Jones made us stay after class."

"Were you sorry about those things?" asked Mom.

"Well, sure," replied Charlie. "But I just keep doing things wrong." He held up his hand as Mother started to speak. "I know . . . I know," he said. "God forgives when we're sorry and confess what we've done, but I think he'd get awful tired of forgiving us over and over again." Before Mom could reply, Charlie went to his room.

When Mom came to his door a little later, Charlie was getting fresh water for Snowball, his hamster. "Didn't Snowball bite your finger yesterday?" asked Mom. "How is it?"

Charlie held up his finger. "It's OK," he said.

Mom frowned. "He makes such a mess in his cage, and he bites you," she said. "Why don't you get rid of him?"

Charlie stared at Mom in surprise and stroked Snowball's back. "He's mine!" he said simply.

Mom smiled. "And you love him, right?" she asked. Charlie nodded. "Snowball doesn't deserve your care," continued Mom, "but you care for him and forgive him because you love him—even when he bites your finger. We don't deserve God's care, but he cares for us and forgives us because he loves us . . . much more than you love Snowball."

"Well," Charlie said, "if God loves me that much, then I guess I won't give up on being a Christian." *KEC*

HOW ABOUT YOU?

Have you trusted Jesus as your Savior? Accept the forgiveness he offers, and then do your best to do what you know is right. When you fail, don't give up. God still loves you. Confess your sin to him, accept his forgiveness, and try again.

MEMORIZE:

"Give thanks to the Lord, for he is good! His faithful love endures forever." Psalm 107:1

God Loves You

The Sodium Chloride of the Earth

(Read Matthew 5:13-16)

Steven waited patiently as the food was put on the table and his father offered a prayer of thanks. Then he spoke up. "Please pass the sodium chloride."

Dad laughed. "I know what you're talking about, but where did you hear that?"

Steven laughed, too. "In school today," he said. "We had a lesson on salt. Salt's important," Steven informed them. "Our teacher said that it's used in science and medicine."

"And here at home," Mother added. "Salt is used to flavor food and also to keep it from spoiling."

"Did you know that sodium chloride is mentioned in the Bible?" asked Dad.

"Aw, c'mon, Dad," protested Steven. "In the Bible?"

"Well, not by that name," said Dad, "but it does talk about salt. It tells us that Christians are the salt of the earth. Christians can help preserve and flavor the earth. Unless—" he stopped abruptly.

"Unless what?" Steven asked.

"Unless the salt has lost its flavor."

"So Christians have to be careful to live in such a way that others can see how Jesus has made a difference in their lives," Mother added. "Christians are to be a good influence on those they meet."

Steven was quiet for a long time. At last he spoke. "I wonder if my teacher can tell I'm part of the sodium chloride of the earth. I hope so." *RSM*

HOW ABOUT YOU?

Are you being a "good flavor" to your schoolmates? To your family? Can they tell that Jesus has made a difference in how you live your life? If so, then you are being the salt of the earth.

Be a Useful Christian

MEMORIZE:
"You are the salt of the earth."
Matthew 5:13

January
30

Chameleon Eyes

(Read James 1:8; 4:8)

"Ramon," called Mom from the den, "keep away from the cookie jar."

"Uh-h-h . . . how'd you know I was checking out the cookies? You weren't even here," said Ramon as Mother came into the kitchen.

"Oh, I have eyes in the back of my head," joked Mother. "Every mother does."

Dad laughed as he came in the back door. "I heard that!" he said. He grinned at Ramon. "Mom may not really be able to see in two directions at once, but your chameleon can," he added. "Have you noticed his eyes?"

"Yeah!" said Ramon, going over to the terrarium to check out his new pet. "His eyes are really weird. His left eye is looking at me but his right eye is looking at that fly out on the window screen!"

"Each bulging eye can move independently and can rotate in every direction," said Dad.

"Wow! It would be cool to have eyes like that!" exclaimed Ramon.

Dad smiled. "Well, I'm sure God gave us just the kind of eyes we need," he said. He paused, then he added, "But some Christians seem to think they have chameleon eyes. They seem to try to look at two things at once, too."

"They do?" asked Ramon in surprise.

Dad nodded. "Christians kids sometimes 'look' at all the things other kids are doing, and they wish they could be involved in it all. Yet they want all the benefits of being a Christian, too."

Mother nodded. "I'm afraid it isn't only Christian kids who do that," she said. "Christian men and women are also guilty of the same thing."

"That's right," agreed Dad. "As Christians we should keep our minds focused on godly things." *LJR*

HOW ABOUT YOU?

Do you read the Bible and try to focus on doing good? But then wish you could watch movies you know your parents would not approve of? Ask God to help you do those things that are good and right. This is how you can keep your eyes focused on things that please God.

MEMORIZE:

"Look straight ahead, and fix your eyes on what lies before you."
Proverbs 4:25

Focus on Good Things

Watch Your Opponent

(Read 1 Peter 5:6-9)

Eight-year-old Mitch was excited as he put an *X* on the corner spot of the tic-tac-toe game. He was finally going to win against his big sister, Marcia. He laughed out loud because on the next move, he could win two different ways. It didn't matter where she put her *O* to block him! But his laughter stopped suddenly as Marcia marked an *O* and went on to draw a line through three *O*s in a row! She had won again!

"I hate you!" he shrieked as he threw his pencil across the room and stomped out. A little later Mother found him lying on his bed.

"Marcia told me what happened," she said. "You lost two things—the game and your temper. And you lost both of them for the same reason. It was because you didn't watch your opponent."

Mitch sat up straight and looked at her, a question in his eyes. "That's right," she said. "Marcia was your opponent in the game, but you were so concerned about how you would win that you forgot to think about how she would play. You also have another opponent, a more serious one. The Bible says that the devil is our opponent. We need to be alert and not allow him to get the best of us. You weren't watching out for him when you lost your temper. While it is OK to be angry, it is not OK to hurt other people with our anger."

Mitch nodded sadly. "I guess I let him get the best of me," he said. Then he brightened. "But Jesus will forgive me for hurting Marcia, won't he? I'll ask him, and Marcia, too." *HWM*

HOW ABOUT YOU?

Losing your temper, cheating, and gossiping are some of the sins we are all tempted to do. But the Bible verse for today tells us to resist the devil by not giving in to temptation. Ask God to help you the next time you are tempted.

Resist Satan

MEMORIZE:
"So humble yourselves before God. Resist the Devil, and he will flee from you." James 4:7

The Fence

(Read Exodus 20:1-17)

Sooki, the dog, yelped and whined to be let off her chain. Dad looked over at Todd. "Why don't you bring Sooki in for the night?" he asked.

So Todd brought Sooki in and sat down on the floor beside her. "Silly dog," he said, patting her fondly. "We have a nice fence around the yard so you can run all around and still not get hit by any nasty old cars, but do you appreciate it? No, you dig out, so then we have to chain you even though you hate it. It's your own fault, see?"

"If Sooki could understand how much we love her and want her to be safe and happy, I bet she wouldn't try to get loose," observed Carrie.

Mom nodded. "She's a lot like us, isn't she?" said Mom. Everyone turned and looked at her. "God loves us, so he has put up a 'fence' for us, too. He has set limits for us," she explained. "He does this so we'll be safe and still have all the room we need for our activities. But sometimes we think there must be something better outside the 'fence.' We think God's laws limit and restrict us too much, though they actually give us freedom."

"I bet the Ten Commandments are the 'fence' God has set for us, right?" asked Carrie.

"Yes, the Ten Commandments along with all the principles for living found in God's Word," said Dad. "They're a guideline for us, but when we realize God's goodness and love for us, we find that we want to live to please him because we love him. Then the 'fence' God gave doesn't feel like something that hinders us in any way, but rather like something that keeps us safe."

"Well," said Todd thoughtfully, "whenever I start to feel that God's laws are too strict, I'll think about Sooki and how fences keep people safe."

"Me, too." Carrie nodded. She gave the dog a squeeze. "You're a good teacher, Sooki," she added. *RSS*

HOW ABOUT YOU?

Do you realize that God has set up limits for you because he loves you? What are some of those limits? Ask him to help you stay within his laws—to trust that they are for your good.

Stay within God's Limits

MEMORIZE:
"Loving God means keeping his commandments, and really, that isn't difficult." 1 John 5:3

The Balloon that Burst

(Read James 4:6-10)

"I was sure I'd win the Bible quiz contest last night," said George with a sigh. "I can't figure out what went wrong."

"Yeah," agreed Tyrone. "You always win everything."

"Now Allen will go to the state contest instead of me," George added. "And he'll be honored at the church party tonight."

Mr. Loveland held out some crepe streamers. "Hurry, boys," he urged. "The party begins soon. Hang up the rest of these while I blow up some balloons. Tell me about the contest while you work. I couldn't attend last night."

"I was awful," George said as he fastened streamers to the ceiling. "I couldn't remember the answers, and I misquoted Bible verses."

"But he's smarter than Allen," said Tyrone.

"Sure I am," said George confidently. "Besides, he just started going to church last year."

"Did you study for the contest?" asked Mr. Loveland.

"Oh, I don't need to study much anymore," replied George, "because I know the Bible so well."

Mr. Loveland looked at the balloon he was blowing up. "Allen told me he'd studied a great deal," he said. He blew hard on the balloon. It grew bigger and bigger. Then *BANG!* It burst into little pieces. "Well! The balloon was puffed up so much it burst," observed Mr. Loveland. "You know, George, I think you're like this balloon."

"You mean by not studying I was acting 'puffed up' about my Bible knowledge?"

"Exactly," said Mr. Loveland. *MRP*

HOW ABOUT YOU?

Are there times when you think everything's going your way and then you fall flat on your face? Could pride be the trouble?

MEMORIZE:
"It is better to live humbly with the poor than to share plunder with the proud." Proverbs 16:19

Pride Brings Shame

The Missing Ingredient

(Read 2 Thessalonians 3:10-13)

"I'm sick of working!" grumbled Lynn when it was time to begin the chores. "Life is supposed to be fun!"

"It's nice to have fun times," said Mother, "but God has made work a part of life, too, and he gives us the ability to enjoy it. In fact, life would be pretty dull without it."

"I don't think so," pouted Lynn.

Mother smiled. "All right," she decided, "we'll let you have the day off. OK?"

"OK!" agreed Lynn. So while the rest of the family worked on the lawn and garden, Lynn talked to some friends, read, and watched television. To her surprise, she was soon bored. *What can I do?* she thought to herself. *Oh, I know! I'll make a cake. That will surprise Mom!*

Lynn had just finished frosting the cake when her family came inside. "A cake!" exclaimed Mother. "How nice! But you didn't want to work today."

"I guess I got a little bored," admitted Lynn. "Here—try the cake, everybody. It's the kind Mother always makes."

Lynn's brother eagerly took a big bite. "It's good," he said, "but it tastes different."

Lynn took a bite herself and frowned. "Alex is right," she agreed. "There's not a lot of flavor to it. It's just kinda sweet, like sugar."

"Did you follow the recipe exactly?" asked Mother.

Lynn nodded. "Sure—except for the lemon juice. I thought it would make the cake sour."

"It would have given it a lemon flavor," said Mother, "but the sugar would keep it from being sour."

"Sometimes we like something super-sweet," said Dad. He glanced at Lynn. "But often we prefer something with a little more flavor. It's sort of like that when it comes to playing all the time. That can be fun, but often we're happier if we first accomplish something by doing some work."

"I guess we do need both work and play," said Lynn. *BJW*

HOW ABOUT YOU?

Do you complain when you have to work? Everyone needs some fun and relaxation, but a life of all play is dull and meaningless. God intended you to work. He planned that honest, hard work would bring many rewards.

Work—then Play

MEMORIZE:
"Work brings profit." Proverbs 14:23

4

Does It Pay?

(Read Psalm 37:1-8)

As Brandon dragged his snow shovel toward home, the cold air seemed to go right through to his bones. Shoveling Mrs. Walker's driveway and front walk had been a big job—especially since he'd had to do it alone!

Brandon was glad to find that his mom had a cup of hot chocolate waiting for him when he got home. "Mmmm . . . thanks," he said with a sigh as he slumped into a kitchen chair. "Mom, it just doesn't seem fair. Sometimes I wonder if doing right really pays."

Mother looked surprised. "What makes you say that?" she asked.

"Well, Chad and Adam and I all agreed to shovel Mrs. Walker's driveway after school today," Brandon explained, "but then Mr. Wilbert offered to pay anyone who would come and help clear his long driveway. Of course, that sounded good to Chad and Adam, so they went and did that instead. Not only did they break their promise, but they also got paid for it!"

"That doesn't seem fair," agreed Mother. "You know, Brandon, it often seems to us that people benefit from doing what is wrong. However, the Bible tells us not to envy those who seem to be rewarded for wrongdoing."

Dad had been listening from the living room. Now he entered the kitchen with a smile on his face. "I'm proud of what you did today, Son," he said. "I'm sorry to say that I regularly work with businessmen who seem to benefit by being dishonest or breaking promises, and it sometimes doesn't seem fair to me, either. But it helps to remember that God will reward us for doing right. After all, God is the one we are really working for."

After talking with his parents, Brandon began to feel better about the situation. He knew God had seen his actions and would one day reward him for doing what was right. *DLR*

HOW ABOUT YOU?

Does it seem like others benefit from doing what is wrong? Do you know kids who seem to get away with cheating? Stealing? Lying? God tells you not to get tired of doing what you know is right. He will reward you for it.

MEMORIZE:
"Trust in the Lord and do good."
Psalm 37:3

Keep Doing Right

Growing Two Ways

(Read Colossians 1:10-12)

It was time to measure again. Bill was eager to see how much he'd grown. For four years now, Dad had marked the new height on his closet door.

"When Aunt Alice comes from the mission field," Bill said, "she'll see a big change in me!"

"Four years makes quite a difference," his dad agreed. "Just think, she'll be here next week."

Bill remembered the day Aunt Alice had left for the mission field. It was the same day he'd made his decision to live for Jesus Christ and let him be Savior and Lord. Aunt Alice had been so pleased. She'd hugged him when they saw her off at the airport. "I suppose you'll be practically grown by the time I come home again," she had said. "Be sure to grow in grace, too!"

And now Aunt Alice was due to return. Bill knew she would see a difference in his physical growth. But would she see spiritual growth as well? He decided to ask Dad about it.

Dad smiled. "That's a good question," he said, "one we should all ask ourselves. Now, let's see—in what areas have you had problems? I seem to recall that you used to have a terrible time with your temper. Has that changed?"

"I got mad at Joe last week, and I told him off," Bill confessed. "But I did apologize."

Dad nodded. "I'd say that's progress, wouldn't you? I'm also thinking of the boys you've been inviting to Sunday school. I think you've made progress in witnessing. How about Bible knowledge? Do you know more about God than you did when Aunt Alice left?"

Bill nodded. "Quite a bit, I think. I've learned lots of verses and worked hard on my Sunday school lessons."

Yes, Bill thought, *maybe Aunt Alice would see some spiritual growth. RIJ*

HOW ABOUT YOU?

Have you taken inventory to see if you've grown spiritually? Do you spend time with God, learning from his Word and talking to him? Do you witness more than you once did? Are you more friendly, kind, and loving than you used to be? If marks could be put on the wall for spiritual growth, how would your chart look?

Grow Spiritually

MEMORIZE:
"But grow in the special favor and knowledge of our Lord and Savior Jesus Christ." 2 Peter 3:18

At Least a Tenth

(Read Malachi 3:8-12)

Andrew stirred his soup thoughtfully. Finally he looked across the table. "Does everybody have to tithe?" he asked. "I mean, do we have to give God ten cents out of every dollar?"

"Well, the Bible says we should give 'as we are able,' and often that would mean giving more than a tithe," replied Dad. "Many people believe the Bible suggests that giving a tenth is the least we should do. It seems to me it is, too."

"But if I do that, I'll have hardly anything left!" Andrew complained. "Besides, if everybody else gives a tenth, that's an awful lot of money. The little bit I might keep wouldn't really be missed, would it?"

"Well, let's think about that," said Dad. "Do you know what our tithes and offerings are used for?"

"Well, they support our missionaries," said Andrew. "They pay the pastor's salary. And I guess sometimes they buy Sunday school books and food for needy people."

"Right. And how about the upkeep of the church?" suggested Dad. "Things like electricity and insurance and janitor's supplies and the church bus and gas and . . ."

"And your scholarship to camp," interrupted Mother, "and . . ."

"OK! OK!" Andrew grinned. "But I'm still not sure that my small offering would be missed."

"That's not the point," added Mother. "Giving God 10 percent is very little compared to what God has given us."

Andrew nodded soberly. "OK," he agreed. "Ten percent it is!" *RG*

HOW ABOUT YOU?

Do you feel that tithing cuts too deeply into your allowance? Have you thought about how that money is spent in God's service? Discover the joy of giving.

MEMORIZE:

"But the one who plants generously will get a generous crop."
2 Corinthians 9:6

Give Cheerfully

The Clown Who Wasn't Smiling

(Read Psalm 139:1-4, 23-24)

"The chimpanzee was really funny," said Peggy when the circus show had ended.

"I like the clown best because he made me laugh," said six-year-old Timothy. "He was always happy and smiling."

They filed out of the "Big Top"—the huge gray tent that housed the circus ring and the crowds who came to see the circus. On their way out, Timothy suddenly clutched his father's arm. "Daddy, look! There's the clown." They stopped to watch. "He's taking his face off!" screamed Timothy in terror.

Peggy hooted with laughter. "Timmy! It's not his face—that's just a mask," she said.

The clown mopped his brow with a big white handkerchief. He didn't look young and energetic any more. He looked old and tired. There were tiny, wrinkled worry lines around his eyes, and his mouth wasn't smiling any longer.

"He looks sad," commented Mom.

"My clown was happy and smiling," said Timmy. "What happened, Mommy?"

"He wasn't really smiling. The mask just had a big smile painted on it," she explained.

"You know, Timmy, we all wear masks sometimes," said his father.

"I don't," said Timmy. "I don't have a mask." Peggy and Brian looked surprised, too.

"Not the type of mask the clown wears," said Dad. "But when we pretend to be something we're not—like pretending to be honest, when we're really telling or acting out a lie—it's like we're wearing a mask. Or when we try to impress people by making them think we're being good, when really we're not, that's another kind of mask."

"We need to remove our masks, like the clown did," said Mother, "and be honest with ourselves and God."

"Yes," agreed Dad. "Remember, God knows our heart; he knows what we're really like. We may fool other people, but we can't ever fool God with our masks." *MTF*

HOW ABOUT YOU?

Do you pretend to be something you're not? Do you pretend to be kind and loving when all the while you're nursing anger or hatred? Remember, God knows your heart. He knows all there is to know about you. Masks can't fool him. Confess your sin, and ask him to help you be an honest, genuine person, living in a way that pleases him.

MEMORIZE:

"Search me, O God, and know my heart; test me and know my thoughts. Point out anything in me that offends you, and lead me along the path of everlasting life." Psalm 139:23-24

Be Genuine

Names in Stone

(Read 1 Peter 1:3-5)

"The last avalanche of rocks at this site took place in 1970," Jody read from the plaque at the rest stop. He turned to look at the huge boulders along the side of the mountain road. "So all these rocks landed here over 30 years ago," he said thoughtfully.

"Johnny and Sue were here then, too," said Mom, pointing to another big rock showing those names and "1970" in faded spray paint.

"I guess it made them feel important to have their names written on stone," said Dad. "Everyone wants his name to live on forever."

"Well, these lasted quite a while, but they're fading away," observed Mom. She frowned. "It's a shame to spoil the mountain that way!"

"You know," said Dad with a little smile, "I once had my name written in a special place, too."

"Bill!" scolded Mom. "You didn't!"

"Yup." Dad nodded. "When I was younger . . . before you met me."

"Neat!" exclaimed Jody. "Where is it? Do you think it's still there?"

"It sure is," said Dad. "I know it's still there, because the Bible says so. My name is written in heaven."

"In heaven?" asked Jody. "On stone?"

"Nope." Dad shook his head. "It's in the Book of Life. When I became a Christian, Jesus wrote my name in his special book where no avalanche can bury it, and no sun can fade it. When I die," continued Dad, "my name in that book will prove that I belong in heaven, and God will welcome me in."

"I gave my life to Jesus," said Jody, "so my name is written there forever, too. Right?"

"It sure is," said Mom, "and so is mine." *HMT*

HOW ABOUT YOU?

Is your name written in heaven? If not, receive Jesus as Savior today. Then your name will be written in a place where it can never be destroyed or removed.

MEMORIZE:

"Rejoice because your names are registered as citizens of heaven."
Luke 10:20

Your Name Can Be Written in Heaven

New Mission Field

(Read Romans 10:12-15)

Adam was not in a very good mood. His father had just come home with the news Adam dreaded most. They were going to move again. "Doesn't the army know that we've moved often enough already?" he grumbled.

"I know how you feel," said Mother. "I used to take these moves in that same way."

"And now you like moving?" asked Adam with a pout on his face.

Mother shook her head. "No, not really. But Daddy and I decided long ago that each move meant a new mission field for us."

"A mission field?" asked Adam. "It seems to me that moving just means giving up my friends and trying to make new ones and going to a new school and church and things like that."

Mother nodded. "I know . . . it does mean those things. But do you remember when we moved here and Mrs. Evans stopped by the very day we moved in?" Adam remembered—mostly because she had brought a great big plateful of chocolate chip cookies. "Through that visit, I was able to invite her to church and later she became a Christian." Adam remembered that, too. Mother was still talking. "It seems that at every place we've been, God has had someone there for us to witness to and others for us to help. Now he's sending us to another field of work." After a moment she added softly, "I wonder who the Lord will send our way at the new place."

As Adam thought about his mother's words, he remembered the day he had surrendered his life to God. But somehow it had always seemed like that was for some future work God would have for him. Now he sat back in his chair and thought about all the moves they had made through the years—lots of them. *Maybe God is sending me from place to place to get me ready for work he has for me later,* he thought. *Maybe moving isn't so bad after all! RIJ*

HOW ABOUT YOU?

Maybe you aren't moving, but are you thinking about your school and your neighborhood as a mission field? The people there need to hear about Jesus, too. Let God use you wherever you are.

MEMORIZE:
"You will receive power and will tell people about me everywhere— in Jerusalem, throughout Judea, in Samaria, and to the ends of the earth." Acts 1:8

Enjoy God's Leading

Never Again

(Read Romans 14:7-12)

"OK, kid. We've been watching you. Come with us." Cold fear chilled the back of Bob's neck. The woman who had spoken signaled a big man nearby, who immediately moved to Bob's side.

Where's Chuck? wondered Bob. *Taking a few candy bars was his idea, and now he's just disappeared into thin air.* Bob's thoughts raced through his mind as he walked with bent head between the two security guards.

In a small room the unsmiling woman said, "Open your jacket and put everything on the table." Then Bob was asked questions about everything: his name, address, school, parents, friends. Had he ever shoplifted before? Was he alone in the store? On and on. Bob thought it would never end. "OK, Bob. Call your parents," the lady guard said finally.

"Oh no, please," protested Bob. "I'll never do—"

"You have to call them," interrupted the woman.

When Bob heard his mother's voice on the phone, he tried not to cry while he explained the awful thing that had happened. "I'll be right there," said Mother.

Mother came, but Bob couldn't look at her. She spoke gently. "Why, Bob? You know better." The sadness of her tone made him feel like a slug. And the worst wasn't over yet. He still had to face his father.

When Bob's father heard about it, he said, "You've made your mother and me very sad today, Son, and you've made it necessary for us to punish you. But I want you to think about something else. As a Christian you represent God to other people, too."

Bob nodded solemnly. "I've told him I'm sorry," he replied quietly. "I'll never do it again. I promise." *PIK*

HOW ABOUT YOU?

When you do something you know is wrong, is it hard to face people? When you know you've hurt your parents, is it hard to look them in the eye? Just as you are accountable to your parents, you are also accountable to God. Confess those things you've done wrong and receive his forgiveness.

MEMORIZE:

"Yes, each of us will have to give a personal account to God."
Romans 14:12

You're Accountable to God

The Red Cellophane

(Read Romans 5:6-11)

"What's that, Grandpa?" Steven pointed to some small cards and pieces of shiny red paper on the kitchen table.

Grandpa smiled. "Grandma found these when she was cleaning the attic the other day," he replied. "When I was a boy, we used to get these as prizes in cereal boxes."

"Wow!" Steven was impressed. "They're really old! What are all the shiny red papers for?"

"Ah, that's what makes these cards interesting, Steven," replied Grandpa. "Here, look at this one. It has a picture of Babe Ruth on the front. Now, see this question on the back of the card? It says, 'What was Babe Ruth's given name?' To find the answer, we put this shiny red paper—cellophane—right over the question, like this. Now what do you see?"

"It says 'George Herman Ruth,'" answered Steven. "The question disappeared, and the answer showed up!"

"Right," said Grandpa. "This little piece of paper taught me a great lesson." Steven wrinkled his nose. "What do you mean?"

"When I was young, we had revival meetings at our church," began Grandpa. "I knew I needed Jesus in my life. I was the church rascal." Steven laughed. "I had often heard that only the blood of Jesus could wash away sin," continued Grandpa. "One night, the evangelist called me up to the platform. He said he saw these cards sticking out of my pocket and wanted to use them as an illustration. Well, he took this Babe Ruth card, put the red paper over the question, and said, 'Bert, read the question for me.' I said I couldn't see the question, only the answer. Then he said, 'That's how it is with God. When you accept Jesus as Savior, the blood of Jesus washes away your sin. Just as you can't see the question when the red paper covers it, God can no longer see your sin when it's covered by the blood of Jesus. Just as you see only the answer on the card, God sees only Jesus living in you.' "

Steven nodded. "I'm glad God sees only Jesus in me." *PR*

HOW ABOUT YOU?

What does God see when he looks at you? Does he see your sins, or are they covered by Jesus' blood so that he only sees Jesus living in you? If you haven't done so before, talk to a friend or trusted adult about how you can accept Jesus as your Savior.

MEMORIZE:

"I myself no longer live, but Christ lives in me. So I live my life in this earthly body by trusting in the Son of God, who loved me and gave himself for me." Galatians 2:20

Jesus' Blood Covers Sin

Help from Hurts (Part 1)

(Read Psalm 84:9-12)

John was tired when he got home from the Children's Orthopedic Center where he was taking treatments for cerebral palsy (or C.P., as it's called). The disease affected his muscles and caused difficulty in walking and speaking.

Being in therapy was hard work, and now John also had been given exercises to do at home. *Oh well,* he thought, a*t least I won't have to do them before dinner. By then maybe Mom and Dad will forget about the exercises.*

"That was a good supper," Dad said when they had finished. Then he turned to John. "Why didn't you eat your vegetables, Son? You know they're good for your body."

"Yuck!" John said. "I don't like them, Dad."

"I talked to the nurse at the orthopedic center," Dad went on, "and she said you've also been trying to skip your physical therapy treatments. They're also good for your body."

"But, Dad," protested John, "those treatments hurt! When they stretch my legs and arms, they pull so hard."

"I know they do, Son," said Dad, "but they're doing it to help you. If you want those muscles of yours to grow stronger and healthier, you'll have to be in therapy each time your teacher sends you."

John sighed. "I suppose. But why doesn't God just heal me? Then I wouldn't have to worry about exercises."

Mother smiled sympathetically. "I don't know why God doesn't heal you, John. That is just something we may never understand. But we can still trust that God has a wonderful plan for you. Can you trust him?"

John looked thoughtful as he nodded. "I get so tired sometimes," he said slowly. Then his face broke into a smile. "But I do trust him. He's very good to me!" *GM*

HOW ABOUT YOU?

Do you have some special problem? Perhaps it's some disease. Or perhaps it's something that only you and God know about. If you're a Christian, will you trust God to do what is best for you? Will you accept his decision? He gives what is good.

MEMORIZE:

"No good thing will the Lord withhold from those who do what is right."
Psalm 84:11

God Answers Some Prayers "No"

Help from Hurts (Part 2)

(Read Romans 13:1-6)

After supper the Hill family had devotions together, and then John sat down to read a book. Soon he was deep in one of the adventures of *The Black Stallion*. As he was starting a new chapter, the list of exercises he was supposed to do at home flashed through his mind. *Oh no!* he thought. He glanced at Mother and Dad. *I guess they forgot about my exercises, too. Maybe I can get away with skipping them today. At least I can try.* He settled down to read again, but somehow he couldn't get interested in his book. He seemed to hear the voice of his therapist repeating over and over, "Be sure to do your home exercises regularly. They will help strengthen your muscles."

"Oh, phooey!" muttered John as he put down his book.

Mother glanced up in surprise. "What's the matter?"

"My therapist says I have to do exercises at home," John said slowly. "Since you didn't remind me, I was going to skip them. But I know the therapist wants me to do them."

Dad smiled and nodded. "Remember the verses we read for devotions tonight?" he said. "God says we're to 'submit to,' or obey, those in authority. It goes on to say that God provided them for our good. This doesn't mean obeying only your mother and me. It means obeying the pastor and Sunday school teacher at church. It means obeying your teacher at school, and your therapist, too." *GM*

HOW ABOUT YOU?

Are you obeying your mom? Dad? Teacher? They love you and want what is best for you! Above all, are you obeying God?

Obey Authority

MEMORIZE:
"Obey the government, for God is the one who put it there. All governments have been placed in power by God."
Romans 13:1

February
14

Warm, Brown Toast

(Read Luke 11:5-10)

"Hey, Paul! You forgot to pray for Carter," exclaimed Lizzy after Paul finished his prayer at the breakfast table.

"I gave up praying for him," declared Paul. "It wasn't working. He's not interested in coming to Sunday school or Bible Club or anything."

As Mom put bread into the toaster, Lizzy looked at her brother. "You prayed for Carter for only three days," she said.

"God could save him in three seconds if he wanted to," Paul answered smugly. "Remember the story of Saul? God came to him in a blinding light, and he repented right away!" Mom leaned over and popped the bread out of the toaster. "Is my toast done already?" Paul asked, glad to change the subject.

Mom held out the piece of bread. "It doesn't look like the toaster is working, does it?" she said.

"But you left it in for only a few seconds," Paul complained.

Lizzy smiled knowingly. "Just like you prayed for Carter for only a few days," she reminded him. "Right, Mom?"

Mom nodded. "You're right about one thing, Paul," she said. "God can save Carter in a second, and he will, as soon as Carter responds to his invitation." She held up the limp piece of bread. "If this bread were thin, it would toast quickly. If it were frozen, it would take quite a long time to toast. We need to leave it in the toaster as long as it takes to make a perfect piece of toast. If it doesn't get toasted the first time we put it down, we have to put it down again." She paused. "It reminds me of how we need to pray for people."

"I guess you're saying that some people don't respond as quickly as others," murmured Paul.

"That's right," said Lizzy. "Our job is to pray and pray again and again if we don't see results right away." *HMT*

HOW ABOUT YOU?

Have you prayed for somebody who doesn't know God? Does it sometimes seem like nothing is happening? Keep praying anyway. God hears every prayer, and he will be faithful to answer—when his time is right.

MEMORIZE:

"Keep on praying."
1 Thessalonians 5:17

Keep on Praying

The Big Event

(Read John 14:1-6)

When Kent's Sunday school teacher suggested that the class go together to watch the space shuttle launch, Kent was thrilled. He had been wishing he could somehow have a really good view of the event. The week seemed to pass slowly, but finally Saturday arrived. Kent and six other excited boys met Mr. Marshall at church, and it was a wide-awake group that boarded the church van.

"Hope we're early enough to get a good view," exclaimed Kent—and they were! About an hour after they reached their viewing point the big space shuttle was launched. The bright red light and the trail that followed the liftoff was something Kent would never forget.

Back in the van, Mr. Marshall turned on the radio so they could listen to an announcer review what had taken place. They also heard the space control center talk with the astronauts.

"Well," said Mr. Marshall, "whenever you think of what you saw this morning, I want you to remember that all Christians will participate in a 'liftoff' someday."

"Hey, that's right," said Kent. "You mean when Jesus comes, don't you?"

"Exactly," answered Mr. Marshall. "When he returns, he'll be taking all Christians to live in heaven with him."

"And we won't even need a spaceship, will we?" asked one of the boys.

"No," agreed Mr. Marshall. "It will all happen quick as a flash, or as the Bible puts it, 'in the twinkling of an eye.'" He looked at the boys. "I'm glad you all made it to the liftoff today. My prayer is that each of you will also be ready for that wonderful event when Jesus comes again." *RIJ*

HOW ABOUT YOU?

When Jesus returns in the clouds, those who have confessed their sins and asked for God's forgiveness will rise to be with him. Are you one who has done that? If not, talk with a trusted friend or adult to find out more.

Be Ready for Christ's Return

MEMORIZE:
"When everything is ready, I will come and get you, so that you will always be with me where I am."
John 14:3

Ready and Willing

(Read Philippians 3:7-10)

Blake, Tammy, and their parents strolled through the museum peering into each display case. "Look at these old shoes," said Tammy. "They look uncomfortable. I'm glad we have sneakers today."

"Me, too," agreed Blake.

They walked along, commenting on the things they saw. Just before leaving, they stopped to look at things from the Revolutionary War period.

"Check out this wig," said Blake. "It reminds me of pictures I've seen of George Washington. Do you think he wore a wig?"

Mother nodded. "At that time, men often wore wigs for special occasions," she said.

"It looks silly," remarked Tammy. "Oh, look! Here's the Minuteman display! We read all about them in my history class. They were called Minutemen because they would be ready to follow their leader into battle at a minute's notice."

"It meant leaving all they had," said Mom. "Families, businesses, and possessions were left for a cause they believed in. When the word came, they had to be ready and willing to go."

"That must have been hard," said Blake. "I wonder if I could leave everything I owned in a moment's notice." He shrugged his shoulders. "Well there are no Minutemen today, so I guess I'll never know."

"In a way, there are Minutemen," said Dad. "When Jesus calls, we should be ready immediately to follow him wherever he leads. It may mean leaving everything we have and everyone we know."

"Missionaries do that," observed Tammy.

Dad nodded. "They often do," he agreed. "Wherever God wants us is the place we'll find contentment and happiness as we commit our life to him and yield to his will." *SSA*

HOW ABOUT YOU?

Would you be willing to follow Jesus whenever and wherever he leads? Is there something you know the Lord would like you to give up to follow him? It is hard. Ask him to give you the courage and strength to do so today. You'll find it brings real joy.

MEMORIZE:

"All those who want to be my disciples must come and follow me, because my servants must be where I am. And if they follow me, the Father will honor them." John 12:26

Be Ready to Follow Jesus

Salty Songs

(Read Colossians 4:2-6)

Many of Kyle's classmates had gone to a rock concert. Kyle had stayed home because he knew that the words of many of the songs the group sang were not pleasing to God.

For several days after the concert, the kids sang some of the songs they'd heard. Soon Kyle knew the words, too, but he didn't sing along. A Bible verse he had learned in Sunday school kept running through his mind, and it kept him from joining in. The verse was, "You are the salt of the earth," and Kyle recalled his Sunday school teacher's words. "When Christians do wrong things just because others are doing them," Mrs. Drake had said, "they've lost their 'salti-ness'—their usefulness."

After a week or so, the kids lost interest in the concert songs and turned to other subjects.

One afternoon Kyle hummed a tune as he walked home. Ben, a classmate, heard him. "That's a nice song you're humming. What is it?" asked Ben.

"It's 'God Is So Good,'" said Kyle. "We sing it a lot in Sunday school."

Ben shook his head. "I've never heard it before. Sing some more."

Kyle sang different verses including the one, "Christ died for me."

"What does that mean?" asked Ben.

Kyle smiled and explained how Christ came to take everyone's punishment for sin, so all who believe can go to heaven. After reaching Kyle's house, the boys sat on the front steps and talked awhile longer. Kyle was pleased when Ben agreed to go to church and Sunday school the next weekend. How glad he was that his song had been "salty!" *CEY*

HOW ABOUT YOU?

If you love Jesus, you can be "salty" in many ways, even in the songs you sing. Although some songs used by popular groups are all right, many are not.

MEMORIZE:
"You are the salt of the earth. But what good is salt if it has lost its flavor?" Matthew 5:13a

Be a "Salty" Christian

A Higher View

(Read Romans 8:28-32)

Katie and Derrick grinned at one another as their family rode the elevator to the observation deck of the Sears Tower in Chicago. Their ears popped as they whizzed by floor after floor, going higher and higher. Getting off the elevator, the children ran to the window to look out at the view below.

"Everything looks so tiny!" Katie exclaimed. "The cars look like toys."

Mother nodded. "You can see a long way from here. See the boats on the lake?"

"Look way ahead, over to your right," Dad instructed.

"Traffic's stopped there."

"Yes, but look right below us," Derrick said. "See that red car? It keeps changing lanes, trying to get ahead of everyone else."

"Probably in a hurry," Katie suggested.

"Probably," agreed Dad. "That guy is in such a hurry he's driving dangerously. But he's going to be slowed down because it looks like there's a roadblock up ahead. That will stop him."

"Too bad he can't see the roadblock like we can," Katie said. "Then he wouldn't be in such a hurry."

"You know," said Dad, "as Christians, we sometimes act a lot like that fellow. God has a plan mapped out for each of our lives, but we often try to hurry ahead of him. We complain when we have to wait, but we don't stop to think that there is a purpose for the delay."

Mother nodded. "The higher view is better, isn't it?" *JLH*

HOW ABOUT YOU?

Do you fret when your plans are changed? Do you grumble when someone gets sick or hurt, making it necessary to cancel an activity? Changes aren't always pleasant, but they are a part of life. Trust God to work out what is best for you despite your interrupted plans.

MEMORIZE:

"If God is for us, who can ever be against us?" Romans 8:31

God's Ways Are Good

Beware!

(Read James 1:13-15)

"Hey, Rod," whispered Max. "Look over there by the bushes."

"Wow!" Rod whispered back. "Mr. Jones must have a new dog. He's big, but he looks harmless."

"I think we can still take our regular shortcut through his backyard," said Max, a little bit louder.

"But look, Max." Rod pointed to a sign on a tree. "It says, 'Beware of the Dog.'"

"Sure! Just look at that baby face!" exclaimed Max as he slowly walked toward the dog. The dog began to growl. "Nice doggy, nice doggy," repeated Max.

"Hey, Max," warned Rod, "maybe we better not go any closer."

"He's as gentle as a lamb. You'll see," Max assured him. "You just have to have a way with animals, Rod."

Suddenly, the dog lunged toward Max. "Help!" yelled Max as he frantically tried to free his pant leg from the dog's teeth.

The boys heard a shout. "What are you doing in my backyard?" Mr. Jones asked angrily as he walked towards the snarling dog. "Come here, Dude!" Dude wagged his tail and trotted to his master. "You boys should read signs more carefully," Mr. Jones said firmly. "You were trespassing. See that it doesn't happen again. Dude may look gentle, and most of the time he is, but he's been known to scare a few people. Warnings are given for a reason."

Max and Rod were quiet as they walked home. "Max," Rod broke the silence, "Mr. Jones sounded a lot like Rev. Parker."

Max nodded. "Yeah." They were remembering Sunday's evening message. "Sin may look harmless," Rev. Parker had said. "But God warns against all sin. Heed this warning. Say no when Satan tempts you." *VLR*

HOW ABOUT YOU?

Would you like to be like some of your more daring friends once in a while? Do you think it wouldn't hurt you to go where they go and do what they do, even though you know they are doing wrong sometimes? It will hurt you. God warns that sin has consequences.

Beware of Sin

MEMORIZE:
"These evil desires lead to evil actions." James 1:15a

February
20

Grandpa Forgets

(Read Luke 12:6-7)

"Hi, Grandpa!" exclaimed Dennis. "Is Grandma here, too?" Dennis had come home from the supermarket with his father, who was picking up a cake mix and some ice cream for his birthday party the next day. But what was wrong with Grandpa? He didn't say anything. Grandpa just stared at him as if he didn't know him.

Just then Grandma appeared. Seeing Dennis, she gave him a quick hug. "Are you ready for your birthday party?" she asked.

"Party?" asked Grandpa. "Who's having a party?"

"Dennis is. We talked about it at breakfast," said Grandma patiently. "Don't you remember?" She took his arm and led him into the kitchen.

That night as Mother tucked him into bed, Dennis told her about Grandpa's strange behavior. Mother looked concerned. "Grandpa isn't well," said Mother. "Do you remember when we took him to University Hospital not long ago?" Dennis nodded. "The doctors discovered that he has a disease called Alzheimer's. It causes people to forget names, places, and even people they love."

Dennis swallowed hard. "But Grandpa and I are friends—he said so himself. And friends aren't supposed to forget each other."

"Honey, Grandpa can't help it when he forgets," said Mother. "Thank God for the good times you've had together. Thank him, too, that Jesus is always there for you—that he's a friend that sticks 'closer than a brother'—or even than a grandfather."

As Dennis snuggled down, he thought about his mother's words. Dennis thanked God that he would never leave him. *CJB*

HOW ABOUT YOU?

Do you feel sad because a friend moved away, chose someone else, or just simply forgot you? Aren't you glad that God will never forget you? Thank him for that, and let him heal the sad place in your life.

MEMORIZE:

"There are 'friends' who destroy each other, but a real friend sticks closer than a brother." Proverbs 18:24

God Never Forgets You

Close-up Christian

(Read Psalm 19:12-14)

"Hello, Mrs. Rodgers." Len smiled nicely at a lady picking out some oranges in the produce department at the grocery store. "This is my mother," Len continued. "Mother, this is Mrs. Rodgers, my art teacher."

"You have a wonderful son," Mrs. Rodgers told Len's mother. "He's so polite and helpful—such a happy, cheerful child."

After Mrs. Rodgers went on her way, Len turned to his mother. "Are you about done?" he asked. "I'm tired of grocery shopping. I don't see why I had to come along." Soon they were on their way home.

At home, Len grumbled when he had to help put away the groceries. Then he picked a quarrel with his brother, Craig. Finally he announced, "I'm starved. Can I have a pear?"

Mother nodded. "There are just two left. You and Craig can each have one."

"I get the biggest," said Len quickly. He snatched the larger piece of fruit from the bowl while Craig took what was left. Len was about to take a bite when he let out a wail. "Oh, no fair! This one's no good. Look!"

Mother looked at the pear Len held out. At first glance, it looked fine, but when she looked closely, she could see that it was bruised. "This pear reminds me of you," Mother said.

Len scowled. "What's that supposed to mean?"

"Well, you act like one kind of person at school, the happy and cheerful you. Then here at home you act like the grumbling and complaining you. It's as important to be helpful and kind at home, where most people don't see you, as you are when other people do see you." *HWM*

HOW ABOUT YOU?

Do you talk nicely at church and then grumble when you get home? Are you eager to help your teachers and unwilling to help your mother? You need to show your love for Jesus by being the same person at home and away.

MEMORIZE:

"But the wisdom that comes from heaven is first of all pure. It is also peace loving, gentle at all times, and willing to yield to others. It is full of mercy and good deeds. It shows no partiality and is always sincere."

James 3:17

Be Nice at Home

Not Sticky Enough

(Read 1 Corinthians 13:4-7)

As Kip and his sister Tina drove home after a shopping trip with Mother, they saw a couple walking along, holding hands. "There go Mr. and Mrs. Glue," said Kip. "They're so sticky."

"Mr. and Mrs. Glue?" asked Mother.

Tina nodded. "That's what the kids call them because they're so stuck on each other," she said. "Yvonne thinks everything Clay says is so cute. And she's always running her fingers through his hair."

"Yuck!" responded Kip. Just then he spotted someone else. "Oh, and there goes Mr. Know-It-All," he added.

Tina looked. "That's Brent," she said. "He's OK. You just don't like him because he's smarter than you."

"Nobody likes him," retorted Kip.

"Brenda does, and that makes you mad, because you like Brenda," taunted Tina as Mother pulled into their driveway. "I don't see why you like her. She's a snob." Kip made a face at his sister as they got out of the car.

In the kitchen, Tina pulled a big bottle of glue from a bag. "I really need this for my science project," she said. "Snobby Brenda used up half of my last bottle."

"She's not a snob," said Kip. "She's pretty and you're just jealous."

Mother sighed. "I have no doubt that the couple we saw earlier are too sticky, as you put it," she said. "But I get the feeling that the two of you are not sticky enough. I think you need a little more 'glue' in your lives." Tina looked at the bottle she held in her hand. "Not that kind," continued Mother. "But tell me—what does glue do?"

"It holds things together," replied Kip.

Mother nodded. "And the best glue—the best thing for holding people together—is love. God says we're to love each other. Were you two displaying God's love when you talked about your classmates? Were you showing love by fighting with each other? Think about it!" *HWM*

HOW ABOUT YOU?

Is there plenty of "glue"—plenty of love—displayed in your life? Are your words and thoughts loving and kind? Display God's love in your life.

MEMORIZE:

"So now I am giving you a new commandment: Love each other. Just as I have loved you, you should love each other." John 13:34

Love One Another

Being Different (Part 1)

(Read Romans 10:9-13)

Lan closed her locker and hurried toward the door. Her first day in the new school had been just as she expected. She felt as if everyone stared at her because she looked different from most of the girls in her class. But then, they had not been born in Korea, and she had. She sighed. She was glad there were at least a few other Asian girls in the class, and she hoped she'd soon get to know them better.

"Lan," someone called. "Wait for me." Lan turned abruptly and saw a short blonde girl coming toward her. "I was hoping I'd get to meet you," the girl said in a friendly voice. "My Sunday school teacher told me you and your folks had just moved next door to her."

Lan nodded. "She wanted me to go to church with her yesterday," the Korean girl confessed. "But . . . ," she stopped again.

"My name is Gina Ellers," the other girl said. "I wish you had come to church yesterday. You would have liked it. There are lots of nice people there."

Lan shook her head. "No," she said shyly. "They would just look at me and say I'm different."

"Oh, I don't think so," Gina replied. "Most of them know nobody is really different."

Lan looked at the blonde girl in surprise. "That's silly. You sure look a lot different from me."

"Well, we look different on the outside," Gina admitted. "But it doesn't matter how different each one looks on the outside because God sees the heart, and he knows that we're all the same inside," she explained. "He knows we've all done wrong things, and we need to be forgiven."

"I never heard that before," Lan said thoughtfully. "Maybe I will come to your church and hear more about it. Or maybe you can tell me more." *RIJ*

HOW ABOUT YOU?

Maybe you're a different color or nationality from others in your school. That makes no difference to God. He gave his Son for everyone, including you. Have you asked him to forgive you for the wrong things you have done, and make you his child? If not, talk to a trusted adult or friend to find out more.

All Have Sinned

MEMORIZE:
"Anyone who calls on the name of the Lord will be saved." Romans 10:13

February
24

Being Different (Part 2)

(Read Mark 8:34-38)

Gina and Lan became good friends, and it wasn't long before Lan accepted Jesus as her Savior. She was beginning to feel more at home in her new school, too. The two girls talked about it one day. "You know something?" said Gina. "You've been afraid of being different, and so have I."

Lan looked at her in surprise. "You? Why would you be afraid of anything like that? You look just like all the other kids in school."

Gina nodded. "Maybe I look like most of them," she admitted, "but I've still been afraid of being different. I hardly ever talk to anyone about church or God or anything like that—all because I'm afraid they might laugh at me."

"You mean you've never talked to anyone like you talked to me?" Lan asked in surprise.

Gina shook her head. "I've been a Christian for three years," she said, "and I guess I've just been afraid the other kids would laugh at me." She paused for a long time. "Yesterday in Sunday school, when our teacher read those verses about Jesus being ashamed of us before his Father if we are ashamed of him down here on earth, I really felt sad. I don't want him to be ashamed of me anymore."

Lan was not sure she understood everything Gina was saying. It was still all so new to her. But she did know what it meant to be different. "Maybe we've both been wrong," she said slowly. "Maybe sometimes it's good to be different. I don't want Jesus to be ashamed of me either. Let's be different together." *RIJ*

HOW ABOUT YOU?

Are you afraid to let your Christian testimony show for fear that someone will think you are a little different? Maybe "being different" in your actions and speech will be the very thing that will cause someone to see that you are a Christian. Perhaps it will give you the opportunity to talk about the Lord with some of your friends.

MEMORIZE:

"If any of you wants to be my follower, you must put aside your selfish ambition . . . and follow me."
Luke 9:23

Be Different for Jesus

That's Ridiculous

(Read 1 John 4:7-11)

It was the most ridiculous thing Steve had ever heard! "Let your brothers and sisters know you love them," Mrs. Johnson, Steve's Sunday school teacher, had said. "And don't just tell them—show them, too." Well, obviously Mrs. Johnson didn't know Todd, Steve's brother. He was a pain!

When Steve got home, Moppet, his dog, looked up from his basket. "Hi, Baby," crooned Steve. As he sat down to pet him, Todd walked through the kitchen. Moppet promptly jumped from his basket and followed Todd outside. Steve glared after the dog. "Hey," he complained, "you belong to me, you know." Steve went to his room to change his clothes.

Later that evening, Steve saw his brother sitting in the living room, watching TV. He could tell that Todd wasn't very interested in the program. He hadn't thought about it before, but Todd didn't have many friends. And he didn't spend much time talking to Mom and Dad. Neither of them did, because their parents always seemed busy. Steve never talked to Todd much, either, except to fight with him. He always kept busy with his own friends.

As Steve thought about it, he remembered how he felt when Moppet chose to follow Todd instead of him. It annoyed him, but it made him feel kind of sad, too. *Is that how Todd feels?* he thought. *Sad, and maybe lonely?* He thought of Mrs. Johnson's words. Actually, he did love Todd, even though he didn't always get along with him.

Steve went to the kitchen and got a Coke. He took it to the living room and handed it to his brother. Todd looked up in surprise. "Todd," Steve said softly as he sat down next to him, "I . . . I just want you to know that I . . . I love you."

Todd gave him a funny look. "At least somebody does," he mumbled.

It wasn't much, but it was a start. *LMW*

HOW ABOUT YOU?

Do your brothers or sisters know you care about them? Sometimes it's harder to get along with family members than with anyone else, but it's important that you do so. Ask the Lord to help you be creative in showing love to your family.

Show Love to Your Family

MEMORIZE:
"And God himself has commanded that we must love not only him but our Christian brothers and sisters, too." 1 John 4:21

February
26

Satisfied Customer

(Read 2 Corinthians 3:1-6)

"Sean, turn off that horrid music!" exclaimed Mother as Sean was watching television after school one day. "I've told you before—you are not to listen to that kind of music in this house!"

Sean laughed. "It's a commercial," he said. "It says that Kleaner King is the 'king of all cleaners.' Don't you want to get some, Mom?"

"After a commercial such as that, I wouldn't use the stuff even if they were giving it away!" Mother said with a scowl. Dad walked into the room as Mother went on. "I can think of a couple of other products I wouldn't buy because I can't stand their ads."

"This conversation reminds me of our discussion yesterday about how we should advertise for the Lord," said Dad. "You bring up a good point. A commercial or advertisement should draw people to the product, not cause them to turn away. As representatives of the Lord, we want to attract people to him."

"How can we be sure to do that?" asked Sean.

"Well, let's think about some ways," suggested Mother. "I'd say a neat appearance would help. What else?"

"We shouldn't be grumpy," said Sean, "or nobody will want to listen to us."

"Right," agreed Dad. "A happy smile is more attractive than a gloomy look."

"And we shouldn't use bad language," added Sean, "or swear and use God's name in vain."

Mother nodded. "Let's be careful always to live in a way that will make people want to know more about the Lord." *HWM*

HOW ABOUT YOU?

Does your life back up your witness for the Lord? People notice the places you go, the friends you keep, and the way you look and talk, as well as what you say. When they watch you, will they be attracted to the one who changed your life? Ask the Lord to help you live, as well as speak, for him.

MEMORIZE:

"But the only letter of recommendation we need is you yourselves! Your lives are a letter written in our hearts, and everyone can read it and recognize our good work among you." 2 Corinthians 3:2

Attract People to Jesus

Shut Out

(Read 2 Thessalonians 1:5-12)

"I'm finished sweeping," Jacob called to his Uncle Bill, who was janitor at the school. He was helping his uncle get the auditorium ready for the school play.

"Would you like to see the play?" asked Uncle Bill. "I have an extra ticket for the Saturday afternoon matinee." But Jacob thought it sounded boring, so he didn't take the ticket.

On Saturday afternoon, Jacob changed his mind. *I'll go see if Uncle Bill is at school,* he thought. *Maybe I can still get in.*

When he arrived at school, the play had already started. It was a comedy, and he could hear the crowd roar with laughter. Jacob inched past the door to get a better look. "Wait a minute, young man. Do you have a ticket?" asked an usher.

"No-o-o, but I'm looking for my uncle—Bill Reed," Jacob said in a hopeful tone. "He works here."

"Sorry, but you can't get in without a ticket," said the man.

Jacob went back outside and sat down on the steps, feeling disappointed and left out. He knew he had no one to blame but himself. If only he had accepted the ticket, he could be having a good time right now. Hearing footsteps, he looked up to see his uncle. "Uncle Bill, do you still have my ticket?" Jacob nearly shouted.

Uncle Bill shook his head. "I gave it to another boy. I'm sorry, Jacob," he said, sitting down beside him on the steps. They sat quietly a few minutes, then Uncle Bill said, "Jacob, I know you're disappointed at missing the play—and it occurred to me that the way you feel is a little like the way people will feel who have turned down their chance to get into heaven. They'll be shut out of not just a play, but the most beautiful place you can imagine. Have you ever asked Jesus to come into your life and forgive your sins so you can live with him in heaven some day?"

"Not yet, but I do have a lot of questions," answered Jacob.

"Well, why don't you ask me a few of your questions. Perhaps I can answer them for you." *CEY*

HOW ABOUT YOU?

Have you been turning down a ticket into heaven? You can't get in unless you have asked Jesus to forgive your sins. If you want to know more talk to a trusted friend or adult.

Accept Jesus

MEMORIZE:
"They will be . . . forever separated from the Lord and from his glorious power." 2 Thessalonians 1:9

That'll Be the Day!

(Read James 2:1-9)

Tom eagerly leafed through one book, then another. He loved to read and study. "Thanks for the encyclopedias, Dad," he said. Tom picked up the *S* book and started flipping through the pages. He paused and looked at a picture in the book. "Sur-i-nam toad," he pronounced loudly. Then he laughed. "Hey, that looks just like Frankie Webster. Look at those beady eyes . . . and those big feet. If that toad had messed-up hair he'd be the spittin' image of Frankie!"

"Tom, that's not very nice," scolded Dad. "Instead of making fun of Frankie, you should try to be his friend."

"That'll be the day, when I have anything to do with him!" exclaimed Tom. "None of the kids like him."

"That's enough, Thomas," said Dad sternly.

As Tom continued flipping pages, the words "Ships and Shipwrecks" caught his eye. He read a little out loud to his dad.

Dad replied, "That's interesting stuff. But I have a question for you. If you were shipwrecked on a desert island and discovered that Frankie Webster was the only other person on that island with you, how would you feel about Frankie then?"

"I think I would want to talk to him," said Tom. "Otherwise we'd both be lonely."

"I think Frankie is already lonely at school," suggested Dad.

As Tom thought about his dad's comment, he felt ashamed as he remembered his remarks about Frankie. Neither he nor Dad said anything for a few moments, but Tom made a decision. "Hey, Dad, remember when I said, 'That'll be the day, when I have anything to do with Frankie Webster'?" he asked. Dad nodded. "Well . . . today's the day!" announced Tom. He walked over to the telephone, looked up Frankie's phone number, and began dialing it. *SRS*

HOW ABOUT YOU?

Would you be embarrassed if a Christian with messed-up hair and tattered clothing wanted to be your friend? Jesus loves all believers the same, and so should you. Think of someone who is unappealing to the other kids and see what you can do to help him or her.

MEMORIZE:
"Dear friends, since God loved us that much, we surely ought to love each other." 1 John 4:11

Love Others

The Vaccination

(Read Job 42:1-3)

Randy looked sad as he sat with his dog, Pal, in the waiting room at the veterinarian's office. "What's on your mind, Son?" asked Dad. "Feeling sad about Mom today?"

Randy shrugged. "I feel sad about her all the time," he said.

Dad nodded and gave Randy's shoulder a squeeze. "I know," he agreed. "I do too."

"I just don't understand why Mom had to get cancer," said Randy angrily. "The Bible says God works everything out for good, but I'd sure like to hear his explanation of why Mom has to go through all those treatments and be so tired all the time."

"Maybe we just need to trust him without knowing the reason why," Dad replied. Just then the vet was ready to see Pal, so Randy and Dad led their happy, jumping puppy to a room.

"Pal, we're going to get you vaccinated so you won't get rabies," Randy told his dog.

When the vet came in and stuck the needle into Pal's thigh, however, the puppy barked and yelped and jumped right off the table! Dad, the vet, and Randy all had to work together to lift the scared dog back up for his next shot.

"Pal," said Randy, holding his dog down, "we're not trying to hurt you. It's because we love you. You don't want to get sick, do you? Are you mad at me, Pal?" Pal stared at Randy with scared, sad, brown dog eyes. Randy patted his dog. "I can't make you understand, but you've just got to trust us," he said. As he spoke, a thought flashed through his mind, and he gave Dad a little, lopsided smile.

When they were on their way home, Randy turned to Dad. "I've been like Pal was today, haven't I?" he said. "I've had a hard time trusting that God will work all of this out about Mom."

Dad nodded. "Me, too. But let's try to remember that he loves us—even more than you love Pal," he said. Randy smiled as he scratched Pal's ears. *DAG*

HOW ABOUT YOU?

Have you wondered why God let a hurtful thing happen to you? Do you get angry or try to figure out the reason? God wants you to remember that he loves you. And he wants you to talk to him about your hurt, sad, and angry feelings. Trust him even when you don't understand.

MEMORIZE:
"For just as the heavens are higher than the earth, so are my ways higher than your ways and my thoughts higher than your thoughts."
Isaiah 55:9

Trust God's Wisdom

One Chance

(Read Acts 26:28-29)

Joe peered down the long hallway. He saw his friend Ben standing beside his locker. Joe hurried to talk to him. "Hi, Ben," he said. "I've been meaning to ask you—want to play ball with my team?"

"Some other guys asked me to play with them," Ben said, pulling books from his locker.

"But we're good friends," protested Joe.

Ben grinned and nodded. "Friends forever," he said.

"The other guys from church really want you to play with us, too," said Joe.

Suddenly Ben slammed the locker shut. He spun around and stared hard at Joe. "Church team!" he exclaimed. "I suppose they'd want me to come to church with them, too. I told you before—I don't care to hear about all the church and Jesus stuff!"

"But it's important to know Jesus," Joe began as a small, noisy group of boys rushed down the hall toward Joe and Ben. "He's . . . ."

"Hey, Joe," interrupted the tall boy in the lead. "Ben here is going to play on our baseball team. Want to play with us, too? We play in a Sunday morning league."

"I love to play ball," said Joe. "But on Sunday mornings I go to church and Sunday school."

"Joe goes to Sunday school. Isn't that sweet?" called a boy in a blue shirt. All the boys started laughing.

Joe swallowed hard. "Play with our team," he urged, looking at Ben. "This could be real important to you."

"This is important all right," said Ben. "I'm the new pitcher." He grinned. "This is my big chance to pitch. Maybe it's the only chance I'll ever have."

"Come on. Let's go," called one of the boys. Ben pulled his baseball cap on while the other boys grouped around him. Soon they were laughing and joking as they headed for the exit.

Joe stood alone in the quiet hallway. He silently prayed that one day Ben would become a Christian. *SIZ*

HOW ABOUT YOU?

Have you trusted Jesus as your Savior and best friend? If not, talk with a trusted friend or adult to find out more.

MEMORIZE:

"Indeed, God is ready to help you right now. Today is the day of salvation." 2 Corinthians 6:2

Trust Jesus Now

Time to Get Up!

(Read Psalm 122)

"Robbie," Mother called. "I told you to get up long ago. Now hurry! We'll soon be leaving for church!" Robbie sleepily opened his eyes. It was so hard to get up in the morning! He put one foot on the floor, then the other. It was cold. He wrapped his blanket around him. "Robbie, are you hurrying?" Mother called from the hallway.

"Yeah, yeah. I'm hurrying," Robbie answered, but he didn't hurry at all. He put on his shirt and pants and then flopped down on the bed again. In fact, the next time Mom checked on him, he was fast asleep.

"You're going to have to get to bed earlier," his mother sighed as she woke him again.

The following day was Robbie's birthday. All weekend his family had been giving him hints about a very special gift, and as soon as Robbie heard his dad and mom get up, he jumped out of bed, too. He didn't mind that it was early and cold. He threw his clothes on as fast as he could and then ran downstairs to open his gift.

"Hmmmm," Mother said. "This is funny."

"What's funny?" asked Dad.

"It's funny how easy it was for our sleepyhead to get out of bed this morning," said Mother.

"Today's a special day, Mom!" said Robbie, eyeing the big box standing in the center of the table.

"Sundays are special days too, Son," replied Mother. "Sundays are days we set apart to learn more about God's Word and to worship him."

"Right," agreed Dad.

Robbie looked at his birthday present. He knew his parents were right. Then and there he decided he was going to take the ribbon from the birthday gift and pin it to his bulletin board. It would be a reminder that Sunday was a special day. *LMW*

HOW ABOUT YOU?

Do you have trouble getting up for church? Maybe sometimes you don't get there at all! Or maybe Sunday morning is a hassle at your house because your dad and mom always have to be yelling at you to hurry up and get moving. Treat Sunday as a special day. Get to bed early on Saturday.

MEMORIZE:
"This is the day the Lord has made.
We will rejoice and be glad in it."
Psalm 118:24

Sunday Is a Special Day

Lifeprints

(Read Colossians 3:8-9, 12-14)

When the school bell rang, Tyson pushed past several children and hurried to the drinking fountain. He edged in at the front of the long line. "No cuts!" called several children, but Tyson took a long drink. When he went to hang up his coat, he found a coat on the hook nearest the door. He moved it to a place down the line and put his own coat in his favorite spot. Somehow, he managed to be the last one to his seat.

It was the start of a typical day. Tyson spent a lot of time daydreaming instead of studying. At recess he tried to be the first one out the door and the last one back in. "No fair," he grumbled when he had to stay in to finish his work during the afternoon recess. He glared at his teacher.

After school, Tyson invited Jerry over to play. "I got a new detective set," he said. "Let's see if we can lift fingerprints."

The boys played until Tyson's grandpa came home from work. After Jerry left, Tyson told his grandpa about the "detective work" they had been doing. "You leave prints on everything you touch, you know," said Tyson.

"That's right," said Grandpa. "What kind of prints have you been leaving today?"

Tyson squinted at his grandpa. "The same kind as always, of course," he said. "Your fingerprints don't change."

"True," agreed Grandpa, "but wherever you go, you leave other 'prints,' too. Let's call them 'lifeprints.' Everything you do makes an impression—or a 'lifeprint'—on other people. What kind of impression do you think you made today on your teacher and the other kids at school?" Tyson hadn't thought of that before! "Unlike fingerprints," Grandpa was saying, "we can change the kind of 'lifeprints' we make. But we need God's help."

Tyson nodded slowly. Changing his work and play habits wouldn't be easy. He would have to pray about that. *HWM*

HOW ABOUT YOU?

What kind of "lifeprints" are you making? Do others see selfishness and laziness in your prints, or do they see kindness, courtesy, faithfulness, and friendliness? Do they see Jesus? Ask God to help you live in such a way that the prints you leave are a good testimony for him.

MEMORIZE:

"Since God chose you to be the holy people whom he loves, you must clothe yourselves with tenderhearted mercy, kindness, humility, gentleness, and patience." Colossians 3:12

Witness through Actions

Patching the Hole

(Read Colossians 3:12-15)

The back door banged shut, and Brian stomped into the kitchen where his dad was making a pie. "What's wrong?" he asked when he saw Brian's face.

"It's Ryan. He stepped on my new remote control car," replied Brian. "Look at it." He held out the mangled pieces. "He said he was sorry and that he'd pay to have it fixed, but I bet it can't even be fixed."

"Easy, Brian," cautioned Dad. "Come here. I want you to see something." He pointed to a small, rough spot in the crust in the bottom of the pie plate. "What do you see?" he asked.

"I don't know," grumbled Brian. "Looks like a patch."

"That's exactly what it is," Dad told him. "I accidentally tore a hole in the crust when I was spreading it in the pan. So I flattened a small bit of dough, dampened the edges, and pressed it over the hole. With the patch, the crust is strong enough to hold these blueberries." He picked up the berries and started pouring them in. "Now . . . what kind of friend is Ryan?"

"He was my best friend," mumbled Brian.

Dad nodded. "Often something unpleasant tears a hole in a friendship, even a best friendship, and even between Christians. So the two friends have to 'patch the hole.' Ryan did his part."

"I guess. But this was my special car," whined Brian.

"What's more important? A toy car or a best friend?" asked Dad.

Brian said nothing for a while. "OK, I'll forgive him," he mumbled at last. "How long until supper?"

Dad put the pie in the oven and smiled warmly at his son. "You have time to go see Ryan and patch a friendship," he said.

"Thanks, Dad!" Brian grabbed an apple from the fruit bowl on the table and dashed out the door. *DTC*

HOW ABOUT YOU?

Aren't you glad that God freely forgives and doesn't hold grudges? When friends who upset you apologize, do you forgive them? Don't let the hurt fester until the friendship is lost. And when you've hurt someone—or God—never be too proud to say, "I'm sorry. Please forgive me."

MEMORIZE:

"Instead, be kind to each other, tender-hearted, forgiving one another, just as God through Christ has forgiven you."
Ephesians 4:32

Friends Forgive

Almost Passing

(Read Acts 26:1-3, 22-23, 27-29)

Ted was having trouble with math. He hated the subject, and he often hurried through his assignments. But when report cards came out, he was dismayed to see the low grade he had earned—somehow he didn't think it would be quite that bad!

Ted's parents were equally unhappy with his grade. They wanted to teach him a lesson, but they didn't think punishing him would be the best way. "You know we have wanted to buy you a horse for some time now," Dad told him, "but we think you should do a little to earn it. So, if you work hard and bring your math grade up to a passing grade, you'll get the horse. But if you don't, no horse."

Ted was excited. "Wow! Now I've got to pass!" he exclaimed.

Ted really did study hard for a while, but as days became warmer, he studied less and played more. When exam time arrived, he knew he was failing in math. So the night before exams, Ted got out his math book and spent several hours pouring over its pages. "How do you work this kind of problem?" he asked his mom or dad from time to time. He listened carefully as they explained.

After taking his math exam, Ted waited anxiously for the results. Would he pass? When he finally got his paper back, he saw that he had not quite made it. He had learned a lot in that last night of frantic study, but he had started too late!

"I'm sorry, Ted," said Dad when he saw Ted's grade.

"But, Dad, I tried hard! I almost passed," pleaded Ted.

Dad shook his head. "Almost isn't enough," he said. *HCT*

HOW ABOUT YOU?

Are you, like King Agrippa in today's Scripture reading, almost persuaded to be a Christian? Just as almost passing a test isn't enough, so almost believing in Jesus isn't enough either. God has prepared wonderful things for those who love him and believe in him. If you have questions about what it means to believe in Jesus ask an adult or trusted friend.

MEMORIZE:

"Jesus replied, 'I assure you, unless you are born again, you can never see the Kingdom of God.'" John 3:3

Almost Believing Isn't Enough

Rhambau's Treasure

(Read Ephesians 2:1-9)

Rhambau, an elderly pearl diver in India, clung to the hope of earning his way to heaven. "The gods not be pleased with one who is not working for a place in heaven," he told Mr. Grayson, a missionary. Pointing to a man on the street, he added, "That pilgrim goes perhaps to Bombay—or Calcutta. He walks barefoot and picks the sharpest stones to step on. See how he sometimes kneels down and kisses the road? That is good!" Rhambau sighed. "I am getting old. I must prepare for the life to come," he added. "The first day of the New Year, I also begin my pilgrimage. I shall make sure of heaven. I shall go to Delhi—on my knees. The gods will reward me with heaven."

"But, Rhambau," pleaded Mr. Grayson, "Jesus died to purchase heaven for you. You must simply believe and accept his free gift of salvation. Can't you see that, my friend?"

"No. No, that is too easy," insisted Rhambau.

Shortly before Rhambau was to leave for Delhi, he showed Mr. Grayson a beautiful pearl. "My son, a diver, found this pearl," said Rhambau, "but he stayed under the water too long! He died soon after. I want you to have it, my best friend."

"Oh, I'm so sorry about your son's death," exclaimed Mr. Grayson, "but let me buy the pearl from you."

Rhambau shook his head. "No one in all the world has enough money to pay what that pearl is worth to me," he answered sadly. "You may have it only as a gift."

"But that is too easy," exclaimed Mr. Grayson. "I must pay for it—or work for it."

Rhambau spoke quickly. "Don't you understand? I would never sell this pearl—its value is in the lifeblood of my only son. Just accept it in token of the love I bear you."

Then Mr. Grayson explained. "Rhambau, don't you see?" he asked gently. "God offers you salvation as a free gift. It is so great and priceless that no one could pay for it. It cost God the life blood of his only Son to make it possible for you to enter heaven. In a million years—or in hundreds of pilgrimages—you could never earn entrance to heaven! All you can do is accept it as a token of God's love for you." *AGL*

HOW ABOUT YOU?

Are you trying to work your way to heaven? Obeying your parents, going to church, giving money to missionaries, being a nice person—all these are good to do, but they will not buy heaven for you. You must simply believe and accept God's free gift.

MEMORIZE:

"God saved you by his special favor when you believed. And you can't take credit for this; it is a gift from God. Salvation is not a reward for the good things we have done, so none of us can boast about it." Ephesians 2:8-9

Salvation Is Free

A Son Forever

(Read Luke 15:11-24)

Brian was sprawled on his bed with a book when his big brother, Mark, came into the room. "Guess what, Brian? Bert Klein was just here, and he accepted the Lord as his Savior," said Mark. "Isn't that great?"

"I guess so," Brian answered halfheartedly. He frowned. "But what happens if he sins again? Or even you—what if you sin again?" he asked. "I mean . . . right now you're a good Christian, but what if you start doing things like smoking pot or stealing? Would you still belong to God then?"

"You mean you think I don't sin?" Mark asked with a smile. Then he became very serious. "I'm God's child forever," he said. "When I do something wrong, I confess it to God and ask him to help me stop doing wrong. But that doesn't mean I'm not saved any longer."

Brian still wasn't so sure. "I'm going to wait to accept the Lord till I'm sure I can live right," he decided.

One day Brian's family learned that Bob Phiefer, a boy from the neighborhood, had run away from home. "Mr. and Mrs. Phiefer are so upset," Mother told the boys. "They're hoping and praying they'll hear from him soon."

Mark turned to his brother. "Hey, Brian, too bad Bob's not a Phiefer anymore, isn't it?" he said.

"What are you talking about?" asked Brian. "Even though Bob ran away, he's still a son of Mr. and Mrs. Phiefer. They still love him and want him to come home."

"Exactly," Mark said. "You see, just as Bob still belongs to the Phiefer family, a Christian who sins still belongs to God's family. But he needs to apologize to God for what he's done wrong and then try not to do it again."

Slowly, Brian nodded his head. He was beginning to understand. *AGL*

HOW ABOUT YOU?

Have you put off accepting Jesus because you're worried about whether or not you can live as a Christian should? You'll need God's help to do that, but the important thing to remember is that once you've been born into God's family, you're his child forever. Nothing can ever change that.

MEMORIZE:

"I give them eternal life, and they will never perish. No one will snatch them away from me." John 10:28

Salvation Is Forever

Not by Might or Power

(Read Ephesians 6:13-18)

Kendall, who was a new Christian, came home one day with a swollen lip and a black eye. "Kendall!" exclaimed his big brother, Dan, "have you been in a fight?"

"We-e-ll, yeah," said Kendall. "The Bible tells us to fight if we have to, doesn't it? It says we're supposed to be soldiers and warriors—and I read a verse the other day about fighting a good fight. This one was a real winner!"

Dan sighed. "Those Bible verses aren't talking about neighborhood squabbles," he said. "They're talking about defending our faith—about boldly witnessing for Christ."

Kendall spoke quickly. "That's just what I was doing! See, Bill Jones heard me say I had become a Christian. And he told me that Christians are a bunch of sissies."

"So what did you say?" asked Dan.

"I just picked up a stick and put it on my shoulder, and I told him if he thought he was big enough to knock it off, to try it," Kendall replied. "The next thing I knew, he hit me! But I won, anyhow. He's got two black eyes!" Kendall grinned. "Then I sat on his back and twisted his arm and made him apologize for saying that Christians were sissies. Then I gave his arm a good twist and asked him if he didn't want to be a Christian, too."

"Oh-h-h," moaned Dan, "you didn't, Kendall! You can never force anyone to be a Christian. A person has to decide of his own free will that he wants to be saved, not because somebody is twisting his arm."

"Well, I was fighting for Jesus," insisted Kendall.

"But God says in his Word, 'Not by force nor by strength, but by my Spirit'!" replied Dan. "The Spirit of Christ was that of love and kindness."

Kendall stared at Dan. "You mean, I should be kind to Bill when he makes fun of me?"

Dan nodded. "People made fun of Jesus, and he didn't get into fights," he answered.

Kendall was thoughtful. "You think I should apologize?" he asked.

"I think so," said Dan with a smile. "Try to be his friend. You're much more likely to win him to the Lord that way." *HCT*

HOW ABOUT YOU?

Do you become angry if others laugh at you? Are you fighting battles for Jesus with the right weapons? Today's Scripture lesson does not mention fists. It mentions truth, righteousness, peace, faith, salvation, the Word of God, and prayer. Use those things instead of physical strength.

MEMORIZE:

"It is not by force nor by strength, but by my Spirit, says the Lord Almighty."
Zechariah 4:6

Witness with God's Spirit

In a Minute

(Read Psalm 119:57-64)

When Dad told Luke to take out the trash, he agreed promptly. "Sure," he said. "I'll do it in a minute." When Mother told him to clean his room, Luke answered, "OK—in a minute." When asked to mow the lawn, "Just a minute—I'm busy now," was the answer. But the "minute" always stretched to many, many more, and often he had to be told several times before the work was done.

"Will you fix me a snack?" Luke asked one Saturday. "I'm starving!"

"Sure," agreed Mother. "In a minute." But she didn't, and by the time he asked again, it was too close to dinnertime. So he had to wait until then to eat.

After dinner, Luke asked Dad to play catch with him. "Sure will, Luke." Dad nodded. "Just a minute."

Luke went out and bounced his ball while he waited. Finally, he went to find Dad. "When are you coming out to play catch?" he asked.

Dad looked up over his newspaper. "Oh, in a minute," he replied.

Luke waited awhile, then asked again—and again. Each time he asked, he got the same answer. "But, Dad," protested Luke at last, "you've said that four times now. It's been thirty minutes already."

"Hmmm," murmured Mom, who had just come into the room. "Your dad reminds me of someone else in this family."

"Who are you talking about?" asked Luke. Actually, he was afraid he knew.

"I'm talking about you, Luke. You often tell Dad and me you'll do something 'in a minute,' but then you don't do it quickly at all," Mom explained.

Dad nodded. "We decided to give you a little dose of your own medicine today," he added.

"Wouldn't it be terrible," said Mother thoughtfully, "if we needed God and he said, 'Just a minute—I'm busy'? We all need to obey promptly." *BJW*

HOW ABOUT YOU?

Do you quickly obey when you're told to do something? Or do you like to put things off for "just a minute"? Notice how often you do that today. Ask God to help you go through each day doing your tasks the first time you're asked!

MEMORIZE:
"I will hurry, without lingering,
to obey your commands."
Psalm 119:60

Obey Promptly

No Lemon Juice

(Read Exodus 16:8-12)

Julie felt grouchy as she sat on the couch at the home of her Sunday school teacher, Mrs. Watson. She didn't really want to be on what she called "this stupid old Parents' Night planning committee." She had to miss her favorite TV program to attend this meeting. Marla and Danny, the other committee members, seemed to be enjoying it, however—or at least they had been. They had made several suggestions, but Julie just scowled about all of them. Now the others seemed to be losing their enthusiasm, too.

"Julie," said Mrs. Watson finally, "why don't you help me prepare the snacks? Marla and Danny, I like your ideas. Keep thinking."

Glumly, Julie followed Mrs. Watson into the kitchen and arranged cookies on a plate while Mrs. Watson prepared hot chocolate. "Maybe I'll add just a little lemon juice to the chocolate," Mrs. Watson said.

"Lemon juice?" Julie was surprised. "That'll make it sour!"

Mrs. Watson looked at the bottle of lemon juice she held in her hand. "You're right, of course," she agreed. "And you know, Julie, just like a little lemon juice can ruin this hot chocolate, so, too, a bad attitude from just one person can ruin the special night we're planning. We want this to be a great Parents' Night. Marla and Danny have come up with some good ideas, but you've 'soured' them all."

Julie bit her lip and stared at the floor. "I'm sorry," she said at last, and she really was. "I'll apologize to Marla and Danny. I really do like their ideas. Oh, and Mrs. Watson?" she added.

"Yes, Julie?"

Julie grinned. "Please put the lemon juice away." *LMW*

HOW ABOUT YOU?

Are you a complainer? Do you often get into a bad mood if things don't go the way you want? You might be surprised how quickly your moods can spread.

MEMORIZE:
"In everything you do, stay away from complaining and arguing."
Philippians 2:14

Don't Be a Complainer

The Wrong Place

(Read 1 Corinthians 8:8-13; 10:23)

"Mom, can I go with Joe to Pete's Poolroom?" asked Tony. "It's a new place downtown, and we want to play the video games."

Mother shook her head. "I really don't want you going there, Tony," she said.

"Why not?" asked Tony. "What's wrong with video games?"

"Some of the games may be OK," said Mother, "but I've heard it's the kind of place where people drink too much alcohol and gamble."

"But good people go there, too," argued Tony.

"Perhaps," agreed Mother, "but you're a Christian. If you go into Pete's place, it could be a poor testimony. Maybe other kids who see you go there would think that if it's OK for you to go to such a place, it's all right for them, too."

"Aw, Mom," protested Tony, "if anybody follows me there, they can see that I'm just playing video games."

"But what if, by following you there, someone finds himself in a situation where he's not strong enough to say no to temptation?" asked Mother.

"It wouldn't happen. I still don't see how the place should make any difference if the game's all right," grumbled Tony.

At supper, Tony's father talked about his day as a wildlife officer. "What do you think I hauled out of Cotter's Creek today?" he asked.

"Probably someone's pet," Tony suggested.

"It was an animal all right," said Dad with a smile, "but no pet. It was an eight-foot alligator. It probably swam into the creek when the water was so high after all that rain we had."

"Oh, dear!" exclaimed Mother. "There are houses along there, and I've seen lots of kids playing along the creek, too."

"Yeah," said Tony. "An alligator's OK in a swamp, but not in a creek near houses."

Mother nodded. "That's kind of like what I was trying to tell you this afternoon," she said. "Some things may not be wrong in themselves, but they can be dangerous in the wrong place." *JLH*

HOW ABOUT YOU?

Do you go to places that may cause you to sin, or where your presence may be a bad testimony to others? Ask yourself this question: Could I take Jesus there as my guest? If not, you shouldn't go there either!

MEMORIZE:
"And do not give the devil a foothold." Ephesians 4:27, NIV

Go Places Jesus Would Go

Caged by Sin

(Read John 8:31-36)

Spring break had come at last, and Jason could hardly wait for the trip to the zoo that Mom had promised. They packed a picnic lunch and started out. Mom glanced at Jason. "Remember, this zoo has only local animals," she said. "There won't be any tigers or elephants. Still, I think you'll enjoy what is there."

"I know I will," said Jason. "Eric told me they had wolves and coyotes and even a mountain lion."

When they reached the zoo, Jason sprang from the car. He could see the fences and gates. Mom paid the fee, and they entered the zoo.

They walked past the wolves, who stood together far beyond the fence. "Wow! They have a lot of room to run," Jason said.

Mom smiled. "I think they are happiest that way," she said.

Jason admired the mountain lion. It stretched above them on rocks that were enclosed behind a tall fence. Then it lazily closed its eyes.

At last they came to a cage that housed a large bird. "Look! That's a bald eagle. But what's it doing in this little cage?" Jason asked.

Mom pointed to a sign. "It says this bird was injured and has to stay caged until its wing is healed. Then it will be released to fly away."

"I feel sorry for the eagle," Jason frowned. "I'd hate to live in a little cage."

Mom looked thoughtful. "There are a lot of people who live in cages," she murmured.

Jason laughed. "I've never heard of a people zoo. Where is it?"

Mom shook her head. "I was just thinking that when people choose not to accept Jesus as their Savior, they're trapped by their sin, just like these animals are trapped in cages," she said.

Jason nodded. "I'm glad Jesus has set me free," he said. "It feels good to be forgiven and fly free like an eagle." *KEC*

HOW ABOUT YOU?

Have you asked God to set you free from sin? You may be a "good" person—a member of a Christian family or of a church. That's nice. Many of the people Jesus talked with were "good," too . . . good, that is, in people's eyes. But Jesus said they needed to be set free by the Son—by him. You do, too.

Let Jesus Set You Free

MEMORIZE:
"Bring me out of prison so I can thank you." Psalm 142:7

Not Close Enough

(Read John 3:1-3, 16-18)

"Let's go on the Blue Streak next," called Matt. "That's a really big roller coaster."

The boys scurried over to the line for the Blue Streak, getting there just ahead of a large group. But a lady stopped them as they were making their way through the turnstile. "Hold on, young man. Let's see how tall you are," she said, smiling at Matt as she held up the measuring stick. Matt looked nervously at his older brothers and stood as tall as he could while the lady held the stick behind him. "I'm sorry," she said, "but you're about an inch too short to go on this ride."

"But, ma'am, it's so close! Can't you just let him on?" pleaded Bryan. "He's not scared. I know he'll be fine."

Matt smiled weakly as the lady looked down at him once more. "I'm sorry," she said, shaking her head, "but for safety reasons, every rider must be at least forty-eight inches tall."

Three disappointed boys turned around and walked away. "I'm sorry, guys," Matt said apologetically. "I can't believe that lady wouldn't let me ride when I was so close."

"It's not your fault, Matt," said Bryan. "But never mind—you'll be tall enough next year. C'mon. Let's go try the Mine Ride. I'll beat you there." Laughing, they dashed off toward the smaller roller coaster.

That evening, the boys told their parents about it. "Don't you think they should have let me ride on the Blue Streak today?" asked Matt. "I mean . . . only one inch! That should be close enough, shouldn't it?"

Mom shook her head. "Close doesn't count in a lot of things."

"That's right," agreed Dad, looking up from his newspaper. "For example—a lot of people think they come close enough to meeting God's requirements for getting into heaven. But what they don't understand is that they need to be born again." *LDC*

HOW ABOUT YOU?

Do you do lots of good things? Perhaps you obey your parents, help around the house, respect your teachers and others in authority, treat other people well, and in general, do what's right. That's nice, but God says you still need to be "born again" by trusting Jesus as Savior. If you have questions, talk to a trusted friend or adult.

MEMORIZE:

"Unless you are born again, you can never see the Kingdom of God."
John 3:3

You Must Be Born Again

Batter Up

(Read Proverbs 4:5-9)

Jacob squatted behind the batter and watched the ball sail toward his glove. He raised his mitt to catch it. Suddenly the batter swung wildly and lost his grip on the bat. He missed the ball and his bat hit Jacob's mask. Jacob fell backward. He felt dizzy.

Everyone rushed forward to see if Jacob was OK. Someone lifted the mask, and he heard his mother's voice. "Jacob, are you all right?"

Jacob rubbed his chin. "I think so," he said. "It's just sore." He got up and put his mask back on. "I'm fine," he assured everyone. The game went on and Jacob's team won.

After supper the next Wednesday night, Jacob hesitantly approached his mother. "Can I . . . ah . . . can I skip our youth group Bible study tonight?" he asked. "There are lots of other things I could be doing instead of studying Bible lessons and memorizing verses every week. I'm a Christian now and that's what counts anyway, right?"

Mother looked at Jacob. "It is most important that you've accepted Jesus," she agreed, "but Bible study is important, too. It will help you grow in your faith." She paused, then asked, "Remember when that batter accidentally hit you with the bat?"

Jacob rubbed his chin. "I sure do."

"You don't want to quit wearing your catcher's mask now, do you?"

"Of course not," said Jacob. "But what does that have to do with Bible study?"

"The catcher's mask offers protection when you play ball, and studying the Bible offers protection in your everyday life," said Mother.

Jacob frowned. "I don't get it," he said.

"As you grow up, people may question your faith, and if you don't have a solid belief in the Bible, you may begin to doubt," explained Mother. "Understanding God's Word is protection for your faith."

Slowly, Jacob nodded. "So I keep wearing my catcher's mask to protect my head, and I keep going to Wednesday night Bible study to protect my faith, right?" he asked. Then he grinned. "OK," he said, "I'm on my way." *KEC*

HOW ABOUT YOU?

Do you learn all you can about God and his Word? What you learn from the Bible can help you when troubles or temptations come along.

Use God's Protection

MEMORIZE:
"A final word: Be strong with the Lord's mighty power." Ephesians 6:10

Spring Cleaning

(Read 1 Samuel 15:18-22)

The junior high Sunday school class was getting geared up for its annual "Spring Cleaning Give-Away." Each year, members of the class brought books, games, and other articles that they were no longer using to give to the Pine Crest Children's Home.

"What can I give this year?" Paul asked his mother as he fumbled through his closet. "With Dad out of work part of the year, we barely had enough money to get the things we needed, let alone anything extra."

Mom smiled. "Oh, I'm sure you can come up with something," she said. "Maybe there's something in your locker at school."

The next day, Paul searched hopelessly through his locker. Lots of old papers, broken pencils, and even a dirty pair of gym socks were soon piled up on the floor. Then he spied a baseball that he had borrowed from Randy long before. *Randy's probably forgotten about this,* Paul thought, pulling the ball from the back of his locker. He tucked the ball in his jacket pocket and headed home.

That evening Paul showed the ball to his friend Joey. "I'm gonna help Randy do a good deed," he said. "I'm gonna give this to the kids at the home."

Joey frowned. "Whoa!" he said. "You can't give something that isn't yours."

"But it's for a good cause," insisted Paul.

"Doing something wrong can't be justified by saying that you're doing it for God," Joey told him. "King Saul, in the Bible, tried to do that. God had told him to destroy all the cattle and sheep in a certain city, but King Saul kept some of the best animals—he said he wanted to sacrifice them to God. But God was not pleased. He'd rather have had Saul obey him than offer sacrifices."

"Well, I don't want to be like King Saul," answered Paul. "I guess I'll have to find something of my own to give." *DLR*

HOW ABOUT YOU?

Are you ever tempted to steal or disobey in some way in order to do what seems to be a good thing? God doesn't want you to decide whether or not to obey his commands, depending on your situation. When God says "don't steal" and "keep yourself pure," that's exactly what he means!

MEMORIZE:

"Obedience is far better than sacrifice.
Listening to him is much better
than offering the fat of rams."
1 Samuel 15:22

Always Obey God

Delayed Action

(Read Ecclesiastes 8:11-13)

Mark's Uncle Jeff was scheduled to have surgery on his back. "It's a funny thing," Dad told the family. "The doctor says it's an old injury that's causing the trouble. I had forgotten that Jeff was butted by a goat years ago."

"Butted by a goat?" echoed Mark. "How'd that happen?"

"Jeff and I had an uncle who always kept animals—among them a mean old goat," said Dad. "Our Uncle Ted warned Jeff and me not to go into the stall where the goat was, but Jeff did anyway. When he tried to get out, the goat got him."

"Was he hurt bad?" Lisa asked.

"Pretty bad, but he never told anyone what happened because he was afraid he'd be punished," answered Dad. "He pretended he fell. He was really stiff for a long time, and he had a big bruise. Now that spot is giving him a lot of trouble."

"Then he really didn't get away with it," said Mother.

"No," agreed Dad. "It took a while, but he's paying for his disobedience now."

The next week, Dad and Mark came home with a shrub Mother had been wanting. She came out to watch as Dad started to dig a hole, and Mark suddenly remembered something! A few months ago he had tossed a ball in the house and had broken his mother's best vase. He had buried the pieces in this very spot. Sure enough, in a few minutes, Dad turned up some broken pieces of pottery.

"Oh," Mark said sorrowfully, "I guess I'm just like Uncle Jeff." Then Mark told his story and apologized. "I'm sorry, Mom. I'm so ashamed."

"Oh, Mark, I would have forgiven you the day it happened if you had told me," Mother answered. "All sins are uncovered sometime, and it's always unpleasant. Actually, it's best to tell what you did wrong at the time you did it." *AGL*

HOW ABOUT YOU?

Are you hiding some sins, thinking they will never be found out? Do you think you are getting away with something? God knows all about it. Confess your sins, take the consequences, and receive forgiveness.

MEMORIZE:

"But I know! I, the Lord, search all hearts and examine secret motives. I give all people their due rewards, according to what their actions deserve." Jeremiah 17:10

Confess Right Away

True or False

(Read Ezekiel 18:30-31)

"The answer is no, Peter. That's final!" Mother was firm. As Peter stomped out of the room, a swear word exploded from his lips. "Peter! Come back here!" Mother ordered. "Did you say what I think you said?" Peter gritted his teeth and stared at the floor. Mother sighed deeply. "Son, what is the matter with you?" Peter did not answer, and tears filled Mother's eyes. "You will have to be punished for swearing."

"But, Mom, I didn't mean to," Peter pleaded. "It just slipped out. I'm sorry. Really I am. All the guys at school say those words, and they stick in my mind. I promise I'll never do it again. I'm sorry. Honest!"

Mother sighed and looked at him closely. "I believe you are," she decided. "Very well. We'll forget it this time."

Later that evening, loud, angry words burst from Peter's room. "How many times have I told you to stay out of my stuff?" he roared.

As Mother started down the hall, she heard Tina cry, "But, Peter, I just wanted to borrow a pencil. I didn't mean to break your model. I'm sorry."

"That's what you said when you broke my watch. You're not really sorry! You're just sorry you got caught. You cry and think I'll forget about it." Peter did not see his mother come into the room as he bent over to pick up the broken model, swearing softly.

"Peter!" At the sound of Mother's voice, Peter jumped and dropped the model. "Peter, look at me," Mother said. "Tina isn't the only one whose apology is false. Didn't you tell me this afternoon you were sorry you swore?" Peter nodded slowly. Mother continued. "True repentance is more than saying, 'I'm sorry.' It's being sorry enough for what you have done to stop doing it." *BJW*

HOW ABOUT YOU?

Do you ever say "I'm sorry" simply to keep out of trouble? False apologies might fool others for a while, but they never fool God.

MEMORIZE:
"Turn from your sins! Don't let them destroy you!" Ezekiel 18:30

Be Truly Sorry for Sin

The Way to Heaven

(Read Matthew 7:13-14)

One Saturday, Anoli and Jil sat on the front steps, discussing the sermon they had heard the week before. Pastor Peterson had said that people pass by every day who don't know the way to heaven, and that it's the responsibility of Christians to tell them how to get there. "I told him it was a good sermon," said Jil, "and he asked me what I was going to do about it."

"What did you tell him?" Anoli asked.

"Well," Jil shrugged, "I said I guessed I had better obey it. But I'm not alone in this, Anoli. He preached that sermon to you, too!"

"I know. He's right, too," Anoli agreed. "OK. Let's go talk to our friend Ahmed. While one of us is talking, the other can be praying."

It took a lot of courage, but the kids walked over to Ahmed's apartment building.

As they were shooting baskets Anoli asked him, "Do you know how to get to heaven?"

"Have you ever been there?" Ahmed asked.

"No, but . . . ," began Anoli.

"So you don't know the way!" Ahmed interrupted. "You have never been there and don't know anyone who has."

Jil joined the conversation. "That isn't true! Jesus was there, and he . . ." Jil paused. "Wait here just a minute. I'll be right back." He dashed to his house and soon returned with a Bible and a map. "Look," he said, holding out the map, "I've never been to Chicago, but this map can show you how to get there because someone who has been there gave us these directions." Then Jil held out his Bible. "And I have a book with directions on getting to heaven. The God who made the world and heaven, too, wrote this book. If we can trust a map that was made by a man, don't you think we can trust God's directions?"

Ahmed listened thoughtfully. "You know, you have something there," he said. "I'd like to talk about this some more." *AGL*

HOW ABOUT YOU?

Have you told anyone how to get to heaven? Do your friends in school know the way? The Bible says that Jesus is the way. Pray for your friends to want to know more about God, Jesus, and heaven. Then when they ask, you will be ready to tell them what they want to know.

MEMORIZE:
"I am the way, the truth, and the life. No one can come to the Father except through me." John 14:6

Share the Way to Heaven

Get Out of the Dump

(Read 2 Peter 3:10-14)

Steve and his family lived in an area where there was no trash pickup, so he and his dad would put the garbage cans in the back of their truck and take them to the county dump. One afternoon, as he was helping his dad unload the truck at the dump, Steve noticed some mice among the trash heaps.

"I can see why a mouse would love to nest in that trash," Dad said when Steve pointed them out. "There's always plenty of food and lots of papers and things for building materials. But those mice are in for a big shock. Tomorrow night some men from the county are going to burn all this trash. Most of the mice will escape, but their homes, their young ones, and everything else will be lost in the flames."

As Steve and his dad drove away, Steve couldn't resist one last look at the mice, who were cheerfully scampering about as though they had nothing in the world to worry about. "That's too bad about the mice," he remarked, "but I guess they don't know any better."

When they arrived home, Steve went to his bedroom to change his clothes. As he opened the door, he glanced around. He saw his posters, his records, and his comic books. He saw his baseball mitt, his football, and his model ships. He saw his books and his Boy Scout manual. *Hmmm,* thought Steve. *These aren't bad things, but I wonder if I am spending too much time on these things! I'd hate to be like those mice, spending all my time on things that are temporary. Maybe it's time I got "out of the dump" and started spending more time on things that really matter! SLK*

HOW ABOUT YOU?

How do you spend most of your time? Are you involved in sports, school projects, and social activities? These are good things, but you need to make sure you are balancing your fun times with times of work and times of getting to know God better.

MEMORIZE:

"Since everything around us is going to melt away, what holy, godly lives you should be living!" 2 Peter 3:11

Live for Jesus

The King's Son (Part 1)

(Read Philippians 2:14-16)

Tom was excited about the special program his school was putting on. He had the part of Prince Gregory in a play, and his parents watched proudly as the scene opened.

Prince Gregory (played by Tom) was unhappy with his life. He had a private teacher who was with him most of the day. Besides studying all the usual school subjects, he had to learn the history of his father's kingdom, proper court etiquette, and all the responsibilities of a king. "Why must I study all day?" grumbled the prince. "Who cares what my great-great grandfather did? The village children play and have fun. Why can't I ever have fun? All day I hear, 'You must never do this.' 'A prince must always remember to do that.' 'Be careful what you say.' 'Everyone watches what you do.' It's tiresome!"

"Prince Gregory!" exclaimed his tutor. "You should feel honored to be the king's son and to have all the privileges you have!"

The prince frowned. "Well, does that mean I can't be human?" he asked. "Does it mean I must never lose my temper in public? I must never break a law? I must always look neat and clean and always say just the right thing?"

"Of course." The tutor nodded. "You must never do anything that would bring shame to your father. You are an example to the village people, remember?"

"Will I ever stop hearing all those do's and don'ts?" grumbled the prince. "I'm sure the village children don't hear them all day long."

"You are not a village child," came the answer. "You are the son of King Gregory the Third. You must study and learn the ways of a king, for the village people are watching you. They expect you to display kingly qualities. If they look at you and see that you have no respect for your father, for his reputation, and for his laws, they will also lose their respect for your father and won't obey his commands. As a prince, you must bring honor to your father's name."

Tom's parents clapped loudly as the first scene ended. *BJW*

HOW ABOUT YOU?

If you're a Christian, you're a child of God—a child of the King of kings! Are you studying the ways of God in your Bible and at church? Does your life bring honor to the King?

Honor God

MEMORIZE:
"A son honors his father." Malachi 1:6

The King's Son (Part 2)

(Read Colossians 1:10-14)

"A king's son should have the right to do as he pleases! He should be able to play and have fun. I'm sick of studying! I'm going to the village," muttered Prince Gregory in the next scene of Tom's play. The prince (played by Tom) ran off the stage.

When he returned, he wore dirty, torn clothes. Two children approached him. "What's your name?" asked one.

"I'm Prince Gregory," was the reply. "I've left the palace—I tore my clothes when I sneaked out. I'm tired of rules and lessons. I'm out for some fun."

"Sure! And I'm Peter Rabbit, and this is Goldilocks!" one of the children mocked. They shook their heads and ran off.

Prince Gregory walked around for a long time without seeing another child. Finally he asked a woman where all the children were. "Working in the fields," she replied. "They go to school, and then they work until supper." She asked who he was, and then she immediately invited him to stay with her family. "There isn't much food, but please join us," she said. "We'd be glad to give you a place to sleep, too."

Prince Gregory stayed. The children finally came home, and he ate with them. No one had second helpings, and for the first time in his life Prince Gregory went to bed hungry. He slept poorly, too, because he had to share a bed.

At daybreak, the prince was awakened by a call. "Time for chores!"

"What? It's still dark!" the prince muttered, half asleep.

"It's almost daybreak. We have to do chores before school," said the oldest boy. "Do you want to come along?"

"No, I'm going home," answered Prince Gregory. To himself he said, "My tutor was right. Being the king's son is a great privilege even though it has responsibilities. I really am blessed, and I won't complain any more."

The curtain fell, ending the play. *BJW*

HOW ABOUT YOU?

Are you a Christian? If so, do you complain about having to be an example for other kids? Think about who God, your heavenly Father is! He's the creator and ruler of all the universe, yet he's interested in you! What a privilege to belong to such a great God! Be thankful; it makes doing what's right a more joyful task.

MEMORIZE:

"We pleaded with you, encouraged you, and urged you to live your lives in a way that God would consider worthy. For he called you into his Kingdom to share his glory."
1 Thessalonians 2:12

God's Children Are Blessed

Curiosity's Captive

(Read Luke 5:27-31)

"Uncle Perry makes me so mad!" said Jimmy as he slammed down the telephone. "That was Dee, and she was crying. The electric company threatened to turn off their electricity if Aunt Helen doesn't pay their bill by tomorrow. Uncle Perry's off drinking with his buddies."

Dad looked over the edge of the newspaper. "I feel sorry for Perry," he said.

"I feel sorry for his family! Uncle Perry is selfish and mean!" Jimmy said.

"He hasn't always been an alcoholic," Dad reminded him. "We need to pray for Uncle Perry. He's like a prisoner of alcohol."

"He could get loose if he wanted to! He just—" Jimmy was interrupted by a banging sound from the garage. "What's that?"

"I don't know." Mother looked puzzled. "We had better find out. Copper's out there." When they opened the door, the strangest sight met their eyes. Copper had a plastic pitcher stuck on her head, and she was bumping into everything.

Mother called softly to the frightened dog and gathered her in her arms. Holding her body, she tried to pull off the pitcher. She frowned. "I can't get it off."

Dad quickly got out his pocketknife and carefully cut the pitcher from the dog's neck. "Poor baby!" Jimmy crooned. "Your curiosity almost killed you that time."

"She must have stuck her nose in it, then pushed it up against something to hold it as she pushed her head further inside," Mother reasoned.

Dad nodded. "Having us scold her and tell her how foolish she was wouldn't have helped her at all," he observed. "She was caught and couldn't do anything to help herself. She needed us to help her. Jimmy, Uncle Perry is like Copper. Curiosity started him drinking. Now he is caught in a trap so powerful he cannot break loose. God can deliver him. It may be that God wants to use us to help Perry. If so, he will show us how." *BJW*

HOW ABOUT YOU?

Do you know people who are caught in the trap of sin? It might be alcohol or drugs or many other things. Are you tempted to dislike them? Ask God to give you compassion for them, and pray for them.

MEMORIZE:

"Finally, all of you should be of one mind, full of sympathy toward each other, loving one another with tender hearts and humble minds."

1 Peter 3:8

Care for Others

Something Special

(Read Romans 8:26-31)

Jon propped his chin in his hand as he watched his grandmother mix shortening and sugar. "I'm making your favorite cake, Jon—chocolate." As Jon smiled faintly, Grandma added, "Why so quiet? Is anything wrong?"

Jon snorted. "Everything's wrong! Dad's getting transferred, so I have to leave all my friends. Mom says I have to give up my dog, too. And the doctor says I have to wear a brace on my leg for two years. How can I ever make new friends wearing a metal monster? If God loved me, he wouldn't let all this happen to me." Jon slammed his fist on the table. "It's not fair!"

"Here, have a taste," Grandma handed him the cocoa.

"Yuck!" Jon drew back.

"Then how about this?" Grandma dipped a spoon into the shortening and sugar mixture.

Jon frowned. "No way am I going to taste that!"

Grandma raised her eyebrows. "Then how about some flour, or baking soda, or this egg?"

Jon grinned. "Awww, Grandma, you're teasing me."

Grandma smiled. "You know, the Bible says all things work together for good in the life of a Christian. It doesn't say all things are good. Cocoa or a raw egg isn't good alone, but when I mix all the ingredients together . . ."

"Yummmm, yummmm, good!" Jon sang.

"So in life," Grandma continued as she sifted flour into the batter, "when God gets through mixing a Christian's experiences together—the bitter, the sweet, the happy, the sad—life comes out good. Moving and wearing a brace are bitter experiences for you now, but trust God, Jon. He'll add some 'sugar' and some 'flavoring,' and in the end it will be good. Even better than my cake."

"Maybe so," Jon agreed. Then he grinned. "Grandma, may I lick the beater?"

BJW

HOW ABOUT YOU?

Have you had to "swallow some bitter experiences" lately? Be patient. All the ingredients are not in yet, but God will make your life come out good, too.

MEMORIZE:

"And we know that God causes everything to work together for the good of those who love God and are called according to his purpose for them." Romans 8:28

All Things Work Together for Good

Watching You

(Read Psalm 139:1-12)

Jay didn't really mean to cheat. But Kenny pestered him for a look at his test paper, and Jay weakened and allowed him to see it. Then he felt guilty. He felt that, as a Christian, he should tell Mrs. Grant about it. "Why?" demanded Kenny. "You weren't cheating. I was. And nobody saw."

"God did," Jay told him. "He watches everything we do."

"Aw, I don't believe that," protested Kenny. "That sounds like God can't trust us, so he sits up round-the-clock to spy on us. Look—let it go this time, and we'll never do it again."

That evening, Jay invited Kenny to go with him and his parents to visit a family out in the country. On the way back home, Dad exclaimed, "I do wish that driver would dim his lights! He's blinding me, so I can't see."

Finally, when the car was almost past them, the driver did dim his lights, and a moment later, Mother cried out, "Don! Look out! There's a . . ."

The car brakes squealed, there was a loud thump, and they felt themselves spin around. A moment later, they discovered that no one was hurt, but they had hit a cow.

"What an evening!" exclaimed Kenny when they finally reached home. "It was lucky that none of us got hurt."

"It was more than luck, Kenny," said Jay's mother. "God chose to protect us from harm tonight."

"That's it!" said Jay excitedly. "That's what I meant earlier today, Kenny. God does watch us, but it's not just to catch us doing wrong. He watches to protect us, too."

Dad nodded. "Right," he said. "The Bible says God watches 'everywhere, keeping his eye on both the evil and the good.'"

Kenny was thoughtful when he saw Jay the next morning. "I've been think-ing," he said. "And, well . . . if you still want to tell Mrs. Grant about the test, I . . . I'll go with you. Say! Do you suppose God will see that, too?"

"He sure will," answered Jay. "And you know what? I've just got a feeling that he'll smile at us." *BJW*

HOW ABOUT YOU?

Are you pleased to have God watching over you? Is he pleased with what he sees? Remember, he watches over us because he loves us.

God Sees All

MEMORIZE:
"The Lord is watching everywhere, keeping his eye on both the evil and the good." Proverbs 15:3

The Leper

(Read Isaiah 53:4-11)

"Mom, I don't understand my memory verse," said Dan one afternoon. "Wanna hear it?" Mom smiled and nodded. "It's 2 Corinthians 5:21," said Dan. He quoted it. "For He made Him who knew no sin to be sin for us, that we might become the righteousness of God in Him."

"Good," approved Mother. "What don't you understand?"

"Well, I know it's talking about Jesus," answered Dan. "But what does it mean when it says he was made 'to be sin for us'? Jesus was sinless, wasn't he?"

"Yes, he was," answered Mother, "and being made 'sin for us' is what caused him to suffer so much. Let's see . . ." She reached for a book from the bookcase. "Look here," she said. "Maybe this picture of a leper will help you understand."

Dan frowned as he looked at the picture. "That man sure looks awful," he said. "He hasn't got any fingers or toes! Just ugly little stumps!"

"Yes," agreed Mother, "and he's blind—and so thin! Now, you're a Christian, Dan. What could you do for him?"

Dan answered, "I could give him a drink of clean water and some food," he suggested.

"But he's dying," answered Mother. "Would you love that poor man enough to get down on your knees beside him, and take him into your arms, and tell him that if he will trust in Christ, he will go to heaven? Could you do that?"

Dan hesitated, then spoke hesitantly. "Maybe if I forced myself, I could."

"Now," continued Mother, "in order to really help him—and if you had the power to do it—would you allow all of his sickness to flow into your body and allow all of your strength and health to flow into his body?"

Dan cringed at that idea. "That's asking too much!" he objected.

"But, you see, Dan," explained Mother, "this is what Jesus did when he was made to be sin for you and me. Jesus hated sin, even more than you hate leprosy. Yet he bore all our sins in his own sinless body on the cross."

Dan thought it over. "I'm beginning to understand," he said. *HCT*

HOW ABOUT YOU?

Do you realize that Jesus took your place on the cross? He not only suffered the pain of being physically crucified, but also the shame and horror of taking your sin upon himself. He did it because he loves you that much!

MEMORIZE:

"For He made Him who knew no sin to be sin for us, that we might become the righteousness of God in Him." 2 Corinthians 5:21, NKJV

Jesus Took Your Place

Iguana

(Read 1 John 2:15-17)

Andy looked up with a grin as Dad read a bedtime story to Andy's little sister, Joy. The story was about an iguana—a kind of lizard—who was not happy with how she looked. She wanted to look like everyone else she met. Whatever anyone else had, she wanted, too. She managed to glue on a hairy mane and a cardboard trunk. She painted on stripes and fastened feathers to her back.

Andy chuckled as he glanced over at his little sister's book. "That iguana looks absolutely crazy," he said.

"You know, Andy, you're right," agreed Dad. "Do you kids ever act like that?"

"What do you mean?" asked Andy.

"Well, a lot of people don't want to be themselves. They're always trying to be like someone else. They do this by the way they dress and the things they say and do," explained Dad. "And then, like Iguana, they often end up looking silly because they are not being who God created them to be."

"Let's finish the story, Daddy!" Joy said eagerly.

"OK, let's finish it and see what Iguana learns," agreed Dad.

So Dad read on. "Iguana's friends had a costume party, and to her surprise all of them came dressed up like iguanas! Iguana, who always wanted to be like everyone else, rushed to her room, intending to copy them . . . but instead, she just had to be herself. She won a prize for being the best iguana, and she learned that that was the way her friends liked her the best anyway. And so Iguana learned to be herself," finished Dad. "She learned that she shouldn't try to be like the rest of the world." He closed the book. "That's a good lesson for us, as Christians, too," he said. "We should not feel like we have to be like all the other kids. Jesus is the one we should copy." *TJE*

HOW ABOUT YOU?

Do you try to be like Jesus? Or do you want to be like the kids who don't know him? Be your own person. Better yet, be God's person. Dress, talk, and act the way you believe Jesus would want you to.

Don't Let the World Be Your Guide

MEMORIZE:
"For God knew his people in advance, and he chose them to become like his Son, so that his Son would be the firstborn, with many brothers and sisters." Romans 8:29

March
28

Sight Unseen

(Read John 20:24-29)

Shawn had agreed to attend Sunday school with his friend Matt. But he frowned as the teacher talked about Jesus. "It's Jesus who saves us," explained the teacher. "If it weren't for him and his death on the cross, we'd have no hope of going to heaven. It's his blood that washes away our sins."

"I don't get it," said Shawn as he and Matt talked later. "How could Jesus' blood help me? He lived years and years ago. I've never even seen him. It's impossible!"

"You can believe without seeing him," Matt told him. "I do." But Shawn just shrugged and shook his head.

A few days later, Shawn fell and cut his arm badly. He was rushed by ambulance to the hospital, but by the time he arrived there, he had lost a lot of blood and needed a transfusion. "You'll be fine now," the doctor told him cheerfully as he watched blood flow through a tube into Shawn's arm. "This blood saved your life."

As Shawn grew stronger, he often thought about what the doctor had said. "They gave me someone else's blood. Whose was it?" he asked his mother one day.

"I wish I knew," replied Mother. "I'd like to thank that person. But that blood came from the blood bank, and I'm sure it belonged to someone we don't even know. It seems strange, doesn't it, to know that blood from someone else's body—someone you've never even seen—saved your life!"

Shawn nodded. Suddenly he thought of something else. "Hey! That's something like what Matt was telling me. He's right! If the blood of someone I've never seen can save my life here, the blood of someone I've never seen can save me for heaven, too. I can believe in Jesus—sight unseen." *HCT*

HOW ABOUT YOU?

Does it seem strange that someone who lived and died a long time ago is able to save you? Jesus not only lived and died, but he rose from the dead. He is alive, and even though you can't see him, you can know him. You don't have to "see" to believe.

MEMORIZE:
"Blessed are those who haven't seen me and believe anyway." John 20:29

Believe on Jesus

The Ugly Duckling

(Read Romans 3:10-12; 5:6-8)

Ducky, a little stuffed toy, was no longer pretty—his fluff was all rubbed off, and he was limp and faded. But to Peggy, he was adorable, and she loved him dearly. Her brother, Aaron, on the other hand, thought he was awful. He called her toy "The Ugly Duckling."

One day Peggy ran to Mother in tears. "Ducky's gone!" she wailed. "Aaron took him. I know he did!"

Aaron was called in and questioned. He declared that, though it was a good riddance, he knew nothing about Ducky's disappearance. Everyone searched, but no Ducky.

Several days later, Mother again had a talk with Aaron. "Have you noticed that Peggy is very unhappy since she lost Ducky?" she asked him.

"Yeah!" said Aaron. "I never thought she'd feel so bad about that ugly piece of rag and sawdust. How can anybody love anything so ugly?"

Mother smiled. "Love is a strange thing, Son," she said. "You know, Peggy's love for the Ugly Duckling, as you call him, is like God's love for us. He loves people just the way they are. And what's more amazing is that he loves people even when they do wrong things like lie, cheat, and steal."

Aaron's face turned red. "I'm glad he does, Mom," he admitted. He paused before adding, "I . . . I lied about Ducky. I hid him. He's on the top shelf in my clothes closet."

"Yes, I know," Mother answered. "I saw him there, but I thought I'd let you tell me about it."

Aaron was ashamed. He asked, "Do you really think God loves me anyway—like Peggy loves Ducky?"

"Even more," Mother assured him. *HCT*

HOW ABOUT YOU?

Is it hard to think of yourself as an "ugly duckling"? The Bible says we have all sinned (done wrong, ugly things). In spite of this, God loves you and sent Jesus to take your punishment for sin. Have you accepted God's wonderful gift of salvation? If not, talk to a trusted friend or adult to find out more.

Christ Died for Sinners

MEMORIZE:
"But God showed his great love for us by sending Christ to die for us while we were still sinners." Romans 5:8

March
30

Why Him?

(Read Matthew 5:43-48)

"Jamie, why don't you ask Ben to come to Sunday school with you this week?" asked Mother as they were returning from picking up a puppy at Grandpa's house. Jamie sighed. Ben used bad words, he cheated on tests, and he'd even gotten into trouble for shoplifting a couple of times. *He just isn't the kind of kid I want for a friend,* he thought. *I should think Mother would know that, but she keeps suggesting that I invite him.*

"Jamie, what's wrong?" Mother asked. "Every week you come up with a reason why you can't invite Ben to Sunday school. That's not like you. You've invited lots of kids in the past."

"But they weren't like Ben," Jamie explained, and he told his mother how Ben acted.

"I know Ben has some serious problems, Jamie," agreed Mother. "But that doesn't mean you can't be friendly and invite him to church." When Jamie didn't answer, Mother motioned toward the puppy Jamie cuddled on his lap. "Why did you pick that puppy, Jamie?" she asked. "Didn't you think some of the others were cuter? Grandpa says this one is the runt of the litter."

"But that's just it, Mom!" said Jamie in surprise. "Grandpa says lots of people will want the other ones, but this little puppy needs a good home, too! Besides, I like him. I think he's cute."

"He reminds me of Ben," observed Mother. "In some ways, he may not be the most popular boy, but he certainly needs to know Jesus, doesn't he? And Jesus loves him just as he loves all of us, right?"

"Well . . ." Jamie thought about it. He knew his mother was right. "OK. I'll invite him to Sunday school this week," he decided. *LMW*

HOW ABOUT YOU?

Do you invite only your "nice" friends to Sunday school? Do you wish that boys and girls with "real problems" would stay away from your church? Maybe there has been a child with a serious problem attending your Sunday school. Have you gone out of your way to be friendly—or have you ignored that person, hoping he or she wouldn't come back? Remember, Jesus loves everybody. He doesn't play favorites. That child with the serious problem needs to know Jesus just as much as you do!

MEMORIZE:
"For God does not show favoritism."
Romans 2:11

All People Need the Lord

Alive!

(Read 1 Corinthians 8:4-6; 1 Thessalonians 1:9-10)

"We're going to my grandmother's for spring vacation," said Alan as he and his friend, Karim, walked home from school. "She lives in Pennsylvania, and we always have fun at her house. On Easter Sunday, we go to Grandma's church, too. They have an early morning service—a sunrise service. We meet outside and watch the sun rise. It's cool."

Karim shrugged. "Come in for a minute," he said as they approached his house. "I'll show you something." Alan followed Karim into the house. "Look!" said Karim, pointing to a shelf in the kitchen. "That's our god—Buddha." Alan stared. There, on a shelf, stood a strange-looking little statue. Alan had heard a lot about idols, but he had never seen one before. "You can't even see your god," continued Karim, "but our Buddha is right in our kitchen."

"But the Bible says there's only one true God," protested Alan.

"Nah," scoffed Karim. "My mom says it doesn't really make any difference which god you believe in, just as long as you're sincere and do your best. I'd rather have a god you can see than an invisible one."

Alan wasn't sure what to say. He was still thinking about it as the boys walked to school the next morning. When he saw a large stone along the sidewalk, he had an idea. He picked it up. "Hey, I think I'll make this my god," he said. "It will fit right in my pocket, so that way I can have it with me all the time and pray to it whenever I want to."

"You've gotta be kidding," said Karim in surprise. "That's just an old stone. It can't hear you when you pray. It can't take care of you!"

"Well, your Buddha can't, either," retorted Alan. "It's just a piece of brass!" Karim looked a bit startled. "Even if I can't see him, Jesus is alive," continued Alan. "I'd rather have a God I can't see but who is alive and can hear me than one I can see but that can't hear me. Think about it." *LMW*

HOW ABOUT YOU?
Have you ever seen an idol? Don't you wonder why people think a man-made figure can hear them pray? If you're a Christian, be thankful that you know the true, living God.

God Is Alive

MEMORIZE:
"Tremble with fear before the God of Daniel. For he is the living God, and he will endure forever." Daniel 6:26

Like a Candle

(Read 2 Corinthians 12:7-10)

Jesse trudged home from school with an angry frown on his face. The day had started off well. His class sang "Happy Birthday" to him, morning recess was fun, and even lessons went well. But then, during the last recess, everything went wrong. "I lost my temper again today," he blurted out when he saw his mom. "We played ball, and some of the guys said I was out when I knew I was safe! I lost my temper and said some things I wish I hadn't said."

Mom studied him. "Since you became a Christian, you've been working hard on not losing your temper, haven't you?"

Jesse nodded. "I really try hard . . . I even counted to ten before I said those things, but I still said them. I guess it's hopeless."

"It's not hopeless," Mom assured him, "but I think maybe you're trying to change a difficult habit without depending on God." She thought a moment, then pointed to a birthday cake standing on the cupboard. It was shaped like a baseball and had yellow candles on top. Jesse's frown disappeared when he saw the cake. "What do you think would happen if we'd take your cake outside and light the candles?"

"The cold wind would blow the candles out," exclaimed Jesse.

"You're right," Mom said. "And we're a little like candles."

"We are?" asked Jesse.

Mom nodded. "God tells us to let our lights shine for him," she said.

"And we let our lights shine by doing what is right," replied Jesse.

"That's right," answered Mom. "But sometimes temptation acts like a cold wind. If we give into it, then our lights (the right things we do) temporarily go out. We need to depend on God to keep our lights burning brightly."

"Maybe I should talk to God first, then count to ten the next time I feel angry," suggested Jesse.

"Good idea," said Mom. *KEC*

HOW ABOUT YOU?

Do you ask God for strength to master whatever sinful habits you may have? Your own self-discipline is good, but you need God's help, too. Rely on him. He is the source of power over temptation.

MEMORIZE:

"So humble yourselves before God. Resist the Devil, and he will flee from you." James 4:7

Rely on God

The Shadow

(Read 1 Timothy 4:12-16)

Paul and his friend, Matt, went to watch the work going on at a construction site, and four-year-old Ricky tagged along as usual. "See that open gate over there?" asked Matt after they had watched awhile. "Let's go up closer and look around. If we act like we know what we're doing, no one will ever question us. C'mon!"

Paul hesitated. "But the sign says, 'Keep Out,'" he said.

"Be a baby and stay here if you're scared," sneered Matt. "I'm goin' in."

"Wait," called Paul. "I'll come." He turned to Ricky. "You sit right here and wait for me," he ordered. "I'll be only a minute." So Ricky watched the older boys go inside the fence.

Soon Ricky was bored and went in search of his brother. As he wandered through the gate, the machinery started up. Bricks began flying as an old building was torn down. "Hey!" yelled a workman who spotted Ricky and snatched him up. "You tryin' to get killed?" Soon Paul and Matt were also discovered, and the three children were returned to their homes.

As punishment for his part in the escapade, Paul was grounded for a month! "You boys could have been seriously hurt," scolded Dad. "That workman said Ricky came within inches of being killed."

"I told Ricky to stay outside," protested Paul.

"But you didn't stay outside," Dad pointed out. "I know you and your friends sometimes call Ricky 'The Shadow' because he follows you so much. You have a big responsibility to lead him only where he should go. You need to be careful who you follow yourself, knowing that Ricky will be right behind you. Do you see that?" Slowly, Paul nodded. *BJW*

HOW ABOUT YOU?

Do you have a "shadow"? Is there a little brother or sister, or maybe a neighbor, who follows you? Someone may be watching and imitating you even though you don't know it. Be careful to be a good example. To do that, you need to have a good leader, and the best leader of all is the Lord Jesus. Teach others to follow Jesus, as you do.

MEMORIZE:

"Don't let anyone think less of you because you are young. Be an example to all believers in what you teach, in the way you live, in your love, your faith, and your purity."
1 Timothy 4:12

Follow Jesus

No More Idols

(Read Exodus 20:3-5)

"Pam, it's time to leave for the missionary conference at church," called Mother. "Are you ready?" When Pam didn't respond, Mother headed to her room. Hearing her mother's footsteps approaching, Pam slipped a book under her pillow and quickly changed the dial on her radio. "What were you listening to?" Mother asked. "I called and called, and you didn't seem to hear me."

"Oh, I was just looking for some good music," said Pam.

"Well, are you ready to leave for church?" asked Mother.

Pam reluctantly stood up. "I suppose," she muttered. But she was grouchy all the way to church because she really wanted to stay home and watch her favorite television program.

Pam expected to be bored, but when the missionary showed slides, she watched intently. "Many of our people worship idols and practice black magic," the missionary said. "When they accept Christ as Savior and become new creatures in him, they no longer want to do many of the things they did before. This last slide shows a big bonfire where they're burning their idols, magic books, and special potions. They're getting rid of anything that would keep them from living for God. They're often persecuted for their stand, but Jesus means more to them than being popular." He turned off the projector and waited for the lights to come on. Then he asked, "Is there anything you need to 'burn'? Anything you need to get rid of so that it won't keep you from living for God?"

Pam thought about the heavy metal music she had listened to before her mom had come to her room. She remembered the book she didn't want her mom to see, and the way she had wanted to watch a television program instead of coming to church.

Pam bowed her head to pray. Just like those people in Africa, she, too, had some idols to destroy in her life. *JLH*

HOW ABOUT YOU?

Does Jesus have first place in your life, or are you letting TV, video games, a new bicycle, or friends control your thinking and actions? Examine your life. If there are some "idols" you need to put away, take care of it today.

MEMORIZE:
"Dear children, keep away from anything that might take God's place in your hearts." 1 John 5:21

Put Away Your Idols

A Special Love

(Read 1 John 4:7-10)

"I really don't see what's so incredible about Jesus dying to save people," Erik said bluntly.

His mother regarded him thoughtfully for a minute before she answered. "Well, here's a question for you. Erik, would you die for a thousand grasshoppers?"

A broad grin spread over Erik's face. "You kiddin'?"

"No, I'm very serious," said Mother. "Don't you suppose we look like grasshoppers to God?"

Erik frowned. "I never thought of it like that, Mom."

Erik had always pictured God as just another man. It was a bit frightening to think of himself as a little grasshopper with a great big God looming over him.

"But, Erik," continued Mother, "there's one important difference between how you see a grasshopper and how God sees you. You don't care a thing for the grasshopper, but God loves you because he created you! The Bible tells us that while we were still sinners, Christ died for us. Love makes all the difference in the world."

Erik replied thoughtfully, "I guess it must."

His mother hugged him. "You know, Erik, if you had been the only person in the world, Jesus would have died just for you. In fact, he did die for you—for you, personally." *BJW*

HOW ABOUT YOU?

Jesus died to take the punishment for your sin. What love! Do you appreciate what he did for you? Have you accepted his gift of salvation? If not, why don't you talk to a trusted friend or adult so you can find out more.

MEMORIZE:

"But God showed his great love for us by sending Christ to die for us while we were still sinners." Romans 5:8

God Loves You

Hear That Bird

(Read Romans 10:12-17)

"Do you hear that bird?" asked Mike as he and Joseph were walking through the park. Mike motioned with his hands as he spoke.

Joseph looked at his friend. "I don't hear any bird," he said in sign language, "and you don't either. You're deaf."

Mike grinned. "He's in those trees." Mike pointed to a group of pine trees. "I saw him a minute ago. He's called an oven bird, and people who study birds say his song sounds like someone saying 'teacher.'"

Joseph looked at Mike in amazement. "I don't understand how you know so much about birds! You're deaf and have to read my lips and watch me sign words in order to know what I'm saying, yet you can tell me about bird songs! Where did you learn all that?"

"Well, I've always liked birds, so I read books about them and study their pictures," Mike explained. "I memorize their colors and shapes and their flight characteristics."

"Wow! You sure know a lot more about birds than I do," exclaimed Joseph.

Mike smiled. "Mom says I've made up for the fact that I can't hear by studying. She calls it compensation. But you know what? There's more than one way to be deaf."

"What do you mean by that?" Joseph wanted to know.

"Well, it's true that I can't hear anything with my physical ears, but it's not true that I can't hear anything," answered Mike. "I can hear spiritually. The Lord says that hearing comes 'by the Word of God,' and I can read the Bible as well as anyone. But you don't seem to care about God's Word, so I think that maybe you're spiritually deaf. That's even worse than being deaf like me."

Joseph thought about Mike's words. "Maybe you're right," he admitted slowly. *LMW*

HOW ABOUT YOU?

Are you spiritually deaf? In other words, do you just ignore what God says to you through the Bible and other people? You can change all that. First of all, trust Jesus as your Savior. Then ask him to help you "listen" to and obey his Word.

**Read and Heed
God's Word**

MEMORIZE:
"Yet faith comes from listening to this message of good news—the Good News about Christ." Romans 10:17

The Wrong Book

(Read Genesis 1:1-31)

Getting out his science book, John sat down at the kitchen table to do some homework. "Wow!" he said to himself after reading a few pages. "This sure doesn't sound like what it says in the Bible." Feeling confused, he went to talk to his dad, who was replacing some spark plugs in the car. "Dad, my science book doesn't teach creation like the Bible does," said John. "According to my book, many scientists believe that the earth and people and everything just 'happened' to come into existence. They call it evolution."

"Well, Son," Dad responded, "some books are wrong. They have been written by man, and man can sometimes make mistakes. But the Bible has no errors!"

"Because the Bible was inspired by God?" John asked.

"That's right," Dad replied. "That's why we call it the Word of God, and it tells us that God created everything. In addition to that, our common sense tells us that man couldn't have just 'happened.' What if I told you this car just 'happened'—that nobody put the engine, the body, the seats, the wheels, and all the other parts of this car together?"

"Why, I'd tell you that was the craziest thing I ever heard," said John with a smile.

"You'd be absolutely right," Dad replied. "And the human body is far more complicated than this car. We're not accidents. We are part of God's plan and creation." *CVM*

HOW ABOUT YOU?

Have you heard people talk about evolution as if it were fact? Don't you believe it! God made the whole world and everything in it. He made you. He loves you, and he has a wonderful plan and purpose for your life.

MEMORIZE:

"In the beginning God created the heavens and the earth." Genesis 1:1

God Made Everything

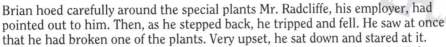

Brian's Big Break

(Read Psalm 103:8-12)

Brian hoed carefully around the special plants Mr. Radcliffe, his employer, had pointed out to him. Then, as he stepped back, he tripped and fell. He saw at once that he had broken one of the plants. Very upset, he sat down and stared at it.

Suddenly a young man stood before him. "What's the trouble, Brian?" the stranger asked kindly. Brian told him what had happened. "I see," said the young man. "Well, don't worry about it—I promise you, it'll be all right. You'd better get on with your work. I'll check on you later."

Brian sighed and got busy again, but he was very unhappy. He knew he'd have to tell Mr. Radcliffe what had happened. About noon the young man returned. "Come with me," he said, and he led Brian toward the place where he had fallen. As they approached, Brian was shocked. A lovely, blooming shrub, just like the one he had broken, now stood in its place.

"D-did you put a new plant there?" Brian asked.

Brian's new friend nodded. "I ordered it from a plant nursery."

"But why?" asked Brian. "Who are you?"

The man smiled. "I'm Jason. My father owns this house," he said. "You see, I understand how bad you felt when you broke that plant. I once broke something I couldn't fix, and the Son of the Owner took care of it for me."

"What did you break?" asked Brian eagerly.

"I broke God's greatest commandment—to love the Lord with all my heart, soul, and mind. His Son, Jesus, made things right for me and gave me a new life," Jason told him.

Brian had heard about Jesus before—and as he looked at Jason, he realized what a great thing Jesus had done for him. Having to answer to Mr. Radcliffe for the broken plant was not nearly as bad as having to answer to God for breaking his laws. Brian was very grateful to Jason for what he had done, but he realized he should be even more grateful to Jesus for what he did. He smiled at Jason. "Thank you for helping me," he said. "Now will you help me again by telling me more about Jesus?" *AGL*

HOW ABOUT YOU?
Do you realize that you have broken God's commandments—his rules? Jesus, God's Son, paid the price to remove your sin and give you a new and clean heart. Confess to God that you are a sinner, and accept what Jesus did for you.

MEMORIZE:
"For God so loved the world that he gave his only Son, so that everyone who believes in him will not perish but have eternal life." John 3:16

Jesus Paid for Your Sin

8

An Inheritance (Part 1)

(Read 1 Peter 1:3-5)

Joey liked to visit Great-Uncle Hank's dairy farm. He liked to throw down feed from the silo. He liked to swing on ropes in the hayloft. He liked to ride on the tractor. But most of all, he liked to work with Uncle Hank on the old Model T car in the shed behind the tractor barn.

The old car had been Uncle Hank's first, and he was working to restore it to its original condition. It had been taken apart piece by piece, and then each piece had been cleaned. Worn parts had been repaired or replaced. The old paint had been stripped off the body, the rust had been removed, and a new coat of paint had been applied. Now the work was nearly done. Joey would polish the car until it shone, as Uncle Hank put the engine back together.

As they were working on the car one day, Uncle Hank turned to Joey and asked, "How would you like to have this car?" Joey grinned, and his eyes lit up. Uncle Hank smiled. "Someday it will be yours," he said. "It's going to be your inheritance from me."

That evening Joey excitedly told his parents about Uncle Hank's decision. Mom smiled. "What a nice thing for Great-Uncle Hank to do," she said.

Dad nodded. "It certainly is," he agreed. After a moment he added, "You know, this reminds me of what God has done for us. He has promised that whoever trusts in his Son, Jesus Christ, will someday enjoy all the blessings of heaven, just as you'll someday enjoy owning that car. Aren't you glad you belong to him?" *TVB*

HOW ABOUT YOU?

Is there an inheritance waiting in heaven for you? There is if you have become a Christian. If you haven't yet done that, why not talk to a trusted friend or adult to find out more?

MEMORIZE:

"All honor to the God and Father of our Lord Jesus Christ, for it is by his boundless mercy that God has given us the privilege of being born again. Now we live with a wonderful expectation because Jesus Christ rose again from the dead." 1 Peter 1:3

Receive God's Inheritance

An Inheritance (Part 2)

(Read Ephesians 1:11-14)

As soon as he could, Joey visited Great-Uncle Hank and helped him work on the Model T again. After a while, Uncle Hank stuck his head out from under the hood and looked at Joey. "I thought you might like to know that I had your inheritance of this car added to my will," he said. "I'd like you to have a set of keys for it now."

"Wow!" Joey's eyes glistened as he thanked his uncle.

That night Joey happily showed his parents the keys. "So you're really going to own that car," said Dad with a smile.

Joey nodded, but he had a question. "You said Christians will receive the blessings of heaven as an inheritance from God. How can we be sure of that?"

"Well," replied Dad, "how can you be sure Uncle Hank will really give you the Model T?"

Joey answered quickly. "I trust him to do what he said because I've never seen him lie to anyone. He even gave me a set of keys to prove that he intends to give me the car."

"That's right," answered Dad, "and it's much the same with God. We know we can trust him to do what he said, too, because he has never lied. He also sends the Holy Spirit to live in us to prove that we really belong to him."

"But how can we know the Holy Spirit is living in us?" asked Joey.

"Well, one way is that his Spirit somehow tells me so," added Mother. "He causes me to be interested in the things of God, and he gives me a peace in my heart."

Joey looked at the keys he held. They were a good reminder of a very important "proof" of an inheritance. *TVB*

HOW ABOUT YOU?

Do you know what an inheritance is? It is something that someone promises to give you. God promised to give us the Holy Spirit and to take us to heaven one day. Because God has promised these things we can be sure we have them if we are Christians.

Christians Have the Holy Spirit

MEMORIZE:
"For his Holy Spirit speaks to us deep in our hearts and tells us that we are God's children." Romans 8:16

Spiritual Milk

(Read 2 Timothy 3:14-17)

"Can you recite the next verse, Mark?" asked Dad.

"What?" Mark looked up at his dad with a blank look. The Bible was open to the day's verse and the family was watching him, waiting for an answer. "Um, I missed the last part," he mumbled.

"Did you hear any of what I just read?" Dad asked suspiciously.

Mark tried to recall even a little bit of what his father had read, but he couldn't remember a word. He shook his head. "I was watching the puppies," he admitted. In a box next to his chair, his dog was feeding her newborn pups. He leaned down and picked up the smallest puppy. "Little Rusty still won't eat," he said, stroking the puppy's fur. "Maybe he's sick."

Dad closed the Bible and took little Rusty in his big hands. "He will be sick if he doesn't eat soon," Dad agreed, "but there's nothing we can do since he won't drink from a bottle."

"He can have one of my pancakes," offered Mark's little sister, April.

"No, honey," said Mom, "he needs milk."

Dad put Rusty down. "If you kids were starving and all you had to do was drink the milk in front of you, would you do it?" he asked.

"Sure," Mark answered, and April nodded in agreement.

"Well," Dad continued, placing his Bible in the middle of the table, "this is the richest source of spiritual 'milk' there is. As we 'drink it in' and 'digest' it each day, it helps us stay spiritually strong and healthy."

Mark knew Dad was talking to him. "I'll try harder to listen," he promised.

Dad opened the Bible and read a few verses again. "Now I know the next verse!" exclaimed Mark. "It's my memory verse from last Sunday!" He quickly recited it. Then he looked at Rusty, and his eyes lit up. "Look!" he shrieked. "Rusty is eating!"

"Not just Rusty," said Dad with a smile. "Now you're both eating!" *HMT*

HOW ABOUT YOU?

Are you enjoying the "milk" of God's Word? Do you take time each day to read your Bible and learn from it? As you learn what pleases God, do you obey him? Thank God that you have a Bible to read. Read it as though you're starving. Then as you practice what it teaches, you'll see how good it is!

MEMORIZE:

"You must crave pure spiritual milk so that you can grow into the fullness of your salvation. Cry out for this nourishment as a baby cries for milk."
1 Peter 2:2

Feed on God's Word

Surprise Dessert

(Read Revelation 21:3, 18, 21-23)

Jim took a bite of his meat loaf. "We learned about heaven in Sunday school today," he said, "but there's something I don't understand." He frowned. "I know heaven is supposed to be wonderful and all that. But won't it be boring just walking around on the golden streets, singing hymns?"

"I'm sure we'll be doing more than that," Dad said with a smile, "though the Bible doesn't tell us a lot about it. But the wonderful part about heaven will be being together with Jesus."

"Right," agreed Mother. "I know it's hard to understand that at your age. Maybe it would help if you think about how glad you always are to see Grandpa and Grandma when they're able to come or when we can go to see them."

"I guess so." Jim shrugged as he ate the last bite of his mashed potatoes. "I wonder why God didn't tell us more about what heaven will be like."

"For one thing, it would be impossible for our minds to understand all the wonderful things he has planned for us," said Dad. He looked over at four-year-old Eric. "Finish your carrots, Son. We're almost ready for dessert."

"What is it?" Eric asked.

Mother just smiled. "It's a surprise," she said. "But I promise you'll like it."

"Can I have mine now, Mom?" asked Jim.

Mother shook her head. "Let's wait till Eric's ready. It's his favorite. If he sees it, he'll get so excited that he won't want to finish his carrots."

A short time later they were all enjoying strawberry shortcake. "I just thought of another reason God didn't tell us exactly what heaven will be like," Jim announced with a grin. "If we knew, we'd get so excited, we'd never be happy on earth, doing the things God wants us to do now."

Dad and Mother smiled. "You may be right," agreed Mother. *SLK*

HOW ABOUT YOU?

Do you ever wonder what heaven will be like? The Bible gives us some ideas about it, but we won't really know what God has in store until we get there. Trust him and believe that he knows best how to make us happy. In the meantime, keep busy doing God's will on earth and telling others about Jesus so they can go to heaven, too!

Heaven Is Wonderful

MEMORIZE:
"You will show me the way of life, granting me the joy of your presence and the pleasures of living with you forever." Psalm 16:11

Gate to Heaven

(Read John 10:1-9)

Tim ran into the house. "Mom," he said excitedly, "you know Brandon—that new boy down the street? He and I want to go for a hike in the park, OK? He's my age and he's the nicest boy I've ever met! I bet he's a Christian."

Mother looked up at Tim. "That will be fine," she said. "Just don't be back too late." She smiled. "Brandon does seem very nice. Is he a Christian?"

"Well, he just said he tries his best to be real good," admitted Tim.

"I see. But you know that doesn't make a person a Christian," replied Mother. Tim just shrugged and hurried out to meet Brandon.

The boys had a great time hiking, and before they knew it, it was time to head for home. "We'd better be going," said Tim.

"Yeah," agreed Brandon. He looked around. "Hey, Tim," he said. "Look! From up on this hill you can see a long way."

"You sure can," agreed Tim. He pointed. "See that yellow dot over there? That's your neighbor's house."

"Wow! Yeah!" said Brandon. "Let's take a shortcut down the side of this hill and across that valley."

The boys set off, and as they expected, they soon came to the road on which they lived. "Oh, no!" groaned Tim. "I forgot about the high chain-link fence between the road and this park. We won't be able to climb over it, either. There's barbed wire at the top."

The boys followed the fence for a while, looking for a hole, but there was none. They had to go all the way back to the path that led out of the park.

"I'm really tired," said Tim when he reached home. He explained what had happened. "We were sure we could get home this other way. We were so close, but we couldn't get here. I guess the only way home from the park is through the entrance gate."

Mother nodded. "You know, I'm reminded of what we talked about earlier. Brandon is a very nice boy, and he may be close to becoming a Christian. Yet the only way to get into heaven is through the gate. And Jesus is that gate."

Tim nodded thoughtfully. "I'm going to pray for Brandon and tell him more about Jesus," he said. "Maybe he'll come to church with me, too." *AGL*

HOW ABOUT YOU?

Do you have friends that are not Christians yet? Be sure to pray for them.

MEMORIZE:

"Yes, I am the gate. Those who come in through me will be saved. Wherever they go, they will find green pastures." John 10:9

Jesus Is the Way to Heaven

Flying High

(Read Psalm 37:1-8)

Andy watched the red kite soaring in the bright sky. His brother, Mike, grinned. "Looks like fun, huh, Andy? Would you like to be able to fly high like that?" asked Mike.

"Sure would!" Andy grinned back. "But if I were that kite, I'd want to break loose and fly away, high into the sky." His small hands clutched the spool of kite string, trying to make sure his kite didn't do that.

Mike laughed. "But if you broke loose, you'd crash to the ground instead of flying away," he said. "Without the string, that kite would just fall down here on the field."

Andy turned to his father. "Would it, Dad?"

"Yep." Dad nodded. "Without that string, it would soon fall."

"Oh." Andy held the spool of string even more tightly.

"You know," Dad mused, "in a way, we're something like that kite. The string guides the kite, and God guides us. Sometimes it's hard to act the way he wants us to, and we try to break loose and fly our own way. But if the bond that holds us to him would ever break—if he'd let us go—we would crash, like a kite whose string has broken."

"That's kind of scary," said Mike seriously.

"Would God ever let us go, Daddy?" asked Andy.

"No, Andy. If you have become a Christian, he'll never let you go," Dad assured him. "The Bible says that nothing can ever separate us from his love. But it's important to let God lead our life and not fight against it. He'll give us the power to be strong and graceful and beautiful for him."

"Like the kite flying way up there," said Andy with a smile. *JKB*

HOW ABOUT YOU?

Do you sometimes resent the "strings" you feel God has put on your life? Do you feel you'd like to be free to go wherever you want, to choose your own friends, or to pick your own TV programs? Do you wish you could be rid of an illness, a teacher you dislike, or discipline from a parent? Everyone feels like that sometimes. But God has a reason for everything he allows to happen in your life. Trust him.

MEMORIZE:
"Commit everything you do to the Lord. Trust him, and he will help you."
Psalm 37:5

Submit to God's Control

The Flashlight

(Read Philippians 2:13-16)

"Tom finally agreed to go to Sunday school with me," Bill told his mother, "but then this afternoon he changed his mind. I wonder why." Mom looked thoughtful when she heard this.

That night shortly after Bill went up to bed, he came running back downstairs. "Mom, my new flashlight doesn't work!" he exclaimed. Mom watched while he unscrewed the end. "Look!" he gasped. "There are old rags stuffed in here where the batteries should be!" He began pulling them out. "Look! They have words on them," he reported. He read them aloud. "Selfishness . . . disobeying . . . lying . . . complaining." Bill turned to his mother. "What is this?" he asked. "Who put these in here?"

"I did, Bill," answered Mom. "You see, I couldn't help but notice the look on Tom's face this afternoon when you were bullying some of your other friends. I wondered if that had something to do with his changing his mind about coming along to Sunday school. So I decided to illustrate something." Bill looked puzzled, and Mom explained. "Just as the old rags in the flashlight kept its light from shining, the things written on the rags will keep your light from shining for Jesus," she said. "I've noticed you doing some of those things quite often lately, and maybe Tom has, too. The Lord wants you to get rid of these things and really shine for him. Then Tom and your other friends will be able to see that you're a Christian."

Bill was ashamed as he thought over the day. He knew that Tom had heard him tell his teacher he had finished a reading assignment, and that wasn't true. Tom had also seen Bill lose his temper and show poor sportsmanship on the playground. And then Tom had seen him acting like a bully. "I guess I need to talk to Tom," he said slowly. "If I shine for Jesus, maybe Tom will want to know him, too." *AGL*

HOW ABOUT YOU?

Are sins clogging your life so your light can't shine? Is there laziness? Lying? Disobedience? Selfishness? Talk with Jesus. Tell him about the wrong things you are doing and ask him to help you turn away from them.

MEMORIZE:

"In the same way, let your good deeds shine out for all to see, so that everyone will praise your heavenly Father." Matthew 5:16

Let Your Light Shine

The Best Hamburger!

(Read 1 Corinthians 13:1-3)

"Dad sure looks tired lately," said Jenna to her brother, Jeremy. It was Saturday morning and the two children were playing catch in the front yard. Just a few minutes earlier, they had watched their dad slowly walk down the road to the bus stop. Even though it was the weekend, he had to go to the office.

"Dad's tired because of that big report he's writing for the convention next month," Jeremy explained.

"Mom's been busy, too," Jenna continued. "It's not easy teaching at church and working a full-time job. Wish we could help them."

"Well, we have helped Mom with the cleaning," said Jeremy, "but there are some jobs kids just can't do!"

They threw the ball back and forth for a while, then Jenna spoke excitedly. "Jeremy, how much money do you have?"

Jeremy grinned. "I'm rich! All last week I helped Mrs. Parker clean out her garage and attic, remember? And she said she could use me later, too. Why?"

"I've got baby-sitting money saved up," said Jenna, "and I thought maybe we could take Dad and Mom out for dinner. We don't have to go to the most expensive place in town, but it would let them know how much we appreciate them."

And that's just what Jenna and Jeremy did! Their parents were very surprised. "You know," said Dad as they were eating, "this is the best hamburger I've ever tasted!"

"I agree." Mom smiled. "It's terrific to know that our children care about us!"

Jenna and Jeremy grinned at each other. They were glad they had given their parents a special treat! *LMW*

HOW ABOUT YOU?

When was the last time you did something special for your dad and mom, or told them how much you appreciated the hard work they do? Dads and moms sometimes become very busy and therefore very tired. Read 1 Corinthians 13, a chapter in which the apostle Paul talks about love. Then show that kind of love to your parents.

MEMORIZE:
"'Honor your father and mother.' This is the first of the Ten Commandments that ends with a promise."
Ephesians 6:2

Show Love for Parents

Now Let Us Assume

(Read 2 Timothy 1:9-14)

"I hope you don't get upset with me, Dad," said Trent, "but, well, I really like my science teacher, and he believes what Darwin says about evolution. Sometimes it sounds pretty logical."

Dad smiled. "I'm not at all upset with you, Son," he said. "I gave evolution a lot of thought when I was young, too." As he talked, he walked over to the bookshelves and pulled out a book. "Most kids your age don't get to see this book," he said as he held it out to Trent. "It's about evolution, and it's pretty hard to understand. But I'd like you to look through it and see how many times you can find such words as *let us assume, perhaps,* or *probably*—words indicating uncertainty. I'll come back later to see what you've found."

Trent opened the book as he sat down in a nearby chair. Soon he was busily reading. He looked up as his dad walked into the room some time later. "Nine times, Dad," Trent said, even before his dad could ask a question. "Nine times in ten minutes."

Dad took the book. "Imagine how often you'd find such words if you read this from cover to cover," he said. "To assume means to suppose or pretend. Trent, wouldn't you rather know?" Dad handed him another book. "Here's the world's best textbook, the Bible! It tells how we can know our Creator. We can know where we came from and where we're going." *PR*

HOW ABOUT YOU?

Do you know the God who created you? You can know him through his book, the Bible. It tells how you can have a personal relationship with God through his Son, Jesus Christ.

MEMORIZE:

"And that is why I am suffering here in prison. But I am not ashamed of it, for I know the one in whom I trust, and I am sure that he is able to guard what I have entrusted to him until the day of his return." 2 Timothy 1:12

You Can Know God

Happy Birthday

(Read Psalm 138)

David frowned when he looked outside. "It can't rain today," he grumbled. "It will spoil everything!" It was David's birthday, and his grandparents were coming for a picnic.

Just then the phone rang, and Mother went to the kitchen to answer it. "Grandma wants to talk to you, David," she called a little later.

"Some birthday," David muttered when he had finished talking with his grandmother. "Grandpa hurt his back and has to stay in bed. They'll come next week instead of today."

Mother hugged David. "I'm sorry things aren't working out the way we planned. But we'll do something else today, and we'll celebrate your birthday next week."

"I have an idea," said Dad. "Who else might be lonely today?"

"Maybe Jeff," said David. "His father died a couple of months ago. Maybe I can call and see if he wants to come over."

Jeff was delighted with the invitation, and he and David had a great time together. David was surprised to find that the two of them had many things in common.

Before bedtime, David and his dad had a talk. "I expected my birthday to be perfect," David said, "and then everything went wrong. But I found out that things don't have to be perfect to be fun."

"I'm glad to hear that," said Dad. "You know, some Christians figure that once they become Christians, everything will be perfect, and they won't have any troubles. But it just isn't so. Jesus doesn't guarantee an easy, happy life, but he does promise to be with us. And if we'll allow him, he'll use those things that seem like trials to bring us a blessing." *JLH*

HOW ABOUT YOU?

Have you found that things don't always work out the way you hope? Remember, happiness comes from Jesus, not from circumstances. So when your plans go astray, cheerfully look to see what other plans he may have for you.

**Make the Best
of Situations**

MEMORIZE:
"The Lord will work out his plans for my life—for your faithful love, O Lord, endures forever. Don't abandon me, for you made me."
Psalm 138:8

A Bitter Spring

(Read James 3:5-12)

The camping trip for Nathan's church class was lots of fun. He loved the outdoors, and in no time at all, his tent was up. When Mr. Charles, his teacher, suggested that the class hike up a mountain trail, Nathan was eager to go.

The boys were delighted when they came across a spring of fresh water. Nathan took a long, satisfying drink, but Mr. Charles stopped the other thirsty boys. "Perhaps we shouldn't drink this water," he said. "It might be bitter."

Nathan gave Mr. Charles a peculiar look. "No way!" he exclaimed. "This is a freshwater spring. I just had some of the water."

"I know," said Mr. Charles, "but how can we be sure the next person to try it will get fresh water?"

Nathan frowned. "A spring doesn't give two kinds of water," he said.

Mr. Charles smiled and nodded. "Good point," he said. "Do you know that the Bible makes that point, too, when it speaks about controlling our tongue? Just as salty water can't come from a pure spring, unkind words shouldn't come from a heart filled with love for Jesus."

Nathan was startled. His parents frequently reminded him that he needed to be more careful about what he said when he was teasing somebody.

"Always remember that words can sound very cruel," continued Mr. Charles. "When I was your age I sometimes just meant to tease someone. I didn't intend to be mean, but the things I said hurt the person I was talking to. I asked God to help me show love, even when I was teasing. When he did that, my words were like fresh water instead of bitter water. He smiled as he glanced around the group of boys. "If you have a problem with your words, ask God to change you. He will." He grinned. "Now, who would like a drink from this spring?" *DLR*

HOW ABOUT YOU?

Does your "joking around" often sound biting and cruel? Ask the Lord to give you real love for others. Then when you're tempted to make a taunting remark, examine it. Will it hurt the person you're teasing? If so, think of something nice to say instead—and say it.

MEMORIZE:

"He who guards his mouth and his tongue keeps himself from calamity."
Proverbs 21:23, NIV

Speak Words of Love

The Right Nose

(Read Isaiah 45:6-7, 9-12)

"I have an ugly nose!" said Ryan as he looked into the mirror.

"Let's not worry about noses now," said his big brother, Ted. "We've got to get going if we want to stop at the zoo today."

It was a beautiful, sunny day. Ryan and his brother enjoyed a leisurely stroll, looking at all the animals. "My! The elephants have long trunks, don't they?" commented Ted as they stopped to watch the great beasts. "I'm glad my nose isn't that long."

"Come on, Ted," protested Ryan, "that's what makes an elephant an elephant!"

At the rhinoceros's cage, Ted laughed as he pointed to the horns on their noses. "Oh, dear! That kind of nose would be even worse!" Ryan gave him a curious look, but said nothing. As they walked along, he noticed that Ted had a comment to make about almost every kind of animal's nose. When they reached the baboons, Ted turned to him. "Their noses are much too stubby, don't you think? Wouldn't they look better if they had noses more like the tigers?"

Ryan was annoyed. "No, they wouldn't!" he snapped. "I like them just the way they are. The animals wouldn't be very interesting if they were all alike. Besides, God made them the way they are, and he knows best how they should look."

"Exactly," replied Ted. "He knows best how animals should look, and he knows best how people should look."

"Oh!" exclaimed Ryan. "I get it! I'm the way I am because God made me this way. I guess I should thank him rather than complain. Besides, if God likes my nose, who am I to say it isn't a good-looking nose?" *PR*

HOW ABOUT YOU?

Do you sometimes complain about the way you look? If everyone had the "perfect" nose, mouth, eyes, and teeth, we would all look alike! Wouldn't that be dull—and confusing! Remember, God made you, and he loves you just the way you are.

MEMORIZE:
"For the Spirit of God has made me, and the breath of the Almighty gives me life." Job 33:4

God Made Me Special

Tattoos

(Read 1 Samuel 15:22-26)

After supper one evening, Mike made an announcement. "Dave says he's going to get a tattoo when he's thirteen—and his parents don't care. He even has it picked out already. He can hardly wait!" Mike paused a minute, then added, "Next month when I'm thirteen, I'm going to get one, too."

"A tattoo!" exclaimed Dad. "Why would you want one?"

"They're cool!" replied Mike. "Everyone is getting a tattoo!"

"Oh, now, Mike," said Dad, "I know that not everyone has one." He shook his head. "I don't think it's a good idea, and I can't give my permission for you to get one."

"I don't see what's wrong with it!" protested Mike.

"Well, for now you'll just have to accept my decision on this," said Dad firmly. Mike started to argue but then turned angrily and left the room.

After school a few days later, Mom noticed a tattoo on Mike's arm. "Michael!" she said sternly. "You know what Dad said about getting a tattoo!"

Mike scowled. "Oh, Mom," he said crossly, "you always overreact! It'll wash off."

"Then go and wash it off," ordered Mom. Mike hesitated. He glared at his mother for a long time, then went to wash off the tattoo. When he came back, Mom looked at his arm. "That's better," she said, "but Mike, I'm concerned about your attitude. It needs to change. You could wash off your pretend tattoo, but your attitude can't be washed away with soap and water."

"Oh, Mom," grumbled Mike, "it's not that serious."

"You may not see your attitude as serious, Mike, but God does. I think it's time that you do, too. You need to seek his forgiveness and help." *SKV*

HOW ABOUT YOU?

What is your attitude toward your parents and teachers and others in authority over you? What tone of voice do you use when you talk to them or talk about them? Rebellion (not doing what you know is right) begins with an attitude. Check yours.

MEMORIZE:

"Evil people seek rebellion, but they will be severely punished."
Proverbs 17:11

Rebellion Is Serious

The Whole Clock

(Read 1 Corinthians 12:12-27)

"This must be a clock you've already fixed," Kyle said, looking at a large clock standing on the counter in front of him. He was watching his Uncle Bill work on clocks and watches that had been brought to his shop. "This one seems to be ticking all right."

Kyle's uncle laughed. "Yes," he agreed. "It's ticking all right, but that's all it's doing."

Kyle looked at the clock more closely. "Hey, it doesn't have any hands on it," he remarked, feeling embarrassed because he hadn't noticed that immediately.

"That's right." Uncle Bill nodded. "So even though the clock is ticking, it isn't doing its job—it isn't giving the correct time, is it?"

Kyle shook his head. "Not without the hands, it isn't."

"I use my clocks as illustrations when I teach Sunday school," Uncle Bill told Kyle. "Sometimes kids—and adults, too—think they're the important ones in a project. They seem to think they can handle things by themselves. But the clocks prove that it takes a lot of different pieces to get a job done. The inside works can be clean and running well, but that still doesn't give you the time. Or you can pick up the hands and look at them closely, but you won't learn the time of day that way, either."

Kyle thought he understood. "But put the two together, and you've got it made, right?"

"Wrong," was his uncle's reply. To explain, he picked up the inside works of a clock and attached some hands to the front. "Does it give you the time?" he asked.

Kyle shook his head. "You've got to put the face on it so I can find the numbers."

"Exactly." Uncle Bill smiled. "It takes everything working together to get the job done. That's the way it is in the Lord's work, too. It takes people working together. Pastors, church teachers, musicians, nursery workers, the congregation—all need to work together to bring others to Jesus."

Kyle nodded. He had learned a very valuable lesson. *RIJ*

HOW ABOUT YOU?

Do you sometimes try to be the "whole clock" in your youth group or Sunday school class? Or do you go to the opposite extreme and decide that your small part is not important? Remember, it takes many parts to complete the job. Do your part faithfully and allow each other member of the group to do his. Work together for the Lord.

MEMORIZE:
"Now all of you together are Christ's body, and each one of you is a separate and necessary part of it."
1 Corinthians 12:27

Work Together

April 22

The Real Thing

(Read 1 Timothy 4:1-2, 7-8)

"Look at this!" Keith stuck the newspaper in front of his mother's face. She backed away a few inches and read the headline, "All Religions Lead to Heaven." As she finished reading, Keith spoke again. "Everyone knows that Jesus is the only way to heaven."

"No, I'm afraid everyone doesn't know," Mother said as she reached for her sweater. "Want to come along to the bank?" she asked.

At the bank, Keith and his mother got in line at one of the windows. The teller and the bank manager were talking to a customer. "Mr. Baker, do you know where you got this bill?" asked the manager as he held out a $20 bill.

"Why, no," replied Mr. Baker. "At my store we take in $20 bills every day. Is something wrong with that bill?"

"Yes, I'm afraid it's a counterfeit," replied the bank manager. "We've been warned that they're circulating in this area. Come into my office and we'll make a report on this."

When Keith and his mother got up to the counter, Keith asked, "How did you know that was a counterfeit bill?"

The teller smiled at him. "Part of our training is to study real bills, and I've handled and examined them for years. When you're well acquainted with the real ones, it's easier to spot the counterfeits."

On the way home, Keith studied a dollar bill. Suddenly he snapped his fingers. "I've got it!" He turned to his mother. "People are fooled by other religions because they don't learn enough about Jesus."

"You're right." Mother nodded. "If we become well acquainted with Jesus through studying his Word and praying to him, we're less likely to be led astray by false religions."

Keith was thoughtful for a few minutes, still looking at the dollar bill in his hand. Then a twinkle came to his eye, and he turned to his mother with a grin. "I sure wish I had a five-dollar bill to study so I could avoid ever taking a counterfeit one. Could you help me out?" *BJW*

HOW ABOUT YOU?

How well do you know Jesus? He's the only Savior of the world. Start today to learn more about him. Read his Word. Talk to him. Get to know him well. Then you won't be fooled by counterfeit religions.

MEMORIZE:

"I am the Lord, and there is no other Savior." Isaiah 43:11

Know the Savior

A Sure Guide

(Read Psalm 18:24-33)

The Johnsons—Rebecca, Bob, Mother, and Dad—had spent the past few days with Grandpa and Grandma Johnson. They treasured the long talks, the jokes, and the delicious food. They hated to leave. It was going to be a long good-bye, for it would be four years before they would meet again. In less than a week, the Johnsons were going to Peru as missionaries.

As they finally prepared to go home, fog settled in. "Oh, dear," moaned Mother, "I just knew we should have left earlier." Since they had brought several items to store in the grandparents' attic, she had driven the family car while Dad drove a truck they had borrowed. "John, how will I ever see the way home?" she murmured as she and the children got into the car.

"The fog lights on this truck will pierce through the mist pretty well, so I'll lead the way," said Dad. "Just follow me and keep your eyes on my taillights. I won't go very fast. Trust me."

Mother nervously gripped the steering wheel, but as the children prayed and sang, she gradually relaxed. It seemed like the trip home would never end, and it wasn't easy, either. When they got home safely, they thanked God for his protection.

"As I was driving, I couldn't help but think that God was using this fog to teach us something about our upcoming trip to Peru," said Dad. "Just like we couldn't see very far ahead in the fog, we can't see very well what our future is going to be like either. The people, customs, and language are unknown to us, and we don't know just what's ahead, but God knows all about it. He'll take care of us."

"That's right," agreed Mother. "I had your taillights to guide me, and we have Jesus to guide us as we go to Peru. We can trust him." *JLH*

HOW ABOUT YOU?

Does an unknown future upset you? Do you worry about a different school, an unfamiliar town, a new family or stepparent, or a new challenge awaiting you? God knows your fears and your future. Read his Word for instruction and encouragement. Pray to him for wisdom. He'll guide you because he loves you.

Jesus Will Guide You

MEMORIZE:
"For that is what God is like. He is our God forever and ever, and he will be our guide until we die." Psalm 48:14

All Play, No Work

(Read 2 Peter 1:5-10)

"Yummy! Fudge!" Steve grinned as he came into the kitchen. "Can I . . . I mean, may I have a piece, Grandpa?"

"Yes, you may," said Grandpa, heading for the door. "I'm going to take some to Uncle Wilbur, and I want you to clean your room and do your homework while I'm gone, Steve."

"OK," Steve mumbled, his mouth full. He was just ready to start his work when the doorbell rang.

Steve's friend Nate was at the door. "How about a basketball game of one on one?""Sure!" answered Steve with a grin. When Grandpa returned, they were playing basketball on the driveway.

At dinnertime, Steve's little brother Adam pushed his food around his plate. "What's the matter?" asked Grandma. "Aren't you hungry?"

"He couldn't be." Grandpa spoke up. "He got into the fudge while I was gone."

Adam pushed his chair back from the table. "I don't feel good," he whined. Grandma suggested that he go and lie down.

After dinner, Grandpa turned to Steve. "I saw that you still need to clean your room," he said. "And is your homework done?"

"I was going to do it, but Nate wanted to play basketball," Steve mumbled.

"You remind me of Adam," said Grandma. "A little candy is good, but too much is bad news. A little play is also fine, but you also need to do a little work. God says we are to use moderation in all we do," continued Grandma. "That means we must use self-control and not overdo anything. It means being balanced—balancing candy and healthy food, work and play. Moderation helps us stay healthy."

Grandpa stood to clear the table. "Go start on your homework and then clean your room, Steve," he said. *BJW*

HOW ABOUT YOU?

Do you balance work and play? Is there a task left unfinished so you can spend time watching TV? Are your chores sometimes left undone while you're off playing with your friends? God made boys and girls with a desire to play, but he knows that work is needed, too. When you balance your play with work, life will be more enjoyable. You'll feel much better, too.

MEMORIZE:

"A person without self-control is as defenseless as a city with broken-down walls." Proverbs 25:28

Balance Work and Play

Study to Know

(Read 2 Timothy 3:14-17)

"Well, Greg, what's on your schedule for tomorrow?" asked Dad as he sat down in his recliner.

Greg snapped off the TV and picked up the paper. "Oh," he said, "tomorrow afternoon we have a youth group party." He quickly read through the comic page while his dad took off his shoes. Then, handing Dad the newspaper, Greg added, "We're having a Bible quiz at the beginning of the party. Maybe I'll just go late."

"Oh?" asked Dad. "You used to enjoy quizzes. Why don't you like them now?"

Greg leafed through a sports magazine. "Because Joel always wins, that's why. They're no fun anymore."

"Do you know what chapters the quiz will cover?"

"Yes," replied Greg. "But it doesn't matter what chapters they are. Joel will know everything in them. That guy really knows his Bible. The other day in science class, Joel and our teacher got into quite a discussion about creation, and Joel did really well. He quoted verses from the Bible and talked about why he believed they were true. He really knew what he was talking about."

"Good for Joel!" cheered Dad.

"I've heard him do the same kind of thing in history class. I wish I knew the Bible like that." Greg sighed and began reading an article.

Dad watched Greg for a moment, then he asked, "How do you suppose Joel learned so much?" Greg shrugged. "Well," said Dad, "I don't think it came from reading magazines or newspapers or watching TV. If you want to know the Bible, you have to study the Bible."

Greg looked at Dad thoughtfully. He looked down at his magazine. Then, putting it down, he got to his feet. "Excuse me, please." He grinned at his dad. "I have to go study a couple of chapters in my Bible. Joel's gonna get some competition tomorrow!" *HWM*

HOW ABOUT YOU?

Do you wish you had as much Bible knowledge as your pastor, your Sunday school teacher, or even a friend? It's available to you, too, but it won't come automatically. Listen carefully when God's Word is taught in church and Sunday school. Also, study it for yourself.

MEMORIZE:
"Work hard so God can approve you. Be a good worker, one who does not need to be ashamed and who correctly explains the word of truth."
2 Timothy 2:15

Study the Bible

World of Wars

(Read Matthew 24:4-14)

"Boy, have I got a hard assignment tonight," Daryl announced as he and his brother and sister sat down at the kitchen table to do their homework. "I have to memorize a bunch of dates about the Civil War. We're going to be tested on it tomorrow."

"And I'm learning about the different battles of the Revolutionary War," said John.

"All I have to do is go through the newspaper and cut out articles for our current events project," Jana told her brothers. "That doesn't sound too hard compared to what you guys have to do."

"Just make sure you don't cut any of the comics," said Daryl, grinning.

The three children worked quietly for a while, then Jana sighed. "Almost all the articles in this paper are about troubles and wars in one place or another."

"I wonder how come," said John. "Politicians are always talking about making the world a better place, but things just seem to be getting worse!"

"That's true," agreed Daryl, "but as Christians, we shouldn't be surprised. The Bible says there will always be wars and rumors of war. Men talk about peace, but their desire for power gets in the way. God is left completely out of the picture."

"It's kind of scary," Jana said. "It makes me glad I'm a Christian."

"Right," Daryl said. "As Christians, we can have peace of mind no matter what happens here on earth." *LMW*

HOW ABOUT YOU?

Do you ever wonder why the world is not getting better as so many politicians promise? Do you wonder why there are so many wars? People, because they are human, cannot get along with each other. They refuse to listen to God and follow his ways. Isn't it good to know that in spite of the chaos in the world around you, you can put your trust in God and have peace?

MEMORIZE:

"If you do this, you will experience God's peace, which is far more wonderful than the human mind can understand. His peace will guard your hearts and minds as you live in Christ Jesus." Philippians 4:7

God Gives Peace

He Knows His Own (Part 1)

(Read John 10:1-5, 11-14)

Gary settled back in his seat as the shades were pulled. Today his science class was watching a movie about penguins. Gary shivered as he saw the penguins swimming in the Antarctic. It was a cold and lonely place. How did they survive?

Gary watched as the penguins swam toward the coast in the spring. They slid and waddled across the icy land, searching for a nesting place. How funny they looked! Soon they stopped at a rocky place that was called a rookery. Large numbers of penguins would lay their eggs and raise their young there. The rookery was very crowded. A million penguins could live in a single rookery, but each penguin had her own nest.

When the lights came on, Gary had several questions for his teacher. "If thousands of penguins live in one spot, how can a penguin tell which babies are hers?" he asked. "They all look dressed alike to me." The class laughed.

"That's a good question, Gary," his teacher said. "Each penguin has a different voice. The parents can pick out their own children from thousands of other penguins just by the sound of their voices. They know their own children, and they take care of their own children."

That evening Gary told his parents about the penguins. Dad smiled and nodded. "You know, God does the same thing for us," he said. "Millions and millions of people are scattered all over the world, but God knows those who belong to him—those who have trusted Jesus as Savior. If they should stray away from him, God will call them back to himself by his Word. He knows his own children, and he takes care of them."

"I'm glad I belong to Jesus," Gary said to himself, "for I know God will always take care of me." *JLH*

HOW ABOUT YOU?

Do you sometimes worry about having food to eat or clothes to wear? Do you feel alone and forgotten? Do you wonder if God cares about you or your circumstances? If you are a Christian, you belong to God. He knows you by name. He cares about every detail of your life. He has promised to care for you. Trust him.

God Knows His Own

MEMORIZE:
"The Lord knows those who are his."
2 Timothy 2:19

He Knows His Own (Part 2)

(Read Hebrews 10:22-25)

After seeing the movie about penguins, Gary decided to do a report on them for extra credit. He was reading a book on penguins when his dad came into the family room. "How's your report coming, Gary?" Dad asked.

"Good, Dad. I'm learning some really neat stuff," Gary replied. "Did you know that when the penguins head for land and search for a nesting place, they march in single file for miles? They don't have any landmarks to guide them, but they never get lost. They use the sun to guide them. Aren't they smart?"

"Yes, and it's because God gave them certain instincts when he created them," Dad explained. "God cares about his creation."

"Listen to this," Gary continued. "When the penguin chicks are about three weeks old, they get so hungry that both parents must go out and hunt for food. Then the chicks gather into groups of fifty or sixty. In bad weather they huddle together to keep warm. They stick together for safety, too. If they wander off alone, a sea bird will try to capture them."

"That's a good illustration of Christians in a local church," Dad said. "They need to stick together so they can help each other, too."

"Wow! I'm getting lots of lessons from the penguins. They sure are good teachers!" laughed Gary. *JLH*

HOW ABOUT YOU?

Do you attend a good Bible-believing church? Do you listen as the Bible is taught? Do you make friends with the people there? These friends can encourage you as you live for Jesus. They can pray for you. Knowing they are there to help you makes it easier to stand up for Jesus in the world.

MEMORIZE:

"And let us not neglect our meeting together, as some people do, but encourage and warn each other, especially now that the day of his coming back again is drawing near."
Hebrews 10:25

Don't Neglect Church

The Binoculars

April
29

(Read Job 31:4-6; Psalm 33:13-15)

Daven eagerly tore the wrapping paper off the birthday present his parents had given him. "Oh, wow! Binoculars! Thanks!" he exclaimed, quickly pulling them out of the box. He turned them over and over in his hands. "Can we go to the state forest reserve? It has some good lookout points where I could try these out. I bet I can see a long way."

"Sounds great!" agreed Dad. "Let's go!"

Before long, Daven and his dad stood together on one of the park's lookout points and took turns looking through the binoculars. As Daven took a turn, he silently watched something for a moment. "Dad! I see a doe and twin fawns," he whispered. "They're so cute! Look!" Dad took the binoculars his son offered and soon located the animals. He watched them for a minute. "Aren't they neat?" whispered Daven.

Dad laughed and handed the binoculars back. "Yes, they are," he said out loud. "But you don't need to whisper."

Daven looked again. "Just think, those animals have no idea we're watching them," he said in awe. "We can see every move they make, but they're so far away that they don't even know we exist!"

"That is amazing," agreed Dad, "and it reminds me that we're being watched, too."

"We are? Who's watching us?" Daven wanted to know.

"God is. He's watching every move we make, whether it be right or wrong," explained Dad. "He sees the mistakes we make, and he sees the good things we do. Yet we're often unaware of his presence, just as the doe and fawns are unaware of us."

"I knew that, but I never thought about it quite that way," said Daven. "I think I'll be more careful of what I do if I remember that God is always watching." *VLR*

HOW ABOUT YOU?

Are you aware that God sees you 24 hours a day? Next time you're tempted to do something wrong, remember, God is watching! Next time you become discouraged in your efforts to do what is right, remember, God is watching! He sees you all the time.

God Is Watching

MEMORIZE:
"For the Lord sees clearly what a man does, examining every path he takes."
Proverbs 5:21

30

The Solo Part

(Read John 21:17-22)

"It's not fair!" Troy whined. "I go to children's choir practice every Saturday morning. I've never missed once. And I've been practicing the solo part for weeks, but now Mr. Widmark says that Joel gets to do the solo when we sing next Sunday." The nine-year-old boy was fighting tears as he rode home in the car with Mom.

"Now wait a minute, Troy," said Mom. "Did Mr. Widmark ever say that you were going to sing the solo?"

"Well, no," choked Troy, "but I'm the most faithful boy in the choir. I just took it for granted that I'd get to sing it. I've got the best voice in—"

"Stop it, Troy," Mom reprimanded. "You do have a nice voice, but evidently Joel does, too. Maybe Mr. Widmark is hoping that Joel's parents will come to church if he has the solo. Or maybe Joel has the better voice. Whatever the reason, it shouldn't matter to you who sings the solo part."

"But Mom, doesn't being faithful for all these weeks of practice count for anything?" asked Troy. "Joel has only been coming for a few weeks."

Mom sighed. "I can understand how you feel," she said gently, "but I think you need to remember the reason for being in the choir. You remind me a little of the apostle Peter at the end of the book of John. Peter had just been told by Jesus how he would die, and Peter immediately wondered how John would have to die. Jesus said, 'What is that to you? You follow me!'"

Now Troy was quiet for a long time. Finally he said, "So Jesus just wants me to follow him and not worry about what Joel does. It will be tough not to be jealous of him, but I will try hard to be happy for him." *REP*

HOW ABOUT YOU?

Have you ever been upset because, as you tried to serve the Lord, it seemed someone else got more attention than you or had an easier time of it? Peter had the same problem. He wondered if John was gong to get to live a normal life, when he, Peter, was going to have to die for Jesus. You should not worry about what other people get to do. Your job is to follow Jesus.

MEMORIZE:

"Jesus replied, 'If I want him to remain alive until I return, what is that to you? You follow me.'"
John 21:22

Follow Jesus

No Looking Back

May

1

(Read Luke 9:57-62)

Scott had been a Christian only a short time. His old friends kept after him to join them in the wrong things they used to do, but he knew from experience that they often got into trouble. It was a real struggle for him.

"Scott, I need some help getting my garden ready for spring planting," said Mr. Lockwood, Scott's church teacher. "Would you care to come over after school tomorrow and help me?"

"Sure," responded Scott. He really liked Mr. Lockwood.

The next day Mr. Lockwood started the garden tiller and showed Scott how it worked. "Start here, and don't take your eyes off that post down there," said Mr. Lockwood, pointing to the other end of the garden. "Make a straight row toward it. When you come back this way, you follow the furrow you've just made."

Scott began eagerly, hoping he would do a good job. Soon his confidence began to build as row after row of neatly turned earth appeared. He was almost finished when he saw that his teacher had a big glass of lemonade for him.

"Shut it off and take a break," shouted Mr. Lockwood.

Grinning, Scott turned back to shut off the machine. To his dismay, he saw that the tiller had made a big swerve to the right while he had been looking back. Mr. Lockwood saw what had happened, too. "Come and have your lemonade," he said, "and then we'll see what can be done to straighten this last row."

As they sat under a tree and drank the lemonade, Scott mentioned the problems he was having with his old friends.

"Hmmm," murmured Mr. Lockwood thoughtfully as he gazed over the garden. "Looking back messes up a field, and looking back often messes up a life, too." *REP*

HOW ABOUT YOU?

Do you have old friends who want you to join them in doing wrong things? Do those old ways seem attractive? Ask the Lord to help you not to look back. It may be necessary to replace old friendships and old habits with new ones.

Look to Jesus

MEMORIZE:
"Anyone who puts a hand to the plow and then looks back is not fit for the Kingdom of God." Luke 9:62

A Beautiful New Body

(Read 1 Corinthians 15:51-57)

Geoffrey lay in the warmth of the bright sunshine watching the beautiful butterflies flit from one flower to another. "This is the saddest day of my life," he said to his brother, Steven, who rested on the ground next to Geoffrey.

"Yeah, mine, too," said Steven as he drew lines in the grass with a stubby piece of stick. "I can't believe Grandma died. She wasn't sick or anything!"

"But she was pretty old, and old people die," said Geoffrey.

The back door opened, and the boys' mom came out carrying two glasses of lemonade. "May I join you?" she asked, as she handed each of them a glass. The boys scooted apart, and Mom sat down between them. They could tell she had been crying. Her eyes were puffy, and her nose was red. She closed her eyes and lifted her face toward the warm sun. "The sun feels so good, doesn't it? I'm glad God gave us such a beautiful day," she said thoughtfully. "Look at all these butterflies!"

"Grandma showed me these cocoons a few days ago," said Geoffrey, handing a couple of gray casings to his mom. "She told me they had caterpillars in them. Today I noticed that the butterflies had hatched."

Mom smiled and nodded. "And those caterpillars have a new life now, flying around as butterflies," she said. She put an arm around each of the boys. "Grandma also began a new life today, just like all these lovely creatures," she added, as tears gently spilled onto her cheeks. "Can you imagine what she might be doing today?"

"I hadn't thought of it that way," said Steven. "She's in heaven with Jesus, isn't she? I bet she's walking on that street of gold!"

"That sounds neat!" said Geoffrey. "She always did like to walk. I bet she's having a really great time! And I bet she's beautiful, too, just like these new butterflies." *DLW*

HOW ABOUT YOU?

Have you ever been sad that someone you love died? Did you know it's OK to cry because of the sadness? Even Jesus cried when his friend Lazarus died. But when Christians die, their souls go to heaven. If you're a Christian, too, you'll see that person again someday and you'll both have what God calls a glorified body. We don't know exactly what that will be like, but we do know it will be wonderful!

MEMORIZE:

"Listen, I tell you a mystery: We will not all sleep, but we will all be changed." 1 Corinthians 15:51, NIV

We'll Be Changed

Temporary Permanent

(Read Psalm 48:9-14)

Tim poured a glass of milk to drink with the snack his mother had left for him because she was out getting a permanent. Tim was usually hungry after school, but today the food seemed to be as tasteless as sawdust. He sighed as he thought about his troubles. First, he'd lost his science assignment, and his teacher said he would have to do it over. At recess he'd ripped a hole in the knee of his new jeans. His best friend had ignored him all day, and Tim didn't know why. Finally, Tim hadn't understood the afternoon English lesson, but he was too discouraged to ask for help.

"Why the unhappy face?" asked Mother, coming in the door and interrupting his dark thoughts.

"Everything went wrong today," mumbled Tim. As his mother sat down, he noticed her hair. "Your hair looks nice, Mom. Will it always stay curly now?"

Mother laughed. "I wish it would. But after a while it will start to lose its curl," she said.

"Well, why is it called a 'permanent' then?" asked Tim.

Mother smiled. "I think it's misnamed," she replied. She gave Tim a hug. "Many things we call 'permanent' don't last forever. But there's something that does—God's love. It's really permanent. Even when things go wrong and it seems he's forgotten us, he really hasn't. His love is still there, strong and true."

Tim smiled. "That's nice to remember after the kind of day I've had," he said. "Thanks, Mom. When I look at your temporary permanent, I'll remember that God's love is really permanent." *CEY*

HOW ABOUT YOU?

When things go wrong, especially one thing after another, it's easy to get discouraged and forget God's love. But God doesn't forget you. His love is there, whether you're feeling it or not. It's an everlasting love.

MEMORIZE:

"I have loved you, my people, with an everlasting love. With unfailing love I have drawn you to myself."

Jeremiah 31:3

God's Love Is Permanent

Instruction Manual

(Read 2 Timothy 3:14-17)

Brian squirmed impatiently in his chair. "I've got to get my things packed so I'll be ready when Aunt Marge comes for me in the morning," he said. Brian was completely off his chair now, excited about going to visit his aunt and uncle on their farm.

"We're going to have our Bible reading first, Brian," replied Dad. Brian reluctantly slid back onto his chair and sat quietly.

The next day, Brian was waiting when Aunt Marge pulled up in her new car, and soon they were on their way. Brian looked at the car clock. "Aunt Marge, your clock is wrong," he said as they drove down the street. "It says nine o'clock, but it's really ten o'clock."

"Oops!" said Aunt Marge. "Looks like nobody changed the clock when the time changed this spring."

"Can I fix it?" asked Brian. "How do you do it?"

"Actually, I don't know," said Aunt Marge. "I'll have to get out the instruction manual to see how it works." She glanced out the back window, then over toward Brian. "Brian, will you adjust that side mirror?" she asked. "It needs to be tilted up a little."

"Don't you have a button that moves it from the inside?" asked Brian.

"Yes," admitted Aunt Marge, "but I never had one on that side before, and I can't remember how it works."

"You just turn that little knob." Brian grinned. "You better read your instruction manual, Aunt Marge. It sure won't do you any good in the glove compartment," he teased as he adjusted the mirror.

Aunt Marge grinned. "That's true," she agreed. "Instruction manuals are meant to be read and followed, not just stashed away. This reminds me that just last Sunday our pastor pointed out the importance of reading our 'manual for living.' Do you know what that is?"

"It must be the Bible," guessed Brian. "I guess that's why Dad makes us read it every day." *THB*

HOW ABOUT YOU?

Do you listen carefully when God's Word is read? Do you follow its instructions? Use it regularly so that you will know how God wants you to live and what he wants you to do.

MEMORIZE:
"You must crave pure spiritual milk so that you can grow into the fullness of your salvation." 1 Peter 2:2

Read God's Instruction Manual—the Bible

Trusting or Testing

(Read Luke 4:1-14)

Mark placed the ladder against the garden shed and climbed carefully onto the roof. He stood up slowly.

"Mark! What are you doing up there?" called Dad.

"Practicing!" Mark yelled back. "I've got to jump off the roof of the shed at school tomorrow."

"What did you say you're going to do?" exclaimed Dad.

"I said I have to jump off the roof," repeated Mark patiently.

"You'll do nothing of the sort!" said Dad. "Come down at once!"

"But it's to prove my faith," protested Mark.

Dad looked puzzled. "Prove your . . . climb down and explain."

"I was telling some guys at school about Jesus, but they laughed and said it was all rubbish and they don't believe there's a God. Then Nick dared me to jump off the roof—if I do it without getting hurt, he'll believe in God!" Mark climbed down carefully. "I remembered that the Bible says you can move a mountain if you have faith as small as a mustard seed, so I'm praying that God will keep me safe when I jump."

Dad sighed. "Mark, God can move even more than a mountain—nothing is impossible for him. But when you ask him for something, you must make sure it is in keeping with his will. And I don't think jumping from the roof to 'prove' something to a group of boys is God's will! When Jesus was tempted in the wilderness, one of the temptations was to jump down from the highest point of the temple," Dad reminded Mark. "Do you remember Jesus' reply?"

"Do not put the Lord your God to the test," said Mark promptly.

Dad nodded. "And you don't have the right to put God to the test, either," he said. "Your friends have dared you to do something foolish; you don't have to do it! Let's go inside and talk about what you can do to help your friends know more about Jesus." *MTF*

HOW ABOUT YOU?

Jesus has promised that whatever we ask in his name he will do. And asking "in his name" doesn't mean asking for something against God's will, like asking that something bad happen to another person or trying to put God to the test and make him "prove" himself. Next time you ask for something make sure you are truly asking "in his name."

Don't Test God, Trust God

MEMORIZE:
"Do not test the Lord your God."
Deuteronomy 6:16

The Birth Certificate

(Read Romans 10:8-13)

"Dad . . . ," Nathan hesitated. "I think I'm a Christian," he continued. "I've asked Jesus to come into my heart and forgive my sins, but how can I really know God heard me?"

Nathan's dad was delighted that his son was talking his problem over with him. He smiled at Nathan. "Who are your parents?" he asked.

"Dad, you know the answer to that!" Nathan was surprised. "You and Mom are."

"How do you know we are?" Dad continued.

"Well, I just know. You've always been my parents." As Dad opened a desk drawer and took out a piece of paper, Nathan wondered why he was asking such strange questions. Then he saw what Dad was holding in his hand. "That's my birth certificate!" exclaimed Nathan. "It says right on it when I was born. That's proof!"

"And do you believe what the birth certificate says?" Dad asked.

Nathan nodded. "Sure I do."

"Well, Son, the Bible is just as good as this birth certificate—even better," Dad assured him. "You don't doubt what is written on the birth certificate, and you don't have to doubt anything in the Bible. He says if you ask Jesus to be your Savior, you're his child. When you became a Christian, we made a note of it in your Bible. Let's look."

Nathan got his Bible from the shelf, and together they read from the inside cover page, "Nathan accepted the Lord Jesus Christ into his heart on April 10, 1988."

"I think we need to add something there—a verse from God's Word," suggested Dad. After discussing it, Nathan carefully copied Romans 10:13 into the front cover of his Bible. "Now," said Dad, "you can think of this Scripture as another kind of birth certificate—the certificate of your new birth in the Lord Jesus."

Nathan nodded. "Thanks, Dad," he said. *DK*

HOW ABOUT YOU?

Do you ever wonder if you're really a Christian? Talk to a trusted friend or adult and make sure you've accepted Jesus as your personal Savior. Then pick a verse (such as John 1:12, John 3:16, Acts 16:31, or Romans 10:13) that tells you that you now belong to him. Whenever you doubt it, point to that verse.

MEMORIZE:

"Anyone who calls on the name of the Lord will be saved." Romans 10:13

You Can Know You're Saved

The Right Key

(Read Acts 16:25-31)

"Let's see," murmured Gary, looking at the keys he held. His grandparents had dropped him off at their house. They'd be home after Grandma had her checkup at the doctor's office. In the meantime, Gary planned to enjoy milk and cookies. "Grandpa said the silver key with the round top is his house key. But I can't find one like that."

Gary tried each key in the lock, and nothing worked. Then he walked around the house, checking every window and door. They were all locked securely.

After two long hours his grandparents arrived. "Hey, what took you so long?" Gary asked. "I've been outside the whole time. You didn't give me the right key."

"Oh no!" exclaimed Grandpa. "Now I remember that I took it off that ring when I had a duplicate made. I must have forgotten to put it back. I'm sorry, Gary."

After they entered with Grandma's key, Gary said, "It sure was tough sitting out there with all those keys when not one would work!"

Grandma nodded as she began to make supper. "Do you know there's something worse?" she asked. "It's expecting to get into heaven and then finding out too late that you have the wrong key."

"What do you mean?" asked Gary. "You don't get into heaven with keys."

"No, not actual keys," agreed Grandma. "But many people think being in a Christian family or living a good life will get them into heaven. These things are like wrong keys. Jesus said, 'No one can come to the Father except through me.' The right key is 'Believe on the Lord Jesus Christ.'" She paused and then asked, "What key do you have, Gary? How do you expect to get into heaven?"

"Hey, I don't want to be left outside heaven's door!" exclaimed Gary. "And I won't be, either. I do believe in Jesus." *MRP*

HOW ABOUT YOU?

What "key" are you counting on for entering heaven? Good works? A Christian family? Your church? These are useless in opening heaven's door. Jesus is the Door to heaven. Believing in him as your Savior is the only key.

Believe on Jesus

MEMORIZE:
"Believe on the Lord Jesus and you will be saved." Acts 16:31

God's Money or Mine

(Read Malachi 3:8-12)

Dad looked into Ron's room and saw Ron counting money on his bed. "Wow!" Dad exclaimed. "It looks like that paper route is really paying off! Are you planning to buy something?"

Ron stared at the money. "Remember those new roller blades I want?"

Dad nodded. Ron's parents had told him that if he wanted new roller blades, he would have to use his own money. "Have you saved enough?" asked Dad.

"Not quite," answered Ron, "but there's a big competition next week, and I was hoping to have the new roller blades by then. If I use this money—" he pointed to a pile of coins on the bed— "I do have enough. But this is money I put aside for church."

Dad sat down beside Ron. "Do you remember when Grandpa found some money at the fair last year?" Dad asked.

"Sure." Ron nodded. "When he couldn't find out who it belonged to, he gave some to me."

"Yes," said Dad. "How much of it did he let you have?"

"Most of it," Ron remembered. "He just kept a little to buy a souvenir for Grandma."

"Why didn't you ask Grandpa for those last few dollars, too?" asked Dad.

"Dad!" Ron protested. "I couldn't do that. It was Grandpa's money, and he already let me have most of it. It would have been selfish to ask for more."

"You're right," Dad agreed, "and I'm pleased to know that you're not that greedy. That's why I don't think you would really want to be selfish with God's money, either. All your money is his. But God is generous enough to let you use most of it. He asks you to return only a small amount to build up his church. Would you really want to take that, too?"

"Not when you put it that way," Ron admitted with a sigh. "I suppose I could work a little harder and make more money before the competition."

"I think that's a much better idea," agreed Dad. *HMT*

HOW ABOUT YOU?

Has God given you a chance to make some money—maybe through a paper route, baby-sitting, or an allowance? Do you give some back to God? He doesn't ask for much, but if you're faithful to give it cheerfully, he says he will take care of all your needs.

MEMORIZE:

"And God will generously provide all you need. Then you will always have everything you need and plenty left over to share with others."
2 Corinthians 9:8

Let God Have His Share

One Rotten Egg

(Read James 2:8-13)

"Oh, yummy! Chocolate cake!" exclaimed David when he arrived home from school. "That is going to be chocolate cake, isn't it?" he added.

Mom smiled as she beat the mixture in a big white bowl. "It sure is," she said. "How was school today?"

"Good," said David. "Except for Jordan. He came to church yesterday, and today he was telling all the kids that our teacher was goofy."

"He was?" said Mom. "Why does he say that?"

"She used some Bible verses to show that everybody has sinned," said David, "but Jordan doesn't believe that. He says he's not so bad."

"Your teacher—and the Bible—are right," said Mom, picking up another egg and breaking it on the edge of the bowl.

"Yuck!" cried David a moment later. "What's that awful smell?"

"Oh no!" exclaimed Mom. "That last egg was rotten! I've got to get rid of this. It's spoiled my whole cake mixture!" She picked up the bowl, then hesitated. "On second thought," she said, "the flour and sugar and butter were just fine. And so were all the eggs—except just that one. Maybe this will be OK when it gets baked."

"Mom!" protested David. "We can't eat that awful stuff, even if it's cooked!"

"You're right," agreed Mom. "Maybe you should tell Jordan about this."

"Jordan?" asked David.

Mom nodded. "Yes. The Bible says that if we keep all the laws, except just one, we are still guilty. That's like this cake mixture. All my ingredients were fine, except that one rotten egg, and that messed up my whole cake."

"Yeah!" said David. "I bet Jordan wouldn't want to eat that."

"You're right," said Mom, putting the smelly mixture in a plastic bag. "Tell him that no matter how 'good' we think we are, however 'law-abiding' we may be, we've all done at least one thing that's wrong—something 'rotten.' We can go to heaven only because of Jesus—not because we have earned it by anything we do ourselves, but because we trust in him." *MTF*

HOW ABOUT YOU?

Do you know people who think that because they are "good," they don't need Jesus? Remember that even the best person still falls short of God's standard—perfect holiness. That's why everyone, both the "good" and the "bad," needs Jesus.

We Are All Guilty

MEMORIZE:
"And the person who keeps all of the laws except one is as guilty as the person who has broken all of God's laws." James 2:10

Worth the Wait

(Read Ecclesiastes 3:1-11)

"Let me drive, Dad—please!" Craig begged as Dad turned the car onto a country road leading to Grandpa's farm. "There's not much traffic here."

Dad shook his head. "You're not old enough, Son."

"I'm fourteen. Next year I can get my permit," Craig pleaded. "Besides, Steve's dad lets him drive all the time." Immediately, Craig knew he had said the wrong thing. His father was never impressed with what Steve's dad did. When Dad did not respond, Craig knew the subject was closed.

When they arrived at the farm, they found Grandpa in the garden, planting potatoes. Craig's little brother, Tyson, squatted down on the ground and began digging. "I wanna make a garden, too," he said.

Craig headed for the barn. "I'm going to ride Princess. At least I don't need a license to ride a horse!" he mumbled.

As they prepared to leave later that afternoon, Tyson was nowhere to be found. They searched all over, calling his name. Even Dad was beginning to look worried. Then Grandpa came across the yard carrying a tired little boy. "Found him in the garden, sound asleep," Grandpa explained as he put Tyson in his father's arms.

Dad smiled. "What were you doing in the garden?"

"Waitin' for the 'tatoes to come up." The little boy yawned. "But it took 'em so long, I went to sleep."

Dad and Craig were still chuckling as they drove onto the freeway. "Patience is a wonderful thing," said Dad. "It's something God wants all of us to learn. In time, Craig, you'll have your driver's license, and it will have been worth the wait. And in time, Tyson, we'll have our potatoes." *BJW*

HOW ABOUT YOU?

Do you try to "leapfrog" over time to get what you want before the "right season"? God knows the best time for everything. Waiting is hard, but it is important. When you are told to wait, don't fret and fuss. Be patient.

MEMORIZE:

"God has made everything beautiful for its own time." Ecclesiastes 3:11

Be Patient

Stopped in Time

(Read Psalm 37:3-6)

"No, Katie!" Teddy's words startled his little sister as he pulled her hand away from the lamp. Katie started to cry and squirmed out of her brother's grasp.

"What's going on?" asked Mother as she entered the living room.

"Katie almost knocked the lamp over," said Teddy. "She was trying to reach the lightbulb." He lifted her in his arms and kissed her cheek, but she only cried louder. "I guess she doesn't know the bulb is hot and would burn her hand."

"No, Katie doesn't realize she could be hurt," Mother answered. "She wants to touch everything she sees. That's why you and I are here to take care of her."

Teddy smiled at his little sister. "You might not think I'm being very nice, but someday you'll understand."

Later that evening, Mother came into Teddy's room to say good night. She found him sitting on the bed, a frown on his face. "What's wrong?" Mother asked.

"I'm worried about going to the dentist tomorrow," replied Teddy.

"We could pray about it," suggested Mother.

Teddy's frown deepened. "Yeah," he said softly, "but sometimes God doesn't answer my prayers the way I want him to."

Mother put her arm around Teddy's shoulder. "Remember this afternoon when Katie tried to touch the lamp?" Teddy nodded. "You knew your little sister could get hurt," Mother said, "so you stopped her before anything bad happened."

"What's that got to do with my going to the dentist?" asked Teddy.

Mother smiled. "When God doesn't answer our prayers the way we think he should, it could be because he knows more than we do." She pulled Teddy closer. "As Katie gets older and realizes you want what is best for her, she will learn to trust you more."

Teddy thought for a moment. "And I should trust God more, too, right?"

Mother nodded. "So shall we talk to him about it?" *EAA*

HOW ABOUT YOU?

Life may not always go the way you wish. Don't be afraid to tell God how you feel about it. Believe that he hears your prayers and wants to help you. Then trust him even if you don't get your way. He wants the best for you.

MEMORIZE:

"'For I know the plans I have for you,' says the Lord. 'They are plans for good and not for disaster, to give you a future and a hope.'" Jeremiah 29:11

God Can Be Trusted

God's Report Card

(Read Matthew 16:24-27; Romans 14:11-12)

The front door opened quietly. *Good. No one in sight*, Kerry thought. He tiptoed down the hall and into his bedroom. Carefully, he shut his door, cringing at its familiar creak. He quickly slid his report card into his baseball card album. *Mom will never think to look there*, he thought.

When Dad came home, Kerry was outside playing ball. Dad greeted him, then went on into the house, where Mother was making supper. With a smile, Dad took a new baseball card from his pocket. "Look what I got for Kerry," he said. "He's been wanting this. I'm going to put it in his album as a surprise for him." But when Dad opened the album, he found the report card!

"Kerry," Dad called from the back door a few moments later, "come here, please."

As Kerry came running, he saw Dad holding the report card. He slowed his pace. "Oh," he said, breathlessly, "I see you found my report card."

"Yes," answered Dad. "It seems to have gotten lost in your baseball album. I found it when I went to put a new card in there for you."

Kerry looked at the ground. "I . . . I was ashamed of it," he said.

"You should be more ashamed of the grade you would get on God's report card," said Dad.

"God's report card?" asked Kerry.

Dad nodded. "He knows everything we do," he said. "Someday we'll have to stand before him to receive our rewards. What kind of grade do you think you deserve in the subject of honesty?"

"I . . . I deserve a failing grade," answered Kerry through his tears.

"I'm afraid that's true," agreed Dad. "What do you think you should do about it?"

"Ask God to forgive me?" asked Kerry tearfully. Dad nodded. "I will," said Kerry. "I'm sorry I hid that report card. I'll ask God to help me do better in honesty." *LJR*

HOW ABOUT YOU?

If God were to grade you in your behavior, what would your grades be? Make a list of things you know you should do . . . such things as obey your parents, help others, be honest, be kind, etc. For each item, give yourself the grade you think God would give you. Then ask him to help you in areas where you feel particularly weak.

MEMORIZE:

"See, I am coming soon, and my reward is with me, to repay all according to their deeds."
Revelation 22:12

Get Good Grades from God

Plants and Kids

(Read Romans 12:6-11)

Jeff, Sam, and Steve were all sitting on the railing in front of Meyer's General Store. Each had bought a stick of bubble gum, and they were seeing who could blow the biggest bubbles. Splat! Sam's great, big, head-sized bubble popped, and Sam had gum on his face from ear to ear! "When I grow up, I'm gonna invent a bubble gum that doesn't stick to you when it pops!" he grumbled.

Jeff laughed. "You're too late. I heard that someone has already invented it," he said. That got the boys to talking about what they wanted to be. "I'm gonna be a pilot," Jeff stated firmly.

"And I'm gonna be a preacher," said Steve. They both waited for Sam to say what he would be, but he remained silent. "Well," Steve prompted, "what are you going to be, Sam, instead of a bubble-gum inventor?"

"I don't know." Sam shrugged. "I haven't given it much thought."

Just then, Pastor Hawkins pulled up in front of the store. "Well, hello, boys!" greeted the pastor. "What are you so busy talking about on this beautiful morning?"

"We're talking about what we're going to be when we grow up," Steve told him, "but Sam here hasn't got any plans!"

"Well, boys, I've noticed that plants and kids have something in common," said Pastor Hawkins. "I've just been looking at my neighbor's garden. When some plants first come out of the ground, I can't tell what kind they are. Might be green beans, or corn, or something else. But when they grow up, then you can tell what they are. That's the way it is with children, too. They often don't know right away what they'd like to do when they grow up."

"How do they decide?" Sam wanted to know.

"Well, all kids are different. Some kids can work problems better than others. Some are stronger than others. Some can draw better than others," said Pastor Hawkins. "One way God helps us know what we should be is by the talents and abilities he gives us. So, Sam, don't worry if you don't know what you'll be. Just be willing to be anything God wants you to be." *CVM*

HOW ABOUT YOU?

Do you wonder what you'll be someday—whether you'll be married or single, a teacher or a doctor? Be willing to be whatever God wants you to be. If you'll let him, he will lead you!

**Be Willing to Serve
God His Way**

MEMORIZE:
"Never be lazy in your work, but serve the Lord enthusiastically."
Romans 12:11

Feeling Special

(Read Ephesians 2:4-10)

Michael's heart was heavy as he trudged down the road. *Maybe I should run away—but they probably wouldn't even notice I was gone,* he thought to himself. Lately, he felt left out and alone in his family.

Michael's older brother, Joe, always seemed more important to the family than Michael did. When Joe got a home run in a ball game or an A on a report card, Mom and Dad made a big fuss over him. They were excited and happy. But when Michael did something special, it seemed Dad and Mom usually said, "I remember when your brother did the same thing two years ago."

Michael's younger sister, Amy, got even more attention. Everyone in the family, including Grandma and Grandpa, always remarked how cute she looked in her pretty little dresses. They lovingly teased her about her curly hair, and they laughed at the cute things she said.

But—and Michael sighed—no one thought there was anything special about him. He was just . . . well . . . just there.

Michael's thoughts were interrupted when he heard someone crying. Glancing ahead, he saw a small boy standing by a bike. "What's the matter?" he asked.

"My pant leg is caught in the chain," the boy answered through his tears. "I can't get it loose."

Michael bent down to look. "This happened to me once. I think I can help you." He worked at the material until it let loose from the chain, freeing the boy's leg.

"Oh-h-h, thanks," the boy said with relief in his voice. He looked up at Michael with admiration. "You're great!"

Michael began to whistle as he walked on. He felt much better now. *Maybe I am just as important as my brother or sister,* he thought. *I can do things that help others. CEY*

HOW ABOUT YOU?

Do you sometimes feel left out or unimportant in your family? You're important to God—so important that he sent Jesus to die for you so that you could become a part of God's special family of believers. In God's family, everyone is equally important. God delights in each one of his children. He rejoices over you. You are special to him.

MEMORIZE:
"The Lord your God . . . will rejoice over you with great gladness."
Zephaniah 3:17

God Delights in You

Older Than the Hills

(Read Hebrews 1:8, 10-12)

While helping his grandfather in the garden, Randy noticed a strange-looking stone. It was full of tiny holes. "Look, Grandpa," said Randy. "This stone is rotting away."

Grandpa took the stone and looked it over. "You found a very special stone," he said. "It's a fossil."

"What's that?" asked Randy.

"Well, when a living thing, like a plant or an animal, gets buried in mud or clay, the material around it hardens as the years go by," explained Grandpa. "Then the plant or animal dissolves away, leaving openings right in the hardened material. Those openings are exactly the shape of the plant or animal that has long disappeared."

Randy looked surprised. "You mean there was once a plant or animal right in this stone?"

"That's right." Grandpa nodded. "Isn't it exciting to think you're holding something very old?"

Randy grinned. "I guess it's as old as the hills," he said. He looked at Grandpa, then asked, "How old is that?"

"We don't know for sure," answered Grandpa. "But God knows, because he's older than the earth or anything in it."

"Yeah, he's older 'n anybody, isn't he," said Randy. "Even older than Jesus."

Grandpa disagreed. "No," he said, "Jesus is God, too. He was right there when the earth was made. Jesus, along with God the Father, made the earth and everything in it."

"But Jesus was born in Bethlehem," objected Randy.

"Yes, he was born as a baby many years after the earth was made, but before that, Jesus was up in heaven," explained Grandpa. "He is eternal. That means he has no beginning and no ending, because he is God."

"That's hard for me to understand," said Randy.

"For me, too." Grandpa nodded. "But God said it, so I believe it." *CEY*

HOW ABOUT YOU?

Do you find it hard to understand some things about God? This will continue to be true until you get to heaven. Then you'll know much more about him. Until that day, study the Bible and believe that what he says is true.

MEMORIZE:

"In the beginning the Word already existed. He was with God, and he was God. . . . He created everything there is. Nothing exists that he didn't make." John 1:1, 3

Jesus Is Eternal

16

Telltale Chocolate

(Read Psalm 139:1-12)

When Rick opened the freezer compartment of the refrigerator, he spotted a box of chocolate-covered ice cream bars. He took one out, figuring he could probably eat it without its being missed. Although he knew his mother had gone next door to care for old Mrs. Cook and his dad was at work, Rick automatically looked around to see if anyone had seen him. Then he peeled back the paper and took a small bite.

Suddenly the outside door opened. It was his mother! *Why is she coming back so soon?* Rick wondered in panic. He started to open the refrigerator door so he could return the ice cream bar, but the sound of his mother's footsteps told him there wasn't time. Quickly he folded the wrapper around the bar and stuffed it into his back pocket.

"I don't have to stay with Mrs. Cook after all," said Mother as she came into the kitchen. "Her granddaughter just arrived from Detroit, and she'll be with her all day."

Rick leaned carelessly against the wall, hoping his mother wouldn't suspect anything. As he did, he felt the ice cream bar smash in his pocket. Realizing the predicament he was in, he turned and fled toward his room.

"Rick," Mother called, "be sure you change into a clean pair of jeans. When ice cream bars melt, they become very sticky."

Rick whirled about and looked at his mother in amazement. How did she know what he had done?

"You wonder how I know?" she asked before he could get the words out of his mouth. Rick nodded. "It shows," Mother said simply. "There's chocolate around your mouth, and guilt in your eyes. And there's a wooden stick poking out of the back pocket of your jeans."

At first Rick couldn't answer. Then he looked up at his mother. "I guess I thought you wouldn't know, Mom. I'm sorry," he said. "I really am."

"I am, too," she replied. "You see, I planned to serve those bars to you boys at the Cub Scout meeting tomorrow. Now it looks as though someone will have to go without." Rick knew who that "someone" was! *RIJ*

HOW ABOUT YOU?

Perhaps you've sneaked cookies, broken a dish, or read a bad book, and you thought nobody knew. Generally, you're not fooling Mom and Dad as completely as you think you are. You're certainly never fooling God. He sees everything. Instead of trying to hide your sin, confess it.

MEMORIZE:
"You may be sure that your sin will find you out." Numbers 32:23

Sin Will Show

When the Tree Needs Help

(Read Proverbs 6:20-23)

Roger watched his father pull out the stake that had been wired to a small tree ever since it had been planted.

"A small tree often doesn't have the strength or ability to stand alone," Dad said. "This stake acted as a support, but now I believe the tree is big enough to take any winds that may come along." He stood back and looked at the tree. It was growing tall and straight because it had been held in that position by the supporting stake. "That's pretty much like life," added Dad thoughtfully.

"What do you mean?" Roger asked.

"When you were small, your mother and I held on to your hand every time you took a step," Dad explained. "We didn't want you to fall and get hurt. Then as you began to grow and get control of your walk, we let you go by yourself, but we still watched you."

Roger nodded as he thought about it. Even now there were many times that he needed his parents' advice and help. He guessed maybe he would always need them. He mentioned that to his father.

"We'll be to glad to help whenever you call on us," Dad replied, smiling. "When the time comes that we are no longer here, you'll be ready to go on without us. There's a verse in the Bible that your mother and I try to follow as we raise you."

"Which one?" Roger asked.

"It's Proverbs 22:6," replied Dad. "Teach your children to choose the right path, and when they are older, they will remain upon it."

"Sort of like the tree, isn't it?" Roger asked. "When it was small and frail, you had to keep an eye on it all the time so it didn't grow wrong. But now that it's old enough, it will keep growing straight without the supporting stake."

Dad smiled broadly. "That's it," he agreed. "Exactly!" *RIJ*

HOW ABOUT YOU?

How do you feel when you are restricted in some way by your parents' rules and guidance? Maybe you feel angry. That's normal. But remember, every young tree needs help to grow big and strong and straight. Thank God for your "supporting stake"—your parents.

Welcome Help

MEMORIZE:
"My son, obey your father's commands, and don't neglect your mother's teaching." Proverbs 6:20

Strong Links

(Read 1 John 5:1-5)

As Jeff and his dad waited in line to ride the bumper cars, Jeff spotted his classmate, Amy. "I hope she doesn't want to go on with us," he mumbled.

Jeff's dad smiled as Amy approached them. "Hi, Amy," he said. "You're not here alone at the carnival, are you?" he asked.

"No," answered Amy. "My mom brought me, but she won't go on the roller coaster." Amy turned to Jeff. "Do you want to go with me, Jeff?"

"Naah." Jeff shook his head. "Roller coasters make me sick," he mumbled.

"OK." Amy shrugged. "I'll see you on Monday then."

"Since when did they make you sick?" asked Dad suspiciously after Amy was gone.

"They don't," admitted Jeff, "but I don't want to go on it with Amy!" He leaned on a nearby chain row divider. "It was just a little lie," Jeff said, defending himself.

"Jeff," Dad said, " look at that chain you're leaning on. What would happen if one of those links was weak and broke?"

"I guess I'd fall," Jeff answered.

"Do you think it would matter which link it was that broke?" asked Dad. Jeff shook his head. "Nope," he said.

"You're right," Dad agreed. "Try to think of that chain as the law of God." Jeff looked puzzled. "The law of God?" he asked.

Dad nodded. "His law is made up of many links—many commands—and each one is equally important," he told Jeff.

"Well, telling a little lie can't be as bad as stealing or murder," protested Jeff. Dad answered, "God's law is broken when you sin. No sin is small in God's sight."

"Yeah . . . ," Jeff hesitated.

"God's first commandment is to love him," said Dad, "and the second is . . . what?"

"Uh-h-h . . . ," Jeff thought for a moment. "To love our neighbors," he said. Dad nodded. "Do you think you showed God's love to Amy?" he asked.

Jeff answered slowly, "I do like the roller coaster, and actually Amy's a nice kid, too," admitted Jeff. "I guess I'll go see if she still wants to go on it." *HMT*

HOW ABOUT YOU?

Are you ever tempted to ignore what you think is just a small command that God has given? He wants us to obey all his commands.

MEMORIZE:

"And the person who keeps all of the laws except one is as guilty as the person who has broken all of God's laws." James 2:10

Obey All God's Commands

The Broken Watches

(Read Isaiah 46:3-4, 8-10)

Charles ran into the house and slammed the front door. "Mom!" he called. "Is it true, what Beth said? Is Grandpa coming to visit again?"

"Yes, your sister is right," replied Mother. "Dad is going to get Grandpa on Saturday morning. You can probably go along if you like." She sighed. "My watch is broken, and I was hoping one of my old ones would still work. Look, Charles." She held up a small, gold wristwatch. "This was my high school graduation present from Grandpa and Grandma. This one with the leather strap was my official nurse's watch. And this lovely one I wear now—Dad bought this for me on our first wedding anniversary. And now it won't run, either."

Charles nodded, but he went back to the matter at hand. "I don't want to go get Grandpa," he whined. "Why does he have to come again? He spills things and talks funny."

"I thought you loved Grandpa," Mother said quietly.

"I do," Charles said, "or I did before he had that stroke. He used to do stuff with me. Now he just sits around and . . . gets in the way."

Mother looked at the watches on the table. "These bring back precious memories of happy times, but none of them will run," she said. "I'm fond of them and hate to throw them out, but at least they don't have feelings. But people do." Charles looked at the floor. He knew she meant Grandpa. "My heart is full of memories of growing up with Grandpa and Grandma," added Mother. "Grandma is in heaven now, and age and illness have injured Grandpa. But he is still my father and I love him very much."

Charles hugged his mother. "I love Grandpa, too. It's just hard seeing him so different now." *BK*

HOW ABOUT YOU?

Use every opportunity to show older people that you do love and appreciate them. As you give of yourself to them, you'll be surprised to find how much you get back in return.

Respect Old People

MEMORIZE:
"Gray hair is a crown of glory; it is gained by living a godly life."
Proverbs 16:31

May
20

Scattered Seeds

(Read James 3:7-10)

Karen sat in the tall grass, surrounded by bright yellow dandelions, and watched her grandmother set the picnic table. "Grandma," she said as she absentmindedly began to pick some of the yellow flowers, "what do you do when someone tells you something about someone else and all of your friends want to know what you heard?"

"That depends," replied Grandma. "Was what you heard true? Was it something that could possibly hurt the other person?" Karen nodded as she picked a dandelion that was going to seed. "When you repeat such things it's called gossip," continued Grandma. "Gossip can spread very quickly once it's started, and it can never be taken back."

"So I shouldn't repeat it, right?" asked Karen. She blew as hard as she could on the round, white globe of dandelion seeds. The seeds drifted in all directions and landed on the ground like fluffy, tiny parachutes.

"You're right," said Grandma. "You shouldn't repeat gossip." She motioned all around her. "Go and gather up all the seeds you just scattered," she added.

Karen looked at her grandmother in surprise. "That's impossible," said Karen. "The wind took them every which way. I could never find them all."

Grandma nodded. "That's what happens with gossip, too," she said. "Someone tells you something. You repeat it to someone else, who repeats it to someone else, who repeats it to someone else, and so on. It's almost as if the wind has carried it in all directions. If you wanted to stop the gossip and take it all back, it would be impossible." Karen nodded as she twirled the empty dandelion stem in her fingers. "When you take part in spreading gossip, you're just as responsible in God's eyes as the person who started the gossip," added Grandma. "Gossip can be hurtful and can even break up friendships. Don't repeat unkind things you hear about others. Instead, do your best to stop rumors from going any farther." *JJL*

HOW ABOUT YOU?

Are you able to control your tongue? That's one of the hardest things God has asked you to do. If the temptation to gossip strikes, ask God to give you the strength you need to hold your tongue. Repeat only things that build others up.

MEMORIZE:

"So then, let us aim for harmony in the church and try to build each other up." Romans 14:19

Gossip Hurts Others

20/20 Vision

(Read Ephesians 6:1-3)

"Hey, Dad, I went to the eye doctor today, and he said my vision was 20/20," announced David at dinner. "That's perfect, you know!"

"That's right," agreed Mother as she passed the salad. Loud voices, slamming doors, and squealing tires next door interrupted her. When it was quiet again, she murmured, "Poor Mrs. Marler."

"Yes, I'm afraid Chad is worrying her to death," Dad said with a nod.

"I don't know why everybody's on Chad's case," David protested. "I like him. He gave me a ride on his motorcycle."

"Well, you are not to get on his cycle again," Dad ordered.

"Aw, Dad, he's OK," argued David.

"In some ways he's a nice boy," said Mother, "but I don't approve of the way he's been acting lately. The way he talks to his parents is disgraceful!"

"He called his mother 'stupid old woman' the other day," little Cheri reported. "That's not nice."

"It certainly isn't," agreed Dad. "It's too bad Chad doesn't have 20/20 vision. He seems to be blind."

"Chad's blind?" David was horrified.

"Well, in a manner of speaking he is," answered Dad. "He is blind to how his actions are hurting himself and his mother."

As Mother cleared the breakfast table the next morning, she told David, "Chad wrecked his folks' car and was charged with drunken driving last night."

"Oooooh!" David exhaled. "Maybe he is blind like Dad said." Before leaving for school, David paused long enough to pray and ask God to help Chad with his blindness. *BJW*

HOW ABOUT YOU?

Do you honor and obey your parents? Ask God to help you speak respectfully even when you are angry. And don't become blind like Chad to how your actions hurt others, especially your parents.

Honor Your Parents

MEMORIZE:
"Honor your father and mother."
Exodus 20:12

Faith

(Read Matthew 25:14-15, 19-23)

Jimmy was confused. "Mom," he said, "I've been trying to learn the fruits of the Spirit, and the seventh one is faith. I don't understand how that can be one of them since it takes faith to become a Christian in the first place."

Mother smiled. "That's true," she agreed, "but the Bible also tells us to have faith after we're Christians. For example, when we pray, we are to have faith that God will answer. But I think there's something else here, too. Several of the newer translations of the Bible use the word *faithfulness*. Do you understand the word?"

Jimmy nodded. "Dad always says that Tippy is a faithful old dog. I guess that means she's always here when I need her," he said.

Mother laughed. "Yes, we got Tippy to be a companion to you, and she faithfully does her job, doesn't she? In much the same way, we should be faithful in what we do."

The next day Jimmy had a job to do. Mrs. King lived three doors down the street, and she was quite old. At the beginning of the summer she had hired Jimmy to take care of mowing her grass for the whole summer. They had made a bargain that Jimmy would mow the lawn every Friday morning, and she would pay him $3.50 each time. Just as Jimmy was putting gas in the mower, some of his friends approached.

"Hey, Jim! A bunch of us are going to play baseball. C'mon," they urged. "We need a good third baseman."

Now there was nothing Jimmy would rather do than play baseball, so he put the gas can away and reached for his mitt. But just then old Tippy came running around the corner of the garage. Stopping, Jimmy thought about his conversation with Mom yesterday. *The fruit of the Spirit is faithfulness,* he remembered. Reaching down, he patted Tippy on the head and called to his friends, "You guys go on! I have a job to do right now." *REP*

HOW ABOUT YOU?

When someone gives you a job to do, do you do it faithfully, no matter how large or small it is? Perhaps the job God has given you right now is to help Mom, mow the lawn, or be a good student. Are you faithful in whatever it is that he has given you to do? When you stand before him someday, will you hear the words, "Well done, good and faithful servant"?

MEMORIZE:

"But when the Holy Spirit controls our lives, he will produce this kind of fruit in us: love, joy, peace, patience, kindness, goodness, faithfulness, . . ."
Galatians 5:22

Be Dependable

A Fine-Free Day

(Read Romans 6:18-23)

"Oh, boy! This is my lucky day," Steve shouted. "Listen to this, Mom." From the newspaper he read, "Wednesday has been declared Fine-Free Day at the local library. All overdue books may be returned without paying a fine."

Mother laughed. "The librarian will be sorry when she sees *you* coming. Think of all the money they'll lose!"

Very soon Steve was on his way to return all the overdue books. As he pedaled toward the library, old Mr. Burns staggered out of his house. "Drunk again!" Steve snorted in disgust.

"Hi ya, Steve," Mr. Burns slurred. "Where ya goin'?"

"To the library to return overdue books." Steve stopped his bike. "Today is Fine-Free Day."

"Sure wish they'd have Fine-Free Day at city hall. I've paid out a bundle of money down there." Mr. Burns's blurry eyes stared at the boy. "Hey, yer a good Christian. Ya suppose God has a Fine-Free Day?"

Steve blinked, then replied, "Sure he does, Mr. Burns. Today is Fine-Free Day with God, too. Jesus paid our fine when he died on the cross for us. If you'll turn your life over to him, he'll forget the fine. He forgave me, and he'll forgive you!"

Mr. Burns shook his head. "Easy to say, boy. Ya only have *little* sins to yer charge. I've got a whole pack of 'em."

Steve pointed to his backpack, crammed with books. "It makes no difference to the librarian if I have one overdue book or ten. I don't have to pay a fine today. And it makes no difference to God if I have a few little sins or a whole pack of them. Jesus paid the fine."

"Ya really think so, Son?" As Steve nodded, Mr. Burns continued, "I'd sure like ta believe ya." He staggered toward his house. "I'll think that one over. Fine-Free Day, huh? Sounds pretty good ta me." *BJW*

HOW ABOUT YOU?

Are you carrying some sins for which you need to repent? It makes no difference if they're a "few little sins" or a "lot of big ones." They must be paid for. But today is the day of salvation—Fine-Free day! Bring your sins to Christ while there's time. He paid your fine for you.

Jesus Paid Your Fine

Just Joking

(Read Romans 12:9-18)

Tom and Jeff went into the house to get Tom's mitt. As usual, they stopped in the kitchen for a few cookies. "That Colin is so stupid!" Tom remarked as they ate. "I bet he's failed every math test we've had all year."

"Yeah," agreed Jeff, "and when we laughed and asked if he could help us with our math, he got mad. He can't even take a joke." The boys laughed together, but when they saw Tom's mother looking at them, they quickly changed the subject.

The next day Tom was working on his birdhouse. He was hammering away at a nail, when . . . "OUCH!" Tom dropped the hammer and began running around, holding his finger, moaning and groaning. He heard someone laughing, and looked up. "Oh, you look so funny!" howled his sister, Denise. "You should see yourself!"

"It's not funny! It hurts!" Tom wailed.

"I'm sure that does hurt," murmured Mom as she put ice on Tom's finger. "And it didn't help your finger at all when Denise teased you about it, did it?"

"That was mean," said Tom. "I think that made it worse. She needs to apologize."

"I'm afraid Colin felt worse, too, when you laughed at him yesterday," Mom said. Startled, Tom looked up. "But it was just teasing," he protested.

"Sometimes teasing is very painful," said Mom, "especially when you're teased about something that hurts you already."

Tom looked away, ashamed. "I'm sorry," he whispered.

"Good." Mom nodded. "I wonder if Colin knows that?"

Tom frowned. "Do I have to tell him?" he asked.

"Well . . . you thought Denise should apologize to you," Mom reminded him.

Tom sighed. "OK," he murmured. He looked up at his mother. "Hey . . . can I invite him over to help me with my birdhouse?" he asked. "Maybe that would make him feel better." Mom gladly agreed. *MMB*

HOW ABOUT YOU?

Do you sometimes tease people? Teasing can be fun, but remember that jokes can hurt, too. Be sensitive to the feelings of others. God says to rejoice with those who are happy and to weep with those who are sad. He says to love your neighbor as yourself and to love one another as he loved you.

MEMORIZE:

"So now I am giving you a new commandment: Love each other. Just as I have loved you, you should love each other." John 13:34

Don't Tease If It Will Hurt

Tornado Tongue

(Read James 3:2-8)

Don walked into the house and headed straight for the telephone. Some of the guys on the baseball team had told him what Jeremy Carlson was saying about him. They had encouraged Don to call Jeremy on the phone and give him a piece of his mind. "That's the only way you'll get him to stop telling stuff like that. Let him have it," they said. Don couldn't agree with them more.

But one thing bothered him. He was a Christian, and Jeremy was not. On several occasions, he had talked with Jeremy about the Lord. A couple of times Jeremy had seemed to be ready to come along to Sunday school, but then he had walked away, ignoring everything Don tried to tell him. Well, he wasn't going to walk away this time!

As Don picked up the phone, a Bible verse came to his mind. "Father, forgive them, for they know not what they do." That's how Jesus had reacted when people treated him wrong. But Don wasn't Jesus, and he couldn't take it anymore! He dialed the number, but no one answered.

As Don slammed down the phone, his sister Julie walked toward him. "You look angry," she said.

"I am angry," Don responded bitterly. "I'm sick and tired of this guy talking about me, and I'm going to give him a piece of my mind!"

"You mean like a tornado tongue?" Julie asked. "The damage is done in a matter of seconds, but it usually takes years to rebuild the damaged area."

Don thought about his sister's words. If he talked to Jeremy the way he planned, he knew it probably would do all kinds of damage that would take years to correct. The more he thought about it, the more he knew he didn't want to be guilty of having a "tornado tongue." He would still talk to Jeremy and ask him not to tell untrue stories about him, but he would ask the Lord to help him do it in a way that would show Jeremy that Christians truly are different. *RIJ*

HOW ABOUT YOU?

When someone makes you angry, do you give him or her "a piece of your mind" before thinking about the damage you might be doing? Like a tornado, your tongue can do a lot of damage in a few seconds, but it might take years to repair the situation.

MEMORIZE:
"Take control of what I say, O Lord,
and keep my lips sealed."
Psalm 141:3

Control Your Tongue

God's Plan

(Read Genesis 1:1; Psalm 33:4-9)

"Mom, my science teacher said the world made itself after some big explosion," said Tony as he pulled crayons and paper from the drawer. "I thought God made the world."

"Yes, Tony, God created the world," said Mom. She too reached for a piece of paper and several crayons. She placed them on the table and then sat back and looked at them.

Tony watched her for a minute. "Aren't you going to draw a picture?" he asked. "Draw a horse for me, OK? Please?"

"Don't be so impatient," said Mom. "Why don't we watch these crayons a little while? If we wait long enough, maybe, by chance, they'll make a sky and grass and flowers and trees and horses—and even people—all by themselves."

"That's silly!" protested Tony. "A picture can't just draw itself. A drawing doesn't just happen!"

Mom smiled. "You're absolutely right," she said. "A picture can't make itself, and the world couldn't make itself, either. It didn't 'just happen.'" She smiled at Tony. "When you want a picture, you plan what to draw. Then you put your plan into action—you pick up your crayons and draw, right?" Tony nodded. "Well," continued Mom, "God had a plan. He knew every detail of what he wanted his world to be like, from the tiniest germ to the largest dinosaur. Then he put his plan into action—he spoke, and it was done. God's special plan and his word brought the world into existence."

Tony grinned and picked up a crayon. "I think I'll draw a picture full of the things God created," he said.

"Me, too," said Mom, "including that horse you asked for." *GJT*

HOW ABOUT YOU?

Have you been told that the world "just happened" to come into being? Don't you believe it! God planned just exactly how everything—including you—should look. He spoke, and the world was created. Only God could do that! Aren't you glad you have such a great and wonderful God?

MEMORIZE:

"He created everything there is.
Nothing exists that he didn't make."
John 1:3

God Created Everything

Little but Powerful (Part 1)

(Read James 3:12-16)

Jerry had several pets. He loved them all—especially his dog, Sport. But it seemed his farm pets were not enough, for he was always bringing other creatures home in his lunch box. "E-e-eek!" shrieked Mother when she opened his lunch box and found a little snake one day. "How many times have I told you not to put these things in your lunch box! Get rid of this!"

"Where did you find it?" asked Dad, after taking a look.

"He was sunning himself in the road," answered Jerry. "He was such a cute little fella. I just couldn't leave him."

"Do you know what kind of 'cute little fella' this is?" asked Dad. "It's a rattlesnake."

"But he's so tiny!" exclaimed Jerry. "Besides, I don't see any rattles on him."

"This snake will grow rattles as he grows older, and he'll also have fangs and poison—enough to kill a man. He even has poison now," Dad told him.

"Aw, he doesn't look like a killer," protested Jerry. "If you take a baby snake like this and treat him nice and feed him . . . he'd never try to kill you."

"Well, we're not going to experiment," Dad assured him. "Rattlesnakes are dangerous, even when they're little. Now, you take this one out behind the barn and kill it."

Reluctantly, Jerry took the box and carried it away. "I don't see why I have to get rid of the snake," Jerry complained to Sport. "It's such a little one." Sport just growled.

Later that evening, Jerry again grumbled about not being allowed to keep the little snake. "Little snakes get to be big ones," repeated Dad. He looked at Jerry. "This reminds me of the way it is with sin," he added. "It may start out little, but it grows. Sometimes sin may even seem like fun, but it can fill our life with poison." *HCT*

HOW ABOUT YOU?

Is there something in your life that is not right, but it seems small and unimportant? A "little" lie, maybe? Or copying just one answer on a test? An unkind attitude toward someone? Whatever it is, get rid of it. Confess it while it's small.

Don't Allow Sin to Grow

MEMORIZE:
"These evil desires lead to evil actions, and evil actions lead to death." James 1:15

Little but Powerful (Part 2)

(Read Romans 5:6-11)

Some months after Jerry had come home with the baby rattler, his cousin Arissa came for a visit, and Jerry showed her all his pets. "Here's the last one," said Jerry as he led the way to a dark corner of the barn. His dog, Sport, followed. "Promise you won't tell Dad," Jerry added, lifting the lid from a box.

"Oh! A huge snake!" gasped Arissa. Jerry had disobeyed his father. He had not killed the baby snake after all—it was just "too cute"! But now it was not so little anymore.

Jerry lifted the snake from the box. "He likes to lay here in the straw and be petted," he said. "Go ahead—pet him."

Arissa shuddered. "He's horrid!" she declared.

"Here, fella . . . ," began Jerry. "Hey. . . what's the matter?" He looked nervous. "I never saw him curl up like that before," he added. He stood up and backed away. "Look at his head swaying. Jump, Arissa! He's going to strike!"

Arissa screamed. "Oh, he got Sport," she gasped a moment later. Jerry ran to the house to get Dad.

Later, Jerry and Arissa were still shaking, and Jerry had tears in his eyes as he stroked Sport. "The snake is dead, and I've called the vet," Dad told him. "He'll be right over."

Jerry nodded. "Will Sport be all right?" he asked.

"The vet will do his best to save him," Dad said, "but I'm afraid a snake bite can be fatal to a dog, so you must be prepared."

"Poor old Sport," murmured Jerry, wiping his eyes. "I'm so sorry, fella. If only I'd obeyed Dad and killed the snake the day I brought him home."

The vet came and gave Sport a shot of strong serum to fight the poison in his system. He gave instructions on how to care for the dog, and then he left. Fortunately, in a week Sport was his old self.

One night Dad asked Jerry, "Do you remember how we compared sin to that snake the day you found him?" Jerry nodded. "Well, you know, the cure for sin is a little like the cure for the snake bite," continued Dad. "The poison needs to be removed. The only thing that can remove the poison of sin from our life is Jesus' death on the cross for us." *HCT*

HOW ABOUT YOU?

Has the poison of sin been removed from your life? If not, talk to a trusted friend or adult to find out how Jesus can help you.

MEMORIZE:

"The blood of Jesus, his Son, cleanses us from every sin." 1 John 1:7

Be Saved by Jesus' Blood

Two Kinds of Sin

(Read Romans 12:9-16)

Billy was helping Dad in the workshop, and he thought it would be a good time to ask a question that had been bothering him. "Dad, you're always telling me that it's important to confess our sins when we pray. Right?"

"That's right," Dad replied.

Billy then said, "But what if I can't think of any sins to confess? There are some days that I never catch myself telling a lie or doing anything else really wrong. So how can I confess anything?"

Dad looked at him seriously, but there was a twinkle in his eye. "I wish I had that problem, Billy," he said. "I can always think of plenty of sins to confess."

"You, Dad?" asked Billy in surprise. "I don't see you doing any sins."

Dad laughed. "Thanks for the vote of confidence," he said. "Maybe I don't have much of a problem with 'obvious' sins. But I still sin many times a day. For example, I might have sinful thoughts that no one would know about. Besides, Son, there are actually two kinds of sins."

"Huh?" asked Billy. "I thought sin was sin!"

"In a way it is," agreed Dad, "and all sin is wrong. It hurts others and ourselves. But sometimes we sin by doing wrong things, and sometimes by *not* doing things we know we should do. The Bible says that if I know to do good, and don't do it, it is sin."

Billy thought about that. "You mean, when I know I need to tell you or Mom something wrong I did and I don't tell you, it's really a sin?" Dad nodded, and Billy shook his head. "Boy," he exclaimed. "I sure won't have any problem thinking of things to confess any more." *SLK*

HOW ABOUT YOU?

Do you confess obvious sins, such as hurting others with your anger, disobeying your parents, or other things God has said you should not do? You also need to be careful to obey all that God tells you to do. Make use of every opportunity he gives you to do good.

MEMORIZE:
"Remember, it is sin to know what you ought to do and then not do it."
James 4:17

Avoid Evil; Do Good

A Big Nursery?

(Read Luke 17:11-19)

"Did you enjoy working in the nursery this morning, Brett?" asked Mom as they started for home.

"I did—except for one little kid named Jason," replied Brett. "All he said was, 'gimme a cookie,' 'gimme a piggyback ride,' 'gimme, gimme, gimme!' And then he didn't even appreciate what he got. The minute he got what he wanted, he wanted something else!" Brett sighed. Just thinking of Jason made him tired.

"That's what two-year-olds often do," Mom told him.

"As a matter of fact, that's what many adults do, too," added Grandma.

"Adults?" Brett laughed. "They ask for piggyback rides?"

"Not exactly," said Grandma, "but does this sound familiar?" She paused for a moment. "Dear God, please give me a new job . . . and let the kids do well in school . . ."

". . . and help me lose ten pounds . . . ," added Mom with a grin.

Brett laughed. "We all ask for a lot, don't we? I guess the world must seem like a big nursery to God," he said. "Do you think he wishes people would appreciate him more? I know I'd sure like to hear a big 'thank you' from Jason once in a while. If he'd get over asking for things all the time, he'd probably be a lot of fun. He's a nice kid when he gets distracted now and then and forgets to demand something."

"Well then, maybe we can ask God for two more things," Mom suggested. "Patience for you and a grateful heart for Jason . . . and for all of us." *HMT*

HOW ABOUT YOU?

When you ask God for help or for things you need, do you thank him, too? Do you treat the things as a gift from God? God loves to help you, but he doesn't want to be forgotten. Thank him today for all the things he has done.

MEMORIZE:

"Give thanks to the Lord, for he is good! His faithful love endures forever." Psalm 107:1

Thank God for His Goodness

Stay Cool

(Read 1 Peter 3:13-17)

"Hi, John! How was school?" asked Mom cheerfully, lighting the tall white candle that stood in the middle of the dining table.

"Hi," mumbled John, without looking at his mother.

"What's wrong?" asked Mom. "Something happen at school?"

John hesitated. "Well, after baseball practice, I asked Darren if he wanted to come with me to church next week. He asked what we do there, so I told him what I learned at Sunday school last week. Some of the other kids heard me, too, and they laughed at me."

"Then what happened?" prompted Mom gently.

"Tom said anybody who believed in God was stupid," replied John. "That really made me mad. Nobody's gonna call me stupid and get away with it!" He hesitated before adding, "I punched Tom." He sighed. "I felt like I needed to stand up for God."

Mom was silent for a moment, watching the slim white candle standing gracefully in its silver candleholder. "Look at this candle," she said. "It's burning very brightly, isn't it?" John looked at the gently flickering orange and blue flame and nodded. "And you know the flame will be too hot to touch, don't you?" John agreed.

"But how about the side of the candle? Will it burn your fingers?" asked Mom.

John touched the candle lightly. "It's quite cool," he said.

"That's how Jesus wants you to be," explained Mom. "He wants you to burn brightly for him by witnessing in word and deed. But he doesn't want you to get all hot and bothered and lose your temper about it. Instead, stay cool—like the candle!"

John scratched his head thoughtfully. "I guess I shouldn't have hit Tom," he said at last.

Mom nodded. "Instead of getting angry next time, ask the Holy Spirit to help you know what to say," she suggested. *MTF*

HOW ABOUT YOU?

Do you enter into fierce and bitter arguments about your faith? Do you lose your temper if people don't accept what you tell them—what you know is true? Don't get mad. You can't control how they will act, but you can control how you act. Jesus wants you to speak out the truth, but he also wants you to stay calm and cool about it.

MEMORIZE:

"Let your conversation be gracious and effective so that you will have the right answer for everyone."

Colossians 4:6

Witness Calmly

A Hopeless Case

(Read Luke 5:26-31)

Tom and his friends were setting up tents for a campout in Tom's backyard. "Did you invite Mitch?" asked Ben. Mitch lived down the street, but the boys didn't like him very much. They thought he acted "tough," and he sometimes used foul language, too. "I think he'd like to come," added Ben.

Tom shook his head. "No way!" he exclaimed. "Why do you waste your time on such scum?"

"He's not scum to God," said Ben. "Maybe if some of us kids are nice to him, he'll learn that God is more than just a swear word."

"That's a joke! Mitch is a hopeless case," insisted Tom.

The boys had a great time that night. They enjoyed the good camp food—especially the big watermelon Ben's mother supplied.

A whole year passed. Ben continued to be friendly toward Mitch, but most of the boys refused to let him join their activities.

As Tom and his dad worked in the backyard one summer morning, Tom noticed a fairly large plant growing among some weeds near the fence. He looked closely and saw a little green watermelon. "Look, Dad," he said. "This must have started from seeds of the melon we ate on our campout last summer!" As he spoke, someone called to him from the sidewalk. It was Ben, and to Tom's disgust, he saw that Mitch was with him. Tom walked over to chat with them. As the boys talked for a few minutes, Tom was surprised that he didn't hear any bad words from Mitch. "Hey, you've cleaned up your language," he exclaimed impulsively.

Mitch smiled shyly. "Ben and his dad showed me how to become a Christian," he said.

After the boys left, Tom told his dad about it. Dad nodded. "Just like the watermelon seed took root here, God's Word took root in a most unexpected place," he said. *CEY*

HOW ABOUT YOU?

Do you know someone who seems to be a hopeless case as far as ever coming to God? Nothing is impossible with him. He can change the person who seems totally uninterested. Keep praying for your non-Christian friends, talking of God's love, inviting them to church, and showing God's love through the way you act. Trust God to bring results, and don't give up on anyone.

MEMORIZE:
"Everything is possible with God."
Mark 10:27

See the Good in Others

Once Is Too Often

(Read Proverbs 1:20-28)

"Uncle Bob was in a car accident," said Mother as she hung up the phone. "He and some friends had apparently been taking drugs, and they hit another car. That driver was killed, and Uncle Bob is in a coma." Liam and Kyle didn't know what to say. After a moment, Mother continued. "The first time Uncle Bob took drugs he said he just wanted to get high once. He promised not to do it again, but he never quit." Mother turned to leave the room. "Can you play quietly? I'd like some time alone."

"Sure, Mom," they answered sympathetically.

After a few moments, Mother heard a crash. When she went to investigate, she saw pieces of race-car models on the floor. "What happened?" she asked. "You know you're not to handle those cars. They're antique and very fragile."

"Liam said it wouldn't hurt to play with them just once," murmured Kyle, looking at the floor, "and I bumped the shelf trying to get them down."

Liam picked up the pieces. "Can't we fix them?" he asked anxiously. "There aren't many pieces."

"We'll try," said Mother, "but they'll never be the same. And it won't change your punishment for disobeying."

Mother got the glue, and they went to work. "The cracks still show," observed Liam. "Can't you push the pieces together tighter?"

"They look like scars," Kyle added.

"I'm doing my best," Mom answered. "You know, boys, as I try to repair these, I keep thinking of Uncle Bob. His life is full of scars because of drugs. He never finished school, he lost several jobs, and he had this accident." As she set one car down to dry, she turned to her sons. "I'm disappointed that you disobeyed and tried to play with these cars," she said. "When you look at them from now on, I hope you'll be reminded of the results of doing wrong." *SLN*

HOW ABOUT YOU?

Have you been tempted to try drugs "just once" to see what it's like? Once is too often. Doing drugs for pleasure is wrong. It hurts your body, and it could end up hurting you for life.

MEMORIZE:

"God bought you with a high price. So you must honor God with your body."
1 Corinthians 6:20

Don't Try Drugs

Wrong Instructions

(Read Colossians 3:22-25)

"I can do it, Dad. I know how." Ian was eager to help trim the hedge at the back of the yard.

"OK, Son," agreed Dad. "I've got it started, so you can see how much I want cut off. Keep it nice and even. I'm going to run to the store for some grass seed. If you finish the hedge before I get back, you may cut just a little bit off those bushes at the side of the house."

Dad disappeared, and Ian took over the trimming. As he carefully cut the hedge to the same level Dad had started, his friend Barry, who lived in the house behind Ian's, came out. He eyed Ian's work. "You know what?" he said. "If you'd cut that down a little bit more, we'd be able to jump over it and wouldn't have to walk all the way around when we want to go to each other's house."

Ian thought about that. "You're right!" he said. And he proceeded to follow Barry's advice.

Next Ian trimmed the bushes beside the house. Deb, his sister, came out of the house and surveyed his work. "I've always wished we could have these bushes trimmed so they go in points, like in formal gardens," she said. "Can you do them that way?"

"Sure," said Ian, confidently, and he proceeded to show her. The results were not quite what he expected.

When Dad got home, he looked from Ian to the hedge, to the bushes, and back at Ian. "What happened?" he asked. "You didn't do things the way I told you." Ian explained about Barry's and Deb's suggestions. "Who are you working for?" Dad asked quietly. "Them or me?"

Ian was embarrassed. "I'm sorry, Dad," he said. "After this, I'll follow your instructions very carefully." And he did. *HWM*

HOW ABOUT YOU?

Did you know that you are a servant of Christ? As his servant, you need to follow his instructions. Your friends may say, "It doesn't hurt to cheat just a little." But God says, "Be honest." The world says, "A little white lie is OK." God says, "You shall not lie." What worldly advice is someone giving you? Shut it out and follow God's instruction.

Follow God's Instructions

MEMORIZE:
"Oh, that my actions would consistently reflect your principles!" Psalm 119:5

Pay Up!

(Read Ecclesiastes 5:2-7)

Anthony came into the kitchen, slamming the door behind him. "If Luke thinks he's going to be a member of the club, he's sure got another think coming!" he grumbled. "You know that project our club took on—taking some little kids to the circus?"

Mother nodded. "Yes, and I thought it was very nice for a group of young fellows to do that."

"Yeah—very nice," Anthony repeated bitterly, "until it was time to come across with the money for tickets and the food to eat afterwards. Then old Luke says he doesn't have it; he can't swing that much." Anthony shook his head. "He voted for it! He made a promise, and now he's going to wiggle out of it! So the rest of us will have to pitch in and pay Luke's share."

Mother went into the next room and returned with her purse. Pulling out some bills, she held them out to Anthony. "Here," she said softly, "I'll pay Luke's share."

Anthony could hardly believe what his mother was doing. "You shouldn't do that," he insisted. "Luke made the promise, and he should come through on it."

Mother smiled pleasantly. "Oh," she said slowly, "I've done this before."

Suddenly Anthony remembered when she had done it. It was the time he had pledged some money during a missionary conference and later announced that he had spent what he had saved for it. Mother hadn't argued with him. She simply told him she would cover it, and he could pay her back later.

"Yeah," Anthony said, taking the money Mother offered, "I remember when you did that for me. I guess I'd better let you help Luke this time, but I'm going to tell him it's a loan. Once a guy makes a promise, he ought to keep it." He started out the back door and then turned and came in again. "By the way, Mom," he said with a smile, "I get paid tonight for mowing Mrs. Black's lawn, and then I'll pay you back for that missionary pledge." *RIJ*

HOW ABOUT YOU?

Sometimes it's easy to get carried away with the enthusiasm of certain projects. But do you follow through when you make a promise to give or to do something special? Would you be willing to cover for someone else who has carelessly made such a promise? If you've made any promise you haven't kept, take care of it now.

MEMORIZE:

"When you make a promise to God, don't delay in following through."
Ecclesiastes 5:4

Keep Your Promises

Bird Lessons

(Read Jeremiah 29:11-13)

Timothy ran outside to investigate when something crashed against the family room window. Underneath the window, between the flowers, he found a robin flapping its wings frantically. Timothy reached down very cautiously and, anchoring the bird's wings close to its body, he picked it up. "Dad! Come help!" he called.

Dad ran his fingers over the bird's bone structure and spread its wings. "Nothing broken," he said. "I think it just has its wind knocked out."

Timothy lay the bird under the lilac bush in the backyard. Sensing its freedom, it tried to get up, but its efforts were useless. "It can't fly," Timothy said sadly.

"It's just exhausted." Dad pointed to the red breast. "See . . . its chest is moving up and down. Let's leave it and move away so it won't be so frightened."

Timothy nodded. He rode down the sidewalk on his bike, but every now and then he went back to check on the robin.

Some time later, a choir of chirping exploded from somewhere in the hawthorn tree. Timothy peered up through the leaves. At the top, nestled between a thick branch and the trunk, he saw a nest. He glanced back at his patient. Her head was raised attentively. After a struggle, she got onto her feet and ran across the yard. Flapping her wings several times, she rose from the ground, landing on the branch beside her nest.

Timothy ran to tell Dad about it. "She knew the sound of her babies!" Timothy exclaimed happily. "And she flew to them so they wouldn't be scared."

"Great!" exclaimed Dad. After a moment he added, "Jesus is like that . . . he knows us, and he's always there to hear us when we call on him."

"Cool," said Timothy. "That's like my Bible verse last week."

"And what was that?" asked Dad.

Timothy quoted it. "Jeremiah 33:3. 'Call to Me, and I will answer you. . . .'" He grinned at Dad. "The robin heard and answered her babies, and God hears and answers us, right?"

"Right," agreed Dad with a smile. *ECM*

HOW ABOUT YOU?

Do you wonder if God has time for you? If he knows when you are hurting? Be assured that he knows all about what is happening to you and wants only what is best for you. You can go to him anytime and know that he will hear and answer.

God Hears and Answers Prayer

MEMORIZE:
"Call to Me, and I will answer you. . . ."
Jeremiah 33:3, NKJV

6

Keep on Fishing

(Read Lamentations 3:24-27)

"Oh, no! A fish got my bait again!" exclaimed Robbie as he pulled his fishing line out of the water. "That was about the zillionth time I baited that hook. I'm quitting." He laid his pole on the ground. "OK if I go check the frog pond?" he asked. Dad nodded, so Robbie wandered off through the well-known woods on his grandfather's farm, leaving his father to fish alone.

When Robbie returned a half hour later, Dad grinned at him. "Look—I believe I've hooked something!" said Dad. He tugged on his line and brought a flapping, struggling fish to shore. Robbie was surprised to see that there were also several other fish in their pail. "How'd you do it, Dad?" asked Robbie.

"By just keeping at it," replied Dad. "You'll never catch a fish with your fishing pole on the ground."

Robbie picked up his pole and baited his hook again. As they continued fishing, he was thoughtful. "Maybe Todd and Matt are like these fish you caught," he said suddenly.

Dad raised his brows. "I don't think your friends would be very flattered to hear you compare them to the fish," he replied. "What do you mean?"

"Well, I've been trying to win them to Jesus—'fishing for men,' like Jesus said we're to do," explained Robbie. "But they never will come to church or anything. When I try to talk to them about God, they're not interested. Last week I decided I'd just quit, because it didn't seem like it was any use to keep on witnessing to them."

"Now you're wondering about that decision?" asked Dad.

Robbie nodded. "Maybe it's like our fishing today. Maybe I just need to keep at it a little longer."

"That's good thinking," agreed Dad. *MRP*

HOW ABOUT YOU?

Have you become discouraged in trying to help somebody get interested in spiritual things? Have you stopped witnessing to someone, thinking it's just no use? Don't give up. Keep on "fishing," and trust the Lord to bring results in his time.

MEMORIZE:

"Be strong and steady, always enthusiastic about the Lord's work, for you know that nothing you do for the Lord is ever useless."

1 Corinthians 15:58

Keep on Witnessing

Trail of Faith

(Read Hebrews 11:6-10)

Josh squirmed on the wooden bench and poked at the campfire as the other campers headed to their cabins after the missionary finished speaking. Mr. Trent, the missionary, sat down beside him. "Is something bothering you tonight?" asked Mr. Trent.

Josh sighed and shrugged his shoulders. "I just don't understand how people like you can do scary things, like going to Africa. I know I'm supposed to trust God, but I just don't think I could." He stood up.

"Why don't we talk about it a little more," suggested Mr. Trent.

"Maybe in the morning," said Josh. "I have to go to my cabin now."

"No, you better not. It's dark and you might get lost," warned Mr. Trent. "You better stay here until morning when you can see."

"Our cabin is right over the hill," Josh assured him. "I just have to follow this trail. It goes right past it. I'll even be able to see my cabin when I get to the top of the hill."

Mr. Trent smiled. "You mean you're going to exercise some faith?" he asked. "You trust that trail. You know that it has always led you to the cabin, and you have faith to believe that it will do so again. Well, that's something like the kind of faith I have in God. I know that if I stay on the trail he puts me on, I will end up in just the right place." He stood up. "Now tell me what would happen if you refused to move from this spot until you could see the cabin?"

"I guess I'd never get there," Josh answered, "because I can't see it from here."

Mr. Trent nodded. "It's the same with me," he said. "If I wait around until I know God's entire plan, I'll never go, because I can't see his entire plan. So I have to just start out to do what I believe he wants me to do. That's what faith is— moving ahead to where you know you should be going, even though you can't see the end of the trail." *HMT*

HOW ABOUT YOU?

What are some of the things that scare you? Do you worry about having to talk to someone about Jesus, moving to a new town, or doing something else frightening? Faith in God means going ahead and doing it because you know it's the right thing to do and because you know that God will lead you there safely.

MEMORIZE:
"We live by believing and not by seeing." 2 Corinthians 5:7

Faith Starts with Action

A Cat's Nature

(Read Ephesians 4:20-32)

"Look at Smoky lying in the sun! Isn't he pretty?" Jim pointed to one of the family pets, a longhaired cat. A contented purr came from the gray form stretched out on the windowsill, soaking up the warmth of the sun.

A few minutes later, Jim's little sister Jenny bounded into the room. She dashed over to the birdcage and opened the wire door. With a flutter, Chipper, the parakeet, glided gracefully to the floor.

"No, Jenny!" exclaimed Jim. "Smoky's here!" He lunged for the cat. But he was too late. A silent, gray shadow slid down from the windowsill, and a moment later Smoky had the little bird in his mouth. Jim grabbed the cat, held him down, and pried his mouth open. Carefully, he removed the fragile bird.

"Is Chipper hurt, Jim?" wailed Jenny.

"I think he's just badly frightened," said Jim, gently stroking the trembling bird. He placed it carefully back in its cage while Jenny shooed the cat out of the room.

"Smoky's naughty," declared Jenny. "Why can't he be friends with Chipper?"

"It's just his nature," replied Jim. "No matter how tame he is, when he sees a bird, his natural instincts often take over."

"Well, I'm mad at him," stated Jenny.

"And I don't blame you," said Dad. "But Smoky's a lot like us, isn't he?"

"Huh?" asked Jim, looking at his father.

"We have an old nature that likes to take over, too," explained Dad. "When we become Christians, the Holy Spirit comes to live within us. But sometimes we get careless and allow our old natures to take over again."

"Like when you hit me," Jenny accused her brother.

"Well, you called me names," retorted Jim.

"I'm afraid those old natures are peeking out," cautioned Dad. "We need to be on guard! When we know Jesus, we receive a new nature with power to choose to do right.

"The Bible says to 'put off the old man' and 'put on' the new," added Dad. "He gives us the power to do that." *THB*

HOW ABOUT YOU?

Do you often let your old nature take over and cause you to sin? Be on guard against that. Each day ask God to help you let his nature be seen in your life.

MEMORIZE:

"You must display a new nature because you are a new person, created in God's likeness—righteous, holy, and true." Ephesians 4:24

Don't Give in to the Old Nature

The Guardrail

(Read Proverbs 4:1-10)

As the Tylers' car edged up on the mountain road, Jeff pouted in the backseat. "Going on a picnic is boring for a kid my age," he grumbled. "Why couldn't I stay with Lane instead?"

Mother sighed. "We already told you—Uncle Lee and Aunt Sue are out of town, and we don't think you should be over there while they're gone."

Jeff frowned. "You treat me like a little kid."

Suddenly, six-year-old Jessica squealed as she looked out the car window to the valley below. "Be careful, Daddy!"

Dad laughed. "I'll be careful. But if I should happen to slip off the road, the guardrail will keep us from going over the edge."

"Before they put up the guardrail, a car did go over the edge," said Mother. "I remember that it was three days before they found it."

When they reached the picnic area at the top of the mountain, Jeff's spirits lifted. He couldn't stay mad.

The trip home was quiet. After again being assured that the guardrail would protect them, Jessica went to sleep. Even Jeff and Mother dozed.

"Wake up, everyone!" called Dad as he drove into the yard and turned off the engine. "Oh, I hear the telephone ringing." He ran into the house.

Jeff and Mother were unloading the picnic supplies when Dad came back out. "I have bad news. Your cousin Lane had an accident this afternoon on his dirt bike." Jeff stared at Dad in horror.

Later, as they returned from visiting Lane at the hospital, Jeff voiced what they had all been thinking. "If I had stayed with Lane, it could have been me," he said.

Dad nodded. "Uncle Lee told Lane not to ride that bike while he and Aunt Sue were gone, but Lane didn't listen."

"Parents are like guardrails," Jeff said thoughtfully. "They keep us from danger . . . if we obey them." *BJW*

HOW ABOUT YOU?

Do you obey your parents? You need their guidance. Next time you're tempted to disobey, remember that God often uses parents to guard you from danger.

MEMORIZE:

"'Honor your father and mother.' This is the first of the Ten Commandments that ends with a promise. And this is the promise: If you honor your father and mother, 'you will live a long life, full of blessing.'" Ephesians 6:2-3

Obey Your Parents

The Red Car

(Read Leviticus 19:11-13)

What a lot of neat cars, Matt thought. He picked up a bright red car from the store shelf and admired it. *Wish I had enough money to get this*, he thought. He glanced around. *No one's looking*, he thought, and he quietly put the car under his jacket.

Matt was hurrying down the aisle when he felt a hand on his shoulder. "I think you had better come with me, young man." Matt looked up to see a security guard looking at him. "Let me have the car." Frightened, Matt pulled out the car and handed it over.

The guard took Matt to the manager, who questioned him. When the manager learned that he had come to the store with his mother, he paged her over the loudspeaker. Matt cringed when she came hurrying in.

When he finally left the manager's office with his mother, Matt was relieved that they had agreed not to call the police, but he knew he would not go unpunished. As they left the store, he noticed some big mirrors near the ceiling. "Oh, that's how they saw me," he said. "They can see down the aisles and watch for shoplifters. It's like a big eye is watching you from up above."

Mother nodded. "It's a good thing to remember that Someone is *always* watching you from up above," she said. "God would have seen you even if the clerk hadn't. God doesn't need mirrors. He sees everything you do. He also sees your heart and knows even your thoughts. He also knows if you're sorry for what you did—or thought."

Matt was quiet as they climbed into the car. He really was sorry. He was a Christian and knew he had done wrong. He had been unhappy about taking the car as soon as he had done it. Quietly he bowed his head. *Dear Jesus, I know it was wrong to take the car,* Matt prayed. *I'm sorry. Please forgive me. I don't want to do it ever again. Amen.* As they started home, he felt much better. He was actually glad the clerk had seen him in the mirror, because now his heart was once again right with God. *LLL*

HOW ABOUT YOU?

Have you ever taken something without paying for it? Perhaps you think no one saw you and you got away with it. You didn't. God saw what happened. He also sees your heart, and he takes that into account. Are you sorry? Then confess what you did and pay for what you took. Ask God to forgive you, too.

MEMORIZE:

"The Lord is watching everywhere, keeping his eye on both the evil and the good." Proverbs 15:3

God Sees Your Heart

Roger's Mouse

(Read James 2:14-20)

School began in the usual boring way—first math, then reading. *We need some action around here,* Roger thought. He peeked into his desk to check on the little mouse he had in a small box there.

A few minutes later, his teacher, Mrs. Madden, had to go to the office. She appointed Jennifer, one of the girls, to be class monitor in her absence. Jennifer proudly took her place behind the teacher's desk. Roger decided this was his chance. Quietly he took the mouse from his desk and released it. It scampered across the floor. "There's a mouse!" some of the kids screamed, and several of them ran to the back of the room.

"Take your seats," Jennifer instructed. "It won't hurt you." The mouse dashed across the floor, running right over Jennifer's foot. "Ahhh!" she shrieked. She climbed onto her chair.

"Quiet," Jennifer ordered. "Everyone sit down. There's nothing to worry about." But she remained on her chair.

Just them Mrs. Madden returned. She dismissed the class for an early lunch. While everyone was in the cafeteria, a janitor removed the little creature from the classroom.

After school, Roger told his mother about Jennifer and the mouse. "It was pretty funny," he said. "Jennifer kept telling the class to sit down because there was nothing to worry about, but she stayed standing on her chair."

"That's a good example of what we discussed in my ladies' Bible study this morning," said Mother. "Just as Jennifer's actions didn't match her words, Christians' actions don't always match what they say they believe about God." *NEK*

HOW ABOUT YOU?

Do you say you believe in Jesus but carelessly lie, cheat, or treat others unkindly? Or do you act out your faith by treating others the way Jesus would treat them? Ask God to help your words and actions match.

Live What You Believe

MEMORIZE:
"So you see, it isn't enough just to have faith. Faith that doesn't show itself by good deeds is no faith at all— it is dead and useless." James 2:17

The Scary Church

(Read Psalm 139:7-12)

"What's it like in a cave?" asked Robb excitedly. "I've never been in one before." He and his family were on vacation, and Dad had said they'd be attending church services inside a cave.

Dad chuckled. "You'll soon know," he promised.

Early Sunday morning, they were on their way. Robb watched puffy clouds float in the sky while the rising sun flung its rosy colors. He felt close to God as he saw the beauty around him, and it made him think of God's greatness. He was eager to get to the cave where the church service was being held. However, when they were finally down in the cave, Robb shivered. It was totally dark, except where electric lights lit the way. Huge stone formations hung down, while others rose up from the floor, casting gloomy shadows. The air was damp, and water dripped down the rocky walls.

In his seat, Robb pulled his jacket close around him to keep out the cold, clammy air. Although it was rather interesting, he didn't really like this dark, gloomy place, and he hoped the sermon wouldn't last long. He glanced anxiously at the dark shadows cast by the stones.

Suddenly it was pitch dark! "Dad! Dad! Where are you?" Robb whispered loudly, reaching out toward where his father was sitting.

"Right here beside you," Dad whispered back, taking Rob's hand. He squeezed it.

The minister had paused in his message, and some children began crying. Some of the adults nervously tried to calm the children. "Don't be afraid. God is here, too," said the minister. "He can see you just as well in the dark as in the bright sunlight. He's omnipresent."

"What does that mean—that big word?" Robb whispered to Dad.

"That means God is everywhere at the same time," continued the minister. "There's no place in this entire universe where God isn't present, even way down in this dark cave. He's watching over you right this minute."

Robb felt glad that God was right there beside him. He didn't feel so afraid anymore. And he was sure he would never forget that big word—omnipresent! *CEY*

HOW ABOUT YOU?

Are you afraid in the dark? God is there with you. Although you cannot see God because he is a spirit, he's close beside you, caring for you. The Bible tells us he is everywhere. He's omnipresent.

MEMORIZE:

"Darkness and light are both alike to you." Psalm 139:12

God Is Everywhere

No Punishment

(Read Romans 2:1-4)

The sound of breaking glass brought Dale running into the dining room. "Ooohhh, Melissa! Look what you've done!" he gasped. Melissa stared in horror at the shattered pieces of crystal on the floor. "You broke Mom's favorite vase!" Dale exclaimed. "It's the one Uncle Don bought her just before he died. Boy, will she be mad!"

"I couldn't help it," said Melissa nervously.

"What's the matter?" The children both jumped at the sound of Mother's voice. Sorrow spread over her face as she realized what had happened.

Melissa burst into sobs. "I didn't mean to. I was just looking for a pencil, and it fell. Oh! I'm sorry."

Mother put her arm around Melissa. "There, there, honey. Don't cry so!"

"Does she have to buy another one?" asked Dale. "It'll probably take all her savings to replace it."

"No. Some things can't be replaced," Mother said sadly.

"Then are you going to ground her?" Dale wanted to know. Mother shook her head. "Spank her?" was Dale's next question. Again Mother shook her head. Dale was astounded. "Aren't you going to punish her at all?"

"No," Mother sighed. "Melissa has learned that she needs to be more careful."

Dale shrugged in disgust. "If I had broken it, I wouldn't have been able to sit down for a week!"

"That's not true!" Mother denied. Then she wisely added, "Don't be jealous when mercy is shown to someone else. Mercy is something for which we should all be very grateful. Who knows? Tomorrow you may need it yourself." *BJW*

HOW ABOUT YOU?

Do you grumble when others are not punished as you think they should be? God tells you to "love mercy," even when it is given to others. If you are merciful, you will receive mercy. And you never know when you will need it.

Love Mercy

MEMORIZE:

"The Lord has already told you what is good, and this is what he requires: to do what is right, to love mercy, and to walk humbly with your God."

Micah 6:8

A Real Man

(Read John 11:32-36)

As Kurt turned his bike into the driveway, he skidded on some gravel and fell, scraping his elbow. "It doesn't hurt," he said as Mother bandaged it. Actually, his arm hurt quite a bit, but Kurt would never admit it. He felt that he had to be brave and not show his feelings.

"Come on," said Mother. "Let's see if the TV news has anything about that house fire this afternoon." As they watched, they saw a film clip of Kurt's father, a fireman, climbing a tall ladder to help a man escape the burning house. "Boy, did you see that?" asked Kurt. "Dad is sure brave. He's a real man!"

Kurt was excited when his father arrived home, dirty and smelling like smoke. "Hey, Dad, we saw you on TV!" Kurt began, but his father didn't smile. Instead, he slumped down in a chair, put his face in his hands, and started to cry. Kurt was surprised!

"What's wrong, honey?" asked Kurt's mother.

Dad wiped his eyes. "I'm all right. But the man we rescued from the burning house died in the hospital. His wife is terribly upset and frightened. I just feel so sorry for her!"

Kurt grew quiet and went to his room. A short time later, his father came in to see him. "Are you all right, Son?" Dad asked.

Kurt looked away. "Well," he mumbled, "I thought that men never—at least, a fireman wouldn't—well, I never thought *you* would cry."

Dad smiled kindly. "You mean you thought men never cried, right?" Kurt nodded, and his father continued. "I know that I don't usually seem very emotional, but I wouldn't make a very good fireman—or a good Christian either—if I didn't care about people. Jesus cried when his friend Lazarus died, remember? You don't think he was a sissy, do you?"

"No," Kurt replied slowly. "I guess I've got a lot to learn about being a 'real man,' haven't I?" *SLK*

HOW ABOUT YOU?

Do you think that men should be tough—that they should hide their feelings to prove how brave they are? Jesus didn't hide his feelings, but he was no weakling either. He accomplished the difficult through the power of God. You can do the same, whether you're a young man or a young woman.

MEMORIZE:

"Then Jesus wept. The people who were standing nearby said, 'See how much he loved him.'" John 11:35-36

"Real Men" Have Feelings

The Perfect Dad

(Read Isaiah 49:14-16; Matthew 5:48; 7:9-11)

"And before we leave, shall we pray to our Father with the prayer Jesus taught us?" said Mrs. Mac. "Think about the words as you say them." The boys and girls in the Sunday school class stood up and together recited the Lord's Prayer.

As the children were leaving, Mrs. Mac smiled warmly at Benny, a new boy in the class. "We're so glad you came today," she said. "We hope you'll come again."

Benny shrugged. Then his eyes filled with tears. "You all said that prayer just now—that one that says, 'Our Father which art in heaven.' Well, I don't want to have anything to do with God if he's a father!"

"Why is that, Benny?" asked Mrs. Mac gently. "What makes you say that?"

Benny scowled. "You know what my father did? He left my mom and Tina and me when I was five years old. He's never showed up since. So who wants another father like that!"

"Oh, Benny. I'm sorry!" said Mrs. Mac, putting a hand on Benny's shoulder. She was silent for a few moments as she prayed for the right words to say. "Benny," she said at last, "we compare God to many things. But because God is perfect, no human example can ever describe him properly." Benny still looked glum. "Benny, tell me about your mom," suggested Mrs. Mac.

Benny's face lit up as he thought about his mother. "Mom's great!" he exclaimed. "She loves Tina and me, and takes good care of us."

"Well, then think of God as someone who loves you and cares about you even more than your mom," said Mrs. Mac. "The Bible tells us that even if a mother forgets her child, God does not forget. In the same way, even though your dad has left you, God will never leave you."

"Really?" asked Benny, hope shining in his eyes.

"Yes, really," said Mrs. Mac. "And don't forget to pray for your dad, too—maybe one day, he'll come back." *MTF*

HOW ABOUT YOU?

Has God blessed you with a loving mom and dad? Then thank him—and know that God is even more loving than your parents. Has a father or mother abandoned you? Be assured that God will never leave you and never forsake you.

MEMORIZE:
"Can a mother forget her nursing child? Can she feel no love for a child she has borne? But even if that were possible, I would not forget you!"
Isaiah 49:15

God Is a Perfect Father

Right but Wrong

(Read 2 Peter 3:15-18)

Darrin sat down on the living room floor and dumped out the contents of a box. "I see you're going to work on your new model," observed Dad.

Darrin nodded as he began to fit some pieces together. "Dad, there's something I've been wondering about," he said. "I was over at Rob Taylor's house and his dad was telling about a man who was really mean to his wife and kids. This guy excused it by saying he was just being the head of the house, like the Bible says." Dad frowned as Darrin continued. "I guess it doesn't always work out right when you try to obey the Bible."

"Now, just a minute," said Dad. "We do need to obey the Bible, but we have to make sure we are following all of God's instructions. It sounds like this guy you spoke of is only using the part of the Bible that he likes and is ignoring some other very important parts. Jesus would never want a father to be mean to his wife and children. " He stopped as Darrin sighed and threw down two pieces of his model.

"This thing won't go together right," Darrin grumbled.

Dad looked at the model closely. "Are you sure you followed the instructions?" he asked.

"Of course!" Darrin looked at the instruction sheet. "It says right here, 'Snap section E onto section D.' But I tried that, and it won't work! The instructions must be wrong!"

Dad pointed to another part of the page. "Ah! But this says, 'While attaching E to D, press down on tab C.'" Dad quickly assembled the sections and handed them to Darrin.

"Wow! That was easy. Thanks, Dad!" Darrin smiled.

"You see, it's not enough to follow part of the instructions," Dad said. "You have to read them carefully enough to make sure you understand them completely." Then he added, "It's the same way with the Bible. When people try to follow only part of God's instructions and ignore the rest, they get into trouble." *SLK*

HOW ABOUT YOU?

Are there things in the Bible that just don't sound right to you? The Bible is God's Word, but it must be read carefully and prayerfully. If you truly desire to do God's will, he'll help you understand more and more as you study his Word.

MEMORIZE:

"Some of his comments are hard to understand, and those who are ignorant and unstable have twisted his letters around to mean something quite different from what he meant, just as they do the other parts of Scripture—and the result is disaster for them." 2 Peter 3:16

Study the Bible Carefully

What's Missing?

(Read Philippians 4:4-9)

"When are we going to buy an electric ice cream freezer?" Ryan asked as he and Dad took turns cranking the old freezer.

"Not until 'Old Faithful' quits doing the job," said Dad with a grin. "To me, all this work is part of making ice cream. Guess I'm a little old-fashioned."

As Ryan took a turn at the crank, he remembered recent taunts of one of the boys on the block. "Sunday school sissy," the boy had called him. "Dad, were you ever laughed at for being a Christian when you were a kid?" asked Ryan.

"Sometimes," replied Dad, "but as my father said, everyone is laughed at for some reason. Some kids are laughed at for being too fat; some for being too skinny. Some are laughed at for being smart; others for being dumb. My dad taught me that when others made fun of my faith, I could still be glad on the inside that I was a Christian."

"Even when kids laugh at you?" asked Ryan.

Dad nodded. "Real joy doesn't depend on what's happening on the outside," he said. "It's an inner feeling that God gives when we obey and trust him."

"It's hard though," Ryan complained. "Even harder than turning this crank."

"Sometimes," agreed Dad, "but with God's help, you can do it. I think the ice cream is ready. Let's call Mom and the girls."

When everyone had been served, Ryan eagerly took a bite. "Yummm . . . ," he began, then frowned. "This ice cream isn't as good as usual. I wonder why not?"

The others tasted their ice cream. "It's not bad, but it tastes kinda empty," Cindy decided.

Mother tasted it. "I bet I forgot the flavoring!" she said. "Vanilla ice cream without vanilla is, like you said, 'kinda empty.'"

"Like a Christian without joy," Dad added.

"Yes . . . well, the Lord can restore joy, but the best I can do for this ice cream is offer some chocolate syrup," said Mother with a smile. *BJW*

HOW ABOUT YOU?

Are you a Christian who is sad and depressed? Does life seem "kinda empty"? Have you lost your joy? Ask the Lord to restore to you the joy of his salvation. He wants you to live a flavorful, joyful life.

MEMORIZE:
"Restore to me again the joy of your salvation, and make me willing to obey you." Psalm 51:12

Rejoice Always

June
18

Marshmallow Church

(Read 2 Timothy 3:1-5; 4:3-4)

"Hey, Mom," said Mike as his family was driving home from a meal with his aunt and uncle, "those marshmallows on top of the sweet potatoes were yummy. Will you fix them that way sometime?"

"I guess so," agreed Mom. Then she added, "Since we haven't found a church we really like yet, we're going to church with Aunt Mary and Uncle Joe next Sunday."

"Oh, I like the one we went to last Sunday," protested Mike. "The pastor told lots of stories and jokes. Can't we go there?"

"Well, we didn't hear much from the Bible there," said Dad.

Mike frowned. "Aw, Dad!" he wailed. "I liked it there. Sounds like they have lots of parties and fun. There's nothing wrong with having fun, is there?"

"No," said Dad, "but there's more to the Christian life than parties and fun!" Mike just scowled.

The next Sunday, they attended church with Mike's aunt and uncle. Mom and Dad seemed pleased, but Mike grumbled about not going to the other church.

Mike cheered up when he came to the dinner table and found that his mother had prepared a new dish. "All right!" he exclaimed. "You made that sweet potato dish!" Mother just smiled. After prayer, she scooped out a big helping for him. He took the first few bites with enthusiasm. Then he stopped, a puzzled expression on his face. "Hey! What is this?" he asked. "There aren't any sweet potatoes in here!"

Mother and Dad both grinned. "I thought you liked marshmallows," said Mother.

"Well, I do," replied Mike, "but this is too sweet."

Dad smiled at him. "Now you know how your mother and I felt about that other church," he explained. "It was 'all marshmallows.' There's nothing wrong with social events and other fun things, but a church needs to be more than just a place of amusement for Christians. We also need good, sound Bible teaching that helps us grow as Christians. All other things are just the 'marshmallows' on top!" *SLK*

HOW ABOUT YOU?

Do you go to church because of the parties, outings, and other fun things? Let God give you an appetite for the "real food" of his Word. You can enjoy the "marshmallows," but don't fill up on them!

MEMORIZE:

"They will betray their friends, be reckless, be puffed up with pride, and love pleasure rather than God. They will act as if they are religious, but they will reject the power that could make them godly. You must stay away from people like that." 2 Timothy 3:4-5

Attend Church to Learn about God

Great Seats

(Read Psalm 95:1-7a)

Greg's cousin was visiting for the weekend. Mark wasn't a Christian, and Greg hoped that he'd become interested in knowing more about God.

On Saturday morning the boys took the bus to the ballpark to see a major league game. They arrived very early. It grew hotter and hotter as they stood in line, and the long wait was rather boring. Mark and Greg were tired of standing on the hot concrete, but they did want good seats! And once they got into the game, they decided it had been worth the wait. They had a super view from the third-base line!

The next day was Sunday, so the whole family piled into the car and headed for church. After Sunday school, the boys went to the church auditorium for the worship service. "Hey! Let's sit back here today," suggested Greg, pointing to the back row. "Mom and Dad are singing in a special musical group today, so we can't sit with them. If we sit in the back we can talk more." So the boys slipped into the back pew.

"Baseball games sure are a lot more fun than church, aren't they?" observed Mark on the way home. "Can you imagine waiting two hours to get the back row seat we had in church this morning?"

Greg was startled. He realized that he had presented the Lord as someone who didn't mean very much in his life! *LMW*

HOW ABOUT YOU?

Do you sit near the front in church and become involved in what is going on? Do you sing, listen, and perhaps take notes on what the pastor is preaching about? Don't sit in back and whisper with your friends.

MEMORIZE:
"Come, let us worship and bow down.
Let us kneel before the Lord our maker."
Psalm 95:6

Worship with Enthusiasm

June

20

Steve's Painting

(Read Psalm 19:12-14)

Steve loved to paint pictures, and each Wednesday afternoon he and his Aunt Meg spent an hour working together on watercolor paintings—Aunt Meg the teacher and Steve the willing student. "I think this is my best painting yet," said Steve one day. He held up his picture of a bright red cardinal perched on a branch with well-shaped leaves.

"Oh, that *is* good!" exclaimed Aunt Meg. She studied it. "But do you think this wing might be a shade darker?" she asked. Without thinking, she touched the wing with her wet brush—something she knew must never be done to another's work. The color ran. "Oh! I'm so sorry!" exclaimed Aunt Meg. They tried to repair it, but the more they daubed and wiped, the worse the painting looked. The bird was ruined.

Aunt Meg was devastated. "Can you ever forgive me?" she asked through her tears.

Steve was quiet. He was so disappointed! He had worked carefully and had been eager to show his "best ever" picture to his whole family. Now it was ruined. But bravely, with a little smile, he said, "I know you didn't mean to do it."

"I'm just so sorry," Aunt Meg repeated several times.

"Honest, Aunt Meg. It's OK." Steve tried to reassure her. He really meant that, but he trudged home with a heavy heart. He still did feel bad about the picture, and he knew Aunt Meg felt even worse.

That evening, he related the incident to his family. "I'm proud of you, Son," said Mother. "I'm sure it was hard for you to forgive and not hold a bad feeling in your heart. God will honor you for your good attitude and forgiving spirit."

"But Aunt Meg still feels so bad about it," said Steve sadly.

"I think we can all learn a valuable lesson from this," observed Dad thoughtfully. "Aunt Meg couldn't make things right no matter how sorry she was or how hard she tried, so she still feels bad—and you do, too. It's like that when we do wrong. Even though others forgive us, we are often left with a heavy heart, and they are, too. Our sin often leaves scars."

Mother nodded. "That's a good thing for us to remember," she said. *DLS*

HOW ABOUT YOU?

Do you realize that when you tell a lie, disobey, or gossip, you are doing wrong? Ask God and whoever you may have hurt to forgive you. Even things that seem like "little" sins may have sad results.

MEMORIZE:

"Keep me from deliberate sins! Don't let them control me. Then I will be free of guilt and innocent of great sin." Psalm 19:13

Sin Leaves Scars

A Lesson for Jamie

(Read Hebrews 10:23-25)

Jamie sat in his room, pouting. It was Sunday morning, and his family was getting ready for church. But Jamie was tired of getting dressed up; he was tired of having to sit still for two hours; he was tired of being the only boy in his class. He just plain didn't want to go to church!

His father opened the bedroom door just as Jamie put Buddy, his new puppy, in the basket. "What's the problem, Jamie?" Dad asked. "Everyone else is almost ready to go. Don't you feel well this morning?"

Jamie looked down as he replied, "I don't feel like going, Dad. Can't I skip church?"

Before his father could say anything, Buddy started whining. "Maybe he wants a drink," said Jamie. He hurried to take care of the pup.

"You know," Dad said as Jamie returned with some water, "Buddy is really dependent on you. He depends on you to feed him and care for him, and he thrives on your love. He really needs you, doesn't he?"

"Yeah, he does," said Jamie. He smiled. It was nice to be needed.

"We're a lot like he is, Jamie," continued Dad. "We all depend on somebody. Who do you depend on?"

Jamie thought for a moment. "On you and Mom," he answered. "You give me food and clothes and a home and stuff."

Dad smiled and nodded. "Right. And Mom and I depend on each other and also on our church family for love and prayers—and sometimes even for food and help. And, of course, we all depend on God and his Word. That's one reason we go to church—we're fed spiritual food as God's Word is taught to us there." He rumpled Jamie's hair. "So I think you better get ready quickly," he added.

Jamie looked up. "OK," he agreed with a smile. *BMC*

HOW ABOUT YOU?

Have you felt more like staying home than going to church? Although you can learn a lot through studying the Bible by yourself, you should also take advantage of the opportunity to be taught and encouraged in growing as a Christian.

Attend Church

MEMORIZE:
"And let us not neglect our meeting together." Hebrews 10:25

No More Work!

(Read 1 Thessalonians 4:11-12)

"See the world! Travel! Learn a special skill, and meet people!" the TV announcer said excitedly. "All you need to do is join the Navy."

"Wow!" exclaimed Benjamin, watching a jet take off from an aircraft carrier. "That looks like something I'd like to do some day. No more homework, no bed to make, no reports to do for school, no chores, no piano prac . . ." Suddenly he stopped. "Dad, you were in the Navy, weren't you? Was it really as exciting as they say on TV?"

"Well, I did get to travel and see several different countries," replied Dad, "but I worked hard on my ship, too. I even had to make my bed, and the inspections we had make your mother's inspections look like nothing. I learned about electronics, but that required lots of homework, reading, and on-the-job practice. I also met a lot of people—Navy people, mostly. I especially remember my boss. He was pretty gruff at times, but we got along."

"Maybe I wouldn't like the Navy after all," grunted Benjamin, "but I'm sick of homework and chores."

"The Bible tells us that work is a blessing," Dad said seriously. "Satan loves to help us find the laziest way to do things, but God knows we need to work, and we should do our best. The Navy was a good experience for me. God used it to prepare me for the work I do today."

"It doesn't sound very much like what they show on TV, though," protested Benjamin.

Dad chuckled. "Those who write ads know that people dream of the easy life—little work and lots of fun. So they use these things to attract attention." He paused, then added, "That ad shows only a small part of Navy life, and right now you only see a small part of your life, Benjamin. But God knows that homework is an important part of it."

"Well, then I guess I better get to work on my math problems," said Benjamin with a grin. *JAG*

HOW ABOUT IT?

Do you try to get out of doing work? Do you sometimes do only half the job? Ask God to help you do each job well.

MEMORIZE:

"Work hard so God can approve you. Be a good worker, one who does not need to be ashamed and who correctly explains the word of truth." 2 Timothy 2:15

Work to Please God

A Gardening Lesson

(Read John 15:1-8)

"Where's Tim?" asked Dad one afternoon.

Mother looked at the clock and frowned. "I sent him to the store to get a loaf of bread, but he should have been back 30 minutes ago."

"When he comes in, send him to the garden to help me," said Dad. He left, whistling.

Fifteen minutes later Tim joined Dad in the garden. "What took you so long?" Dad asked as he handed Tim a hoe.

"I played a few video games with the guys," said Tim. Dad frowned as he knelt beside the tomato plants and began pulling off small stems. Tim watched in surprise. "What are you doing, Dad?" he asked. "Those plants just started growing."

"See these little sprouts between the vine and the branches? If they're allowed to grow, they'll sap the vine of food," Dad explained. "All the strength of the plant will go into producing leaves, and the tomatoes will be few and tiny. The sprouts are called suckers because they pull the strength from the vine." He stood and stretched. "You've been spending a lot of time and money on video games," he said.

Tim bristled. "What's wrong with video games?" he asked. "After all, I don't go down to Barney's Game Room where there's wild music and drug pushers. I play at the store."

Dad nodded. "That's true," he said. "Playing video games is fine, but I think you need to be careful that playing them doesn't become a 'sucker' that gets between God and you."

"Like how?" asked Tim.

"Well, for example, at church tonight the Carsons are going to show pictures of their missionary work, right?" said Dad. "And there will be a special offering to help their work in Central America. Now, if you were to spend the evening playing video games, or if you spent money on games that could be given for the offering, I'd say those games had become suckers that should be removed."

Tim looked at the tomato plants, then at his dad. "Well, I'll try to make sure video games don't become a problem." *BJW*

HOW ABOUT YOU?

Have you gotten rid of "suckers"—things that keep you from growing as a Christian? Or are there things in your life that take too much of your time and money? Ask God to help you to lead a balanced life. Balance work and play and time for God with time for others and yourself. If you do, you will produce good fruit for God.

Use Time and Money Wisely

MEMORIZE:
"Those who remain in me, and I in them, will produce much fruit."
John 15:5

Broken Promises

(Read Deuteronomy 23:21-23)

Chad liked the missionary who was speaking at his church. Mr. Rathburn had told them thrilling stories of his work in a foreign country.

"In that country there are many orphan children," Mr. Rathburn was saying. "If we could build a home for them, we could show them love, and it would give us an opportunity to teach them about Jesus. We are asking Christians to pray about this home. We're also asking you to give up just one cup of coffee or one bottle of pop or perhaps one candy bar a week and give that money to the fund we've started. If you will do these things, raise your hand." Chad's hand shot right up. He was glad to see many hands raised, including those of his friends, Greg and Gary.

One Saturday a few weeks later the three boys were biking home after ball practice. "I'm hot," said Greg. "Let's get some pop at the gas station."

As they were getting out their coins, Chad exclaimed, "Hey, wait! We promised to give up one pop a week. It's Saturday already, and I haven't given up one this week yet, have you?"

"Nah," said Greg. "I'll give up two next week."

"Yeah," agreed Gary. "I'm too thirsty now."

Chad felt hurt as the boys drank their pop. He wouldn't even take a sip of theirs when they offered it. "I don't see how you can break your promise," he told them. All the way home he was mad at his friends.

That evening Chad was reading quietly in his room when he had a thought. *I was mad at my friends for breaking their promise, but I broke a promise, too. I was going to pray for Mr. Rathburn this week and haven't remembered to do it once.*

Chad put his book aside and prayed for Mr. Rathburn and his friends. Then he felt much better. *AGL*

HOW ABOUT YOU?

Have you made promises to God that you haven't kept? God keeps all his promises, and he expects you to keep yours. Be careful about making promises. Ask God to help you keep the ones you make.

MEMORIZE:

"So when you make a promise to God, don't delay in following through, for God takes no pleasure in fools. Keep all the promises you make to him."
Ecclesiastes 5:4

Keep Your Promises

Busy as a Bee (Part 1)

(Read James 3:7-13)

Kyle was glad to be at his grandparents' home in the country. He ruffled the collie's ears as she came to greet him when he arrived. "Shep," said Kyle, "we're gonna have fun this summer." Shep barked in agreement, and Kyle continued, "Anything's better than all the work Dad makes me do at home. Whew! This is the life!"

The next morning Kyle was awakened by the smell of bacon. "Hmmm—I forgot how good Grandma's cooking is," he murmured sleepily.

When Grandpa called him, Kyle complained about getting up so early. Hearing about the chores he was expected to do, he complained again. Grandpa was patching a fence when Kyle said, "Nasty creatures."

"The cows?" Grandpa asked.

"No," Kyle answered. "Bees! There's a swarm of them by that old apple tree."

Grandpa laid down his tools. "A swarm of bees? Good! Come on. We'll catch them."

"Are you kidding?" asked Kyle. "All they'll do is sting us."

"Not if we dress right," Grandpa assured him. "I'll coax them into an empty hive." Kyle wasn't happy with the idea. "More work," he muttered.

That evening the supper table was piled with fried chicken, potatoes, and thick slices of homemade bread. "Please pass the honey," Kyle said. "I love it on bread."

"I thought you wanted nothing to do with bees," his grandpa teased.

"Did I say that?" Kyle grinned. "I sure was wrong."

"You know, Kyle, we all tend to grumble—or, as the Bible puts it, we curse things that really bring us blessing," said Grandpa. "We grumble about bees—but they make honey. We grumble about hard work—but it provided this food. We should be thankful for both difficult and pleasant things. God said that 'blessing' and 'cursing' shouldn't come from the same mouth," said Grandpa.

Kyle nodded. "I'll do better," he promised. "I'll keep busy as a bee myself! Tomorrow I'll get up early and help with the bees again." *JLH*

HOW ABOUT YOU?

What kinds of words come out of your mouth? Do you argue, complain, or tease others one minute and smile, praise, and flatter them the next? The two don't go together. Use your mouth to speak kind words. Offer encouragement and help. Compliment others.

**Be Grateful:
Don't Grumble**

MEMORIZE:
"And so blessing and cursing come pouring out of the same mouth. Surely, my brothers and sisters, this is not right!" James 3:10

Busy as a Bee (Part 2)

(Read 1 Corinthians 3:6-9)

Grandpa taught Kyle many things about bees and how they work together. "There's only one queen bee but many worker bees and drones," Grandpa said. "They all have a special job to do. They need each other to make a hive run smoothly. The workers gather honey, build and guard the hive, and feed the baby bees."

"Look, Grandpa!" Kyle shouted. "That bee must be sick. See it sway back and forth."

"She's doing a honey dance," Grandpa said.

Kyle laughed. "Oh, Grandpa," he said, "quit teasing. I'm serious."

"So am I," answered Grandpa. "That bee has found a large supply of nectar. It's more than she can handle by herself, so she's calling the others to help her. Watch! Soon the other bees will follow her." As Kyle watched in fascination, Grandpa spoke again. "This reminds me of the lesson I'm preparing to teach in my Sunday school class. It's about how God has work for every Christian to do. Some have what we call 'big' tasks, and others have 'little' tasks. Some jobs are noticed, and others are hidden—like the work done inside the hive. We all need each other to help spread the gospel and to do God's work—and we need each other to accomplish the ordinary chores of everyday living as well. Sometimes we forget that."

"So we should all keep busy as a bee and do our share, right?" said Kyle with a grin. "OK. I'll try to remember." *JLH*

HOW ABOUT YOU?

What is your attitude toward work? Do you grumble about it and put off doing it as long as you can? Others need you to do your share. Even the ordinary, everyday chores that you're assigned to do around the house should be done not only for your parents, but for the Lord as well. Such things as chores, schoolwork, and practicing are the work that God has given you to do at this time. Be faithful in doing them.

MEMORIZE:

"We work together as partners who belong to God. You are God's field, God's building—not ours."

1 Corinthians 3:9

Work Together Cheerfully

A Promise Is a Promise

(Read James 4:13-15)

"It's so sunny out today, I wish we could go to our cabin," said Maggie at the breakfast table.

"I was thinking the same thing," answered Dad. "Let's do it. We'll plan to leave as soon as I get home from work tonight—if you help Mom pack."

"Sure thing!" Maggie gave her dad a big kiss as he left.

While Maggie was helping her mother prepare for the trip, she thought about the fun they would have at the cabin. It was four o'clock when her dad called from the office. "I'm so sorry," he apologized, "but we have a big project that has to be completed by tomorrow afternoon. It was coming along fine, but there was a computer error, and now all the figures have to be rechecked. We'll have to postpone our trip till another day."

Maggie slammed down the receiver. "It's not fair!" she stormed, tears streaming down her face. "Dad promised we could go, and a promise is a promise!"

"When Dad's boss asks him to work longer, he needs to do it," Mother answered.

"But he promised!" wailed Maggie.

"Now just a minute," interrupted Mother. "He didn't exactly promise. He did say we'd plan to go, but you have to realize that sometimes it's difficult, or even impossible, to carry out our plans. We get sick, or circumstances change, and there's nothing we can do about it."

Maggie scowled. "Well, if I can't count on my own dad, who can I count on?"

"You can always count on God. He has made many promises to us, and because he is God, we know that we can trust him completely." Mom smiled. "I know you're disappointed, but I'm sure Dad is disappointed, too."

Maggie was quiet. "I never thought about that." *LMW*

HOW ABOUT YOU?

Are you careful to make promises that you can keep? Are you careful not to accuse Mom and Dad of "promising" things when they are merely "planning" them? And when they have to change their plans, do you become upset or do you try to understand the circumstances? Even though it is hard to do, learn to accept changing circumstances and changing plans.

Accept Changed Plans

MEMORIZE:
"What you ought to say is, 'If the Lord wants us to, we will live and do this or that.'" James 4:15

Growing Pains

(Read 2 Peter 3:14-18)

Turning over to avoid the sunlight coming through the window, Cody hoped to catch a little more sleep. Then, suddenly, he realized he was in Arizona visiting Grandma and Grandpa. Quickly he jumped out of bed, got dressed, and went to the kitchen where Grandma was making breakfast. "This will be ready in just a few minutes," she said. "Now might be a good time for you to have your devotions. Did you bring along the devotional book we sent you?"

Cody felt embarrassed. "I forgot it," he confessed.

"Have you been reading it?" asked Grandma. "Do you enjoy it?"

"Well, I've read some of it," replied Cody. "For a while I read it every day."

"But not any more?" asked Grandma. "Didn't it help you grow as a Christian?"

Cody shrugged. "I didn't really see that it made any difference in my life," he said.

"Hmmm," murmured Grandma. "By the way, would you like some fresh oranges from our tree with your breakfast?"

"Do you have an orange tree?" asked Cody.

Grandma nodded. "Don't you remember? We planted it when you were here last time."

Cody nodded. "Does that one have oranges already?" he asked.

Grandma smiled. "Go see for yourself," she said. So Cody took the basket Grandma handed him. When he saw the tree, he was delighted to find that he could fill the basket from one of the lower branches.

"It was neat to pick oranges from a tree I helped plant," Cody said as he handed Grandma the fruit. "I can hardly believe how tall it's grown!"

Grandma nodded. "Grandpa fed and watered the tree regularly, and as you can see, it has done well," she said. "Of course, we didn't notice any great difference from day to day. Trees need time to grow." After a moment she added, "Christians do, too. Don't stop having devotions when you don't see immediate growth, Cody. Keep it up, and ask God to help you become more like him." *EMB*

HOW ABOUT YOU?

Are you praying, reading the Bible, and obeying it? Does it seem like nothing is happening as a result? Growth may be slow at times, but when you regularly practice these things, you can be sure you are growing to be more like Jesus.

MEMORIZE:

"But grow in the special favor and knowledge of our Lord and Savior Jesus Christ." 2 Peter 3:18

Nourish Your Soul Daily

Ragamuffin (Part 1)

(Read Romans 5:6-11)

Rick and Sandy were helping their dad in his meat shop. Part of their job was to take the trash out to the big bin behind the store. Together they carried out empty boxes and trash. Rick lifted the trash bin cover, then he slammed it back down quickly. "Sandy, there's something in there. I saw it move!"

"You're just trying to scare me," laughed Sandy.

"I'm telling the truth," Rick persisted. Bravely he pulled up the lid and poked at the trash with a stick. A loud moan jarred the air, and Sandy screamed.

Dad rushed outside. "What's wrong?" he asked in alarm.

"Something's in the trash," Sandy choked out. Looking doubtful, Dad approached the trash bin and looked inside. "Why, it's a puppy!" he exclaimed. "Let's see if we can help him."

"Can we take him home, Dad?" Rick begged. "He looks like a stray."

"Ugh!" Sandy made a face. "He smells! I bet Mother won't want him."

"He's a mess all right," agreed Dad. "We'll clean him up and see if we can find him a home."

When they arrived home, the children told their mother all about the puppy. At her suggestion they named him Ragamuffin. "You know, children, Ragamuffin will make a good illustration for my Sunday school lesson tomorrow," said Mother as she looked at the bedraggled pup. "What you did for Ragamuffin, God did for us—and even more! God found us lost, and "dirty" from our sins. Yet he reached down to rescue us."

Ragamuffin barked and Sandy laughed. "He agrees with you, Mom. I think Ragamuffin is glad he's been found!" *JLH*

HOW ABOUT YOU?

Have you become a Christian yet? God loves you. He sent Jesus to rescue you from your sins. Jesus wants to be your Savior. If you would like to know more, ask a trusted friend or adult.

Jesus Loves Sinners

MEMORIZE:
"When we were utterly helpless, Christ came at just the right time and died for us sinners." Romans 5:6

Ragamuffin (Part 2)

(Read Psalm 111)

Rick and Sandy enjoyed romping with Ragamuffin, the stray puppy. They taught him tricks and took him on walks. They were delighted that no one answered the newspaper ad seeking Ragamuffin's owners.

But not everything was pleasant. Ragamuffin got into trouble. Sometimes he tracked mud into the house or knocked things over and broke them. Sometimes he chewed slippers and hid shoes. Though Rick and Sandy were patient, the puppy often had to be scolded or punished for misbehavior.

The children worried that Ragamuffin might not like them when they punished him, but he was always loyal. He ran to meet them, wagging his tail and jumping up and down with excitement. He followed them around and constantly wanted to be with them. He treated them as if they were the best thing that ever happened to him. "Ragamuffin makes us feel like we're really important to him," observed Rick one day.

"You are," Mother said. "You rescued him and you take care of him. Ragamuffin knows that, and he loves you in return."

"That's kind of how it us with us and God," said Rick. "He takes care of us and loves us."

"But I wonder if we praise him or thank him enough?" asked Sandy. "I sometimes act mad when God doesn't let things work out the way I want them to."

"And sometimes I get impatient when God doesn't answer my prayers right away," admitted Rick.

Mother added, "I'm afraid we're all guilty of those things. We need to learn to give to God the kind of love and devotion that Ragamuffin gives to you." *JLH*

HOW ABOUT YOU?

Is God important to you? Do you give him your time? Your love? Your obedience? Your service? Do you praise him with your lips and your life?

MEMORIZE:
"We love each other as a result of his loving us first." 1 John 4:19

Be Devoted to God

The Real Thing

(Read John 4:10-14)

"Oh, Mom! Look!" exclaimed Jeremy. "There's water on the road up ahead." Jeremy and his mom were driving on the highway, and it was very hot.

Mom nodded. "It looks like the real thing, doesn't it? But it's just a mirage," she said. "See how it disappears as we get closer. It's kind of like the mirages desert travelers sometimes see."

"We studied that in school," said Jeremy. "Sometimes people got lost in the desert, and they'd become very thirsty when their water supply was gone. Then they'd see a lake in the distance and start running toward it. But as they got closer, it would disappear. Then they'd see another and another. My teacher said it was really sad, because people would go running to all of these mirages trying to find a drink—but when they saw a real lake, sometimes they'd turn away because they thought it was a mirage again. Often they died of thirst."

"That is sad," agreed Mom. "After having tried so many 'false lakes,' they didn't recognize the real one. It's still that way with a lot of people."

"You mean that still happens?" Jeremy asked.

"Actually, I was thinking about people being thirsty for Jesus," Mom told him. "He's the Living Water. The Bible says anyone who 'drinks of him' shall never thirst. But people who are thirsty for joy and peace try to find it in so many different ways—ways that don't satisfy. The Living Water is right beside them, but after being disappointed with other things so often, they don't recognize that Jesus is the real thing. He is the only one who can give us true peace and joy." *BMC*

HOW ABOUT YOU?

Are you "thirsty" for happiness? Have you tried to find it by being busy with friends, going to parties, taking part in school activities? Or maybe you've joined a church, tried to do good things, and read your Bible. These things are something like mirages—they look good, and you may think you can find satisfaction there. But lasting happiness is found only in Jesus—and he's been there all the time. Turn to him, admit your need, and ask him to take over your life.

**Knowing Jesus Brings
True Happiness**

MEMORIZE:
"But the water I give them takes away thirst altogether." John 4:14

Pumped Up

(Read Hebrews 10:19-25)

Every Sunday morning Keith grumbled about going to church. He complained about having to get up early, about his clothes, and about anything else he could think of. "Why can't we stay home once in a while?" he whined. "Why must we always go to church?"

Dad rumpled Keith's hair as he walked by. "It's good for you," he said, "and it pleases the Lord."

That afternoon Keith and his dad decided to take a bike ride. "My tires are a little soft," said Keith as they started out. "I meant to pump them up at the gas station yesterday, but I forgot. I think they'll be fine though."

"We could pump them up before we go," suggested Dad.

"I don't feel like bothering," replied Keith. "They'll be fine. Let's go."

Before long, Keith began to get tired. "Whew, it's hard to peddle with soft tires," he exclaimed. He was glad when they finally reached home. He ran and got the tire pump. After the tires were filled, Keith tried the bike. "It pedals easy as pie now," he said.

Dad nodded. "Good," he said. "But now it's time to put your bike away and get ready for church."

"Aw, Dad," whined Keith, "seems like we just got back from church. I was thinking of taking another spin on my bike."

"I was thinking, too," said Dad. "Just as it's hard work to ride a bike with soft tires, it's hard work to live for God without the things we learn in church. It's hard work to live without the encouragement we get from other Christians. We need to get 'pumped up' regularly with the Bible and with Christian friends. It pays to take time to do that." *CEY*

HOW ABOUT YOU?

Do you sometimes complain about having to go to church? As Christians we need each other. And we need to learn as much as we can about God through listening to Bible stories and prayer.

MEMORIZE:

"Think of ways to encourage one another to outbursts of love and good deeds." Hebrews 10:24

Go to Church

Too Hard to Learn

(Read Psalm 119:9-16)

"I can't memorize these verses!" Gary threw his papers down on the table. "There's no way, so why should I try?"

"You can do it," encouraged Mother gently. "I know it takes time—but it's worth it. Not only will you earn a scholarship to camp this summer, but you will also have God's Word within you."

"I know, I know," groaned Gary, "but I just can't do it!"

"Well, maybe I can help you after supper," suggested Mother. "If we talk about the meaning of the verses, they might be easier for you to learn."

That idea sounded good to Gary. He put his Bible away and went to watch cartoons with his sister, Laura. They watched together for a few minutes, but soon there was a commercial break. As Gary and Laura went to the kitchen for a glass of milk, Gary repeated the advertiser's "blurb" right along with the announcer. Laura giggled. "You should apply for a job," she told Gary. "You didn't miss a word. That's neat!"

"It's amazing!" exclaimed Mother. "You've learned that entire commercial— something that basically has no meaning for you—word perfect!"

Gary grinned. "Well, I've heard that old commercial over and over. No wonder I know it."

"That's a good point." Mother nodded. "It proves that if you would spend as much time going over your Bible verses as you do watching TV, it might not be a problem to memorize them."

Gary hadn't thought of that before. "Maybe so," he admitted. "Maybe I just haven't gone over them often enough. Do you think we could talk about their meanings? Then I'll go work on them by myself." *LMW*

HOW ABOUT YOU?

Do you take time to learn Bible verses? Do you find it hard to memorize? The key to memorization is to go over and over the verses you are learning. Make them a part of your thoughts and find ways to use them. This is how you can hide God's Word in your heart.

Memorize God's Word

MEMORIZE:
"I have hidden your word in my heart, that I might not sin against you." Psalm 119:11

The Empty Roll

(Read Galatians 2:16-20)

"Your hot dog's almost ready, Joey," Aaron told his little brother. Aaron twirled the long fork once more before withdrawing it from the fire. He placed the hot dog on a roll and handed it to Joey. Then he began to roast one for himself.

"Know what, Dad?" Aaron turned his attention to his father, who was roasting two hot dogs at a time. "I think Kendall is a Christian. He's the new boy in my class."

"Well, that's great," replied Dad. "And what makes you think he's a Christian?"

"Well, I know he goes to church, and he's just real nice. He doesn't use swear words or treat people mean," Aaron replied. "He's not like most of the guys."

"Hmmmm. Sounds promising." Dad moved to the picnic table and handed one of the hot dogs to Mother.

Aaron followed. "Joey, you're not eating the hot dog I roasted for you," he complained, looking at the untouched meat on Joey's plate.

"Am too. See?" Joey held up a half-eaten hot dog bun, thickly spread with catsup. "I like hot dogs."

"That's just bread," said Aaron. "It's not a hot dog unless the meat's in it." Joey just shrugged and went on eating.

"Aaron's right," said Dad. "And here's something else to remember—just as a hot dog roll isn't a hot dog without the meat, a person isn't a Christian without Christ. He's like that empty roll. Take your friend Kendall, for instance. I'm glad he's such a nice young man, Aaron, but none of the things you mentioned make him a Christian. You need to find out if he believes in Jesus. Only if he's done that is he a Christian."

Aaron nodded. "Thanks for reminding me, Dad. I'll find out," he promised. "If he isn't already a Christian, maybe he'd like to become one." *HWM*

HOW ABOUT YOU?

Have you asked Jesus Christ to come into your life? You may be a very nice person—but a very nice person without Jesus is not a Christian. If you want to find out more, ask a trusted friend or adult.

MEMORIZE:

"I myself no longer live, but Christ lives in me. So I live my life in this earthly body by trusting in the Son of God, who loved me and gave himself for me." Galatians 2:20

A Christian Has Jesus

A Cushion for Chaos

(Read Luke 6:27-36)

Ding, Dong! The doorbell had been ringing for several minutes, but Matt and his family were so busy arguing that they hadn't even heard it. Loud, angry words were flying back and forth when Matt finally noticed his friend Rob tapping on the living room window. Embarrassed, he quickly went outside and closed the door behind him. "I'm sorry, Rob," he said. "I forgot you were coming over. You see, I was kind of tied up in a—a family discussion." He paused when he saw Rob looking at him sympathetically. "Well," continued Matt, "actually, it was a fight."

"Yes, I heard," said Rob softly. "I didn't mean to eavesdrop, but I couldn't help overhearing."

Matt sighed. "I don't know why we can't get along," he said. "We're all Christians, even though none of us act like it most of the time. I don't want to argue with my parents and my brother. And I don't think they like the fighting, either. But what can I do about it?"

Just then Matt and Rob heard the squeal of brakes and a crash. They rushed out to the street and saw that a car had banged into the back of a truck at a traffic light. The drivers looked the cars over carefully. "I'm sorry I ran into you," said one of them.

The other smiled and said, "I don't see any damage. My rubber bumper guards cushioned the impact."

As Matt and Rob walked back toward Matt's house, Rob said thoughtfully, "That accident made me think of something. The bumper guards were like a cushion, so no damage was done. Maybe you need to be like a cushion whenever someone is grumpy with you. The Bible says, 'A gentle answer turns away wrath.' Maybe if you answer softly and kindly it will help the situation in your house."

"I'll try it," Matt decided. *SLK*

HOW ABOUT YOU?

When someone is angry with you, do you reply sharply? Or do you keep your temper and try to answer quietly and patiently? The way you respond to anger can make a real difference in your life.

Cushion Anger with Kindness

MEMORIZE:
"A gentle answer turns away wrath, but harsh words stir up anger."
Proverbs 15:1

Swimming in Disobedience

(Read Exodus 20:1-17)

This would be perfect if the afternoons weren't so hot, thought Mike, who was spending some time with his grandparents in Florida. *Even the heat wouldn't be so bad if I could go swimming in the lake.* But Grandpa had said it was unsafe for swimming because there had been problems with alligators recently. So while his grandparents napped after lunch each day, Mike sat in the backyard looking longingly at the lake.

One afternoon it got just too hot to bear! *I haven't seen any dumb old 'gator,* Mike thought. *I'm going to wade a little.* And he did. The next afternoon, he jumped right in, but he made sure he was dry again before his grandparents awoke. This continued throughout the week.

On Friday, Mike took his usual dip in the lake. He was having a wonderful time when he noticed two eyes coming toward him. "An alligator!" he gasped. He swam with all his might, but the alligator kept getting closer and closer! "He-e-elp!" he wailed. And then help came! Grandpa, waking up early, had seen what was happening. He sped out to Mike in a boat and was able to rescue him.

It was a very frightened boy who confessed that he had been disobedient all week. "You were very foolish," Grandpa told him sternly. After a moment, he added, "The lake seemed peaceful, quiet, and beautiful, so you ignored the danger and did something you knew was wrong, didn't you? Satan often tempts us by making sin look fun. He can make sin look so inviting it actually seems right. I hope you'll remember this experience whenever you're tempted to sin." *CH*

HOW ABOUT YOU?

Do you think that if something feels right, it can't be wrong? That's a popular theme in the stories and songs of the world today, but it's not what the Bible teaches. God has given definite standards of right and wrong. No matter how right and good something may feel to you, if it violates God's principles, it is sin. Don't be fooled by the attractive appearance of sin.

MEMORIZE:
"Even Satan can disguise himself as an angel of light." 2 Corinthians 11:14

Don't Let Satan Fool You

Never Give Up

(Read Galatians 6:7-10)

The red wagon made a loud, rattling noise as it bumped along the sidewalk. Jim and Bill were getting very discouraged. All morning they had trudged from house to house, trying to sell the vegetables they had grown—but it seemed as though folks either had vegetables from the store or had a garden of their own.

Then Bill and Jim came to Mrs. Brown's house. They had attended a Bible club in her backyard earlier in the summer. "Do you want to buy some vegetables?" asked Bill.

"Well, those vegetables look nice, but . . ." A look of disappointment crossed the boys' faces. "I'll take one tomato," continued Mrs. Brown. "Have you been selling long?" she asked as Jim handed her a big red tomato.

"Yes," answered Bill, "and you're our first buyer."

"I hope you don't give up," said Mrs. Brown. "Those are nice looking vegetables, and I'm sure you'll find customers who want them."

Bill and Jim felt happier as they went on their way. Soon they did make more sales, and by the end of the afternoon, they had sold almost everything in the wagon.

Twice a week the boys went out selling, and when summer ended, they had a nice little sum of money. "Wow!" exclaimed Bill. "I'm glad we didn't quit when we weren't selling anything at first."

The next time the boys saw Mrs. Brown, they told her about the money they had made. "I'm glad you've learned to keep on trying even when you're discouraged," said Mrs. Brown. "We need to do the same thing when we work for God. Remember the stories we had in Bible club about the apostle Paul?"

Bill and Jim nodded, and Mrs. Brown continued. "Paul had all sorts of discouragement and disappointments when he was telling others about Jesus. Many people would have given up, but not Paul. He just kept on preaching. Many people learned of God's love because Paul didn't give up." *CEY*

HOW ABOUT YOU?

Do you get discouraged even though you are a Christian? No one succeeds unless they keep trying. We all face times of discouragement, but we should not give up. Ask God to help you keep on living for him even when you feel like giving up.

Don't Be Discouraged

MEMORIZE:
"So don't get tired of doing what is good." Galatians 6:9

July
8

Strings Attached

(Read Genesis 3:1-6)

"Come here, little crab. I have something you'll like. Come on," Phillip coaxed softly. "A little closer now. That's right. Keep coming. Another nibble. Closer. Closer."

There was a sudden splash in the water. "Gotcha," shouted Grandpa. Holding up the dip net, he exclaimed, "This one is huge, Phillip! Good job! OK . . . toss that chicken wing back in and let's do it again."

Phillip always had a great time when he visited his grandparents in Florida. The thing he enjoyed most was catching crabs for their seafood cookout. When they went crabbing, they didn't have to bother with hooks, sinkers, or even poles. All Phillip had to do was tie a piece of raw chicken on a long string and then toss the chicken into the shallow waters of the river. When he felt the tug on his string, he very slowly pulled the bait toward him, inch by inch. The crab, nibbling the chicken, would follow it right up to the edge of the water. Then in one swift motion, Grandpa would scoop the crab into the net.

"Here's another one, Grandpa. Get ready!" Phillip warned. He laughed as Grandpa scooped it up. "Crabs must really be dumb to get caught like this," said Phillip.

Grandpa smiled. "Well, I'm not sure how intelligent crabs are," he said, "but it occurs to me that even though we are more intelligent than crabs, we often get caught—just like these crabs did today."

"Caught?" Phillip looked up at Grandpa. "How do we get caught?"

"Satan tosses out all kinds of things that look great to us—popularity, lots of money, good times," explained Grandpa. "Just like you coax the crabs, Satan says to us, 'I have something you will like. Closer. Keep coming closer.' If we're not careful, Phillip, we get caught up into sin. What seemed harmless at first ends in disaster."

Phillip grinned sheepishly, "I guess you might say we could end up in hot water, just like these crabs will tonight. Right, Grandpa?"

"That's right," agreed Grandpa. "We must avoid Satan's temptations. There are always strings attached." *LGR*

HOW ABOUT YOU?

Do you think you can sample sin but not get caught? Do you try to see how much you can enjoy and get away with, without getting swept away completely? If you avoid the first temptations, you can avoid getting involved in sins that can quickly pull you into more serious trouble.

MEMORIZE:

"An evil man is held captive by his own sins; they are ropes that catch and hold him." Proverbs 5:22

Avoid Temptation

Gone Fishin' (Part 1)

(Read Matthew 4:18-22)

Todd quickly scribbled a note for his mother—"Gone fishin', Todd." That done, he grabbed his pole and bait and hurried out the door. As Todd reached the river, he saw a boy sitting in his favorite fishing spot. "Catchin' anything?" he asked.

The boy looked up, shrugged his shoulders and mumbled, "Naw, this isn't a very good spot."

Todd couldn't believe his ears. This was the best spot on the whole river! "Well, you gotta be patient when you're fishin'," he reminded the boy.

"Patient! I've been sitting here all morning without any bites," the boy complained, giving his pole such a jerk that his line popped completely out of the water.

"How often do you keep popping your line out of the water like that?" Todd asked.

"Oh, every few minutes—just to see if a fish has eaten the worm yet," the boy replied.

"You fish much?" asked Todd, sure that he already knew the answer.

"My first time," the boy answered without looking up.

"What's your name?" Todd asked.

"Pete Fischer," came the reply.

Todd sat down. "Pete," he said, "we've gotta talk."

At dinner that night, Todd told his family about Pete. "We sure had fun! He's learnin' to fish so he can live up to his name."

"That's funny," Dad said, smiling. "It reminds me of the Peter in the Bible. He was a fisherman too, you know. And one day Jesus came to Peter and said, 'Follow me, and I will make you fishers of men.' Todd, you have a perfect opportunity to 'fish' for Pete." *LH*

HOW ABOUT YOU?

Do you go fishing? You should if you're following Jesus. This kind of fishing doesn't even require handling wiggly worms or slippery fish! It requires a smile, some time, perhaps an invitation to play with you. It requires prayer and knowledge of God's Word. And it's more exciting than fishing for ordinary fish.

Be a Fisher of Men

MEMORIZE:
"Come, be my disciples, and I will show you how to fish for people!"
Matthew 4:19

Gone Fishin' (Part 2)

(Read James 5:7-8)

Todd lay in bed, thinking of what his dad had said about being a fisher of men. He knew that if he was going to use God's Word he would need to have much of it in his heart and mind, memorized and understood. He worked hard the following weeks at learning Bible verses so he would be ready to talk with his new friend, Pete.

Often he asked Pete to go to church or to a church party, but Pete always refused. Pete never seemed interested when Todd tried to talk about Jesus either. Todd was frustrated. "I give up, Dad," he said. "Pete doesn't want to come to church, and he's getting sick of me asking all the time. I'm gonna quit!"

"Todd," Dad reminded him, "you have to be patient when you're fishing, remember? You can't keep popping your line out of the water to see if a fish has taken the bait."

"Huh?" grunted Todd. "What are you getting at?"

"You don't have to ask Pete to go to church with you so often," said Dad. "I suggest that you first strengthen your friendship with Pete. Share with him what you enjoy at church and the fun you have at the parties. Then maybe Pete will become interested enough to come sometime."

For the next three weeks, Todd practiced what his dad had suggested. Finally, he felt the nibble he'd been waiting for. "Dad!" he shouted as he burst into the house. "Guess what happened today!"

"I found your note about going fishing, so I'd say you caught a fish," Dad said, smiling.

"Did I ever!" Todd beamed. "And his name is Pete! You were right, Dad. A good fisherman must be patient if he really wants to catch a fish." *LH*

HOW ABOUT YOU?

Are you an impatient "fisher of men"? Does it seem as though you're never going to get a bite? Don't give up. Check the bait. Are you being a genuine friend? Do you have good times together? Do you pray for your friend? Are you prepared to share God's Word? Then, if you don't get a nibble right away, be patient. The salvation of a friend is worth waiting for.

MEMORIZE:
"You, too, must be patient. And take courage, for the coming of the Lord is near." James 5:8

Witness with Patience

Turn and Run

(Read Psalm 1:1-6)

Shari watched as Jamie took a cigarette out of the pack in his hand. He placed it on the picnic table along with a match. Other kids in the neighborhood had tried smoking that afternoon, but Shari had refused to join them. "You're just scared to try it," Jamie teased.

"I'm not scared," she retorted unconvincingly. "I just think it's dumb to smoke."

But her answer didn't satisfy Jamie. "I'll leave one right here," he said. "Maybe you'll want to try it when nobody's looking."

Shari watched Jamie go into his house next door, and then she looked again at the cigarette on the table. If she could just show him a partly smoked cigarette, maybe he'd quit bugging her about it. She picked it up and rolled it around in her fingers. Suddenly there was a strong urge to take just one small puff. Just then her mother came out of the back door. "Shari, what are you doing out here?"

"Nothing," Shari replied, slipping the cigarette and match into her pocket. Quickly she skipped back to the house and walked briskly into the bathroom. Nervously she pulled the cigarette out of her pocket, lit it, and took a short puff. Ugh! It was awful! Just as quickly, she put it out. Then she heard the back door open and close.

"Shari?" It was her mother's voice. "Are you smoking?"

Mother was waiting, a hurt look in her eyes. Suddenly Shari broke into tears. She explained how Jamie had tempted her and teased her until she gave in.

Shari's mother shook her head. "No, honey, Jamie's teasing isn't why you gave in. You gave in because you didn't run from temptation. You looked at the cigarette, maybe even took it in your fingers to see how it would feel, and finally gave in and smoked it. If you had turned and left it, you would have been better off. Temptations will come. When they do, run away from them." *RIJ*

HOW ABOUT YOU?

Do your friends sometimes coax you to go along to see a dirty movie? Smoke? Look at indecent pictures? When these or other sins tempt you, don't stand around and think about them. Turn and run. Ask Jesus to help you. He will.

Run When Tempted

Guard Duty

(Read Proverbs 4:20-27)

"Mom said you forgot your lunch this morning, so Amber and I brought it for you," said Noah as he handed his dad a paper bag. Dad was a gate guard at one of the factories in town.

"Are you starving?" asked Amber. "We're late."

"I sure am," declared Dad as he took the lunch. "Thanks for bringing this."

Amber and Noah watched as their dad carefully eyed the workers going back into the factory. They saw one man carrying a water jug, but Dad didn't allow him to take it in. When a woman came along carrying several packages of cookies, Dad made her return them to her car. Amber and Noah wondered why.

"Why did you stop that man from bringing his water jug into the factory?" Noah wanted to know.

"Because he didn't have water in the jug," Dad replied. "He had beer. Drinking on the job causes accidents."

"But what's wrong with cookies?" Amber asked.

"She intended to sell them on the job—on company time," answered Dad. "That's against the rules. People often think a guard is mean because he stops certain items from entering the factory, but it's necessary for everyone's safety."

"Yeah, Dad." Noah was proud of the way his father handled his job. "I'm going to be a guard, too, when I'm out of school," added Noah.

Dad smiled. "Why wait? You and Amber can be guards right now," he said.

"Dad!" protested Amber. "I don't even want to be a guard! Besides, you have to be older than us to do that."

Dad shook his head. "Well, I wasn't thinking of a guard at a factory," he said. "I was just thinking that all of us—kids included—need to guard our heart. As Christians, we need to keep bad attitudes and actions out of our life, or they'll hurt our testimony for Christ." He grinned at the kids. "In other words," he added, "I shouldn't be the only one in this family on guard duty every day." *JLH*

HOW ABOUT YOU?

Are you guarding your heart to keep out bad thoughts? Are you refusing to allow things such as dirty pictures, swearing, or bad television shows to enter your life and influence your thinking? Guard your life from things that you know are wrong.

MEMORIZE:

"Above all else, guard your heart,
for it affects everything you do."
Proverbs 4:23

Guard Your Heart

The Dirty Mouth

(Read Psalm 34:11-14)

Daryl dropped his bat on the back porch and flung his mitt against the wall. He went to find his mother. "That Ryan!" he complained. "I wish he'd keep his dirty mouth shut."

Mother shoved the last articles from the hamper into the washer. "Has he been swearing again?" she asked.

Daryl nodded, and his frown deepened. "You know, Mom, nobody likes him! Seems like he'd get the message and start talking decently."

"That would be nice," said Mother. Then she pointed at Daryl's grass-stained, dirt-streaked jeans. "Just look at those pants! They were clean an hour or so ago. Good thing they're your old ones."

Daryl nodded. "We played ball on Nick's lot, and I slid in home," he explained. He grinned at her slyly. "Besides, what are mothers for anyway?"

Mother laughed and rumpled his hair. "You better be thankful for mothers," she said. "It will take a lot of soap and elbow grease to get that dirt out." After a moment, she added, "Soap and water is the remedy for your dirty jeans, but did you know that there's a remedy for Ryan's 'dirty' mouth, too?"

Daryl looked surprised. "What do you mean?" he asked.

"Ryan needs Jesus to help him stop swearing," said Mother. "Have you ever invited him to Sunday school?"

"No," admitted Daryl. He was a little embarrassed.

Just then the doorbell rang. Looking out the window, they could see a boy standing on the front steps. "Well, there's your chance," suggested Mother.

Daryl hesitated. Then he grinned. "All right!" he agreed as he ran to let Ryan in. *RG*

HOW ABOUT YOU?

Do you know someone who has a "dirty mouth"—someone who swears or uses bad language? He needs Jesus to help him stop doing that. Perhaps you can be an influence in bringing him to Jesus. What about your own language?

Use Clean Language

MEMORIZE:
"But now is the time to get rid of anger, rage, malicious behavior, slander, and dirty language."
Colossians 3:8

July

14

A Sad Story

(Read Luke 22:54-62)

David's Sunday school teacher was Bob Carson, a young man who had recently graduated from college. His class of sixth-grade boys liked to call him "Mr. Bob," and he enjoyed teaching them. He often spent his Saturdays taking them fishing, miniature golfing, or doing some other activity. David constantly talked about the neat things Mr. Bob did. Through his teaching, David had grown spiritually, and his parents were thankful for such a good teacher.

One Sunday another man taught the class. Where was Mr. Bob? No one seemed to know.

That afternoon the pastor called David's father. David could tell it was about something serious because of the tone of his father's voice. When he got off the phone, Dad put his hand on David's shoulder. "Son, I have very sad news for you. Mr. Bob wasn't in class today because he was arrested for drunk driving last night."

At first David refused to believe the news, but he finally realized it must be true. "How could he do such a thing?" he exclaimed angrily.

"David, we all have sinful natures and problems," Dad replied. "Because we are human, we sometimes let people down. That's why the Bible tells us to put our greatest confidence and trust in God rather than in another person. People will disappoint us. God won't. You can be thankful for the help Mr. Bob has given you. Now we need to help him by praying that he will ask the Lord to help him overcome this very serious problem." *LMW*

HOW ABOUT YOU?

Has a Sunday school teacher, a pastor, or perhaps a parent let you down by doing something that was seriously wrong? Because people are human they still sin even after they become Christians. It's good that we can learn about God through other Christians, but our greatest hope and confidence needs to be in God, for he never sins. And he will never let us down.

MEMORIZE:
"It is better to trust the Lord than to put confidence in people." Psalm 118:8

Put Confidence in God

Lifesaving

(Read 2 Timothy 1:6-11)

Paula shot from her chair and raced out to the pool. Her younger brother had just run in and reported that a small neighbor boy had fallen into the water. "Bryan can't swim," Leo had gasped, "and neither can I."

Without a thought for herself, Paula dove into the pool. Bryan was thrashing around, trying in vain to stay above the water. His life was in Paula's hands. She knew she had to rescue Bryan or he would probably drown.

By the time Mother ran out, Paula and Bryan were lying on the cement, exhausted. Because of her quick action, he had swallowed only a little water and would be fine.

That evening they were still quite excited about what had happened, but Paula was rather quiet. "Were you scared?" Leo asked for at least the sixth time.

Paula shook her head. "I took that lifesaving course, so I knew what to do," she said. She looked thoughtfully at her parents. "Last Sunday my teacher said that people are 'drowning in sin,' and that Christians know how they can be saved. I've been thinking about that. I didn't worry about whether Bryan would like how I helped him. If I had stopped to think about it, he might have died. But so often I don't tell my friends about Jesus because I'm afraid they won't like me to do that. I've got to start helping them, too—before it's too late." *VLR*

HOW ABOUT YOU?

If you could save someone from drowning, would you do it? Of course you would. How about if you could tell someone how to be saved from sin? Pray and ask God who you can talk to this week.

MEMORIZE:

"Therefore, go and make disciples of all the nations, baptizing them in the name of the Father and the Son and the Holy Spirit." Matthew 28:19

Tell Someone about Jesus

Do You Know Him? (Part 1)

(Read Matthew 28:18-20)

"Hey, Mario, wait up," Jeff called to the new boy in school. "I hear you just moved here from Cal Ripken's home town. Do you know him?"

"Yeah, I know Cal," said Mario, happy to meet a new friend who was interested in baseball. He was eager to share all he knew. "I have all Cal's baseball cards," Mario told Jeff. "I saw him play in Baltimore, and he even autographed a ball for me. I have all his books, too. He taught me all I know about baseball."

Jeff and Mario became close friends. If they weren't playing ball, they were talking ball and making plans to see Cal Ripken play. Mario always spoke proudly of his friendship with Cal. "My mom says I listen to him better than I do to her," he said.

When plans were completed for Jeff and Mario to see a game in which Cal Ripken would play, Jeff could hardly contain himself. "Guess what, Mr. Jones," he said to his Sunday school teacher one day. "I'm going to meet Cal Ripken, the baseball champion! My friend Mario knows Cal. We've got tickets to see him play, and I'll get Mario to introduce me to him. Just think, I'll get to meet him!"

"Really?" exclaimed Mr. Jones. "That's great! Cal's a famous person. I'll want to hear all about it." *JLH*

HOW ABOUT YOU?

Are you like Mario—eager to tell your friends about any important person you meet? Do you tell them about Jesus? If you know him, you should be eager to introduce others to him, too.

MEMORIZE:
"But the believers who had fled Jerusalem went everywhere preaching the Good News about Jesus." Acts 8:4

Share Jesus

Do You Know Him? (Part 2)

(Read Matthew 7:21-27)

Jeff and Mario joined the 32,000 other fans in the stadium to see Cal Ripken play in a big league game. In the last inning, with the score tied, Cal was at bat. "Strike!" called the umpire as the first two pitches came across the plate.

Jeff and Mario could hardly stand the suspense. "Come on, Cal! You can do it," shouted Mario as the next pitch came.

"He's got it! Look at that ball go!" shouted Jeff. "They won! Hurrah for Cal!" The boys stood with the crowd as Cal rounded the bases and then was carried off the field on the shoulders of his teammates. "Let's go to the locker room," said Jeff. "I want to meet him! C'mon, Mario!"

"Naw," said Mario. "He'll be too busy." He headed in the other direction.

"Oh, come on," insisted Jeff. "I've been waiting for this." He grabbed Mario's arm.

Mario pulled away. "We can't do that, Jeff," he said.

"Why not?" asked Jeff. "You know Cal. You can get us in, can't you?"

"Aw, I don't know him that well," replied Mario, and suddenly Jeff knew that Mario didn't really know Cal Ripken at all—he just knew about him.

"Mario sure had me fooled," said Jeff as he told his Sunday school teacher about the game. "How could he say he knew Cal when he really didn't?"

"People often say they know a person when they just know about him," said Mr. Jones.

"They do?" asked Jeff. "I would never do that!"

"Many people read about Jesus' miracles and hear about his death on the cross. They may even go to church," said Mr. Jones. "They know about Jesus and claim to know him, yet they've never invited him to be their Savior. They don't know him personally." He paused and looked intently at Jeff. "I wonder, Jeff, do you only know about Jesus, or do you know him personally as your Savior?"

Jeff didn't answer for a moment. Finally he said, "I guess I've been just as silly as Mario. I need to know Jesus personally." *JLH*

HOW ABOUT YOU?

Is Jesus your personal friend and Savior, or is he just someone you know about? He wants to be your very best friend. Ask him to come into your life. Get to know him better by reading his Word, and talk to him each day as you'd talk to any other friend.

You Can Know Jesus

MEMORIZE:
"There are 'friends' who destroy each other, but a real friend sticks closer than a brother." Proverbs 18:24

July
18

Joel's Machine

(Read 1 Corinthians 6:19-20)

"It's a great machine, huh, Dad?" Joel watched admiringly as his father polished the hood of their new car. It stood glistening in the sunshine, the dark red interior contrasting sharply with the gleaming white paint.

"Yes, Joel, it sure is," agreed Dad, putting the cleaning rags away. He walked into the garage and returned with a large hammer. He held it out to his son. "Here. Slam this into the windshield!" he urged. "Just for the fun of it."

"Dad!" Joel gasped in astonishment. He put his hands behind him and backed up a step or two. "You've gotta be kidding! What would I do that for?"

"I'm glad you have better sense than to do that," said Dad with a smile. "Let's talk a minute." He set the hammer down and put his arm around the boy's shoulders. "When you were born, God gave you a beautiful, precision-built 'machine'—your body," said Dad. "He asks that you treat it well. That's not expecting too much, is it?" Joel shook his head, smiling at the comparison, and Dad continued. "You've seen the TV ads showing young men and women who have drug problems, haven't you?"

Joel nodded. "Yes, Dad, I've seen them," he said.

"Well, Son," continued Dad, "please remember that there may come a time when some friend of yours will suggest that you try it just once, 'just for kicks,' or maybe to prove you're not 'chicken.' But just as it would be crazy for you to slam that hammer into our new car—" Dad nodded toward the driveway—"it would be even crazier to deliberately do something to hurt the wonderful 'machine' of your body."

Joel nodded. "You can trust me to keep my 'machine' in good shape," he said. Then he added, "And thanks for talking about this. I'll remember." *PIK*

HOW ABOUT YOU?
Have you been asked by friends to do something you know is wrong? It may happen, and if it does, ask God to help you "just say no."

MEMORIZE:
"My child, if sinners entice you, turn your back on them!" Proverbs 1:10

Keep Your Body Pure

Attractive Bait

(Read 1 Peter 5:8)

"Uncle John, my fishing line is pulling!" shouted Ron.

His uncle laughed. "That's because there's a fish on the end. Start reeling him in."

Soon the little sunfish was lying on the sand, but it was too small to keep. Reluctantly Ron put it back into the water. It flipped its tail, and in a moment it had disappeared.

"Whoa!" said Uncle John as Ron tossed his line back into the lake. "Aren't you forgetting something?" Ron looked at him with a question in his eyes. "The bait," Uncle John explained.

Ron laughed. "Oh, yeah," he said pulling his line back in. "I guess no fish would be dumb enough to bite on the bare hook, would he? I'll disguise it and make it look good with this juicy worm. The fish won't know there's any danger, and he'll open his big mouth and swallow the hook. Then I'll have him!" With a grin he returned the line to the water once more.

"This reminds me of the way Satan works," Uncle John mused.

Ron was curious. "What do you mean?"

"Well, Satan tries to make sin look attractive," explained Uncle John. "Sometimes we're uneasy about something, or maybe we've been warned that it's wrong. Yet it looks good. Or it feels good. Or our friends are doing it, and we're tempted to try it, too. Satan is a master at disguising sin. He knows how to make bad things look good to us. So when you're tempted by a questionable activity, remember the fish. He wouldn't have gotten caught if he had stayed away from the hook." *PR*

HOW ABOUT YOU?

Does Satan use an interesting story on TV to get you accustomed to hearing bad language so that it doesn't bother you anymore? Does he catch your attention with a "good" movie so that you become careless about what you watch? Does he make playing video games so much fun that you do it even if you know you're spending too much money? What other methods does he use? Be careful. Ask God daily to help you stay away from the attractive bait Satan uses.

MEMORIZE:

"Put on all of God's armor so that you will be able to stand firm against all strategies and tricks of the Devil."
Ephesians 6:11

Avoid Satan's Bait

Home for Supper

(Read John 14:1-6)

Brandon wandered into his room. He didn't feel like playing. A little red truck caught his eye, and he picked it up. It had been Joey's favorite. *Joey*. Brandon closed his eyes. Pictures of his little brother flashed through his mind. There was the day Mom and Dad and Joey had gone to see a doctor. The time Mom had put her arms around him and explained that Joey had a very serious illness. The days Joey had to spend in the hospital for treatments. Joey, growing thinner and more pale. Then came the day Joey went to the hospital and never returned. And just yesterday . . . his funeral, followed by a graveside service.

"Brandon," called Dad, "want to come help me weed the garden?"

Dad and Brandon worked among the carrots in silence for a while. Then, his voice quavering, Brandon said, "Dad, I miss Joey so much. Sometimes I don't know how I can stand it!"

"We all miss him, Son. But maybe I can give you a word picture that helps me," said Dad. He reached over to put an arm around Brandon's shoulder. "Remember last year when we grew that big patch of potatoes? One afternoon, we all worked hard to dig them up and get them sacked before winter, remember?" Brandon nodded. "When Mom went in to fix supper, you and Joey and I stayed out to finish. We were cold, tired, and hungry. But as we looked at the house, we could see the warm lights shining out into the gathering darkness. And we thought of the good hot meal Mom would have ready for us when our work was done." Brandon nodded again. "That's kind of the way I feel right now," said Dad. "We miss Joey, and it hurts so much. But we know he's safe in our heavenly home. God has a job left for us here. But when it's done, we'll all be back together."

A warm feeling stole over Brandon. "OK, Dad," he said. "We'll finish our work for God and then go home for supper!" *CAP*

HOW ABOUT YOU?

Do you know for sure that you'll have a home in heaven when your life on earth is over? You can know! Jesus died to make that possible. Trust him for salvation today! Then you can also look forward to some day joining your loved ones who have already gone to be with Jesus.

MEMORIZE:

"There are many rooms in my Father's home, and I am going to prepare a place for you." John 14:2

Heaven Is "Home"

A Time to Forget

(Read Ecclesiastes 3:1-8)

"Mom, guess what I just heard about our new neighbors. The dad just got out of prison!" Before Mother could reply, Mark rushed on. "He stole a whole lot of money from his employer! I wonder if we should tell Mr. Wilson that he has a thief working for him."

"I'm sure Mr. Wilson knows all about Mr. Smith," Mother replied calmly.

Mark's eyes snapped. "I'm going to be more careful about locking up my bicycle. I told the other guys to watch theirs, too."

"Mark, you should not be talking about Mr. Smith to others. You don't really know anything about it," scolded Mother. "Now, are you going to play at Nathan's?"

"Yeah." Mark nodded. Then he ran down the hall to his big brother's room. As Mother followed, she heard him ask, "Brad, can I take your telescope over to Nathan's?"

"No, I can't trust you," snapped Brad. "You lost my calculator last month."

"But I paid for it," Mark reminded him.

"Yeah," admitted Brad, "but if you lose my telescope or break it, it'll take you months to pay for it."

"But, Brad," wailed Mark, "it's not fair to hold that one mistake against me forever."

Mother spoke quickly. "Neither is it fair to hold Mr. Smith's mistake against him," she said. "He has paid for it, and he has let everyone know that he's sorry about it. Jesus said if we want mercy, we must be merciful. If we want to be forgiven, we must be forgiving."

"Oops!" Brad grinned at Mark. "He also said that we should do unto others like we want them to do to us, so I guess I'll let you borrow my telescope." *BJW*

HOW ABOUT YOU?

When Jesus forgives us for our sins, he forgets them. Is there something about someone that you need to forget? Then do it. How? Stop talking about it and soon you will forget it, too.

MEMORIZE:

"I—yes, I alone—am the one who blots out your sins for my own sake and will never think of them again."

Isaiah 43:25

Forgive Others' Mistakes

22

Healing Tears

(Read John 11:32-36)

"Ooohhh!!" Luis screamed as his bike flipped through the air. A searing pain ripped through his palms and knees. Angrily, he brushed away his tears. "I will not cry!" he said aloud. Picking up his bike, he hobbled home.

Luis's hands and knees ached almost as much as his heart did. Ever since Grandpa had died two weeks ago, tears had been hiding right behind his eyelids.

Luis limped into the kitchen. "Oh, you're hurt!" Mother exclaimed. "Come into the bathroom and let me take care of you." Luis obediently followed her. Gently, she washed away the dirt and poured disinfectant over the wounds. Luis gritted his teeth as the medicine bubbled and fizzed. "I know it stings a bit," Mother sympathized, "but it's cleansing the wounds so they can heal."

Luis took a deep gulp of air and sniffed. Mother put her arm around his shoulders and drew him to her. Luis stiffened and drew away. *I will not cry,* he said to himself. *Eleven-year-old boys do not cry.*

Mother seemed to know what he was thinking. "Honey," she said, "it's OK to cry when you hurt." Luis shook his head angrily. "But it is," Mother insisted. "Don't you know that your Daddy cried when Grandpa died?"

Luis looked startled. "I didn't think men cried," he stammered.

"But they do," Mother assured him. "Even Jesus cried. Tears are like the disinfectant I put on your wounds. Tears help wash our grief and speed the healing process." Mother put her hands on his shoulders. "Look at me, Son," she ordered softly. "God knows we hurt sometimes," she said. "He gave us tears to help us. If you'd let yourself cry, your broken heart would heal much faster."

Then Mother pulled him into her arms. Luis's shoulders heaved. As the tears he had been fighting rolled down his cheeks, he relaxed. It was such a relief to cry. Already he felt better. *BJW*

HOW ABOUT YOU?

God gave us laughter and tears. Both are like medicine that cleanses our hurts. Even men and boys can cry. Jesus did. When you need to cry, don't try to be big and tough. Let the tears flow and the hurt heal.

MEMORIZE:

"Weeping may go on all night, but joy comes with the morning." Psalm 30:5

Tears Heal Our Hurts

How to Beat Boredom

(Read Matthew 25:34-36, 40-45)

Matt sat idly on the porch swing. When Jerry came riding by on his bicycle at top speed, Matt almost didn't see him. "Hey, Jerry," he called to his friend's back, "where's the fire?"

Jerry slammed on his brakes. "No fire," he responded. "I've just got a lot to do today."

"Boy, I don't," Matt grumbled. "I'm so bored. There's nothing to do around here."

"Nothing to do?" echoed Jerry. "I'm really busy! I'm on my way to mow Gramp Norton's lawn. Want to help me?"

"Sure," Matt answered. "How much will we get paid?"

"Nothing." Jerry grinned. "I'm doing it kind of as an offering to the Lord."

"For the Lord?" Matt slapped his forehead. "You're mowing a lawn for the Lord? Does Gramps have a riding mower or something?"

Jerry shook his head. "No, I'm doing it because it's fun to do things for other people. And besides, Jesus said when I do something for others, I'm doing it for him. I've decided to spend this summer working for Jesus."

Matt raised his eyebrows and moaned. But because he didn't have anything else to do, he went with Jerry. He also went with him the next day—and the next day, too—as Jerry "worked for the Lord."

"Say, this is fun," Matt told Jerry as they cleaned his dad's garage without having been asked to do so.

"My mom says we get bored because we think about ourselves too much," Jerry told Matt. "She says it's less likely to happen when we're busy helping others."

"Well, I sure haven't been bored the last few days," Matt said, grinning. "Maybe this summer won't be so dull after all." *BJW*

HOW ABOUT YOU?

Is "I'm bored" your theme song? Could that be because you're thinking too much about yourself? There are many things you can do to keep busy and to help others. Ask the Lord to show you some way you can help another person each day. Then do it. When you do something for someone else, you are doing it for Jesus, too.

MEMORIZE:

"I assure you, when you did it to one of the least of these my brothers and sisters, you were doing it to me!"
Matthew 25:40

Serve One Another

Just the Shell

(Read 2 Corinthians 5:1-2, 6-8)

David always liked it when the family went to the beach. He had been able to get a good-sized collection of shells from their trips. And now here they were again, he and his father, walking up and down the sandy beach, looking for more shells. Suddenly he stopped and called, "Dad, come here! I found something, but I don't know what it is."

Dad soon joined David, who pointed at a strange-looking sea creature. At least that is what David thought it was. Dad knelt down and looked carefully at David's find. As he did so, David begged him to be careful. He didn't want his father to be bitten or snapped at by some dangerous sea animal. "This one will never bite," Dad said. "There's no life in him."

"How come?" David wanted to know.

David's father picked it up in his hands. "Because this is just a shell," he explained, turning it over and over so David could see what it looked like. "It's a lobster shell. There comes a time in the lobster's life when he squeezes out and leaves his shell."

Before David could ask any more questions, his father asked if he remembered when Grandpa Jones died. "Do you remember how I explained that Grandpa had gone to heaven?" Dad asked.

David nodded. "But I didn't understand how he could be in the casket and be in heaven, too," David replied.

"It's very much like this shell that you just found. The lobster is gone," Dad said. "This is just his shell. In the same way, when Grandpa died, he left his body and went to live with Jesus because he was a Christian."

Suddenly David seemed to understand. "Oh!" he exclaimed. "That's why Grandpa couldn't talk to us anymore. He was gone. It was just his shell that was left."

Dad smiled. "That's right," he said, "and though it made us sad because we knew we would miss him, we're glad that he's with Jesus." *RIJ*

HOW ABOUT YOU?

Do you have a Christian relative or friend who has died recently? If so, that Christian has simply left his body and has gone to be with Jesus. Your body is just the house in which you live.

MEMORIZE:

"Yes, we are fully confident, and we would rather be away from these bodies, for then we will be at home with the Lord." 2 Corinthians 5:8

Your Body Is Your Shell

The Vacation

(Read Hosea 10:12-13)

As the Jackson family traveled along, Trent and Traci seemed to quarrel constantly. It was a relief when they reached Cripple Creek.

"This is an old gold-mining town," Mom explained as she parked beside a railroad depot.

"May we ride the train?" Trent asked as they jumped from the car. Mother nodded, and soon they were seated on wooden benches in an open car behind an old steam engine. The engineer served as guide. As they entered a small valley, the train came to a stop. "This is Echo Valley," the engineer told them. "Listen."

He pulled the train's whistle. *Wwwwwoooooo.* A few seconds later they heard a faint reply. *Wwwwwoooooo.* Traci laughed. "Let me try." She cupped her hands around her mouth and called loudly, "Hello!"

"Hello," came the faint reply.

"My turn," said Trent. "Good-byeee."

"Good-byeee," the echo repeated.

Later the tired and hungry family piled into the car. "Let's go to the motel and clean up before we eat dinner," Mother suggested.

"But I'm hungry now," whined Traci.

"Big baby," Trent mocked.

"Big baby yourself!" responded Traci.

"Listen to the echoes," Mother said, grimacing.

"Echoes? I don't hear any," Traci argued.

"I do," Mother insisted. "I hear ugly, hateful words echoing through this car. When Traci called out, 'Hello,' the echo did not reply, 'Good-bye.' When we send out kind words, we get kind words in return. When we spit out mean words, we can only expect to hear mean words in return."

"Let's make an agreement," said Traci. "For the rest of this vacation, let's agree to send out only words we would want returned to us."

"OK," Trent agreed. *BJW*

HOW ABOUT YOU?

What kind of words have you been sending out? Would you like them returned to you? Life is an "Echo Valley." The words you send out will return.

Talk Pleasantly

MEMORIZE:
"Whatever measure you use in giving—large or small—it will be used to measure what is given back to you." Luke 6:38

Like Master, like Dog

(Read Galatians 5:16-26)

"Fetch, Trevor," yelled Adam as he threw the ball across the yard. A rust-colored object streaked past him as Trevor raced after the ball. He caught it after only one bounce and returned to Adam, dropping the ball at his feet. "Great job, Trevor," said Adam as he knelt down and rubbed the dog's ears. "Ready? Here goes another one!" Adam threw the ball again and watched as Trevor dashed after it. This time he caught it in midair and proudly brought it back to Adam.

"Wow!" exclaimed Dad, who was watching from the patio. "Maybe Trevor could join a major league baseball team. How is he at batting?"

Adam chuckled at the thought of a dog joining his favorite team. "He'd make a great fielder, Dad, but he's not so good at batting or throwing," said Adam.

Dad laughed, too. "You've taught him well, Son," he said.

Adam grinned. "It was easy," he replied. "I love baseball so much that it seemed only natural that I teach Trevor to catch. After all, I don't want him to be a sissy dog who walks around with ribbons in his hair—like Mrs. Gibbons's poodle."

Dad smiled. "They say dogs begin to look and act like their master after they've been together awhile," he said. "Take Mrs. Gibbons and her dog, for example. They both go around with their hair perfectly in place, dressed up fancy, and head held high."

"Yeah!" agreed Adam. "And how about Matt Brant and his dog? Matt's a great big bully, and his dog is the meanest thing I've ever seen. He's always snarling and snapping at anything that comes near him."

"Like his master," said Dad. "I hope we resemble our Master, too."

"Our master?" asked Adam. "What do you mean?"

"I mean Jesus," replied Dad. "Christians belong to him, and we should try to be like him." *JW*

HOW ABOUT YOU?

Do your actions show the world that you belong to Jesus? Do you follow his teaching and example? If you're a Christian, your friends and neighbors should be able to see Christ in you.

MEMORIZE:

"But when the Holy Spirit controls our lives, he will produce this kind of fruit in us: love, joy, peace, patience, kindness, goodness, faithfulness, gentleness, and self-control."
Galatians 5:22-23

Live as Jesus Would

Ten Feet Tall

(Read 1 Samuel 16:4-13)

"Mother, why am I so little?" asked Todd.

"Well, Todd, you're only ten," his mother called from the kitchen. "You've got a lot of growing to do yet."

"I know, Mom, but while I'm growing, all my friends will be growing, too. They'll always be bigger than I am!" Todd grumbled. "Whenever we play baseball or football or anything, I'm the worst. I always get knocked over because I'm so small. Nobody ever wants me on their team."

"So you think that God made a mistake when he made you," observed Mother.

"Mother!" exclaimed Todd. "I never said anything like that!"

"Didn't you?" asked Mother. "You just said you didn't like being small. Isn't that the same as saying that God didn't make you right?"

"Well," said Todd thoughtfully, "I hadn't thought about it that way."

"You don't ever need to be ashamed of the way you're made, Todd. God made you just right, and he loves you just as you are. It's how you look on the inside that counts, not the outside."

Todd sighed. "I suppose you're right, Mom." Suddenly he grinned. "I'll give up trying to be big on the outside and start trying to be big on the inside."

"How will you do that?" asked Mother, puzzled.

"I can work hard in school and get good grades," explained Todd. "And I can learn Bible verses and Bible stories so I'll know more about God, too."

"Todd," said Mother, smiling, "You've already got a good start on being grown-up." *DSM*

HOW ABOUT YOU?

Have you ever wished you were taller? Or stronger? Or had brown eyes instead of green or blue? God made you the way you are because he wanted you that way. He never makes mistakes. Don't worry so much about how you look on the outside. Work on growing and being attractive on the inside.

MEMORIZE:

"The Lord doesn't make decisions the way you do! People judge by outward appearance, but the Lord looks at a person's thoughts and intentions."

1 Samuel 16:7

Inner Beauty Counts

Swaying Castle

(Read Proverbs 12:17-22)

"There!" Pete exclaimed as he finished pounding a nail. "This is the best tree house I've ever seen! I can hardly wait to sleep here. We'll be rocked to sleep, the way this tree sways. It's like being in a swaying castle!"

Jon nodded in agreement. "Let's ask if we can sleep out here tonight," he suggested.

"I know my dad won't let me," said Pete. "He wants to check it out first to be sure it's safe, and I know he won't have time to do that today."

"My dad said the same thing," Jon admitted. "Hey! I know! Let's each ask our folks for permission to spend the night with each other. They'll think we're at each other's houses, but we'll really be sleeping in the tree house."

"I don't know. . . ." Pete sounded doubtful, but with Jon's coaxing, he agreed to try it.

Their plan worked, but in the middle of the night they were awakened by a loud crack of thunder! "Hey! I'm getting wet!" yelled Pete. "It's pouring, and the roof is leaking. Come on! Let's get over to my house."

The storm had awakened Pete's parents, too, and they were very surprised when the boys stumbled into the kitchen. "Where have you been? How come you were out in this storm?" Pete's dad asked.

"We . . . ah . . . we were sleeping in the tree house, Dad," answered Pete.

"The tree house? You asked if you could stay at Jon's house overnight."

"Not really," replied Pete. "I just asked if I could spend the night with Jon."

"I see," said Dad. "You used the correct words, but what about your intentions? Since you deceived us in order to sleep in the tree house, you were really disobeying. Do you both see that you were actually lying?"

"Yes," admitted the boys together. They apologized.

"I'm thankful God protected you tonight," said Dad, "but I'm afraid the tree house will be off-limits until you show us that we can trust you again." *AGL*

HOW ABOUT YOU?

Are you guilty of giving false impressions or of telling "fibs" or "white lies"? Every form of lying is wrong. Ask God to help you be a truth teller.

MEMORIZE:

"The Lord . . . delights in those who do [keep their word]." Proverbs 12:22

All Lying Is Sin

A Lesson Learned

(Read 2 Corinthians 9:6-10)

Randy looked at the money he'd earned mowing a neighbor's lawn. "This is going toward a new bike," he decided.

"Yeah? Well . . . how about putting some of it in the church offering?" suggested his sister, Carla. "You know our department is saving up to buy a new tape recorder for our missionaries in Africa."

"Oh, Dad will give us money for the offering," said Randy. "This is *my* money, so it's going to buy that bike."

A few days later, Carla reminded Randy that their mother's birthday was coming up, so he reluctantly agreed to help pay for a box of chocolates. "Mother will love these," said Carla, as they wrapped the gift. "It's her favorite kind."

"They sure look good," said Randy, licking his lips. "I can hardly wait to taste one!"

Mother was very pleased with the gift. She opened the box, selected one, and popped it into her mouth. "Mmmm—delicious!" she said. Then she closed the box. "I think I'll save the rest for later."

Randy's eyes opened wide with surprise. "But, Mom!" he exclaimed. "Aren't you going to share?"

"Why should I?" asked Mother. "You gave the chocolates to me. So they're mine—right?"

"Well, yes," said Randy, disappointed.

"Randy, I'm just doing with my chocolates what you are doing with your money." Randy looked at his mother in surprise as she continued. "I heard what you told Carla the other day, about not wanting to give God part of the money you earned," she told him. "But we all need to remember that everything we have is really from God. If we're truly grateful for all the good things he gives us, we'll be glad to give some back to him."

"Oh—I see," said Randy.

"Now—how about a chocolate?" said his mother, smiling. *SLK*

HOW ABOUT YOU?

Do you remember that everything you have comes from God in the first place? Are you willing to give back to him your money, time—or whatever he asks of you?

Give Freely to God

July
30

Midflight Refueling

(Read Psalm 119:33-40)

"Do we have to have family devotions tonight?" asked Kapeel after supper. "The guys are waiting for me to play ball. Besides, we just went to church yesterday."

Dad looked at Kapeel thoughtfully. "True, we did," he said, "but reading or studying the Bible, either in family or personal devotions, is a little like having midflight refueling."

"Having what?" asked Kapeel.

"When I flew with the Air National Guard, our fighter planes got thoroughly checked over and fueled up at the airfield, but they were often refueled in the air, too," explained Dad. "We'd be 20,000 feet up, and fighter jets would maneuver just 25 feet below us. The operator aboard the tanker would carefully lower the boom from the underside of the plane and then position it to connect with the jet while we were flying at speeds of 400 to 500 miles per hour."

"Wow!" Kapeel's mouth dropped open in amazement.

"Refueling the planes in midflight kept them going," said Dad, "and I think Christians need to refuel in midflight, too. We get a checkup and get refueled on Sunday as we hear God's Word preached and explained, but that's not enough. So we have devotions—even if we have been to church recently. God made us to need time with him, and he wants our fellowship."

"Well, OK. I guess I need to be refueled spiritually. But . . . do you think we could get this refueling done before it gets too dark to play ball?" Kapeel asked with a grin on his face. *LJR*

HOW ABOUT YOU?

Have you been getting midflight refueling? Does your interest in being a Christian seem to run down by the end of the week? Take time each day to "refuel" your spiritual strength by reading your Bible. Ask God to help you practice the things he teaches you in his Word.

MEMORIZE:

"Your commandments give me understanding; no wonder I hate every false way of life."
Psalm 119:104

Refuel Through Bible Reading

Get the Facts

(Read Ephesians 4:14-15)

"You may go to Bill's house," said Mother one Saturday, "but first I want you to wait for the delivery truck from the store. Dad and I have to go out this afternoon, so you'll have to be here to pay the delivery man."

"Oh, OK," grumbled Jim. But as time dragged on, there was no sign of the delivery truck. At two o'clock, he decided to call Bill. "Hi, Bill," he said. "Sorry I'm so late, but I have to wait till a delivery truck comes."

"But they don't make deliveries on Saturday," said Bill.

"Really?" asked Jim. "You sure?"

"Pretty sure," answered Bill. "Just a minute. I'll check." After a brief pause, Bill returned to the phone. "My sister bought some stuff a week ago," he said, "and she says nobody delivers on weekends. So come on over." Jim quickly hung up the phone and hurried to Bill's house.

When Bill returned home two hours later, his mother was waiting for him. "Where were you when the delivery man came?" she asked. "He left this note on the door."

Jim looked at the note. It read, "Called with bike at three o'clock."

"Oh, Mom!" Jim cried. "That new bike you promised me! And I missed it!"

That evening, as Jim's family was having devotions, Dad read, "Then we will no longer be like children, forever changing our minds about what we believe because someone has told us something different or because someone has cleverly lied to us and made the lie sound like the truth."

"What does that mean?" asked Jim.

"Well , , ," Dad thought a moment. "Remember what happened this afternoon?" he asked. "You were told something that seemed to be right by Bill. It was something you really wanted to believe, so you believed it without checking the facts. Christians tend to do that sometimes, so Paul is warning them to check what they hear against the Bible." *AGL*

HOW ABOUT YOU?

Do you believe everything you hear? Have you fallen into the trap of thinking, "It sounds OK, so it must be right"? Don't build your life on the feelings or opinions of others. Read the Bible to find God's wisdom.

**Believe What
the Bible Says**

MEMORIZE:
"Then we will no longer be like children, forever changing our minds about what we believe because someone has told us something different or because someone has cleverly lied to us and made the lie sound like the truth." Ephesians 4:14

God's Plan

(Read Romans 11:33-36)

Adam never forgot the day his new baby sister, Megan, came home from the hospital. Dad and Mother told him that her spinal cord was damaged before she was born and she would never be able to walk. Adam couldn't quite believe it. *Maybe if we all took real good care of Megan, her legs would become well,* he thought. When Adam mentioned this to his mother, she shook her head sadly. "No, the doctor said that unless God does a miracle, her legs will never work. Instead of thinking about that, let's remember that this is somehow a part of God's plan for Megan and our family—at least for now."

Adam slumped into the kitchen chair, his mind determined not to accept this "plan" Mother was talking about.

Mother put down the screwdriver she was using to tighten a screw on a cabinet and sat down by Adam. "Megan is going to need special care because her legs have no feeling," she said. "She will not know whether they are hot or cold, or whether they have been cut or bruised."

"No feeling at all?" Adam blurted out. "She could hurt herself and not even know it."

"That's where you, Dad, and I fit into God's plan for her," said Mother. "It's going to take time and love to protect her from getting hurt and to help her learn about her disability as she grows up. Will you be part of God's plan for our family by helping us take care of Megan?"

Adam was quiet a long time before answering. "I wish Megan could walk someday," he said finally, "but since she can't, I want to help her as much as I can." *GJT*

HOW ABOUT YOU?

Do you have a brother or sister who is disabled? Do you realize that you are a part of God's plan for your brother or sister? Or perhaps you have a disability yourself. You may not realize it, but God wants to use you, too—to be a blessing.

MEMORIZE:
"'My thoughts are completely different from yours,' says the Lord. 'And my ways are far beyond anything you could imagine.'"
Isaiah 55:8

Accept God's Plan

Midnight to Dawn

(Read Revelation 21:2-4, 22-27)

It was just past midnight when Mr. and Mrs. Benson woke their four children—John, Esther, Paul, and Ruth. As they helped the children get dressed, they explained as carefully and gently as they could that they were going to the hospital to see Mr. Benson's grandma. For some time they had known that the doctors did not expect her to get well again. Now she was asking to see them, and they knew she didn't have much time left.

When they arrived at her bedside, Grandma Benson greeted each one lovingly. "I know it's hard to say good-bye," she said, "but when you think of me, remember that I'm going to be with Jesus. Now I just want to see each of you once more." One by one, she called the children to her—first Ruth, the youngest, then Paul, next Esther, and then John. "I love you," she told them, and she recalled the time each had accepted Jesus. To each she said, "Good night, honey. I'll see you in heaven." Then she said good night to Mrs. Benson.

Finally Grandma called her grandson, Mr. Benson, to her. She held his hand as they remembered some precious times from the past. After assuring him of her love, she said, "Good night, my dear grandson. Take good care of your family."

Then turning to the children she said, "I am so glad each one of you has taken Jesus as your Savior, so that one day you will all meet me in heaven."

After that Mr. Benson led all of them in a prayer. Then everyone gave Grandma Benson one last hug and left.

A happy grandmother prayed that night, "Thank you, Jesus, for giving me my family to keep for all eternity." *HCT*

HOW ABOUT YOU?

Do you have a relative who has gone to be with Jesus? If you are a Christian, you will see that person again. Isn't that good news?

MEMORIZE:
"Prepare to meet your God."
Amos 4:12

Be Prepared to Meet God

Come and See

(Read John 1:44-51)

"Hey, Keith," called Michael as he caught up with his friend in the school hallway. "Want to come to church with me this Sunday?" Michael had been praying for months that Keith would come to church.

"No," answered Keith. "I'm gonna watch the baseball game on TV. Nothing's going to get in the way of me watching the Braves!"

"You'll be home in plenty of time to do that," Michael assured him.

Keith laughed. "Well, even if there wasn't a game, I can't imagine wanting to go to church," he said. "It's a stupid place to go."

"Church isn't stupid. It's great!" argued Michael.

"Church is dumb!" insisted Keith.

"Isn't!"

"Is!"

"Isn't!"

"Forget it, Michael," growled Keith. "I'm not going."

Michael walked away feeling angry and sad. *I wish Keith would come, but I shouldn't have argued with him about it,* he thought. He remembered the Bible story of Philip and Nathanael. Philip didn't get angry when Nathanael asked, "Nazareth! Can anything good come from there?" He simply said, "Just come and see for yourself." Michael didn't know if that would work with Keith, but he decided to try it.

"Keith, wait up!" he called, running after his friend. "Look, I'm sorry I argued with you about coming to church, but I would like you to attend some time. Come and see for yourself how interesting church can be." *LMW*

HOW ABOUT YOU?

Do you invite your friends to church? Do they sometimes laugh at you and tell you you're stupid to believe as you do? Don't argue with them. Instead, just be enthusiastic and excited about what you learn at church. Your friends may be curious and willing to "come and see" for themselves.

Be an Excited Christian

MEMORIZE:
"'Nazareth!' exclaimed Nathanael. 'Can anything good come from there?' 'Just come and see for yourself,' Philip said." John 1:46

The Talking Tools

(Read 1 Corinthians 12:14-22)

As Ryan helped Uncle Ken replace Grandma Harper's porch floor, his uncle could tell that something had upset him. He was too quiet. "Your friend Jason's really growing as a Christian, isn't he?" Uncle Ken asked.

"Yeah," Ryan answered shortly.

"He's quite a guy," Uncle Ken said as he pulled nails. "His solo with the junior choir was great." Ryan didn't answer. Uncle Ken looked at him curiously. "Have you two been playing tennis lately?"

"Nope!" snapped Ryan.

"You haven't argued with Jason, have you, Ryan?" Uncle Ken probed.

Ryan sighed deeply. "No," he said, "it's just that he does everything better than I do. I used to sing solos in the choir. Now Jason sings them. He's the star student in Sunday school, too. He brings more visitors, learns more Bible verses, even beats me at tennis."

Uncle Ken nodded. "Ryan," he said, "what if the hammer got mad when we laid it down and started using the tape measure? Or what if the saw said, 'I'm tired of cutting boards. If you don't let me pull nails, I won't work'?"

Ryan grinned. "Oh, you know they won't. They have to do what they're made to do."

Uncle Ken put down the hammer and picked up the saw. "You're right," he agreed, "and, as Christians, we're tools in God's hands. We must do what we are designed to do."

Ryan gulped. "But Jason does everything I do," he said, "only better."

"How many hammers are in my toolbox, Ryan?"

"Two."

"And God doesn't have just one soloist or one witness or one worker," said Uncle Ken. "He has many, and sometimes we have to wait our turn. But when you're a tool, you don't tell the carpenter when you'll work or what you'll do. You simply lie in his hand and let him use you." *BJW*

HOW ABOUT YOU?

Do you sometimes question the way God sees you? Do you tell him what you will do and what you won't do? Surrender your will to God. Be a tool he can use, willing to do whatever he wants you to do.

MEMORIZE:

"If one part suffers, all the parts suffer with it, and if one part is honored, all the parts are glad." 1 Corinthians 12:26

Be God's Tool

Braving the Storm

(Read 1 Peter 1:3-7; 4:12-13)

Toby found it difficult to understand why God had allowed so much trouble to come into his family. First, there had been a car accident in which little Justin was seriously injured, and now Mother had to spend hours each day giving him therapy. Then the company Dad worked for went bankrupt, and Dad was out of a job. The family had to sell their nice home and live in a trailer on Grandpa's farm. Now Dad had a new job, but he had to be gone two or three nights every week.

One evening when Dad was away, a storm came up. The wind blew wildly, and the thunder crashed. "Come quickly," said Mother. "We need to get over to Grandpa's house. We'll be safer there." She picked up Justin, and soon they were all huddled together in Grandpa's basement. Even there, they could hear the storm raging outside.

"Let's pray together," suggested Grandpa. They all bowed their heads, and Grandpa prayed aloud. As he thanked God for the rain, Toby couldn't believe his ears! Grandpa didn't even ask God to stop the storm!

But soon the storm did stop, and they hurried out to look things over. They saw that the plum tree had toppled over. "I expected that," said Grandpa. "The roots just ran along the ground. But look at the old oak tree. It bent with the wind, but its roots go down deep, and it's standing up again. And look at the beautiful rainbow!"

"Grandpa, why didn't you ask God to stop the storm?" asked Toby.

"The storm brought the rain we need so badly," answered Grandpa. He smiled at Toby. "You know," he added, "sometimes it takes storms in our life to bring blessings. The Bible says, 'Always be thankful.' We may find it hard to feel thankful for all the things that happen to us, but God understands that."

Toby looked at him thoughtfully. "Is that how we get deep, strong roots like the old oak tree?" he asked. "By trusting God in the hard times as well as the easy times?"

Grandpa nodded. "That's right!" he agreed. *BJW*

HOW ABOUT YOU?

Are there storms in your life? Problems at home or at school? Trust God and ask him to help you make the best of whatever comes your way. Start thanking him for the rain and look for the rainbow.

MEMORIZE:
"No matter what happens, always be thankful, for this is God's will for you who belong to Christ Jesus."
1 Thessalonians 5:18

Storms Bring Blessings

The Edge

(Read James 1:13-15)

Ted and his dog, Prince, were relaxing in the shade of the old apple tree as Mother left to go to Aunt Lou's. "Your cousin Jim will be sorry you couldn't come," said Mother. "You be sure to stay close to the house and rest."

After Mother had gone, Ted spoke to Prince. "I didn't really lie when I said I was sick, did I, ol' boy?" He grinned to himself. "I really am sick—sick of Jim and his being such a show-off. Last time I was there, he beat me at every game we played, and he outran me, too. Thinks he's so good! I'm sick of him. Yeah, I'm sick all right!"

Ted was dozing when his friend Bryan came over. "It must be 105 degrees in the shade!" exclaimed Bryan. "Let's go down to Miller's pond and fish." Though Ted knew he shouldn't do it, he agreed to go.

But the fish weren't biting, and before long the boys decided to go wading. It was so refreshing that they went deeper and deeper. Suddenly, with a muffled scream, Ted disappeared under the water. "Swim, Ted! Swim!" yelled Bryan when Ted reappeared. And swim Ted did. Soon he crawled from the pond—scared, muddy, and soaked. And to make matters worse, he reached home only to find that Mother had already returned and was looking for him!

Later that evening, Ted and his mom talked about what had happened. "I wasn't really sick, and I should have gone with you in the first place," confessed Ted. "And then one thing led to another. Bryan and I only meant to wade in the shallow water. But before we knew it, we were too deep, and then I stepped in that hole."

"Sin is like that pond, Ted—it's shallow around the edge but gradually growing deeper and deeper, and it's filled with unseen, dangerous holes," said Mom. "It doesn't start with what we consider a big, deep crime. It starts with little things that don't seem important—like jealousy in your heart because Jim is able to do a few things better than you. That led to telling a lie and then to disobedience. It doesn't pay to play around the edge of sin." *BJW*

HOW ABOUT YOU?

Is there some "small" thing you know you should not do, yet it's attractive to you? Perhaps there's jealousy in your heart, or pride, or laziness. Be careful—before you know it, you may find yourself in sin "over your head." Confess your sins, both big and little, to God. Ask him to help you stay away from all sin.

MEMORIZE:

"So humble yourselves before God. Resist the Devil, and he will flee from you." James 4:7

Say "No" to the Devil

Line to Heaven

(Read Psalm 5:1-3)

"This looks good," said Grandpa as he looked over Chuck's science project. "What do you call it?"

"Means of Communication," answered Chuck. He had written reports about the telephone, radio, TV, satellites, and submarine fiber-optic cables. Then he had found pictures and made diagrams to illustrate the project. He was just adding the finishing touches.

Grandpa studied his work a few minutes. "Ah, but Chuck," he murmured, "you forgot the most important form of communication."

Chuck was startled. "I did? What's that?" he asked.

"Communication with God," answered Grandpa with a twinkle in his eye.

"I never thought of that," said Chuck. "In Bible times, God sometimes talked to people through dreams, didn't he?"

"That's right, and at other times he spoke to people directly," Grandpa said. "But he has a different way of speaking to us now."

"I know how," said Chuck eagerly. "Through the Bible!"

Grandpa smiled and nodded. "God also speaks to his children by putting thoughts in their minds—and desires in their hearts. That's the work of the Holy Spirit. And do you know how we can talk to God?"

Chuck nodded. "Sure do. Through prayer." He grinned. "Hey, I've got an idea! There's still room on my chart—I'll add a picture of heaven with a line running to earth where a man is reading his Bible. Then I'll have a line running to heaven from a man who is praying."

"Great, Chuck," approved Grandpa. "And don't forget to make use of this means of communication yourself, too." *AGL*

HOW ABOUT YOU?

Is there regular communication between you and God? Do you read some Bible verses each day? Do you take time to pray? Be sure to talk with God each day, and listen as he speaks to you.

MEMORIZE:

"O God, you are my God; I earnestly search for you. My soul thirsts for you; my whole body longs for you."

Psalm 63:1

Communicate with God

Later Than You Think

(Read Luke 12:37-40)

Ben's grandmother needed some help around the house, so Mom and Dad were going to visit her. While they were gone, Ben was going to stay with neighbors across the road. "But you'll be responsible for the chores at our place," Dad told him. "I've made a list of the things you need to do."

"OK, Dad," replied Ben. "You can count on me!"

Dad was pleased. "Good! I hope we'll be home in about a week," he said. "Do your work well, and I'll have a reward for you. But remember . . . no work, no reward!" With a grin, Ben agreed. He was sure the reward would be a nice one!

Ben was up bright and early the next morning. He turned the cows out to pasture, cleaned the barn, and then started to hoe the garden. Soon he heard a whistle and looked up to see his friend Jerry coming. "Let's go for a swim in my new pool," suggested Jerry. "You can finish your work later." Ben knew he shouldn't go, but he was tired and hot. Going for a swim sounded like such fun . . . so he went!

Each day Jerry came over to play. Four days slipped by, and hardly any work was done. As Ben stood under the oak tree on the fifth day, he heard a car coming up the driveway. It stopped, and his parents stepped out. "Good news, Ben!" called Dad. "We finished the work at Grandma's house more quickly than we thought we would, so we came home early. And guess what! We stopped at Green's Hardware to buy your reward. Mr. Green is sending the truck with that bike you've been wanting."

"O-o-ohh!" Ben moaned. "I . . . I might as well tell you. I haven't done all the things you told me to do." He hurried on as he saw Dad's frown. "Please, Dad . . . can I keep the bike? I'll work hard now. I'll get everything done!"

Dad shook his head sadly. "It's too late now, Ben," he said. "When the bike comes, we'll have to send it back. But if you work hard for the next few weeks you can earn it back again." *HCT*

HOW ABOUT YOU?

Are you doing the things God wants you to do? Have you told others about Jesus? Invited someone to church? Helped your mother cheerfully? You see, if you're a Christian, God wants you to live and work for him. If you're a faithful worker, he'll give you a reward far more wonderful than a bike.

MEMORIZE:

"You must be ready all the time, for the Son of Man will come when least expected." Luke 12:40

Work for Jesus

Messenger Boy (Part 1)

(Read Revelation 22:16-21)

"Jordan!" called Mother from the kitchen. "Janelle is playing next door, but I need her to run to the store for me. Take this shopping list and money out to her, and then I want you to start mowing the lawn."

"OK," agreed Jordan. After Mother left the room, he looked at the list. It said: 1 carton of sour cream, 1 bottle of vanilla, 2 dozen eggs, a large bag of flour.

That doesn't sound very interesting, thought Jordan. Then he had an idea. He found a pencil with an eraser and changed the list so it read like this: 1 carton of ice cream, 1 bottle of root beer, 2 dozen cookies, a large bag of candy. *Now, that's more like it!* thought Jordan. He chuckled to himself as he put the list in his pocket. *I'll see what Janelle says; then I'll change it back.*

When Jordan turned around, he was surprised to see his mother standing in the doorway, watching him. "What were you doing just now?" she asked. "Let me see that list." Reluctantly, Jordan handed it over. Mother read it and looked at Jordan. "Why did you change what I had written?" she asked. "I hope you weren't planning to leave it like this and let Janelle buy the wrong things."

"No . . . it was just a joke. I was gonna tell Janelle the right things before she left for the store," Jordan assured her.

Mother looked seriously at him. "You're sure?" she said. "Well, I suppose I'll give you the benefit of the doubt." As she rewrote the list, she added, "You know, Jordan, what you did reminds me of your request to go to church with your friend Darrell next Sunday. Remember why we said no?"

"You said his church doesn't believe the whole Bible is true," replied Jordan. "They've changed parts to fit their own teaching."

"Yes." Mother nodded. "Just as you changed what I wrote, they've changed what God wrote. Whenever people change what the Bible says, they are doing wrong." She once again handed him the list. "Here you are," she said. "Now be a good messenger—for me and for God." *SLK*

HOW ABOUT YOU?

Do you realize how important God's Word really is? No matter how fine a church or religious group may appear to be, if they change what is written in the Bible, don't believe what they say. It's wrong for people to change what God has said.

MEMORIZE:
"Do not add to his words, or he may rebuke you, and you will be found a liar." Proverbs 30:6

Don't Change God's Word

Messenger Boy (Part 2)

(Read Ezekiel 3:16-19)

As Jordan walked down the driveway, he met his friend Darrell. "Hi! Where ya going?" asked Darrell.

"Next door," replied Jordan. "My sister is there, and Mom wants her to go get some groceries."

"Did your folks say you could come to church with me next Sunday?" Darrell wanted to know.

Jordan knew that this would be a good time to witness to Darrell, but he felt too bashful. So he just said, "No, I can't come this week. Maybe some other time." Then he and Darrell talked about school activities until Jordan heard his mother calling. He hurried home. "Yeah, Mom?" he asked. "Did you want me for something?"

"Well, I expected you back long ago," Mother said. "Did Janelle leave for the grocery store right away? I need some of those groceries."

"Oh, no! The groceries! I forgot to give Janelle the list you gave me," Jordan said sheepishly. "I got so busy talking to Darrell that it just slipped my mind."

Mother answered. "This is the second time you've gotten in trouble over that list," she said. "First you changed the message, and now you didn't deliver it. I'm afraid we're going to have to take away one of your privileges if you can't be a more responsible person. But I'm glad you got to talk with Darrell. Did you explain why we wouldn't let you go to his church?"

"Uh . . .well, not really," murmured Jordan. "I just couldn't think of what to say."

Mother looked at him sadly. "As we both know, Jordan, there are two ways to fail as a messenger," she said. "One is to change the message itself. The other is to fail to deliver it."

"I get your point, Mom," Jordan replied. "I really am sorry I didn't give Janelle your message . . . and that I didn't explain things to Darrell. I'd like to have another chance to do both." *SLK*

HOW ABOUT YOU?

Are you a Christian? Then you have a message to deliver to others—that Jesus loves them. When did you last tell someone about Jesus? Be a good messenger. Tell someone this week.

MEMORIZE:

"Therefore, I declare to you today that I am innocent of the blood of all men. For I have not hesitated to proclaim to you the whole will of God." Acts 20:26-27, NIV

Give Out God's Message

Out of Tune

(Read Philippians 2:1-5)

"Where's my guitar pick?" demanded James. "You've been in my room again, haven't you, Mandy?" His little sister shook her head. "You must have been," James argued. "I left my pick on my dresser, and now it's gone."

"I didn't take it," said Mandy. "Mama says to stay out of your room, and I do."

"Well, someone took it!" James stomped down the hall and slammed his bedroom door. Mandy felt sad as she thought about her brother. He had been acting like this often in recent weeks.

Later that evening James sat at the piano, tuning his guitar. "Where did you find your pick, James?" asked Mother. "Mandy told me you thought she had taken it."

"It was in my pocket," James muttered. He struck a piano key with one finger. *Plunk! Plunk!* Then he plucked a guitar string. *Ping! Ping! Plunk!* After a few more twists and turns, he ran his fingers across the strings and a harmonious chord sounded.

"You're getting pretty good, Son," said Dad.

"Why do you always listen to the piano and the guitar together?" asked Mandy.

"If all the strings aren't in tune with the piano, they don't sound good with each other," explained James.

Mother looked at James. "Just like each of your guitar strings has to be in tune with the piano, so every member of the family has to be in harmony with God, or they are out of tune with each other," she said thoughtfully. "Just one person out of tune can disrupt the whole family harmony."

Dad nodded. "I've been hearing some discord around here. Could it be someone is out of tune?"

James sighed. "All right—I know it's me," he admitted. "I'm sorry. Guess I'd better let the Lord do a little tuning on me." *BJW*

HOW ABOUT YOU?

Are you out of tune with God? Do you have trouble getting along with your family and friends? Now's the time to have a little "prayer meeting" all by yourself, and let God get you back in tune.

Get in Tune with God

MEMORIZE:
"How wonderful it is, how pleasant, when brothers live together in harmony!" Psalm 133:1

Free Sodas

(Read Acts 8:18-22)

Timothy walked down the street, drinking his cold soda. It tasted really good because it was a hot day. What made it even better was that the soda was free! A new store called "The Soda Shack" had just opened up, and they were giving out free samples to advertise their products.

When Timothy reached the park on his street, a neighborhood ball game had just ended. "Hey! Where did you get that soda?" asked his brother Daryl. "I know Mom didn't give you any money when we left."

Timothy grinned. "I got it at that new place called The Soda Shack, and it was free!" he said.

As soon as Timothy said the word "free," a lot of the hot and thirsty players started to ask questions. "Where did you say you got it?" "You had to pay *something* for it, didn't you?" "Did they tell you to come here and advertise? There must be a trick to it."

Timothy just smiled and said, "There are no tricks. The Soda Shack is giving away free sodas today. They said they hoped I'd come again whenever I want a soda."

Some of the kids, including Daryl, took off running toward The Soda Shack, but a lot of the others didn't believe Timothy. "The sodas are free? Oh, sure they are," someone said sarcastically. "You really expect us to believe that?" asked another. Many of the boys walked over to the water fountain for a warm drink. Others just went home.

That evening, Timothy and Daryl told their parents what had happened. "Some of the kids drank warm water instead of cold pop," said Daryl.

"Yeah," Timothy agreed. "Why didn't they believe me, Dad?"

"I don't know, Son," said Dad, "but that reminds me of what happens when we talk about Jesus to people. Some just can't believe God will give eternal life as a free gift. They think they have to do something to earn it, or they think there's a trick to it." He shook his head. "Maybe the store would have let those boys buy some of their 'free' sodas," he said. "But when it comes to eternal life, the only way to get it is to accept the gift God offers." *HLM*

HOW ABOUT YOU?

Have you accepted God's offer of eternal life? You can't pay for it or earn it. It's free! You simply receive it when you trust in Jesus. If you have questions, talk to a trusted friend or adult.

MEMORIZE:

"For the wages of sin is death, but the free gift of God is eternal life through Christ Jesus our Lord." Romans 6:23

Eternal Life Is Free

A Real Working Phone

(Read James 2:15-18)

Jessica hung up the phone. "I wish Amy wouldn't make me feel guilty because I never feel like doing our Sunday school projects," she complained. "She acts like I'm not even a Christian." Jessica sighed. "What's the big deal?" she continued. "After all, we don't become Christians because of good works."

"That's true." Mom bent down to pick up the baby's toy phone and handed it to Jessica. "Why don't you call Amy back and tell her that?"

"Mom!" Jessica chuckled. "This is a toy."

"It looks like a phone," said Mom. "Push the buttons and they beep like a phone. It even rings. And the box it came in said it was a phone."

"A toy phone, not a real phone," said Jessica. "A real phone makes real calls."

"And a phone that won't do what a phone is supposed to do is not much use, is it?" asked Mom. "Do you suppose that's true about Christians, too? That they're not much use if they don't do what they're meant to do?"

Jessica was startled. "What do you mean?" she asked.

Mom sat down beside Jessica. "You were right when you said that doing good deeds doesn't make a person a Christian," said Mom. "But works do set us apart as 'real' Christians, and they're an act of obedience to God. In fact, the Bible says that "He has created us anew in Christ Jesus, so that we can do the good things he planned for us long ago." It sounds to me like they're pretty important."

Jessica thought about her mother's words. "Wow! I guess I should help with the class project after all," she decided. "I better call Amy and tell her I'll come."

Mom smiled and nodded. "Let me get you the real phone," she said. *HMT*

HOW ABOUT YOU?
Can people tell that you're a Christian by what you do? If you truly want to follow God, good works should be a result of your faith.

MEMORIZE:
"We are God's masterpiece. He has created us anew in Christ Jesus, so that we can do the good things he planned for us long ago."
Ephesians 2:10

Do Good Works

A Hurt Finger

(Read James 1:22-25)

Troy grimaced as he struggled to unscrew the lid of a small bottle of paint. Dad had left to run an errand, and Troy wished he would hurry and return. He and Dad were going to use the paint to decorate the model airplane in the kit that Troy had gotten for his birthday.

Troy's face turned red as he tried with all his might to turn the lid. When he failed, he grew angry and impatient. He took the bottle out to the garage, picked up one of Dad's screwdrivers, and tried to pry off the lid. The screwdriver slipped and jabbed his finger. "Ouch!" Troy cried as he watched a tiny trickle of blood run from the cut. He put the bottle down and went in for a bandage.

When he returned to the garage, he met Dad just returning home. "What did you do to your finger?" Dad asked, looking at the bandage on Troy's hand. Troy explained about the lid. "Did you read the directions on the bottle?" asked Dad.

Troy shook his head. "Directions?" he asked. "To open a bottle? I didn't know there were any."

Dad picked up the paint and pointed to the writing on the top of the lid. "It says to push down and then turn."

Troy followed the directions and the lid came off easily. "Guess I should have paid attention," he said. "I didn't even see those directions before."

Dad looked thoughtful. "Remember our discussion last week when you asked why you should read the Bible and memorize your verses?"

Troy nodded. "You said the Bible gives us directions for life," he replied, "and that without those directions, we may do things that are wrong and then we're sure to get hurt. Like I hurt my finger when I ignored the directions on the bottle of paint, right?"

"Right," said Dad. *KEC*

HOW ABOUT YOU?

Do you read the Bible to learn God's directions for your life, or do you attempt to do things your own way? Not following God's directions can result in getting hurt. Read the Bible and do what God says.

MEMORIZE:

"And remember, it is a message to obey, not just to listen to. If you don't obey, you are only fooling yourself."
James 1:22

Follow God's Directions

Wandering Sheep

(Read Hebrews 10:23-25)

Kurt was having a great time spending the summer with his Uncle Jim and Aunt Ann on their sheep ranch out west. Before leaving home, Kurt had promised his parents that he would attend the little church down the road from the ranch, even though his uncle and aunt were not Christians and probably wouldn't go with him. He had gone a few times, but he soon decided he'd rather go riding instead. Kurt also began copying the bad language—and even some of the bad habits—of the cowboys who worked on Uncle Jim's ranch. He tried smoking and drinking, and he pretended he liked them.

One afternoon, as Kurt rode with his uncle to check on a flock of sheep in the hills, they spied something white in the dust by the side of the road. Uncle Jim got off his horse and went to see what it was. "Oh, no!" he said, shaking his head sadly. "It's a dead lamb. A mountain lion must have gotten it."

"That's awful!" cried Kurt in dismay. "How could that happen? You've had two men with the sheep all the time, and Shep is such a good watchdog. He'd never let a mountain lion near the flock."

"Yes, that's true," said his uncle. "A lion wouldn't dare go near the sheep with men and dogs around. But this little lamb must have gotten separated from the others. Once he left the safety and protection of the flock, he was no match for the strong teeth and sharp claws of the lion."

As they rode away from the pitiful sight, a thought struck Kurt. *Didn't the Bible say that Christians were like sheep? Sheep were meant to stay together— not wander off alone, where they would be easy prey for the enemy.* Kurt remembered hearing his pastor back home say that Christians needed to stick together, too. "If they don't," said Pastor Brown, "they find it harder to resist temptation." Kurt knew that had happened to him. *I better get back to church,* he thought. *I'm going to start going this Sunday! SLK*

HOW ABOUT YOU?

Do you realize how important it is to go to church and fellowship with other Christians? Just as a sheep that has wandered away from the flock is easy prey for a lion, so Christians who have stopped going to church are often easily led into temptation. You need the friendship and help of other children of God. Stay with the "flock"!

MEMORIZE:

"Be careful! Watch out for attacks from the Devil, your great enemy. He prowls around like a roaring lion, looking for some victim to devour."

1 Peter 5:8

Don't Skip Church

16

Two Roads

(Read Luke 13:22-27)

"Are we almost there?" asked Scott from the backseat of the car. It was fun to be going on vacation, but he was tired of riding.

"According to the map, I figure we'll be there in about an hour," Mom said.

Scott's mind wandered back to the previous day. He and a friend had decided to get some candy from the corner store. Jim had dared him to take a candy bar without paying for it, but Scott had refused. After he paid for his bar, Jim had called him a goody-goody, laughed at him, and jingled the money still in his pocket. Scott had almost wished he had taken the candy.

Mom's voice interrupted his thoughts. "Here's an article about your old friend Gordon White," she said to Dad. "He's been sentenced to prison for fraud."

"No!" exclaimed Dad. "He was a nice kid."

"Didn't he do bad stuff when you knew him?" asked Scott.

"Well," said Dad, "I remember that he got caught cheating on his final exams one year." Just then they came to a crossroad. "Do we turn here?" Dad asked Mom.

"Mmm," she answered, not looking up from her newspaper.

After Dad turned, it seemed to Scott that they drove on and on and on. He checked his watch. "We passed Glenmore," he said. "Are we almost there?"

"Glenmore?" asked Mom, putting down her paper. She found the road map and studied it. "Oh, no!" she exclaimed. "We turned onto the wrong road. I'm sorry!"

Dad turned the car around and they began retracing the miles. "Reminds me of Gordon," said Dad. "Way back somewhere, he must have made some bad choices and started traveling down the wrong road. Now look where he's ended up."

"Jim dared me to steal a candy bar after school yesterday," said Scott thoughtfully.

"Did you?" Dad asked.

"No," said Scott. Suddenly he was glad he'd made the choice he had.

"Good!" said Dad. "You don't want to start down that road." *VEN*

HOW ABOUT YOU?

Are you sometimes tempted to do things that seem a little bit wrong . . . like copying your friend's homework, lying to get out of trouble, sneaking one small thing from a store? These "little" sins are the first steps down a road that can take you in the wrong direction. Follow God's map, the Bible.

MEMORIZE:

"But the gateway to life is small, and the road is narrow, and only a few ever find it." Matthew 7:14

Follow God's Road Map

Let Him Come In

(Read John 1:1, 10-13)

While Tommy's parents were away one hot summer day, Tommy took his new magnifying glass and a pad and pencil outdoors to work on a nature project. He crossed the neighbor's garden to the edge of the woods, where he picked a wild flower and examined it. Then he placed it on some dry leaves, propped his magnifying glass so he could see the flower through it, and sketched it on his pad. When he finished, he moved on into the woods to find more things to examine.

Some time later, Tommy realized that he had forgotten to pick up the magnifying glass. With a sigh, he retraced his steps. "Oh, no!" he exclaimed as he approached the neighbor's yard. The heat of the sun through the glass had started a small fire—some dead leaves and grass were burning. Tommy ran and stomped out the fire as fast as he could, but it had spread and left an ugly black, burned spot on the edge of the Prestons' garden.

Frightened, Tommy hurried home. A few minutes later, he saw Mr. Preston cross the garden and look over the scorched ground. Then he came to Tommy's house and rang the bell several times, but Tommy didn't answer. As Mr. Preston turned to leave, Tommy's folks arrived. Mr. Preston talked with them a few minutes and then left.

Tommy soon found himself at Mr. Preston's door. He had come to apologize.

"Thank you for coming," Mr. Preston said after Tommy explained what had happened. "If anything like this happens again, I hope you'll tell me right away. When I came to your home, I was ready to forgive you."

Back home, Tommy reported what Mr. Preston had told him. Dad nodded. "That's a lot like Jesus, Son," he said. "He wants to forgive you, too, but first you need to confess your sin and let him come into your life."

"Let him in?" Tommy asked. "What do you mean?"

"If you had been willing for Mr. Preston to come into the house, what would you have done?" asked Dad.

"I'd have opened the door and told him to come in," answered Tommy. Suddenly he smiled. "Oh, that's what I'll do with Jesus!" he exclaimed. "I'll invite him in!" *AGL*

HOW ABOUT YOU?

If you are not a Christian yet, you need to know that Jesus loves you and wants to forgive your sins. If you have questions about becoming a Christian, ask a trusted friend or adult.

MEMORIZE:

"Look! Here I stand at the door and knock. If you hear me calling and open the door, I will come in, and we will share a meal as friends."

Revelation 3:20

Let Jesus In

Cloudy Skies

(Read Psalm 139:1-6)

Scott stared out the plane window, his thoughts swirling like the thick clouds below. *Why did God allow Mom and Dad to be in that accident?* he wondered. *Going to stay awhile with Grandma and Grandpa is nice, but not when it's because Mom and Dad are in the hospital.* Just then the stewardess arrived with lunch, so Scott turned from the window. "Cheer up," encouraged his big brother, Al, as Scott was given his tray of food. "Eat your chicken. It will help you feel better."

"But I'm not hungry," complained Scott. "I keep thinking about Mom and Dad."

Al gave him a lopsided grin. "I know, Scott. I feel the same way, really. But remember, God cares about us, and he knows what we're going through."

Scott nodded, but he wasn't sure he agreed. Picking up his fork, he began to eat. When the stewardess came to pick up his tray, he turned with a sigh to the window again. Immediately the sigh became a long whistle. "Look, Al!" he exclaimed. Pressing his nose to the glass, he stared down at the colorful fields and the cars and trucks that looked like tiny toys. "I didn't know it would look like that," he said. "See that train. It looks too tiny! Ohhh! I like this!" Scott's solemn face had brightened.

Al leaned over. "It's great," he agreed. "You know, all that nice scenery was there below the clouds all the time. You just couldn't see it."

"I hadn't thought of that," replied Scott.

"We can think of Mom and Dad's accident in the same way," continued Al. "To us, the whole situation is cloudy, and we can't see anything good in it."

"And you're saying that God can?" asked Scott.

"Yes," replied Al. "And even if we never understand why this had to happen, we can still trust that God is good and that he loves us." *GW*

HOW ABOUT YOU?

Do you have a "cloudy" outlook? Have things happened in your life that make you think nothing is going to turn out right? Don't let the hard things of life keep you down. Remember that God knows what you're going through. And he loves you.

MEMORIZE:

"But he knows where I am going. And when he has tested me like gold in a fire, he will pronounce me innocent."
Job 23:10

Accept What God Sends

Crocodile Tears

(Read Acts 17:23, 28-31)

"Come, Joey," Mark encouraged as he tugged at Joey's hand. Mark had seen enough of the zoo. "Let's move on."

"In a minute," Joey said as he pulled his hand loose. "I like to look at these cr-crooked-dials."

Mark laughed. "They're crocodiles, Joey."

"That's what I said, 'crook-ed-dials,'" Joey insisted. "Hey, Mark, look at that one. He must not like his dinner."

Mark wrinkled his forehead. "Not like his dinner? Why do you say that?"

"He's eating, but he's crying," Joey explained.

Mark scoffed. "That crocodile isn't crying."

"He is so," argued Joey. "Look at those big tears."

Mark laughed. "Those are just crocodile tears," he said. "When crocodiles eat, the food pushes on the tear glands in the top of their mouths and makes their eyes water. They're shedding tears, but they really aren't crying. The tears don't mean a thing! He's really OK, Joey." As Mark explained, he remembered how Joey had begged—and even cried—when he wanted Mark to take him to the zoo. *Crocodile tears,* thought Mark as he remembered how quickly the tears had stopped when he had promised the zoo trip. But then Mark remembered something about himself. Because he had been careless with his bike, Mother said he couldn't ride it for a while. But he and his friend, John, had planned a bike trip for Saturday. So Mark had shed a few "crocodile tears" and begged to be allowed to go. He remembered that Joey had been watching. Mark felt a bit ashamed as he thought about the example he had been for Joey. "Now let's go, Joey," Mark urged again.

"No! No!" Joey screamed, and tears began to roll down his cheeks. "I don't want to go home."

"Dry those 'crocodile tears,' Joey," Mark said firmly. "We're going home."

Joey abruptly stopped crying. "Crooked-dial tears? Did I really cry crooked-dial tears?" He grinned. "Wait till I tell Mommy what I learned at the zoo!" *BJW*

HOW ABOUT YOU?

Have you ever shed "crocodile tears" to get your way? Have you cried and said, "I'm sorry," but you were only sorry you got caught? True repentance is more than tears; it is "fruits" (doing something about it). God is not fooled by "crocodile tears."

Be Truly Sorry for Sin

MEMORIZE:
"Now turn from your sins and turn to God, so you can be cleansed of your sins." Acts 3:19

The Untamed Tongue

(Read James 3:2-10)

Don and his father were camping at Rainbow Lake—fishing, hiking, and enjoying the outdoors. "I was surprised you didn't suggest that Stan Harper join us for this trip," said Dad as they finished supper one evening.

Don shrugged. "Did you know his mother is in a mental hospital?" he asked.

"Yes, I knew that," answered Dad.

"I knew she was in a hospital," said Don, "but I sure didn't know it was *that* kind of hospital until some of the kids told me. All the kids at church say Stan must be wacky, too, and . . . Dad, don't you think he does strange things sometimes?"

"Not any more strange than anyone else," replied Dad emphatically. "You shouldn't judge everything Stan does by the fact that his mother is ill." Don didn't say anything, but he was not convinced.

Later that afternoon, Don went for a swim. He enjoyed it very much, but as he was drying off, he suddenly let out a shriek. "Yuck! Look . . . look here!" he squawked. Dad hurried over. "Look! Right here on my arm! See this worm? I can't get him off!" exclaimed Don.

"That's a leech, Don," said Dad. "They live in the water and sometimes stick to swimmers. Hold still, and I'll try to pull it off." Dad succeeded in getting the leech off, but Don's arm bled a lot. "Leeches give off a substance that keeps the blood from clotting," Dad explained. "Don't worry—it will soon stop." Don shuddered as he stared at his bleeding arm. "You know, Don," added Dad thoughtfully, "leeches remind me of gossip. Gossip also sticks tight. Even after people quit talking, the other person continues to hurt."

"You're talking about Stan, aren't you?" asked Don. "Talking about him hurts him long after the talk is finished."

"That's right," said Dad. "A lot of innocent people have been hurt by someone else's tongue. In fact, the Bible says no one can tame the tongue."

"I am sorry," said Don. "Do you think it would help if I'd invite him out here?"

"Why don't you ask him?" suggested Dad. *BJW*

HOW ABOUT YOU?

Are you guilty of hurting someone by listening to and passing along gossip? Instead of using your tongue to hurt others, use it to help them.

MEMORIZE:

"I said to myself, 'I will watch what I do and not sin in what I say.'"
Psalm 39:1

Gossip Is Sin

A Foolish Trade

(Read Genesis 25:29-34)

It was Mark's birthday, and he eagerly opened the envelope his sister brought from the mailbox. "It's from my Sunday school teacher," he said. "Look, Merry—ten dimes! And listen to what Mr. Wayne wrote: 'These are special dimes. Be careful how you spend them—and how you spend your life.'" Mark glanced at the dimes. "I wonder what he meant."

Merry's eyes were wide. "Ohhhh! How nice! You can thank him tomorrow morning at Sunday school."

"I'm not going to Sunday school," Mark announced. "That's for sissies. Besides, Mom doesn't care if we go or not, so I'm quitting."

Sure enough, the next morning Mark refused to go to Sunday school. But he was bored at home, so to amuse himself, he took his birthday dimes and went down to the corner service station where he spent them on candy and coke.

That afternoon, Mark had a visitor—Mr. Wayne. Mark thanked his teacher for the birthday card and the money. Mr. Wayne smiled. "Did you figure out what's special about your dimes?" he asked. Since Mark had not, Mr. Wayne continued, "They're silver dimes, and they're worth more than ten cents. Give me one, and I'll show you how to tell a silver dime from an ordinary one." Mark was embarrassed, but he had to admit that he had spent them that morning. "Oh, I'm sorry," said Mr. Wayne. "I intended to tell you about them at Sunday school this morning. In fact, I was going to use them to illustrate today's lesson about Esau. He sold his right to a double portion of all his father's property just for a bowl of beans. He made a foolish trade—kind of like you did with your dimes. I'm sorry you weren't there to hear that lesson."

"Uh . . . I'm too old for Sunday school," Mark stammered.

Mr. Wayne shook his head. "Mark," he said, "You're never too old to learn something new about the Lord." *BJW*

HOW ABOUT YOU?

Do you think you're too old to learn anything new about God? Are you spending your time wisely or foolishly? Ask God to help you live wisely for him.

**Don't Spend
Life Foolishly**

MEMORIZE:
"People ruin their lives by their own foolishness and then are angry at the Lord." Proverbs 19:3

August
22

A Light to Guide

(Read Hebrews 10:22-25)

Peter couldn't decide which way to look. He had never been where there were so many interesting things going on at the same time. *This is so cool,* he thought. *I'll never be able to think of any way to thank Uncle Ted for bringing me to the air show today.*

As the Thunder Jets made their first appearance, people rose to their feet and burst into applause. The four planes were traveling hundreds of miles an hour, but they were in perfect formation—a diamond shape. At exactly the same moment, they all tipped their wings as if to wave at the crowd.

Peter was spellbound for the next half hour as the Thunder Jets made run after run in front of the review stands. They flew with perfect precision, performing intricate patterns together. Sometimes it looked as if their wings were touching.

All too soon the show was over, but Uncle Ted had a surprise for Peter. He introduced Peter to his friend, Mike Jacobs, who had flown in the third position with the Thunder Jets. "Commander Jacobs, how close are the planes really?" Peter asked. "From the ground it looks like they touch!"

The pilot chuckled. "Well, Peter," he said, "most of the time there are three feet between our wing tips! Pilots began flying like that during World War 2. The planes flew in close formation to avoid getting lost when they entered clouds. As long as the pilot could see the light of the plane next to him, he knew he was OK." They chatted a little longer before Peter and Uncle Ted had to leave.

"That was fun!" exclaimed Peter on the way home.

Uncle Ted smiled. "I'm glad you enjoyed it," he said. "Flying a Thunder Jet and being a Christian are a lot alike, aren't they?"

"Alike?" asked Peter. "They don't seem anything alike to me! What do you mean?"

"As long as the pilot can see the light of the next plane, he knows he's OK. And as long as Christians stay close to Jesus, they know they're on the right path," explained Uncle Ted, "even when the way is cloudy." *REP*

HOW ABOUT YOU?

Do you have a "cloudy" problem in your life? Maybe you're having a tough time at school; maybe your parents seem worried about something; maybe your best friend has been ignoring you. Whatever the problem, stay close to Jesus through prayer, Bible reading, and getting together with other Christians. Jesus is the "Light" that will help you through the "clouds." Trust him.

MEMORIZE:
"Draw close to God, and God will draw close to you." James 4:8

Stay Close to Jesus

One Step at a Time

(Read John 12:35-36)

"Will I really get all covered with black soot? " asked Doug excitedly as he and his Uncle Jake left for the coal mines. Uncle Jake nodded and Doug grinned. "I bet Tim and Angie will be jealous!" Doug and his family were visiting Doug's Uncle Jake in West Virginia. Uncle Jake was a coal miner, and he had gotten permission to take Doug down into the mines with him.

As they drove along, Uncle Jake whistled, then hummed, and finally began to sing. He sang a song Doug had never heard before. "The future dark before us lies; the path is hidden from our eyes; and Jesus leads while faith he tries, just one step at a time!" The chorus repeated the phrase "just one step at a time" twice, then said, "That's the way he leads to glory—just one step at a time." The tune was a catchy one, and Doug found himself humming it several times that day.

At the mine, Doug was given a hat with a light on it. Then he and all the men descended by elevator deep into the earth. Doug had never been any place where it was this dark! "Without the light on your hat, you wouldn't be able to see your hand in front of your face," Uncle Jake told him. Doug nodded, but after taking a few steps, he stumbled. Uncle Jake helped him regain his balance and then gave him some advice. "Doug," he said, "you'll never be able to walk in the mine if you try to look far ahead of you. The lamp on your hat will guide you if you let it, but it lights your way just a step or two at a time." With a little practice, Doug figured it out.

On the way home that afternoon, Doug talked excitedly about how dark it was in the mine and how he had to learn to walk in the light. Uncle Jake smiled. "You know—mining is like living for God," said Uncle Jake. "Jesus doesn't usually show us very far in advance what he wants us to be doing. He wants us to take 'just one step at a time' for him." *REP*

HOW ABOUT YOU?

Do you worry about the future? Do you wonder what you'll do for a living? Whom you'll marry? How long you'll live? Trust God to reveal all these things in his own good time. Obey what God has revealed in his Word. Then trust him for "one step at a time," and he will take care of the future!

Trust God "One Step at a Time"

MEMORIZE:
"Seek his will in all you do, and he will direct your paths." Proverbs 3:6

Trip to Chicago

(Read Isaiah 64:6-7; Philippians 3:4-9)

Bryan thought he must be the happiest boy in town. His father was taking him to Chicago on the train! When they arrived at the station, they saw that the train was almost ready to pull out. They made a dash for it, and soon they were settled down in their seats, watching the scenery go whipping by. Bryan was so excited he could hardly sit still. "How long till we get to Chicago, Dad?" he asked.

"I don't know. We'll ask the conductor," answered Dad. "Here he comes now. Get your ticket ready."

The conductor approached, and Bryan proudly held out his ticket. "Thanks, young fella," said the conductor. He looked at the tickets, and then turned to Dad. "Sir, I'm afraid you've either got the wrong tickets or the wrong train. Your tickets are for Chicago, but this train goes to Fort Wayne."

"Fort Wayne!" exclaimed Dad. "How could I have made such a mistake! I was sure I had the right train."

"I'll call you when we get to the next station," the conductor told Dad. "Then you can get off and catch the first train back the other way."

After the conductor left, Bryan asked anxiously, "Aren't we going to Chicago, Dad? I wanted to see Chicago!"

"We will go," said dad. "But we won't be able to stay as long as I would have liked," Dad answered. A moment later he added thoughtfully, "You know, Bryan, a lot of boys and girls are just like us."

"How do you mean, Dad?" asked Bryan.

"Well, everyone wants to go to heaven someday," explained Dad, "but many are trying to reach heaven the wrong way—they're on the 'wrong train.'

"You mean by going to church and trying to be good?" asked Bryan.

"That's right," said Dad. "What's the only way to heaven?"

"Believing in Jesus," answered Bryan. *HCT*

HOW ABOUT YOU?

Are you trying to get to heaven by living a good life? By going to church? By giving money to missions? That's like getting on the wrong train. It won't take you where you want to go. The only way to heaven is by believing in Jesus. To find out what this means, talk to a trusted friend or adult.

MEMORIZE:

"Jesus told him, 'I am the way, the truth, and the life. No one can come to the Father except through me.'"
John 14:6

Jesus Is the Way to Heaven

Pigeon, Be Still

(Read Psalm 46:7-11)

One day, eight-year-old Steven went with his grandma to the park. Grandma bought popcorn from a sidewalk vendor, and they sat down on a park bench to enjoy it. Soon it seemed there were hundreds of pigeons all around their feet. Steven ended up feeding more popcorn to the birds than he ate himself.

"Watch me, Grandma. I'm a pigeon!" Steven said with a giggle. And soon Grandma was laughing at his imitation, for Steven had captured the pigeon walk perfectly . . . head forward . . . stop . . . head back . . . stop!

As they walked home, Steven again imitated the way pigeons walk. "Steven, I read somewhere that a pigeon walks so funny because it can't adjust its eye focus while moving," Grandma told him. "In order to see where it's going, it has to stop and be completely still for a moment and then go on."

"Oh, I wouldn't like that!" exclaimed Steven. "I like to run fast!" He dashed down the sidewalk, then turned and waited for Grandma.

Grandma laughed. "I want to tell you something," she said. "As you grow older—and even now when you're still a child—you need to listen and be still before God sometimes."

"Before God?" asked Steven. "What do you mean?"

"Well, your Christian life can get all mixed up if you don't come to God and be still so he can speak to you," Grandma said. "Just like a pigeon, we have to stop sometimes and get our focus cleared up. I hope you'll take some time every day to be still with God—read his Word, pray, and just 'be still' so he can speak to you."

"Will I hear God's voice, Grandma?" Steven asked.

Grandma smiled. "Not out loud—but in your heart and mind you'll know God is talking to you. And be sure to do whatever he tells you to do!" she replied.

Steven nodded. "OK, Grandma," he agreed. *REP*

HOW ABOUT YOU?

Do you allow God to talk to you, or are you too busy to listen? If you're too busy to spend time with God, you're too busy. You need to learn and practice today's memory verse.

Listen to God

MEMORIZE:

"Be silent, and know that I am God! I will be honored by every nation. I will be honored throughout the world."

Psalm 46:10

Oh Boy!

(Read Isaiah 55:8-11)

"Oh, boy! It's a boy, isn't it?" Jeremy was jumping around the kitchen while his grandmother talked on the phone to Jeremy's father at the hospital. He was so excited, he almost dropped the apple he was holding.

Grandma hung up the phone. "You now have a beautiful baby sister," she said gently. "Her name is Melissa."

"That can't be!" Jeremy dropped his apple. "I've been praying for months for a brother. It's not fair. Cory got a baby brother, and he didn't pray at all."

Grandma sat down in the chair by the coffee table. "I got out the album that has your baby pictures in it, Jeremy," she said. "You sure were a cute little fellow."

"That was a long time ago. I'm in school now and everything," said Jeremy proudly.

"I remember how happy your mom and dad were when they were expecting you," Grandma told him. "When people asked if they wanted a girl or a boy, they said they just wanted a healthy baby."

Jeremy picked his apple up from the floor. "I'm sure they were glad I turned out to be a boy."

"They were mighty proud of you, but I was disappointed. I wanted a grand-daughter," confessed Grandma.

"Grandma!" Jeremy was shocked. "Don't you like me?"

"Oh, yes," Grandma assured him, "but I already had five grandsons. I thought it would be nice to have a girl in the family." She gave Jeremy a big hug. "But you know what? Now I couldn't love anybody more. You'll love your sister, too. You'll see. Thank God for her."

"I still don't think it was fair of you, Grandma, to wish I was a girl," Jeremy pouted.

Grandma's eyes twinkled. "Less fair than for you to wish your sister was a boy?" she asked.

Jeremy looked surprised. "I guess I was unfair, too," he admitted. *RMQ*

HOW ABOUT YOU?

Do you blame God if he doesn't answer your prayers your way? Remember, he knows what is best for us.

MEMORIZE:

"No matter what happens, always be thankful, for this is God's will for you who belong to Christ Jesus."
1 Thessalonians 5:18

God Knows Best

The Balancing Act

(Read Psalm 1:1-6)

Jordan and his friend Tyler were exploring in a park not far from their homes. "Wow, I'd hate to fall that far," said Jordan as the boys peered over the fence that separated them from a massive waterfall.

"Yeah," Tyler agreed as he lit a cigarette. Jordan stared at his friend in dismay. After urging from classmates, Tyler had recently started smoking. "Look!" exclaimed Tyler, pointing to some other boys climbing on the fence. One even walked along the top of the wooden rail while water from the falls plunged down not far from him.

"Wow! That's scary," said Jordan. "My dad says they oughta put a better fence along here. If that guy fell, it would be the end of him." They watched as the boys hopped off the fence and ran away laughing.

Jordan looked thoughtful. "Hey, Tyler, I dare you to walk the fence like that kid just did," he said after a moment.

Tyler looked at Jordan in surprise. "Are you crazy?" asked Tyler. "I'm not that stupid! I'm staying on *this* side of the fence. I'm not getting that close to the edge!"

Jordan sighed. "What's the difference between the edge of that waterfall and the edge you're on right now?

"Huh?" grunted Tyler. "What're you talking about?"

"Well, there are all kinds of hazard warnings about smoking," said Jordan, "but you ignore them. Seems to me you're doing a balancing act just like that kid on the fence—showing off for the guys!"

Tyler blinked thoughtfully at his cigarette. "I guess I did try smoking just because everyone else did," he admitted slowly. He dropped the cigarette on the ground and squished it under the toe of his shoe. Then he turned to Jordan. "But what about *you* and your 'act' of making fun of Daryl? You did that just because all the other guys were doing it."

Jordan was startled. "You're right," he said, "I guess we *both* have something to work on." *JT*

HOW ABOUT YOU?

Do you resist the temptation to show off? Some Christians want the "best of both worlds," and so they "ride a fence," trying to please their friends and God. God knows you're not perfect, but he can help you to stay as far away from temptation as possible if you ask him to.

Please God, Not Others

MEMORIZE:
"My child, if sinners entice you, turn your back on them!" Proverbs 1:10

Some Friend!

(Read Luke 12:8-12)

The police car drew quickly to the curb where Todd was standing with some other children. "Do you kids know Jason Connor?" the officer asked.

"No, sir," answered one of the children.

"I've got to find him in a hurry," the policeman said, looking straight at Todd. Todd said nothing, and the officer drove away.

When Todd later told his friend Kurt what had happened, Kurt frowned. "I think you should have told him that you know Jason," said Kurt. "Jason's our friend, and he's probably playing ball at the park."

"I know, but what if he's in trouble?" asked Todd.

"Well, some friend you are!" scolded Kurt. "Seems like you should stand by him, not act like you don't know him."

Later both boys were sorry to learn why the police were looking for Jason. His parents had been badly injured in a car accident and were hospitalized.

As Kurt and Todd stood in a checkout lane at the supermarket the next day, two men behind them began talking. "I hear your neighbors, the Connors, were in a really bad accident," said one.

"They sure were," replied the other. "They both were really battered. Be out of work at least a month. I wonder where their God was when they got hit. They've been on my back for years about trusting in their God." He glanced down at Kurt, who was staring at him. "Don't let anybody fool you about a loving, caring God, kid. There isn't any."

Kurt looked away and said nothing, but Todd looked up and smiled at the man. "Sir, I know the Connors," he said. "And God *is* their friend, and mine, too. He was with them when they got hurt, and he'll take good care of them. Right, Kurt?"

"Right, Todd," Kurt agreed nervously. With shame he thought of how he had scolded Todd for not admitting he knew Jason. Now by his silence, Kurt had denied his best friend, Jesus. *AGL*

HOW ABOUT YOU?

Do you speak up for Jesus when you have a chance? Or, by your silence, do you deny that you even know him? Ask God to give you the courage to speak up for him.

MEMORIZE:

"For the Holy Spirit will teach you what needs to be said even as you are standing there." Luke 12:12

Speak Up for Jesus

Thorny Words

(Read Ecclesiastes 10:11-14)

Mary and her mother were busy in the garden. "Ouch!" yelled Mary as she trimmed a dead branch off a rose bush. "How come dead branches can still hurt like that? They should lose their thorns when they die!"

"But they don't," said Mother. "Even though they're dead, they can still hurt." She looked at Mary and then asked, "Have you heard of William Shakespeare?"

"Oh, sure, Mom," said Mary. "Miss Abbott read some of his poetry in English class. Sometimes it's hard to figure out what he means, though. They talked so funny back then."

"In one of Shakespeare's plays, someone said, 'The evil that men do lives after them.'"

"What does that mean?" Mary asked.

"Even after someone dies, the bad things he or she has done live on and continue to hurt others," explained Mother. "I had an aunt who had a terrible temper. Shortly before she died, I heard her arguing with my mother—her sister. She said some terrible things that were not true. She died without ever being able to correct what she had said or to ask my mother to forgive her. Even now, my aunt's words still hurt Mother."

When Mom got out the Bible for family devotions that evening, Mary talked more with her mother about her aunt. Mom turned in the Bible to Ecclesiastes 10. "King Solomon had some wise things to say about our speech," she said. "I believe he's telling us that a fool speaks without thinking sometimes, and no one can say what will happen to those words. But the words of a wise man are gracious."

"I just thought of something," said Mary with a smile. "I have a pressed rose in my Bible. It's dead, but it's still pretty. I want my words to be like that—something nice to remember for a long time, not something that keeps hurting people, like hurtful words." *AGL*

HOW ABOUT YOU?

Listen to yourself today. Are your words pleasant to remember, or are they barbs that will hurt someone through the years? Words are often repeated and long remembered. They help or harm people, even people you may never meet. Let your words today be gracious and pleasing in God's sight.

MEMORIZE:
"It is pleasant to listen to wise words, but the speech of fools brings them to ruin." Ecclesiastes 10:12

Words Last a Long Time

Footsteps

(Read Psalm 18:1-3, 30-36)

Chad had spent the whole month of August with his Uncle Robert and Aunt Kate at their log cabin on Pine Mountain. "We'll go up to the freshwater spring today," said Uncle Robert as they took an early morning walk on Chad's last day in the mountains. But as they started up the steep path, Chad had trouble walking. The rain had made the path slippery, and his feet kept sliding. "Follow in my steps," suggested Uncle Robert. Chad placed his feet into the big footprints Uncle Robert made in the soft earth, and he found he could walk without slipping back.

Soon they neared the spring where a mother deer and her fawns were drinking from the water. They watched quietly. "Wow!" exclaimed Chad after the deer had gone. "I could stay here forever. As a matter of fact, I'd much rather stay here than go to junior high!"

Uncle Robert leaned over to pick some wildflowers. "I thought you were excited about going to junior high."

"I am . . . sort of," Chad replied weakly. "But I've heard that math in junior high is really hard. And the older kids laugh at you. They think they're so much bigger."

"Do you remember King David in the Bible?" asked Uncle Robert. "He, too, faced situations that were much bigger than he could handle. But God gave David success even when the enemy seemed really tough. David said it was as if God had gone before him, and made big footprints for him to walk in."

"Like I walked in your footsteps on the way up here," remembered Chad.

"Right!" said Uncle Robert. "Don't forget that God will be with you through junior high just like he was with David through his hard times." Uncle Robert smiled as he got up to head back to the cabin. "Come on. Let's go see what Aunt Kate has fixed for breakfast." *DLR*

HOW ABOUT YOU?

Do you worry about situations that seem too big to handle alone? God doesn't want you to face them alone—he's with you and he understands just what you're going through. Ask him for wisdom and courage for any situation and trust him to help.

MEMORIZE:

"You have made a wide path for my feet to keep them from slipping."
Psalm 18:36

God Prepares the Way

Grow Up

(Read 1 Peter 1:13-16)

"I give up!" Brad slammed his books on the kitchen table. "I've tried, but I just can't do it. I give up."

"Can't do what?" Mother wanted to know.

"Can't be perfect. I tried all day. Then just before the last bell, I lost my temper. It seems the harder I try to be perfect, the more I goof up."

Mother smiled. "I know the feeling. But why this sudden interest in being perfect? Oh, I remember. Our verse this morning was about being perfect." Mother paused, then spoke again as Brad opened the refrigerator door. "You don't have time for a snack, Brad. We're going to Aunt Melody's to see the new baby."

Later, Brad proudly held his new cousin. "Oh, she's beautiful," he gushed. "Crystal is perfect, isn't she?"

Mother curled the sleeping baby's fist around her finger. "Yes. She is a perfect baby."

Brad wrinkled his brow. "Crystal is perfect. I wish I was."

"Perhaps you have the wrong definition of 'perfect,' Brad," suggested Aunt Melody. "When the Bible speaks of 'perfect,' it often means 'grown-up.' Crystal can't walk or talk or eat meat, yet she is a perfect newborn infant. However, if she stays like this for six months, we will be worried. She would not be perfect anymore."

Brad frowned. "I still don't understand."

"To be perfect is to be complete for your age," Aunt Melody continued. "You know more and can do more than Crystal because you're a ten-year-old. To be a 'perfect' Christian doesn't mean we never make mistakes. It means we grow, and overcome, and learn from them."

Mother nodded. "For example, being perfect doesn't mean you'll never lose your temper, but it does mean you will learn to say you're sorry when you do."

The baby wiggled in Brad's arms and puckered her lips. Aunt Melody laughed. "Better let me have that perfect baby, Brad. She's about to lose her temper." *BJW*

HOW ABOUT YOU?

Are you growing in Christ? Do you learn from your mistakes? That's a sign of growth. Each day you should become a little more like Jesus.

Become like Jesus

MEMORIZE:
"So let it grow, for when your endurance is fully developed, you will be strong in character and ready for anything." James 1:4

First Impressions

(Read 1 Samuel 16:1-7)

"Mom," Lizzy whispered through the shelf of library books, "look at that girl by the checkout. She's in my class at school."

Mom frowned when she saw the girl Lizzy was referring to. The teenager had long, dangly earrings, and also a small gold hoop through her bottom lip. She wore shorts with a tube top.

"It looks like she's more interested in showing off her body than she is in library books," observed Mom.

"Oh, Mom," protested Lizzy, "you're not judging her fairly. I've talked to her quite often, and she's a lot of fun and really smart, too."

"That may be true, but that's not the side of herself that she's letting people see. Come over here." Mom motioned to Lizzy, and they peered through another shelf at some people in the reading area. "See that man standing in the corner?"

"The security guard?" asked Lizzy.

"How do you know he's a security guard?" Mom wanted to know.

"Because of his uniform," Lizzy answered.

"What about that girl at the first table? What can you tell me about her?" asked Mom.

"She has a university jacket on, so she must be a student," Lizzy said.

Lizzy's mom then pointed out a businessman in a suit and tie, and a Muslim man in a turban. "You can guess a lot about a person by looking at his or her appearance," Mom said, "but as you pointed out, that doesn't mean you're always right. Maybe I was wrong about that girl at the checkout. Perhaps she is here to study and learn, but that's certainly not the first impression you get about her."

"I guess not," admitted Lizzy. "And I guess we have to be very careful about what first impressions we're making, especially since we represent not only ourselves but God." *HMT*

HOW ABOUT YOU?

What impression are you giving to others? Does your appearance reflect your heart? It's very hard to change a first impression.

MEMORIZE:
"Man looks at the outward appearance, but the Lord looks at the heart."
1 Samuel 16:7, NIV

Make a Good Impression

Open Hands and Heart

(Read Psalm 37:3-7)

"I hate this town!" stormed Timothy, dumping his bag on the table.

"Oh, Timothy, we've not been here very long," said Mom. "Give it a chance."

"The worst part of all is that Brad's not here," grumbled Timothy. "I know I'm never going to like it here."

Just then three-year-old Kayla came in. "Hey, Kayla! I've got a treat for you," said Timothy, digging into his pocket. Kayla immediately held out her hand, her tiny fist clenched tightly. "Open your hand," commanded Timothy. But Kayla just smiled sweetly at her big brother and waited. "What on earth have you got in there?" demanded Timothy.

Mom smiled. "It's that odd-shaped yellow stone you gave her yesterday," she said.

"Oh, drop that thing, Kayla," said Timothy, "and I'll give you this treat. And I won't take your old stone away either."

"Give! Give!" cried Kayla impatiently, still holding the stone tightly.

"Open your hand, Kayla," coaxed Timothy. "Don't you trust me?" Baby Kayla shook her head. "I won't take your stone," he promised. "After all, I gave it to you in the first place, remember? Besides, this treat is nicer anyway."

"I know that and you know that," said Mom, "but Kayla's afraid to risk it."

"She should know I won't do anything bad for her!" exclaimed Timothy.

Mom grinned. "Kayla's not the only one who's got her fist clenched," she remarked. "What about you, Timothy?"

"What do you mean?" asked Timothy, frowning. "I don't do dumb things like that, Mom!"

"Well, aren't you refusing to trust God in this new town?" asked Mom. "Wasn't it God who gave you Brad as a friend? And now you don't want to let go of all the old things. Why won't you trust his plans for you in this new place, too?"

Timothy was thoughtful. "I didn't think of it like that," he admitted. *MTF*

HOW ABOUT YOU?

What is it that you are clutching so tightly that you are not willing to let go? Is it possessions? Friends? If God wants you to let go of any of these, are you ready to trust him and do so? Maybe God has something better in store for you.

MEMORIZE:

"You parents—if your children ask for a loaf of bread, do you give them a stone instead? . . . If you sinful people know how to give good gifts to your children, how much more will your heavenly Father give good gifts to those who ask him." Matthew 7:9, 11

Trust God

Invitation to Join

(Read John 1:35-42)

"Did you invite Roger to the game?" asked Ted's father.

"Yeah," Ted answered with a frown, "but he's going to a Boy Scout meeting instead."

"Oh, really?" asked Dad in surprise. "I didn't know he was a Scout! Would you like to be a Boy Scout, too?" asked Dad.

"Yeah, I might," replied Ted. "I know they learn neat things . . . like they have camp outs and learn how to find their way out of the woods if they get lost—stuff like that. I don't know how you join, though."

"If you really want to join, we'll find out how," Dad said.

Ted frowned. "But maybe Roger doesn't want me to join," he said. "If he did, seems like he'd have told me about it and asked me." He jumped up to answer the phone, and the subject didn't come up again.

A few days later, Ted and his folks were leaving a school program when a classmate ran up to Ted. "Hey, Ted, want to go with my dad and me to the Rockets' game Sunday?" he asked.

"Sounds like fun, but I can't, Justin," replied Ted. He hesitated. "I go to church on Sunday."

"You do?" asked Justin. "I didn't know that." He turned to go. "See ya later," he said.

As they started home, Dad spoke thoughtfully. "Do you suppose Justin thinks you don't want him to come to church?" he asked.

Ted frowned. "Don't want him to come?" he asked. "Why would he think that?"

"Well, I remember that you were a little annoyed with Roger for not asking you to join the Scouts," said Dad. "You thought maybe he didn't want you to join because he never mentioned it to you. Apparently you've never mentioned church to Justin."

"No," Ted admitted. "I haven't." After a moment, he spoke again. "I'll invite him to come now," he said with determination. "I'll make sure he knows he's wanted there." *AGL*

HOW ABOUT YOU?

Do you attend church regularly? Do your friends know about it? Do they know they are welcome to come, too? Invite them. Then perhaps the following verse may be said of you.

Invite Others to Church

MEMORIZE:
"Then Andrew brought Simon to meet Jesus." John 1:42

September

4

Consider the Ant

(Read Proverbs 6:6-11)

"How do I get so lucky?" wondered Brian aloud as the family ate dinner one Sunday noon. "I ask a simple question and get stuck with doing a report."

Mother smiled as she asked, "How did that happen?"

"Today's memory verse was 'Take a lesson from the ants, you lazybones. Learn from their ways and be wise,'" explained Brian. "I asked my teacher what was so special about ants, and she said I could make a study of them and write a report for next week."

"That should be interesting, and it might be helpful with another problem, too," observed Dad. "You know, Brian, Mother and I have talked to you often about your habit of putting things off until the last minute . . . and also about always being late. Maybe the ants will have a few lessons to teach you." Brian shrugged. He supposed he should do things a little more promptly, but he doubted that making a report on ants would get him out of bed any earlier in the morning or help him get his schoolwork done on time.

It took a little prodding, but Brian finally got busy on his report. He discovered that there were many different kinds of ants, and he found them all fascinating. He read that an ant can carry a load 52 times its own weight. He learned that one kind gathers grain at harvesttime and stores enough to last a whole year. Another kind can strip all the leaves off a small tree in one night. Still another tends herds of aphids and "milks" them like cows.

"Ants are such busy little creatures! No wonder the Bible says to consider their ways," he reported in Sunday school. "If all Christians were more like these ants, the world would be a better place."

And at home he said, "I've decided that if ants are smart enough to get food ready for a whole year, I should be smart enough to get ready on time for school." *JWC*

HOW ABOUT YOU?

Are you generally on time? Or are you a procrastinator—someone who puts things off? Be honest now—are you a lazybones (a lazy person)? Don't let the little ant put you to shame. Resolve to do your work promptly and well, both at school and at home. Learning to be on time and not put things off is a big step in building a strong Christian character. Ask God to help you . . . then get busy and do it.

MEMORIZE:

"Take a lesson from the ants, you lazybones. Learn from their ways and be wise!" Proverbs 6:6

Don't Be Lazy

A Time to Sleep

(Read Mark 6:30-32)

Toby and the other fourth graders of Faith Christian School were on the way to the zoo. As an assignment, they were to notice the animals that were asleep.

The first sleeping animals they saw were raccoons. The little ones were up in the tree, and nearby was the mother. They saw birds sleeping, too. A stork stood on one leg, its head tucked into its feathers, fast asleep. On the opposite side of the room an owl had its eyes closed. Its claws were locked tightly around the tree branch as it slept. Toby thought the Australian koala bear was the most interesting. It was snuggled between some branches way up in a tree. Toby learned that this animal spent most of the day asleep.

When the class returned to school, they discussed what they had seen. Their teacher talked about the importance of rest. "*Our* bodies need rest, too," she said. "God made us that way. When Jesus lived on earth, even he became tired and had to stop for rest."

Toby thought about the animals and then about what the teacher had said. He knew he needed rest, but he didn't always want to go to bed when it was time. And sometimes when he went to bed too late, he didn't get all the rest his body needed. He knew it showed up in his schoolwork the next day.

"Animals show more intelligence than people in some ways," his teacher was saying. "God made our bodies to be useful for him. But if we spend our energy and then refuse to get the rest we need, we're not taking good care of our bodies."

Toby nodded. *I'm going to take better care of the body God gave me,* he decided. *Mom will be surprised at how fast I jump up when she says it's time to go to bed tonight. RIJ*

HOW ABOUT YOU?

Do you grumble at bedtime? Do you stall instead of going to bed when you should? Sometimes staying up late to watch a TV program, read a book, or play a game is not using good judgment. Your body gets tired from the day's activities, and you need to stop for rest. Go to bed cheerfully, knowing that God will renew your energy and prepare you for another day.

MEMORIZE:
"I lay down and slept. I woke up in safety, for the Lord was watching over me." Psalm 3:5

Bodies Need Rest

At Hilltop Farm

(Read Matthew 10:29-31)

"Come here, Mr. Wiggle Worm," said Peter as he put a worm in a can. He and Dad were going fishing. "Dad, are worms good for anything besides bird food and fishing bait?"

"They sure are," said Dad. "They help the earth breathe."

Peter laughed. "You mean they're like lungs?" he asked.

Dad smiled. "As worms burrow through the ground, they let fresh air into the soil. And when they eat and digest the soil, that's like when Mother sifts flour to make a cake," he explained. "The more the soil is digested and fertilized by worms, the better it is for growing things. You see, God has a purpose for everything."

"Yeah . . . and I'm glad one purpose for worms is to make fishing bait," said Peter. "Haven't we got enough? Can we go fishing now?" Dad agreed, and they were off.

That evening they had fish for supper! "Oh, yummy!" exclaimed Peter. "These fish are almost as much fun to eat as to catch. Wish I could go fishing instead of to school."

Mom laughed. "That would be overdoing it a little, don't you think?" she asked. "Besides, you like school, don't you?"

"Yeah—except science," said Peter. "I just don't believe some stuff Mrs. Moore teaches—like that we evolved from a lower form of life. God made the world and us and the stars and . . . and even worms, didn't he?"

"He sure did," said Mom. "Everything works together just perfectly, and it's amazing that people can't see that there must be a God who planned it all."

Dad nodded. "There are so many illustrations of that here on the farm," he said. "For example, when the leaves fall from the trees, they rot and become fertilizer. Birds eat insects, and that's good. The sun is just the right distance away so we can live comfortably. Everything works out just right."

"Hey—I just thought of something!" said Peter. "If God planned all those things, he must have a plan for me, too."

"He certainly has," agreed Dad. *HCT*

HOW ABOUT YOU?

Aren't you glad that the God who planned and made the whole world wants to take charge of your life? Give yourself wholly to him and trust him to work out what is best for you.

MEMORIZE:

"So don't be afraid; you are more valuable to him than a whole flock of sparrows." Matthew 10:31

God Has a Plan for You

Better than the Coast Guard

(Read Romans 5:6-11)

Jason talked excitedly about the Coast Guard ship he had just toured at the Sea Festival. "And just think—our guide said the Coast Guard saved at least 6,000 lives last year!" he exclaimed. "He said storms sometimes come up fast and people can't make it back to shore. Other times boaters are foolish and don't pay attention to the warnings. The reason people are in trouble doesn't matter to the Coast Guard. They do their job. I bet they save more lives every year than anybody!"

"They do save a lot of lives," agreed Dad. "They're well trained and ready to rescue those in danger. Do you know what their motto is?"

Jason nodded. "Yep. Our guide told us. *Semper paratus*—always ready." He grinned at Dad, proud of his knowledge.

"The Coast Guard does a good job," said Mother, "but I can think of some-body who saves even more lives every year than the people in the Coast Guard do. Can you guess who that might be?"

"Who?" asked Jason in surprise.

"I think I know," said Dad. "I think Mom means Jesus. He's willing to save anyone who will trust him."

Mom nodded. "You know, I can't imagine anyone struggling in the water, refusing help from the Coast Guard. But people who are struggling in sin often refuse to accept the salvation Jesus offers. They just keep trying to save them-selves, and they never can." *LLL*

HOW ABOUT YOU?

Have you let Jesus rescue you from your sin? You can never save yourself—not by going to church, not by giving money, not by being a good person. But Jesus died to rescue you. Don't refuse his help. Trust him today.

Let Jesus Save You

MEMORIZE:
"And I, the Son of Man, have come to seek and save those like him who are lost." Luke 19:10

God's Strength (Part 1)

(Read Mark 4:36-41)

Scott glanced nervously out the school window. All day it had looked stormy. He knew it was tornado season, and he hoped there wasn't going to be another tornado alert today. They always made him afraid. Sighing, he tried to concentrate on his math lesson.

As Scott began the first problem, a bell rang. "Tornado drill," said Miss Greely. "Take a large book and file quietly into the hall, children." Quickly they obeyed, taking their places in the school's inner hall and putting the books over their heads as they had done many times before. But there was something different today. Scott could hear a siren blowing, and as he listened, he knew it came from a nearby fire station. It was a signal that a tornado funnel had been seen nearby!

Scott had never been so scared before! But as he sat, trembling, he remembered something Dad had said just the weekend before. They had gone swimming, and as Dad walked out into the deep water, Scott's little brother Brian hung on to Dad's shoulder. "Are you scared in the deep water, Brian?" Scott had asked.

Brian had shook his head and said, "Nope, Dad's got me."

Dad had laughed as he replied, "Good boy! I'm in control here, and I'm glad you trust your father." Then he had added, "I hope both you boys will remember that you can always trust your Father in heaven, too. He's in control of all the circumstances of your lives." As Scott remembered that, he felt better.

A few minutes later, Scott heard a roaring sound. It began softly but got louder and louder. It almost sounded like a train rushing by. He had heard that a tornado sounded that way. *I'm still scared,* Scott thought, *but not so awfully scared. God's my heavenly Father, and he's in control.*

After the "all clear" whistle sounded, the children returned to their classrooms and were soon dismissed to go home. They learned that a tornado had indeed passed by, not far from their school. Much damage had been done, but no one had been hurt. With his family, Scott thanked God for watching over them. *HWM*

HOW ABOUT YOU?

Storms can be frightening, can't they? They are powerful and can cause a lot of damage. But God is even more powerful. Remember that God is in control.

MEMORIZE:

"Who is this man, that even the wind and waves obey him?" Mark 4:41

God Controls Nature

God's Strength (Part 2)

(Read 2 Corinthians 12:7-10)

The tornado that passed close to Scott's town was the subject of conversation for many days. Scott and his family heard stories of strange things that had been caused by the strong winds.

One day Dad came home with a piece of a log. "What's that for?" asked Scott.

Dad held it out, and Scott saw that, sticking out from the wood, was a piece of straw. "One of the fellows at work found this on his property," said Dad. "His place was right on the edge of the storm. Isn't it amazing how the wind could take that little straw and drive it right into the wood without even bending it?"

"Wow!" marveled Scott. "I don't see how it could do that. It sure wouldn't work to try to pound it in."

"No," agreed Dad. "It took a stronger force than we could exert—a special kind of power. I've been thinking about that all afternoon, and I've decided to teach that class of boys I've been offered."

"What's that got to do with this wood?" asked Scott.

"Well, I wanted to take the class," said Dad, "but I was afraid I wouldn't be able to hold their interest. This afternoon the Lord showed me that I have a special kind of power available to me—the Holy Spirit. This straw was weak, but powered by the storm, it became very strong. I'm weak, too, but empowered by the Holy Spirit, I believe I can be of help to those boys. I thought about you, too."

"Me?" Scott was startled.

Dad nodded. "I heard Mrs. Jarvis, the choir director, asking you to sing a solo on youth night. She said she heard you sing and that you have a fine voice."

"But I get so nervous," began Scott, "and I . . ." He stopped. "But I have a special power available to me, too, don't I? I think I'll call Mrs. Jarvis. God will help me sing for him." *HWM*

HOW ABOUT YOU?

Do you feel too scared to sing, talk about Jesus, make posters, or take part in some other activity for which God has given you a talent? If you're a Christian, a special power—God's power—is available to you. Are you using it? Ask him to help you, and then say yes to the opportunities he gives to serve him.

MEMORIZE:

"Since I know it is all for Christ's good, I am quite content with my weaknesses and with insults, hardships, persecutions, and calamities. For when I am weak, then I am strong." 2 Corinthians 12:10

God Gives Power

One Small Candle

(Read Matthew 5:13-16)

"How was school today, Trent?" asked Mom.

Trent laughed. "My new teacher is nice," he said, "but she just can't keep the class quiet. She talks so softly and looks at us with such big, scared-looking eyes. No one pays any attention to her. We had so much fun, but I felt kind of sorry for her, too."

"Then you can help her by being quiet and doing what she says," said Dad.

Trent shrugged. "What's the use? The other kids will still talk and play games." As he spoke, the lights went out. "What's wrong with the electricity?" asked Trent.

"I don't know," said Dad. "A power failure somewhere, I guess."

"Well, I hope it comes back on soon!" said Trent. "Can we light some candles, Mom?" Mom agreed, and Trent hurried to the kitchen to find them. "All I can find is one little birthday candle," he said when he returned. "I'll light it. I found some matches, too."

"Only one candle?" asked Dad. "And a small one at that. No use lighting it. What good would one little candle do in this huge, big darkness?"

"Well, one light will be better than none," insisted Trent. He lit the tiny red and white striped candle. "Hey! This gives more light than I expected!" he exclaimed.

Dad smiled. "Trent," he said, "I hope you'll light your candle in school, too."

"What candle?" asked Trent, puzzled.

"I mean your 'light' for Jesus," Dad told him. "He says we are to let our lights shine, remember? In your case, that means you are to do your part in class by keeping quiet and obeying your teacher."

Mom nodded. "And if you do, just maybe some of the others will do the same," she suggested.

Slowly Trent nodded. "But even if they don't, one little light does make a difference, doesn't it?" he said thoughtfully. *MTF*

HOW ABOUT YOU?

Do you sometimes feel that you are too small, too insignificant, too shy to make a difference? Remember that Jesus didn't say, "You are to change the whole world." He simply said, "You are the light of the world." That means all Christians—including you! No matter who you are or what you look like or what you own or how clever you are, if you know Jesus, he has given you a light. It's up to you to shine!

MEMORIZE:

"In the same way, let your good deeds shine out for all to see, so that everyone will praise your heavenly Father." Matthew 5:16

Shine for Jesus

Unbreakable

(Read Ephesians 5:8-10)

David went to sit beside his mother. "Mom," he said, "Mr. Scott has really changed." Mr. Scott was their neighbor. "He used to yell at us all the time," continued David, "and he'd get mad and swear at us if a ball went in his yard. I wonder how come he's so different now."

"He's a Christian now," Mom told him.

"I know," said David, "but why does that make such a difference?"

Mom smiled and looked at the yarn in her hands. "This yarn is made up of four strands, called 'plies,'" she said, snipping off a length of yarn. She separated the yarn into four threads and handed one of them to David. "Take this in both hands and tug," she instructed.

David tugged on the single strand of yarn. It snapped in two. "That yarn isn't very strong," he said, handing her the two torn pieces.

"No," agreed Mom, "and that's why I don't knit with just one ply at a time. I leave the four plies twisted together." She dropped the smaller of the two pieces into the wastebasket and twisted the longer piece with the three strands she had removed. Then she handed it to David. "Try to break that," she said.

David pulled and tugged and yanked on the yarn, but this time it wouldn't break. "Wow!" he said. "It broke so easily before; I can hardly believe how strong it is now."

"That's a little like what happens when we accept Jesus as Savior and Lord," said Mother. "That first piece of yarn doesn't have just its own strength now. It has three more plies to make it a good, strong, almost unbreakable strand. And Mr. Scott no longer has just his own strength either. He now has the strength of God the Father, God the Son, and God the Holy Spirit to help him."

David yanked on the yarn again. "I get it," he said. *GJT*

HOW ABOUT YOU?

Do you have a problem with your temper? With obeying your parents? With your behavior in school? Are you trying to improve and finding it impossible? Perhaps you're trying in your own strength. Ask God to help you change.

MEMORIZE:

"What this means is that those who become Christians become new persons. They are not the same anymore, for the old life is gone. A new life has begun!" 2 Corinthians 5:17

Jesus Will Change You

Mary's Cake

(Read 1 Chronicles 29:10-13)

"I like being at your house," said Mary's friend Kara as she got ready to go home. "Everybody is so nice to each other. At my house, it seems like all we do is fight. Even Mom and Dad fight a lot. I wonder what makes your family different."

Mary shrugged. "Maybe we work harder at it than some people do," she suggested.

After supper that evening, Mother brought in a dessert—a chocolate cake that Mary had made. "This tastes great, Mom!" exclaimed Mary's brother. "You should make it more often."

"It's one of the best cakes I've ever tasted," agreed Dad.

"Thank you," said Mom, winking at Mary.

"Mom! No fair!" exclaimed Mary. "*I* made the cake."

"*You* made it!" exclaimed Dad. "Good for you."

Mom grinned. "Oh, that's right . . . you did make it, didn't you?" she teased. She turned to Dad. "Actually, she made it all by herself!"

As Mom and Mary cleaned the kitchen after dinner, Mom put the rest of the cake away. "You know, honey," she said, "I've been thinking about something. It wasn't fair for me to take credit for your baking, but you weren't fair today, either. When Kara asked what made your family different, you didn't give God credit for being the center of our life. One reason we get along so well is that we love him. His Spirit is in us. We can't take the credit for that."

Mary bit her lip. "But Kara wouldn't understand that," she said.

Mom smiled. "Maybe; maybe not," she said. "But tell her anyway. Give God the credit he deserves." *KEC*

HOW ABOUT YOU?

As you accept God's blessings, do you remember to give him credit? Let your friends know why your life is different. Tell them about God.

MEMORIZE:

"I will praise the Lord at all times.
I will constantly speak his praises."
Psalm 34:1

Give God Credit

Down, but Not Out

(Read 2 Corinthians 4:5-10)

David's mom came into his room to check on his homework. "How's your report coming?" she asked.

"It's not," David barked, "and I don't want to do it anyway."

"You sound upset, David. Are you still fretting about yesterday?" Mom questioned.

David's eyes got misty. "I wanted to be class reporter for the school paper so bad," he said. "And what did Mrs. French say? 'You have a good imagination, but you don't check facts. A reporter must be accurate. Work on it, David. Maybe you can be a reporter next year.'"

"I know you're disappointed, David, but don't give up," encouraged Mom. "Now, what school report are you working on?"

"I have to write about some famous person," David muttered. "It can be anybody."

"I know who will be a real help to you! Come with me. Let's look in the encyclopedia." David's mother helped him find some books. Then she left to fold clothes.

When Mother returned, David looked up. "I can't believe it, Mom," he said. "Abraham Lincoln was one of our greatest presidents, but this book says he lost several important political races!"

"That's right," agreed Mom, "but he's remembered for his successes, not for his failures. Often it's easy to give up when we fail, but we don't grow that way. It's not what God would have us do either. He wants us to learn from our experiences and to try harder the next time. We must learn to depend on him to help us turn failure into success."

David gave his mom a big hug. "Thanks, Mom," he said. "I see what you've been trying to tell me. I won't give up. I'll make this report so accurate that even Mrs. French would be proud of it." *JLH*

HOW ABOUT YOU?

What happens when you fail at something? Do you give up and quit trying? Don't get discouraged. Learn from your mistakes and realize that it takes time to learn to do things well. Depend on God to help you.

Try Again

The Dead Letter Office

(Read Psalm 66:16-20)

When the doorbell rang, Micah came to the door. The postman stood there, a letter in his hand. "Micah," he said, "did you address this letter? You didn't put down the zip code or the city and state. It's going to end up in the dead letter office."

"Oops!" exclaimed Micah. "I was going to ask Mother for Aunt Julia's full address, but I forgot. What's the dead letter office?"

"It's a department of the post office. Mail that can't be delivered goes there," explained Mr. Zachary. "Then clerks open it and look for return addresses inside. If there is one, the mail is returned to the sender."

"What if there isn't any return address?" asked Micah.

"Most of the letters are destroyed," said Mr. Zachary. "The contents of parcels are sold, and the money goes into the post office funds."

"Well, I don't want Aunt Julia's letter to end up there," declared Micah. "Thanks, Mr. Zachary."

At family devotions that evening Micah began his prayer: "Dear heavenly Father, thank you for a beautiful day and for my parents, and for . . ." He stopped. "I think my prayer is going to God's dead letter office," he said, right in the middle of his prayer. His parents looked at him in surprise. "I need to make something right first," added Micah tearfully. "Daddy, I took five dollars from your wallet last week. Please forgive me. I'll pay you back from my allowance."

"Of course I forgive you, Micah," said Dad. "But you need to confess your sin to God, too."

Micah nodded his head. "I know," he said. "I'm going to do that right now." *MRP*

HOW ABOUT YOU?

Isn't prayer a wonderful privilege? But if you have done wrong things and not made them right, it is hard to pray with a pure heart. And God loves to hear his children pray with a pure heart.

MEMORIZE:
"But God did listen! He paid attention to my prayer." Psalm 66:19

Pray with a Pure Heart

Renewed Power

(Read John 15:4-8)

"Did someone pack the flashlight?" asked Dad. The family was all set to leave for a weeklong camping trip.

"I did," said Keith. "I took the one with rechargeable batteries. Is that OK?"

Dad nodded. "OK. Let's go," he said, and they were off!

They found a camping spot at the lake and were soon having a great time—swimming, hiking, fishing, playing ball, and riding bikes. Evenings were cool, and they generally huddled beside the cozy fire and enjoyed hot chocolate. Then Keith and his little brother Corey would take the flashlight and walk off into the darkness to the washroom.

One particularly cool night, Keith didn't feel like leaving the warm fire. But Mother insisted that he go with Corey, so he stomped into the tent to get the flashlight. On the way to the washroom, the flashlight's beam got dimmer and dimmer. It flickered out just as they got there.

When they were ready to go back to the campsite in the dark, Corey hesitated. "I'm scared," he whimpered.

"Don't be a baby," said Keith, pulling on Corey's hand.

"I'm not a baby." Corey started to cry and Keith stalked off. "Wait for me!" Corey's wails filled the night. Keith went back, grabbed Corey's hand, and together they made their way back to the campsite.

"The flashlight gave out," said Keith, answering the questioning look in Mother's eyes. "And Corey got scared."

"I guess it's been too long since the batteries were recharged," said Dad. "But that flashlight's not the only thing that gave out," he added. "Your patience also gave out. Perhaps you need to hook up to your power source to recharge that as well."

"*My* power source?" asked Keith. "What's that?"

"Jesus," replied Dad. "He gives power to overcome sin and to display the qualities he wants to see in us. Spending time with God is one way to renew our spiritual energy. And then as we live our daily lives, we need to obey the things he has taught us." *VEN*

HOW ABOUT YOU?

Do you read your Bible and learn about God? Do you ask him for strength to do what's right? God is the one who can help you have right attitudes and actions throughout the day.

Jesus Is Your "Power Source"

MEMORIZE:
"For apart from me you can do nothing." John 15:5

A Good Gift

(Read Matthew 7:7-11)

Noah walked home alone, kicking a pebble along the road. It was his first week in a new school and most of the kids there had known each other since kindergarten. So far, he hadn't found where he fit in.

When Noah got home, he opened the back door and set his books on the kitchen table. Mom looked up with a smile. "How was school?"

Noah frowned. "We moved here because Dad felt God was calling him to be the minister of the new church, right?" he said.

"That's right," agreed Mom.

"You and Dad said this calling was a gift from God," said Noah, "but I don't think it was a gift for me. I don't like the new school, and nobody likes me."

Mom set aside the vegetables she was peeling and studied Noah. "Do you remember when you were younger and had trouble learning addition?" she asked. Noah nodded. "I bought you a set of flash cards," continued Mom. "You didn't think that was much of a gift at the time, especially since I made you study them every day. But later you thanked me because it helped you become good at math."

"I remember," said Noah. He grinned. "I'm still good at math."

Mom smiled. "Perhaps moving here is a little like that gift," she suggested. "You don't see the value now, but maybe you should give it a little time."

Noah sighed. "I'll try," he promised.

The next week, he came home from school one day with a grin on his face. "Guess what?" he said eagerly.

Mom set a plate of cookies on the table. "You had a good day?" she asked.

"I sure did," said Noah. "I've always wanted to get good enough to play basketball in high school and maybe in college, but there was never a coach at my old school so we never had a team. Today some of the guys told me this school has a coach and a team. I'm going to try out. I can see now that moving here was a gift from God to me after all," he said. *KEC*

HOW ABOUT YOU?

Do you ever feel as though God has let you down? You may even feel hurt and angry at times. Maybe you expect God's gifts to make you comfortable or happy immediately. However, his gifts may not always seem good at the time you receive them.

MEMORIZE:
"Hope in God, who richly provides us with everything for our enjoyment."
1 Timothy 6:17, NIV

Trust God When Disappointed

Big Little Things

(Read Ephesians 4:24-32)

It had been a terrible day for Larry! In the first place, Mother had said they were out of bread and Larry would have to buy his lunch at school. Mother knew he hated to wait in line! Why hadn't she bought bread yesterday? Then Dad had refused to take him to school—it was only five miles out of his way—so he had to ride the bus.

Larry was mad when he went to school. He was madder when he came home. But he was maddest now! Why couldn't he stay up another 30 minutes? He was old enough to know when to go to bed without being sent there like a baby! He started to kneel, but changed his mind. He didn't feel like talking to God.

Larry had just pulled the sheet over his head when there was a gentle knock on his door. He sighed heavily. *Here comes the scolding!* he thought.

Dad opened the door. Handing Larry his robe, he said, "Put this on, Son. There's something outside I want you to see." Larry did as he was told. Outside, Dad pointed to the moon.

"It looks so big and close—almost like you could touch it," murmured Larry.

Dad reached into his pocket. "Now hold this dime in front of you like this." He held it out from his face an arm's length. Then he handed it to Larry. Puzzled, Larry obeyed. "What do you see?" Dad asked.

"Just a dime," Larry replied.

Dad nodded. "You can completely block out something as big and beautiful as the full moon with one little dime," he said. "And you can completely shut yourself off from a lot of beautiful things—love, friendship, happiness—when you make a big fuss about little things. Little things can even get between you and God."

Slowly Larry handed his father his dime. Then he gave him a quick hug. "I'll try not to make such a big deal out of something small in the future." *BJW*

HOW ABOUT YOU?

Do you make a big fuss about little things? Do you know the most common cause of anger? It's selfishness, and it can ruin your day, your week—even your life. Make up your mind now not to let little things get between you and happiness—or between you and God.

**Don't Fuss about
Little Things**

MEMORIZE:
"A little yeast spreads quickly through
the whole batch of dough!"
Galatians 5:9

Hiding Place

(Read Psalm 143:7-12)

Tim wriggled into the little thicket of shrubs behind the garage. It was his own special hiding place where he always came when he was feeling sad and wanted to be alone. Today he felt very bad because he'd missed a shot in his basketball game, and several kids had teased him. He sighed deeply as he thought about it.

A little bird rustled in the bushes, and the wind sighed softly overhead in the trees. Tim listened to the sounds and began to forget his sadness. He always felt better in his hiding place. Then he heard Mother calling, "Tim! Grandpa's here!" Tim scrambled out.

Tim and Grandpa sat down on the porch to visit—just the two of them. "Where were you just now?" Grandpa asked.

"I was feeling bad about a ball game and went to my special hiding place," Tim said, knowing Grandpa would never tell anyone.

"Say, that's a good idea," said Grandpa sympathetically. "I had a hiding place of my own when I was a boy. It was in the hayloft of the barn." Grandpa's face beamed as he added, "Even at my age, I still have a good hiding place."

Tim looked surprised. "You do?" He wondered what kind of place someone Grandpa's age would use to hide out.

Grandpa nodded. "Run and get your Bible," he said, "and I'll give you a clue as to where I go."

When Tim returned, Grandpa said, "Find Psalm 143:9, and you'll find the answer."

They read it together: "Save me from my enemies, Lord; I run to you to hide me."

"That's right," said Grandpa. "I go to God with all my hurts and sadness. God's presence is the best hiding place of all."

"Next time I'm sad, I'm going to go to the same hiding place you do, Grandpa," Tim decided. "And I can do that right in my other secret hiding place." *CEY*

HOW ABOUT YOU?

Are you sometimes sad and troubled? Do you take your problems and sadness to God? He's ready and waiting to hear and to help you. He wants to hear about anything that is bothering you—trouble with schoolwork, disappointments with friends, or problems in your family. The next time you need help, go to the best "hiding place" of all—the Lord!

MEMORIZE:

"Save me from my enemies, Lord; I run to you to hide me." Psalm 143:9

Go to God for Help

No Laughing Matter

(Read John 12:37-43)

Jose scuffed the toe of his shoe in the playground dirt. He didn't feel very good inside. He didn't really think the words some of the boys were saying were very funny, and he knew they were wrong. But he didn't want to walk away because he was afraid the other boys wouldn't let him play with them anymore if he did. He wanted to be like the other boys, and he wanted those boys to like him. So Jose stood in the small circle of boys, laughing at the words when the other boys laughed.

That night, as usual, Jose read his Bible before going to bed. He read from John 12. He came to verse 43 and read, "For they loved human praise more than the praise of God." Jose saw that he had done the very same thing on the playground. He had wanted praise from the other boys more than praise from God. Kneeling by his bed, he whispered, "Dear God, I'm sorry for laughing at words and jokes that are wrong. Help me to walk away the next time others are talking that way, no matter what they say about me."

A few days later the same boys stood together in a corner of the playground. The tallest boy began to use bad language. Everyone laughed—except Jose. He turned and began to walk away. "Hey, what's the matter, Jose?" someone jeered. "Can't you take it?"

Jose continued to walk away, each step becoming a little easier. He heard footsteps behind him, and then Kendall was walking along with him. "I don't really like that kind of language either," said Kendall.

"Hey, do you collect baseball cards?" asked Jose.

"I sure do," answered Kendall, pulling some out of his pocket. "I've got some right here." That was just the beginning of a new friendship, and the two boys had many good times together. *CEY*

HOW ABOUT YOU?

Whose praise do you seek? Do you care more about what the kids at school will say than about what God will say? Do you dare to be a friend to an "odd" person? To not laugh at dirty jokes? Make sure that the words of today's verse can never be said about you!

Seek God's Praise

MEMORIZE:
"For they loved human praise more than the praise of God." John 12:43

A Bridge to the Gospel

(Read 1 Corinthians 9:19-23)

"Hey, Alec," said Nathan to the new boy in his class, "I go to a neat Bible club on Tuesdays after school. How about coming with me tomorrow?"

"No . . . I don't think so," Alec replied as he hurried out the door for recess. Nathan was disappointed. The week before, his Bible club teacher had talked about the importance of being a witness for Jesus.

The next Sunday, Nathan listened eagerly to a missionary speaker at his church. "When we first went to Africa," said Mrs. James, "the people in our village didn't want to hear the gospel. But, as you know, we established a hospital. This has been a wonderful bridge to the gospel. After several people were treated, they and their families were ready to hear about Jesus." A light seemed to go on in Nathan's head. Ideas began to form. *Maybe I need to make friends with Alec before I can witness to him,* he thought. *Maybe I could get him involved in a game during recess.* Alec didn't know many of the kids yet, and he usually went off by himself to dig in the dirt or fiddle with the branches of a bush. *Maybe I should try to get to know Alec away from school, too. Maybe he could go camping with us.* Nathan could hardly wait to discuss his idea with Dad.

When Dad heard Nathan's plan, he nodded. "I think that's a great idea," he said.

The next day at recess, Nathan found Alec on the playground. "I've been looking for you," he said. "You wanna come camping with my dad and me Friday night? Dad said I could ask you. We'll go fishing and cook our dinner and have lots of fun."

Alec seemed surprised. After a moment he nodded. "I'll ask my mom," he said.

"Great!" exclaimed Nathan. "Come on. Let's go play kickball." *EMB*

HOW ABOUT YOU?

Do people resist your efforts to tell them about Jesus? Can you think of a way to build a bridge to the gospel? Perhaps you could take a gift to someone who is sick. Or help someone with homework. Maybe you know someone who just needs a friend. Do something this week to "build a bridge."

MEMORIZE:

"Yes, I try to find common ground with everyone so that I might bring them to Christ." 1 Corinthians 9:22

Reach Others for Christ through Friendship

The Early Bird

(Read Matthew 20:20-28)

"I get the bathroom first!" yelled Jon. He rushed past Cindy, yanked open the bathroom door, and scurried in. A moment later he stuck his head out. "The early bird gets the worm!" he shouted triumphantly.

At breakfast, Jon made a grab for the cornflakes. "Me first!" he declared, shaking out crispy, crunchy cornflakes into his bowl. "The early bird gets the worm—we learned that in a story we read at school," he announced smugly.

After breakfast, Dad had a surprise gift for Jon and Cindy. In great excitement they tore open the wrapping and peeked inside. It was a box of magic tricks. "I'm going to try them out first," shouted Jon.

"No, let me," said Cindy. "You always get things first."

"Well, I spoke first," said Jon. "The early bird gets the worm, you know."

"I'm getting tired of hearing you say that," complained Cindy. "What does it mean anyway?"

"It means that if you're first at something, you get what you want, just like the first bird to come out in the morning is the one who gets the worm for his breakfast," explained Jon. "I like being first."

"Jon," interrupted Dad, who had been listening to their conversation, "it's not always best to be first. Think about the worm."

"What about the worm?" asked Jon.

"Well, perhaps the worms were all fighting to be first—like you and Cindy. Now what happened to the 'early worm'—the one who was first out of the ground?"

Jon thought for a moment. "The bird ate him up," he said slowly.

"Ah!" said Dad with a grin. "That's right! It's not always best to be first— sometimes you might be like the early worm instead of the early bird! But the real reason you shouldn't insist on being first is that putting yourself first is not what God wants you to do. He wants you to put him and others first." *MTF*

HOW ABOUT YOU?

Do you always try to be first? Jesus is God; he could have been first in every way, yet he chose to be the servant of all. He wants you to be like him by putting others first and serving them. Next time you want to be first, ask yourself, "What would Jesus do?"

Put God and Others First

MEMORIZE:
"And whoever wants to be first must be the slave of all." Mark 10:44

Puppy Color

(Read Galatians 3:25-28)

The day finally arrived for Jodi and James to go to their uncle's farm to pick out a puppy. "Mom, I want the little white puppy with the black nose," said Jodi as she zipped her jacket.

"Not me!" said James. "l want the black puppy."

When they arrived at the farm, the kids rushed to the barn where the puppies were. "Oh, they're all so cute!" exclaimed Jodi. "I was sure I wanted this white puppy, but that black one has a cute little white spot right by his nose. The brown one is cute, too."

"Yeah," agreed James. "I'm not sure anymore which one I want, either!"

Jodi and James took turns holding first one puppy, then another. "Let's get the white one," said Jodi at last. "I already decided on a name for her—Crystal."

"OK," agreed James. "Works for me." So, after thanking their uncle for the puppy, they headed home.

A few days later, James reminded Mom of his upcoming birthday party. "I'm not forgetting," Mom assured him. "You said you have a new boy at school—Brandon. Did you invite him?"

"No." James hesitated. "I'm not sure I should. He's a different color than we are."

Mom raised her eyebrows as she looked at the puppy snuggled in James's arms. "James," she said, "do you think you could love the black puppy, or even the brown one, as well as this white one?"

"Sure," said James. "They're all cute. Why?"

"Well," said Mom, "if the color of a puppy's fur doesn't matter to you, why does the color of a person's skin matter? Couldn't someone be as good a friend and just as much fun no matter what color his skin is?"

James nodded. "That's true," he agreed. "I'll invite Brandon to my party as soon as I get to school tomorrow." *CIR*

HOW ABOUT YOU?

Do you shy away from people who have skin a different color than yours? Have you made an effort to be their friend? Skin color is not important to God, and it shouldn't be to you, either.

MEMORIZE:

"From one man he created all the nations throughout the whole earth." Acts 17:26

Color Doesn't Matter to God

Getting Even

(Read Romans 12:17-21)

Justin groped for the doorknob. His eyes were clinched tightly shut. "Eric threw dirt in my face," he sobbed as Mother hurried to let him in. "I can't see! I can't see!"

While she talked calmly, Mother washed the dirt from his eyes. Finally the last speck was out. "I'll get even with Eric if it's the last thing I do," Justin threatened.

Mother frowned. "Eric was wrong, but getting even won't accomplish anything."

"It'll teach him not to throw dirt in people's eyes," Justin argued.

At bedtime when Dad read Romans 12:17-21, Justin scowled. "Does that mean I'm supposed to be good to Eric to make him ashamed of the way he treated me? Is that how I get even?"

Mother shook her head. "You're not supposed to try to get even. The nineteenth verse says, 'Never avenge yourselves. Leave that to God. For it is written, "I will take vengeance, I will repay those who deserve it," says the Lord.'"

"How's the Lord going to repay Eric for what he did?" Justin wanted to know.

"Maybe he knows Eric has already suffered enough," Dad replied.

"I'm the one who got hurt!"

"Yes, but Eric has a load of guilt and worry to carry," Dad explained. "He's probably one really scared fellow, wondering how badly you were hurt."

"But the Bible says to heap coals of fire on our enemy's head," Justin pointed out. "Isn't that getting even?"

"That was written before people had matches. If their fire went out, they had to borrow live coals from a neighbor, and they carried these in a pot on their heads," Dad explained. "So this verse is telling you to *help your enemy*. Don't get revenge. Overcome his evil with your good."

"That sounds hard," Justin grumbled.

"Not nearly as hard as it would be to keep fighting with him," Mother reasoned. "Wouldn't you really prefer to have Eric for a friend than an enemy?

Justin grinned. "I guess you're right about that." *BJW*

HOW ABOUT YOU?

Has someone mistreated you? Are you planning to get even? Ask God to give you a forgiving spirit. Start overcoming evil with good.

MEMORIZE:
"Don't let evil get the best of you, but conquer evil by doing good."
Romans 12:21

Overcome Evil with Good

September 24

Special Carrots

(Read Romans 12:3-8)

"Hi, Mom." Steven greeted his mother, who was sitting on a stool in the garage. "What are you doing?" he asked.

"I'm cutting tops off the carrots I picked from our garden," replied Mom, tossing the top of a carrot into a basket. "How was school today?"

"Terrible. I don't fit in!" grumbled Steven. "I'm not smart or cool or good at sports. The kids think I'm weird, and they're right."

"Steven! That's not true!" exclaimed Mom. "You may have different interests than most of them, but that's OK." She picked up a twisted carrot and looked at it. She sighed. "I planted a new kind of carrot," she said. "According to the catalog, this kind is sweeter than other carrots, but they sure look strange. I think I should have stuck with all the old kind." She tossed the whole carrot into the basket with the carrot tops.

"Did you taste them?" asked Steven.

"No, but I can't imagine they're any good." Mom picked up another one. "This one's crooked, too . . . they all are." She threw it in with the tops.

"But you should try them before you throw them all away," protested Steven. "If the catalog said they're sweet, maybe they are. Let's try one."

"Well, OK," agreed Mom. "I'll wash it first."

Mom and Steven moved to the family room to eat their carrot. "This is really good!" Steven exclaimed. "The catalog was right! These really are sweet . . . and you wanted to throw them away just because they're different!"

Mom took another bite of carrot. "You're right," she said. "These are extra good!" She grinned at Steven. "These carrots remind me of you. You feel inferior—like you're not worth much—because you think you don't fit in at school. You've forgotten that just like there are different purposes for different carrots—some are grown for size, and others for flavor—God has different plans for everybody. God has a special plan for you, Steven. He gave you abilities and talents that are different from everyone else's. Find ways to serve God with those gifts."

Steven grinned. "Want to share another carrot?" he asked. *HLA*

HOW ABOUT YOU?

Do you worry because you don't seem to fit in with the kids at your school or church? Remember, God has a great plan for your life! He gave you special gifts, abilities, and talents. Find ways to serve God in whatever area he has gifted you.

MEMORIZE:

"God has given each of us the ability to do certain things well." Romans 12:6

God Has a Plan for You

God's Helping Hands

(Read 2 Corinthians 4:1-7)

"Why do we have to pick up Mr. Adams?" asked Bob. "The nursing home is a long way from our house."

"If we don't pick him up, he won't get to come to the church picnic," answered Dad as he drove. "Besides, it makes him happy to be with a family from time to time. This is a small job we can do for the Lord."

Bob thought about that. "It seems like a funny way to help God," he decided. He grinned as he added, "I mean, God could take Mr. Adams to the picnic on a flying carpet if he wanted to. He doesn't really need us, does he?"

Just then they drove up to the nursing home. Mr. Adams was standing outside, waiting—just as he did each Sunday when they picked him up for church. But today he had a small brown bag which he waved in the air. "I remembered it was a picnic," he said. "I brought some lunch."

At the park, Bob's family spread their lunch on a picnic table. They had brought fried chicken, potato salad, rolls, pickles, crisp celery and carrots, a giant chocolate cake with cherries on top, lemonade, and a watermelon. Bob saw Mr. Adams open his bag at the next table. He took out a bologna sandwich. Bob's mother walked over to Mr. Adams. "Please don't eat all by yourself, Mr. Adams," she said. "Come on! Bring your lunch and put it with ours. There'll be plenty."

Mr. Adams grinned and came to Bob's table. He carefully placed his sandwich next to the basket of golden rolls. *He might as well not have bothered with that,* thought Bob. They prayed and began to eat. To Bob's surprise, his little sister, Susan, immediately reached for the bologna sandwich.

Bob's father leaned toward his son. "Bob," he whispered, "we 'help' God in much the same way Mr. Adams is 'helping' us. God has all the power and all the resources, but he allows us to put in our small effort, too. We bring almost nothing to God, yet he uses what we bring, and we receive great blessings from him." *CR*

HOW ABOUT YOU?

Do you feel as though the Lord doesn't need you to help him perform his will on earth? He is all-powerful, yet he has chosen to use your small efforts to bring about large blessings. Thank him for the privilege of serving him. Be a "helping hand" for him.

MEMORIZE:

"But we have this treasure in jars of clay to show that this all-surpassing power is from God and not from us."
2 Corinthians 4:7, NIV

You Can Serve God

Your Burning Bush

(Read Exodus 3:1-6)

"We read about Moses and the burning bush in Sunday school today," said Kelly as the family sat down to Sunday dinner. "We learned that God talked to him from the burning bush and told him what he wanted him to do. Our teacher says God still speaks to people."

Kevin jabbed his fork into a potato. "Maybe, but not through anything as interesting as a burning bush," he said. "I'd like to see a burning bush!"

"Yeah!" agreed Kelly. "Imagine God speaking through one of Mom's bushes!"

Mom smiled. "Make it a bush at the back of the yard, will you?" she said. "I don't want the whole place set on fire!"

They all laughed. "But isn't it too bad God doesn't do that anymore?" said Kevin, turning serious again. "It would be really something to have God speak to you like that."

"Kevin," said Dad suddenly, "what about Jim?"

Kevin looked surprised. Jim was the boy next door. He'd been in a bad accident the year before and was confined to a wheelchair. "What about Jim, Dad?" asked Kevin.

"Maybe he's your 'burning bush,'" suggested Dad softly. "Your call to attention."

Kevin looked startled. "I don't get it," he said slowly.

"It doesn't require a real bush for God to speak to us," explained Dad. "He can catch our attention and speak to us through any situation or any person, if only our eyes and ears and hearts are open to him. But do you think God would have spoken to Moses if Moses hadn't taken the trouble to go over to the bush and examine it?"

Kevin frowned. "I guess not," he said, "but . . . I still don't get it."

"Well, you pass Jim every day on your way to school," explained Dad, "and on your way back, and on your way out to play with your friends . . . and I've seen him watching you with a hopeful look in his eyes. So maybe God wants you to go over to Jim, stop awhile, talk to him, and help ease his loneliness. If you do that, maybe God will speak to you through him. What do you think?" Slowly, Kevin nodded. *MTF*

HOW ABOUT YOU?

Have you thought that God no longer speaks to people today? He speaks, first of all, through his Word. He also speaks in other ways—not always in a dramatic way, but by using circumstances and people to get your attention.

MEMORIZE:

"'Amazing!' Moses said to himself. 'Why isn't that bush burning up? I must go over to see this.'" Exodus 3:3

God Still Speaks

Size Isn't Everything

(Read John 15:1-8)

"This will probably be the last picking of tomatoes," said Matt's mother as he followed her into the garden. "It's about time for a frost."

"Yeah," Matt said gloomily.

Mother glanced at him. "What's wrong?" she asked as she put tomatoes in her basket.

"Ahhhh, nothing," Matt mumbled. But Mother knew better, and she had a good idea what the problem was. She had seen Matt measuring himself against the door frame several times lately, and she had heard his friends bragging about how fast they were growing. She knew they sometimes teased him about being the runt of the class.

"Remember when we planted these tomatoes?" asked Mother. "The plants were all the same size." Then she pointed to the smallest plant. "This one didn't grow as fast as the others, but look at the tomatoes on it now."

"It's about half the size of the others," said Matt.

"Size isn't everything." Mother stood and stretched. "Some of these plants put all their energy into producing leaves, but this little plant produced fruit. You don't have to be the tallest or biggest to be the most productive."

"Huh! You don't know what it's like to be the runt."

"Don't worry about being short, Matt," Mother said. "God made us all different in some way, and our goal should be simply to do our best. So you are the shortest." Mother shrugged. "It doesn't matter. You can be the kindest and the friendliest. The important thing is to bring forth fruit for God—to do what he wants you to do. And who knows? By next year you may be the tallest."

Matt grinned. "Maybe," he said, "but I doubt it. I know you're right, though. I'll try to quit worrying about my size and think more about the things I can do. *BJW*

HOW ABOUT YOU?

Have you been fretting because you're different from your friends? Remember, we're all different. Don't waste your energy worrying about your size or looks. Think about bearing fruit—doing something for Jesus.

MEMORIZE:

"Remain in me, and I will remain in you. No branch can bear fruit by itself; it must remain in the vine."

John 15:4, NIV

Do Your Best

28

What Are You Thinking?

(Read 2 Corinthians 10:1-4)

David was in the locker room getting ready for gym when he heard some of the boys laughing and joking together. David overhead Ted tell a very dirty joke. The others laughed, but David quickly left the room.

All day the story kept popping back into David's mind. He told God he was sorry he kept thinking about it, but still he seemed unable to forget it. This continued for several days. Finally he decided to talk to his older brother, Ryan, about it. Ryan understood. "Satan wants to control your mind," he told David, "so he keeps bringing back the nasty things you see and hear. Now you know the law of space, don't you?"

"Sure," answered David. "No two things can occupy the same space at the same time. We learned that at school."

"Right." Ryan smiled. "Take this book, for example. It's lying here on the table, and nothing else can occupy that space until the book is removed. It's the same way with your mind. Fill it and keep it filled with the Word of God and with knowledge that will help you to live a wholesome life. Then no wrong things can occupy the space that the good things take up."

"I do read my Bible, Ryan," David said, "but I still can't forget that joke."

"Well, now comes God's part," said Ryan. "When you received Jesus as Savior, you also received the Holy Spirit. He gives you power to overcome evil. Whenever this dirty story pops into your mind, ask for God's Holy Spirit to cleanse your mind, and he will. If you do this, you'll find that you'll think of that story less and less often until finally you forget it." *AGL*

HOW ABOUT YOU?

Do you ever have trouble with your thoughts? Following these suggestions will help you. First, avoid situations where you hear or read wrong things. Second, fill your mind with good things. Third, ask the Holy Spirit to cleanse your thoughts. In this way you can have a pure heart and mind.

MEMORIZE:
"God blesses those whose hearts are pure, for they will see God."
Matthew 5:8

Think Pure Thoughts

The Floating Knife

(Read Hebrews 4:12-16)

Gene and his father were taking advantage of a lovely fall afternoon for one last fishing trip before winter, and they were having a serious discussion. "I know we're supposed to love everyone," said Gene as he stared at the river, "but to tell you the truth, I don't think I'll ever love Bruce. He's such a bully, and he makes me so mad. How can I love someone who acts the way he does?"

Dad was thoughtful as he reeled in his line. "Say, Gene," he said, taking out his pocket knife, "what do you think will happen if I toss this knife in the water?"

Gene took the knife from Dad's hand and examined it before handing it back. "It will sink like a rock, of course."

"I disagree," said Dad. "I think it will stay right at the top—I'll show you. Just watch."

"Don't throw it in the water," protested Gene. "You'll lose it. Give it to me if you don't want it anymore. It won't do anybody any good on the bottom of the river."

But Dad had turned to his tackle box. Taking out the biggest cork bobber he could find, he tied it to his fishing line. Just above it, he attached the knife. Gene watched as Dad threw the whole assembly into the river. It sank beneath the water, then began to float.

"Oh, no fair," protested Gene. "The cork is floating and the knife is just riding along."

"Well, I didn't say it would float by itself," replied Dad, reeling it in. "It would be impossible for it to do that. But with the help of the cork, it's carried along at the top of the water. It reminds me that with God, nothing is impossible. God gives many commands that I can't carry out by myself, but when I trust him to help me, he just 'holds me up and carries me along.'"

"I get the point, Dad," grinned Gene. "I'll ask God to help me love Bruce. But it's probably going to take a long, long time." *HWM*

HOW ABOUT YOU?

Is it unnatural for you to talk to your friends about Jesus? To quit complaining? To be cheerful? To be unselfish? God gives many commands that go against your natural inclinations. By yourself, you can't obey them—but with his help, you can.

God Can Do the "Impossible"

MEMORIZE:
"I can do all things through Christ who strengthens me."
Philippians 4:13, NKJV

Settling Differences

(Read Matthew 26:50-53)

Jacob picked up the phone and dialed a number. "Hi, Trevor," he said. "Do you know what I'm gonna do tomorrow about Tyler?" He paused. "If he doesn't give our soccer ball back tomorrow, I'm going to punch him! I'm tired of that bully." Jacob leaned against the dining room doorway. He was surprised to see his grandfather reading at the table. Jacob lowered his voice. "I've got to go now. Bye." He hung up the phone. *I hope Gramps didn't hear what I said,* he thought.

Jacob walked into the dining room. "Who was on the phone?" Gramps asked.

Jacob shrugged. "No one important," he said. "It was just about some stuff at school." He needed to change the subject. "What are you reading?"

"My Bible." Gramps patted the cover.

"Going over a study lesson?" asked Jacob.

"I started to, then I ran across an interesting passage," said Gramps. "Jesus was being arrested, and even then he taught his followers that physical fighting was not the way to settle their differences. Jesus said, 'Those who use the sword will be killed by the sword.'"

Jacob sighed. "You heard what I said on the phone."

"Yes, I did," said Gramps. "It disappoints me to hear you talk of fighting."

"Gramps, I don't want to fight," protested Jacob, "but if we kick a stray ball, this kid takes it and won't give it back until it's time for everyone to go home."

"So you think punching him is the answer?"

"I guess not," admitted Jacob, "but what is the answer?"

Gramps stood, walked over to Jacob and put an arm around his shoulder. "Think about how Jesus would want you to handle this problem," he suggested. "There may be another reason why this boy hangs around the soccer field," he added. "Think about it."

Later that evening, Jacob found Gramps sitting in the porch swing. He sat down beside him. "I thought about what you said. I'm not going to fight," Jacob told him. "I'm going to do something else—something I should've done before."

"What's that?" Gramps asked.

"I'm going to ask him if he'd like to play!" *RRZ*

HOW ABOUT YOU?

What do you do when someone "bullies" you? Shout? Throw punches? Or do you remember what Jesus taught? Love is your best weapon.

MEMORIZE:

"Dear children, let us stop just saying we love each other; let us really show it by our actions." 1 John 3:18

Show Love; Don't Fight

Guilty as Charged

(Read Romans 3:10-12)

"There has been a lot of note-passing going on lately," announced Greg's teacher. "You think I don't see it, but I do. Anyone I see passing a note during the rest of the week will stay in at noon recess."

At school the next day, Greg watched as Brent and Randy passed notes back and forth. *They better watch it,* he thought. *If they get caught, they're gonna have to stay in for recess.* So Greg wrote a note telling them to be careful.

As Greg slipped his note to Randy, Mrs. Barnes looked up. "Greg, Randy, and Brent—you will all stay in at recess time today," she said sternly. And so they did.

That evening, Greg complained about his punishment. "I wrote only one little note!" he grumbled. "The other guys wrote a whole lot more—especially Brent."

"How many notes did Mrs. Barnes say you could write?" asked Mother.

"Well . . . none," admitted Greg, "but I still think she could have let me play outside at least half the time since the others wrote so many more."

"But even though you wrote only one, you were guilty as charged. So you did deserve the punishment, didn't you," said Mother, "even if you weren't, as you say, as bad as the other boys?" Greg had to admit that was true.

"Your argument reminds me of a Bible verse," said Dad. "Some people seem to think that the Lord should excuse them because they aren't as bad as other people they know. But the fact is that we all have done wrong things. The Bible says that if you break God's law in even one point, you're as guilty as if you broke the whole thing." *HWM*

HOW ABOUT YOU?

Do you think you're pretty good? That you're better than a lot of kids you know? God says all of us do wrong things. But the wonderful news is that Jesus came to take the punishment for our wrongdoing. If you want to know more, ask a trusted friend or adult.

Sin Deserves Punishment

MEMORIZE:
"And the person who keeps all of the laws except one is as guilty as the person who has broken all of God's laws." James 2:10

The Lonely Leech

(Read Romans 12:9-13)

The day I invited Dale to go to church with me I had no idea he'd become a tag-along, thought Jamie. *If I had known that, I probably would never have asked him.* After that one invitation, Dale, his next-door neighbor, had started coming over to the house just about every day. When the weather was nice, he would sit out on his steps and wait for Jamie to come out. *I'm glad Dale goes to church now, but other than that, I don't really care about having him around so often,* Jamie admitted to himself.

"OK if I walk to school with you tomorrow?" Dale asked one day after church.

Jamie shrugged. He didn't really want "the tagalong" with him, but what could he say? "Sure, I guess so. But I leave early so I can practice basketball in the gym."

"Great," Dale responded. "I'll see you in the morning."

But Jamie wasn't prepared for Dale coming to their house every morning after that. Sometimes he would ring the bell, and other times he would just sit and wait for Jamie to come out. "Dale really bugs me," Jamie exploded to his mother one day. "I can't walk out of this place without seeing Dale on the steps. I don't know why he hangs around here like he does."

"Maybe he's lonely," Mother suggested.

Jamie thought about that for a moment. "Maybe," he agreed. "His dad works nights, and his mother goes to work even before his dad gets home."

Mother nodded. "That big house next door could be a very lonely place," she said. "Maybe Dale just wants to be someplace where there are people."

"Should I ask him to come in and wait next time?" asked Jamie.

Mother smiled. "That's a good idea," she said. "He's been coming to church with you, and maybe if he waits inside he'll get interested in some of those Christian books we have."

"Yeah . . . OK," agreed Jamie thoughtfully. *RIJ*

HOW ABOUT YOU?

Does someone hang around you —even when you don't particularly want him to? Do you get angry and tell him to "bug off"? Or do you care enough to find out why he's doing it? Maybe he needs you. And maybe you can help to bring him to the Lord.

MEMORIZE:

"Share each other's troubles and problems, and in this way obey the law of Christ." Galatians 6:2

Help the Lonely

Do-It-Yourself Project

(Read Colossians 3:8-17)

"Mom, may I subscribe to this magazine?" asked Clint as he came into the kitchen. "It shows how to make all this neat stuff." He flipped the pages. "I could make gifts for birthdays and Christmas and Mother's Day. Think how much money I could save!"

"OK," agreed Mother. "It looks like a good investment."

Every afternoon for the next two months Clint asked the same question, "Did my magazine come today, Mom?"

Finally, his mother met him at the door with a smile on her face and a magazine in her hand. Clint spent the entire evening looking at the magazine. "I don't know whether to make this picture or this planter," he said.

When Clint's mother was cleaning out his closet several months later, she found a stack of craft magazines. The pages of several were worn from wear. She was putting the last one back on the shelf when Clint came bursting into the room. "Jason Black makes me so mad! He makes the dumbest rules, and he always has to be first. Just because it's his game or his house, everyone has to obey him or go home. I came home!"

"So I noticed." Mother nodded. "Clint, have you ever made any of the crafts shown in these magazines?"

Clint shook his head. "No, but someday I'm going to."

Mother closed the closet door. "Much of our Christian life is like a do-it-yourself project, with the Bible for a book of instruction," she said. "But many people treat the Bible like you're treating these magazines. They read it and intend to follow its instructions, but they put it off."

"Not me. I do what it says," Clint declared.

"What about the verse we read this morning?" Mother asked. "It says, 'Submitting yourselves one to another.' Could that mean letting Jason be boss sometimes?"

"But, Mom . . ," Clint started to argue. Then he grinned. "I guess you're right. OK, I'll do it." *BJW*

HOW ABOUT YOU?

Do you obey what you read in God's Word? Did you read today's Scripture? Do you obey all that you read there? Maybe you need to cleanse your life of a bad habit, or submit to someone, or change a sour attitude. Whatever the Bible has shown you to do, start now.

MEMORIZE:
"Keep putting into practice all you learned from me and heard from me and saw me doing, and the God of peace will be with you."
Philippians 4:9

Hear God and Obey

A Church Flock

(Read Hebrews 10:22-25)

"Look." Dad pointed to the sky as he and Jeff walked home together. "The geese are flying south. Winter must be coming."

Jeff had been waiting for this chance all day. "Speaking of winter," he began hesitantly, "hockey season starts soon." He paused. "The thing is," he added, "practice will be Sunday mornings this year."

"That's too bad," said Dad. "You know that won't work for you."

"But it's only a few months," pleaded Jeff. "I won't miss church very often! And I promise I'll read my Bible at home."

Another flock of geese flew over, honking loudly. Jeff and Dad watched the geese pass. "Do you know why they fly in a *V* formation?" Dad asked. Jeff shook his head. "I've read that the air behind the leader spreads into a *V*—something like the wake of a speed boat," continued Dad. "If the other birds follow in that *V*, a swirl of air actually gives them a shove forward, making it easier to go a long way without wearing out."

"They're pretty smart," said Jeff. Then he pointed to a bird trailing behind the others. "I wonder why that one isn't in the *V*."

"He probably got distracted or slowed down to rest," guessed Dad. "Now he's having a hard time catching up."

"I bet he'll be pretty tired when he gets there," said Jeff.

"If he gets there at all," Dad added. "God didn't design them to go the distance alone." Dad looked at Jeff. "God didn't design Christians to go it alone, either," he said. "We gain strength from the support of other believers. Without it, we would be like that last goose—alone and struggling."

"Oh, Dad! The church doesn't need me," protested Jeff.

"Sure it does," said Dad. "We all need each other. So why don't you look for a different hockey team to play on this year?"

"Hey!" Jeff's eyes lit up. "Why don't we start a church team? One that practices on Saturday!"

Dad smiled proudly. "Now you're talking like a member of the flock!" *HMT*

HOW ABOUT YOU?

Are you part of the "flock"? Is meeting with other believers a regular part of your life, or do other activities get in the way? God didn't design us to live the Christian life alone. Join the flock—you need them and they need you.

MEMORIZE:

"Let us not give up meeting together." Hebrews 10:25, NIV

Attend Church Faithfully

Are You Listening?

(Read Psalm 46:1-11)

As Todd headed for the door after dinner, Mom reminded him that he had to finish cleaning the garage before bedtime. "You were supposed to move things when you swept it last Saturday, but I think you forgot," Mom said, "so you'll have to do it tonight."

"I didn't hear you tell me I should move things," complained Todd. "I was busy watching TV, and I just didn't hear you."

"You should have listened when I spoke to you," Mom told him. "Anyway, you hear me now, so you can do it now."

The next day Todd got a D on his history test. "Why, Todd! History is one of your best subjects!" exclaimed Mom when she heard about it. "What happened?"

"I didn't hear Miss Mikels say we were having the test," Todd explained. "I'll do better next time."

Later, Mom told Todd he could have an apple before going to bed. But Todd didn't hear her—he was too busy playing with his cars. Soon Mom told him to get ready for bed—without his snack. "I didn't hear you tell me to get it," whined Todd. "It isn't fair."

"This is fair," Mom insisted. "What isn't fair is when you waste people's time by not listening when they speak."

"From now on," said Dad, "when someone speaks to you, I want you to put down what you're doing and listen—listen carefully." He continued thoughtfully, "You know, sometimes I also wonder how much we really listen to God."

Todd looked at him. "What do you mean?" he asked.

"I'm afraid I'm sometimes guilty of letting my mind wander, too—for example, on Sundays when our pastor is preaching," he said.

"And even when we have personal devotions, we often want to hurry up and get done so we can go on to other activities," added Mom.

Dad nodded. "I think all of us need to listen better, both to others and to God." *BR*

HOW ABOUT YOU?

How well do you listen to others? How well do you listen to God? It's important to listen carefully so you can learn what God wants you to learn. Only then can you truly obey him.

Listen to God

MEMORIZE:
"I listen carefully to what God the Lord is saying." Psalm 85:8

I Can't See It

(Read John 20:24-29)

"I'll believe it when I see it!" muttered Kurt as he reached for his favorite cereal.

"Oh, Kurt!" exclaimed Lisa, "I really did see a squirrel without a tail! You never believe anything!"

Mother, who was buttering toast, spoke thoughtfully. "Actually, we all believe quite a few things we can't see. If we didn't, none of us would have become Christians." She put a plate of toast on the table.

"Pastor Baker told me that Jeff Pratt accepted Christ last Sunday," said Mom as she passed the toast.

"I'll believe that when I see it." Kurt spoke the phrase automatically, a doubtful look on his face.

"See what?" Lisa asked. "What do you expect to see?"

Kurt was caught off guard. "Well, when I see . . ." His voice trailed off.

"Kurt," said Mom, "many important things in life can't be seen. Take love, for instance. We see evidence, or results, of love, but we can't see the love itself."

"Or friendship," Lisa added. "You can't tell by looking at a photograph that someone is your best friend."

"And honesty," said Mother. "You can't know if a person is honest just by looking at him. All these things we've mentioned are seen only by knowing the person."

"And what about believing in God?" asked Lisa. "You can't actually see him."

Mom nodded. "Do you remember Thomas in the Bible?" she asked. "He insisted that he had to see Jesus before he could believe in the resurrection. He was allowed to do that, but Jesus said those who believe without seeing him are blessed. That includes Christians today. We believe through faith, and God blesses that."

"And you just wait, Kurt," added Lisa. "You'll see the evidence of Christ in Jeff Pratt, too. You just wait!" *LH*

HOW ABOUT YOU?

Do you think you believe only in what you can see? You believe in air, electricity, and fun, don't you? These are all things that can't be seen—you only see the evidence of them. It's true that you can't see Jesus today, but you can see the evidence of his life in the lives of Christians. Put away your doubts and put your faith in him—he's real.

MEMORIZE:

"Though you have not seen him, you love him; and even though you do not see him now, you believe in him and are filled with an inexpressible and glorious joy." 1 Peter 1:8, NIV

Believe, Then See

Bulldog in a Tree

(Read 2 Samuel 7:8-10)

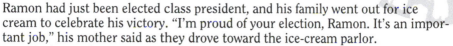

Ramon had just been elected class president, and his family went out for ice cream to celebrate his victory. "I'm proud of your election, Ramon. It's an important job," his mother said as they drove toward the ice-cream parlor.

"And a good opportunity to set a Christian example," added Dad. "Always remember that you . . ."

"Quick, Dad. Turn around!" Miguel shouted from the backseat. "I just saw a dog in a tree!"

"Forget the jokes," said Ramon. "I'm hungry for chocolate ice cream!"

"Honest," Miguel insisted. "I saw it! Turn around, and I'll show you." Dad wasn't convinced, but he circled the block. "See!" Miguel shouted as he pointed. Sure enough! There was a bulldog perched in the crotch of a tree.

"How did it get there?" wondered Ramon. "It sure didn't climb up by itself!"

"No, it didn't," Dad answered. "I'll bet that bulldog is the mascot for the Bulldog football team from Crestview High. Someone must have put him up there as a prank."

"Probably the Warriors from South Ridge High," said Miguel. "They play against the Bulldogs tomorrow."

"Could be," agreed Dad. "When we get to the ice-cream parlor, we'll notify the school so they can come and get him. But that dog in a tree is a good reminder."

"To go to the game?" Miguel asked.

Dad laughed. "That, too," he said, "but I was thinking of what I started saying earlier. That bulldog didn't get there by himself, did he? Someone put him there. And in life no one gets anywhere by himself. Positions of importance and influence are given by God."

"Like my job as class president?" Ramon asked.

Dad nodded. "Yes. Everything we have—our appearance, intelligence, family—was given to us by God." *JLH*

HOW ABOUT YOU?

Do you ever boast about the things you have or the things you can do? Remember, your nice hair, keen mind, and athletic ability have been given to you by God. He is the one who should receive the glory.

Give God the Glory

MEMORIZE:

"For who makes you different from anyone else? What do you have that you did not receive? And if you did receive it, why do you boast as though you did not?" 1 Corinthians 4:7, NIV

Old to New

(Read 2 Corinthians 5:14-17)

As Steve rode to town with his mother, he wore earphones while listening to music on his cassette player. Mom spoke his name twice and finally pulled his earphones off. "Ouch! That hurt my ear," Steve complained.

"Sorry," said Mom. "Why do you wear those things all the time, anyway? What were you listening to?"

"Oh, nothin'," said Steve. He knew Mom would hate the music he'd been playing. In fact, she'd make him get rid of the tape. So he turned the cassette off and listened to what she was saying.

Steve came home from the shopping trip with a lot of new clothes. "Mom," he called as he hung them in his closet, "there's no room for all this stuff. Where will I keep it?"

As Mother came into the room, she chuckled. "Well, Steven, think about it," she said. "Why did we get you so many new things?"

"Because my old clothes are too small," replied Steve.

Mother nodded. "So there's no reason to keep the things you've outgrown," she said. "Put them in this sack for Jeremy. Then there will be room for your new clothes." She grinned at him as she left. "Always keep that principle in mind," she added. "Get rid of the old to make room for the new—in closets and in life!"

As Steve worked, he thought of what Mother had said—"Get rid of the old to make room for the new." *I really like some of my old clothes, but there's no use keeping those that don't fit anymore,* he thought. *It's pretty easy to decide what to get rid of from my closet. But are there things in my life that I should get rid of, too? That's harder to figure out.* As he thought it over, he remembered the tape he didn't want Mom to hear. And he remembered the excuses he sometimes made for getting out of chores. He remembered the way he had treated a classmate he disliked. *Now that I'm a Christian, those things don't fit me anymore,* he thought. *I can't dump them in a bag, but I'll ask God to help me get rid of them, too.* REP

HOW ABOUT YOU?

Do "old things" clutter your life? Are there old habits, old friends, old music, or old books that you should get rid of to make room for the "new things" God wants to put there?

MEMORIZE:

"What this means is that those who become Christians become new persons. They are not the same anymore, for the old life is gone. A new life has begun!" 2 Corinthians 5:17

Make Room for Things of God

Behind the Closet Door

(Read Psalm 139:1-6)

Roger looked around at the mess in his room. He had dropped his shoes in one corner and his shirts in another. There were games and books and magazines strewn around the room. He knew better than to leave things laying around that way, especially right now when his parents were trying to sell the house. But he got careless sometimes.

"Roger," called Mother, "is your room in order? I just got a call, and some people are coming to look at the house."

Roger looked around again. No, it sure wasn't in order! "I'll clean it up," he called back. As he picked up one of the magazines, an article caught his eye. He sat down on the bed to read it.

When Roger heard a car door slam, he jumped up guiltily and looked out of the window. Sure enough, the people were already arriving. In a flash, he picked up his shoes, his shirts, and the games and books. He also gathered up some of the magazines and tossed the whole armful into the closet. Then he closed the door.

When Mother showed the people Roger's room, the lady smiled pleasantly. "What is the closet like?" she asked.

"Oh, it's quite large," Mother replied. Roger had a sick feeling in his stomach. He cringed at the look on Mother's face when she threw open his closet door.

When the people left, Roger looked fearfully at his mother. "I certainly am disappointed today," she told him. "Whatever made you think you could get away with that?" Roger shrugged his shoulders. "I'm sure you know the verse, 'Be sure your sins will find you out,'" added Mother. "Trying to hide your stuff in the closet is like when we try to hide our sins from God. Now go and clean your closet. And the next time you are tempted to do wrong, remember the closet. You can't hide your sins from God. But when you confess them he is gracious and will forgive you." *RIJ*

HOW ABOUT YOU?

Are you trying to cover up your sin? Forget it! God sees and knows everything. He knows all that you do —he even knows your thoughts. Nothing is hidden from him.

MEMORIZE:

"O God, you know how foolish I am; my sins cannot be hidden from you."

Psalm 69:5

God Sees Everything

October
10

Five Finger Discount

(Read Proverbs 4:20-27)

At the department store, Scott met his friends, Jerry and Ken. "Hi," he said. "Whatcha doin'?"

"We're playing five finger discount," Jerry announced, holding up a small pocket knife.

"What's that?" asked Scott.

"You find something in the store that you can pick up with five fingers, and you hide it in your hand," whispered Jerry. "The discount is when you walk out of the store without paying for it."

"That's stealing," gasped Scott.

"Shhh," Ken signaled. "It's just a game."

Scott clapped his hand around a little car he had been looking at. For a long time he had wanted a car like that for his collection. It would be so easy to get the "five finger discount."

"Go on," his friends urged him. "It's easy."

Scott looked longingly at the car. "I'd better go," he said, putting down the car.

"Well, think about it," said Jerry. "You can come back for it tomorrow."

Dessert that night was Scott's favorite—chocolate fudge cake. Mother sat down and looked at her piece. Suddenly she got up and put it back on the cake plate. "When I take dessert, I take it because it tastes so good," she said. "Then when the doctor weighs me at the end of the week, I get upset that my diet isn't working. Sometimes it's hard to resist the temptation of having something now rather than working hard to get it."

Scott knew just what she meant. He had been tempted to do something wrong just for the immediate pleasure of having the little car. Even if he hadn't gotten caught, the car would have cost him a guilty conscience. It would have cost him many uncomfortable moments. He was glad he had resisted. *NEK*

HOW ABOUT YOU?

Are there things you think you need right away? Things you don't want to earn? Trust God to meet your needs in his own good time.

MEMORIZE:

"We reject all shameful and underhanded methods."

2 Corinthians 4:2

Please God First

God's Dress Code

(Read Colossians 3:12-17)

"Our principal is introducing a dress code, Mom!" said Brett indignantly as he came into the kitchen and plopped his book bag down on the table. "Everyone is mad. We're going to protest and make posters, and I'm collecting signatures. Sign right here, Mom!" Brett shoved a list containing a dozen scrawled names under his mother's nose.

Mom read the names out loud. "Are these people for or against the dress code?" she asked.

"Mom!" Brett was shocked. "They're against, of course! Hurry up and sign!"

Mom returned the list to Brett. "You don't want my opinion?" she asked. "You expect me to just sign?" Brett was surprised. His mother was usually supportive of him and always encouraged him to take an active roll in class decision making and discussions. "Did anyone ask Mr. Lewis why he felt a dress code was necessary?" asked Mom. "Maybe he thinks some kids wear clothing that's inappropriate for school. Maybe it's even vulgar or unsafe. A dress code is a way to avoid certain clothing trends and provide a wholesome learning environment. Besides, God has a dress code."

"Whatever do you mean, Mom?" asked Brett. "He doesn't expect Christians to wear a uniform, does he?"

Mother smiled and shook her head. "No . . . but I think our 'clothing' should communicate a message," she said. "In 1 Timothy it says we should wear modest apparel and good works."

Brett frowned. "Good works?" he asked. "I don't get it."

"In the Bible, our 'clothing' refers not only to the clothes we wear, but also to our behavior," explained Mother. "It refers to what we say and what we do. God reminds us to be modest and not show off."

"What's that got to do with a school dress code, Mom?" asked Brett.

"Well, not every fashion or behavior would please the Lord," Mother told him. "Your principal may not have that in mind, but apparently he does recognize that some clothes are inappropriate. I think you should reconsider the whole issue before you continue to get signatures for that petition. What do you think?"

"I think you're probably right," he said. *DDM*

HOW ABOUT YOU?

Would God approve of the things you wear? Would he approve of things you say and the way you behave? Follow God's "dress code" stated in the verse below.

Dress Modestly

MEMORIZE:
"Dress modestly, with decency and propriety. . . (and) with good deeds."
1 Timothy 2:9-10, NIV

12

Let's Take a Chance

(Read James 4:4-10)

Jordan loved to take chances. Such things as climbing a railroad bridge and swinging from the girders tempted him. He often tried talking his friend, Carlos, into joining him.

One day Zach, another classmate, came running up to the two boys. "Hey, guys," he said, "how about going to Steve's house for some real fun?"

"Like what?" asked Carlos.

"Come and see," coaxed Zach mysteriously.

"Sounds exciting!" exclaimed Jordan after Zach had gone on his way. "Come on, Carlos. Let's take a chance on it."

"No." Carlos shook his head. "You know Steve's into drugs."

Jordan, however, decided to go—just to see what was going on. Sure enough, the boys were using drugs. Jordan intended just to watch, but when they challenged him to try it, he took the chance. He didn't intend to ever use drugs again; but he did, and before he realized it, he was unable to stop.

Soon Jordan began to avoid his old friends. He got low grades in school, and he had difficulty getting along with his parents. At first, Carlos couldn't figure out what was wrong with Jordan, but he soon realized Jordan must have become hooked on drugs. So he talked to Jordan about it one day. "You know what drugs can do to you—you need to get help right away," pleaded Carlos.

Jordan knew Carlos was right, and he knew Carlos truly cared for him. "I'll quit if you'll stick with me," he promised.

Carlos smiled. "I'll help any way I can," he said. He hesitated. "Dad and I talked about it—he wants to help, too. But you know who you really need to help you?" he added. "You need God—you need to turn your life over to him. I've been praying for you, Jordan." To his surprise, Jordan didn't even laugh. *AGL*

HOW ABOUT YOU?

Do you enjoy taking chances? Be very careful! Trying drugs is one chance you can't afford to take! But maybe you already have—maybe you're "hooked." If so, talk to your parents and to your pastor. Ask for their help and their prayers. Find out what other organizations are available to help you. Most important of all, turn your life over to God and ask him to help you. It won't be easy, but with God's help you can have victory over every sin.

MEMORIZE:

"Resist the Devil, and he will flee from you." James 4:7

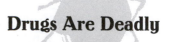

Drugs Are Deadly

Nick's Prayer

(Read Luke 6:27-36)

Nick came running into the house as fast as he could. "Mom! It worked!" he shouted. "Pastor Dunn said that we should pray for our enemies, so all week I've been praying for Todd."

"Isn't he the boy who knocked you off the swing set at school a few weeks ago?" asked Mom.

Nick nodded. "He's mean. Nobody likes him. Anyway, I've been praying, and God answered my prayers. Today Todd had to go to the hospital to have his appendix out, and he won't be back to school for quite a while!"

"What has that got to do with your prayers?" asked Mom in surprise.

"I asked God to make something bad happen to Todd," explained Nick impatiently. "And God did it! Todd will be way behind in school now. Maybe he'll get so far behind that he'll flunk this year and have to stay back!"

"Hold on!" exclaimed Mom. "You prayed for something bad to happen to Todd?"
"Sure."

"Nick," said Mom, "when the Bible talks about praying for your enemy, it means you should ask God to help you be nice to that person and not hate him. You should also ask God to help you set a good Christian example for him and pray that he'll become a Christian, too."

"I guess I've been doing it all wrong," said Nick thoughtfully. "From now on I'm going to pray that God will help me with Todd." *DSM*

HOW ABOUT YOU?

Do you know someone who doesn't like you, or who isn't very nice? Pray for them and not against them. The Bible also says you should love them. It may not be easy at first, but after a while you may find that someone you thought was an enemy really isn't so bad after all. Try it!

MEMORIZE:
"But I say, love your enemies! Pray for those who persecute you!"
Matthew 5:44

Pray for Your Enemies

14

The Game of Life

(Read Romans 13:1-6)

Paul stretched and yawned. "I gotta get to bed early tonight," he stated. "Coach's orders. He says it's important to work hard and eat right, but that nothing will take the place of a good night's sleep."

"Well then, by all means get to bed early—after you work hard and eat right, that is," teased his sister, Alyce. "Be sure to do whatever your football coach says."

"You surely are putting a lot into the game," said Dad. He looked thoughtful. "You know, the game of football reminds me of the game of life. God has provided a big, beautiful field on which to play the game. He created the earth and everything in it."

Alyce grinned. "Oh, and here's an important part—the coaches are our teachers and especially our parents. I bet that's the thing Dad wanted to get across to us."

Dad gave her a playful swat with his newspaper. "You said it, I didn't." He smiled. "You two are getting good at figuring out the lessons I'm trying to teach. Don't forget how important it is to follow the advice of your coaches!"

"Right, Dad." Paul laughed. He stood up and yawned again. "I'm going to do that now by getting to bed. Good night, everybody." *HWM*

HOW ABOUT YOU?

Do you listen to your "coaches" in the game of life? God has given you parents, teachers, pastors, and other Christian leaders and friends to help you make right choices. Listen carefully to what they have to say. God says to obey them.

MEMORIZE:
"For the Lord's sake, accept all authority." 1 Peter 2:13

Obey Those in Authority

Poisoned Minds

(Read James 2:1-4, 8-10)

Thomas, who was a Native American, was the new boy at school. His mother greeted him as he arrived home. "How was school?" she asked.

"Awful!" answered Thomas. "The kids here are so dumb! They think Native Americans wear war paint and feathers and say, 'Ugh! How!'"

"Someone's been teasing you, I see," said Mother with a smile.

"It's not funny," replied Thomas, almost in tears.

Mother was sympathetic. "I'm sorry, honey. I do know what it's like," she assured him. "I'm a Native American, too—but I'm proud of my heritage. Try not to mind the teasing so much, Thomas. No matter where you live, you'll meet people with prejudices."

"Pre-ju-dices? What's that?" asked Thomas.

"Prejudices are opinions people form before the facts are known. They include a dislike of people who are different from oneself," Mother told him. "At one time or another, everyone is laughed at—for being too fat or too skinny or redheaded or freckle-faced or too smart or too dumb. But tell me about the other kids in your class."

"Oh, they're mostly just regular kids," answered Thomas. "There's one girl, though, who's different. Her name is Marsha. Every day a chauffeur in a big, black Cadillac brings her to school and picks her up. She's a snob!"

"Thomas!" exclaimed Mother, "you don't even know Marsha, but you're judging her like others judged you."

"But, Mother . . . ," began Thomas.

"There are other kinds of prejudices besides just racial ones," said Mother. "Some people are prejudiced against other religions, the handicapped, the rich, or the poor. All prejudices are wrong. That's what the Bible is talking about when it says we shouldn't 'show favoritism.' Prejudices poison the mind of the one who has them."

Thomas knew his mother was right. "OK. I'll try not to be prejudiced," he said.

"Good," approved Mother. "And try not to be too sensitive when others tease you. If you can laugh at yourself, it will be much easier for you, and you'll show the other kids that you're very much like they are." *BJW*

HOW ABOUT YOU?
Do you tease or avoid someone who is different from you? Determine to treat those "different" people just as you would want to be treated yourself.

Don't Be Prejudiced

MEMORIZE:
"But if you show favoritism, you sin."
James 2:9, NIV

16

It's Not Fair

(Read Acts 16:22-32)

"I didn't make the basketball team, Mom." Joe slumped down in a chair as he came in from school one day. "I'm not bragging or anything, but I do play basketball well."

"Yes, you do, Son," agreed Mother, "but there were only two openings on the team, and the coach had to choose, didn't he? Who did make it?"

"Kevin, which we all expected. Kevin is good! Then they chose Randy for the other opening. In the tryouts, I made more baskets than he did, and I dribbled the ball longer. But his dad is a teacher at school, and I think that's why he made it," Joe concluded bitterly.

Mother was quiet for a few minutes. She knew there had been other times when Randy was chosen for something because his dad was a teacher. She sighed. "I suppose that may be possible. If you really believe that, perhaps you should ask the coach about it," she suggested, "but do be careful not to make accusations you can't prove. And, Joe, you must learn that life isn't always fair. Another thing you must learn is to maintain a Christlike attitude no matter what happens."

"Aw, Mom," Joe whined.

"Think of Paul and Silas. It wasn't fair that they were thrown in jail for preaching about the Lord," continued Mother, "and yet they sang! They weren't going to let the unfair actions of others get them down. I know this experience is hard for you, but you can learn something from it. Be challenged. Ask the Lord to help you handle the situation. You will come out of it a stronger and more mature Christian."

Joe sighed. He knew his mom was right. It wasn't going to help to be upset. He would ask the Lord to help him turn a bad experience into a growing experience. *LMW*

HOW ABOUT YOU?

Are you ever treated unfairly? It happens to everyone. The next time you're faced with an unfair situation that you can't change, remember Paul and Silas. Instead of complaining, they sang! Maintain a good attitude. Grow through what has happened.

MEMORIZE:
"He is the Rock; his work is perfect.
Everything he does is just and fair."
Deuteronomy 32:4

**Grow through
Unfair Situations**

Dumb Ducks

(Read Ephesians 6:10-18)

Philip watched as his big brother, Steve, got ready to go duck hunting. "What are you going to do with those?" asked Philip, pointing to some painted wooden ducks on the workbench.

"These are decoys," Steve explained, picking one up. "No self-respecting duck will come near if he sees me standing around with a gun in my hands. So I hide, but I put these fellows out on the lake. From the air, they look real. And when the ducks flying overhead see them, they think to themselves, 'If that's a good spot for my brothers to land, it must be a good place for me.' Then down they come."

"Hmph!" Philip was scornful. "What dumb ducks!"

That evening Philip and Steve watched a football game on TV. During a commercial Steve opened a magazine, but he noticed that his younger brother was intently watching a liquor advertisement on the screen. "Don't be a dumb duck," said Steve.

"What are you talking about?"

"Well, I was afraid you might be fooled by the 'decoys' in that commercial," said Steve. "All the people in that ad look as though they're enjoying themselves so much. But they're there to entice you to drink. You're not supposed to realize that alcohol causes all sorts of unhappiness—hangovers and meanness and car accidents. You never see a smashed-up car in those ads. You only see the 'decoys.'"

"Yeah." Philip looked over at his brother. "Don't be a dumb duck yourself," he said, pointing to an ad he spotted in his brother's magazine. "The guy in that cigarette ad looks strong and healthy. Don't be fooled."

"Good thinking." Steve grinned. "Let's both be smart guys, not dumb ducks."
HWM

HOW ABOUT YOU?

Are you fooled by sin? For example, a good report card may make cheating seem worthwhile; a candy bar may make stealing look attractive; being accepted by the other kids may make it seem all right to laugh at a dirty joke. Don't be fooled by the decoys. Sin always ends in sadness.

Don't Be Fooled by Satan

MEMORIZE:
"Put on all of God's armor so that you will be able to stand firm against all strategies and tricks of the Devil."
Ephesians 6:11

Temporary Housing

(Read 1 Corinthians 15:42-49)

Marty groaned as he looked in the mirror and examined his teeth. *I wish Mom and Dad could afford braces for me.* Every time the kids at school called him "Marty the Mouth," he felt like crying. *Why couldn't God have given me straight teeth?*

That evening, Marty went to the grocery store with his mother. They saw a friend from church there—Mrs. Barker. "You recently moved into an apartment, didn't you?" Marty's mother asked her. "How do you like it?"

Mrs. Barker laughed. "We don't like it very much at all," she said. "The furnace doesn't work half the time, and we're tired of the constant dripping in the bathroom sink. The color of the walls is ugly, and the rent is much too high."

"That's too bad!" Marty's mother said. "But you sure seem cheerful about it."

Mrs. Barker grinned. "I guess that's because it's not our final home," she said. "It's just a place to live till the builders are finished with our new home. Every time I feel discouraged because of all that's wrong with the place, I just think of how happy I'll be in our new home. Then I feel cheerful."

When Dad heard what Mrs. Barker had said, he nodded. "That's a good thought for Christians, too," he said. He grinned. "In fact, the next time my back hurts I'll have to remember that this body is just a temporary home. As long as we're on this earth, we're all living in 'temporary housing.' Someday we'll have a new home in heaven—and even new bodies."

Hey, that's right, thought Marty. *I guess I really shouldn't complain so much about my teeth. SLK*

HOW ABOUT YOU?
Are you unhappy with something about your looks? Or do you have a health problem? God didn't make a mistake when he made you. And if you're a Christian, you'll have a new, perfect body someday.

MEMORIZE:
"He will take these weak mortal bodies of ours and change them into glorious bodies like his own, using the same mighty power that he will use to conquer everything, everywhere."
Philippians 3:21

You'll Get a New Body

Braces

(Read Proverbs 4:1-5, 20-21)

Trevor plopped down on the bed. He had been sent to his room without dessert! "So I forgot to take out the trash! So I was 15 minutes late for dinner! So what?" he mumbled. "Every time I turn around someone is telling me to 'do this' or 'don't do that.'"

Later Mom came into Trevor's room. "Do you want to help me plant a peach tree?"

"I guess so," Trevor replied slowly.

After they dug a hole and planted the tree, Mom used stakes and twine to make several braces for it. "This will help it grow straight and tall," she explained.

As they walked back to the house, Mom asked, "How are you getting along with the braces on your teeth?"

Trevor shrugged. "All right, I guess. They aren't as bad as I expected. Six other kids in my class have braces on their teeth, too."

"They may be a bit uncomfortable now, but it will be worth it when your teeth are straight," Mom assured him. Then she added thoughtfully, "We put braces on our trees and braces on our teeth."

"Brenda even has a brace on her back. Her spine is curved," Trevor interrupted.

Mom nodded. "God has given us braces for our life, too," she said. "He wants us to grow straight and strong, spiritually and morally. Right now, Trevor, there are braces around you. I have set rules for you, and I make many of your decisions. I also give you certain responsibilities. Sometimes you resent these braces and pull against them, but some day when you're grown, you'll appreciate them."

Trevor raised his eyebrows. "I'd never thought of it like that," he said. After a few minutes he asked, "When are you going to take the braces off the peach tree?"

"When it's strong enough to stand straight and tall by itself," Mom said. Then she smiled and added, "And we'll remove your 'braces' one day, too." *BJW*

HOW ABOUT YOU?

Do you feel like every area of your life is controlled by someone else? Do you long for the day you can make your own decisions? Stop pulling at the braces. Thank God for them.

Accept Guidance

MEMORIZE:
"May our sons flourish in their youth like well-nurtured plants."
Psalm 144:12

Driftwood

(Read Isaiah 64:4-8)

As Peter walked slowly along the beach, his thoughts were dark. *I'm a nobody,* he said to himself. *Mom and Dad are divorced, and I'm so dumb in school. I didn't make the basketball team, and my teacher never chooses me to be the class monitor.* He sighed and tried to hold back the tears as his thoughts ran on. *I can't do anything right. I wish I'd never been born!*

Just then an old man sitting near a dock caught his attention. The man was chipping bits of wood from an old, dirty piece of driftwood. "What are you doing with that junk driftwood?" Peter asked.

"Carving it into a statue like this," the man answered as he picked up a beautifully carved dolphin and handed it to Peter.

"But that dirty old piece of driftwood looks worthless!" exclaimed Peter. "How could anything this neat come from junk?"

The old man smiled. "It takes time, work, and skill," he said. "I carve the wood carefully, sand it, and polish it." He turned the figurine over in his hand as he peered closely at Peter. "Reminds me of what God can do for us," he added. "Sometimes we feel like we aren't worth much, but we really are—to God. He can take people like us and make us into something beautiful and valuable to himself. Have you allowed him to do that for you?"

Peter shook his head and settled down on the sand at the old man's feet. He was eager to hear more about this. *HCT*

HOW ABOUT YOU?

Do you sometimes feel like everything you do and say is wrong and you might as well give up? Then perhaps you're ready to allow God, the master Creator, to take you and mold something beautiful out of your life. Will you let him do that? First, you need to know Jesus as your Savior. Then, you need to be willing to live the way he wants you to live. Let him make you into what he wants you to be.

MEMORIZE:

"And yet, Lord, you are our Father. We are the clay, and you are the potter. We are all formed by your hand." Isaiah 64:8

Give Your Life to God

Forgetful Borrower

(Read Psalm 37:21-27)

"Where's the book you borrowed from me last night?" asked Sheldon from the doorway of his sister's room.

"I put it on your desk," Natalie replied. "I'll show you." She followed her brother into his room. "Wow! Alert the National Guard! This is a disaster area!" she declared as she pointed to his desk. "I put the book right there, but the way you've thrown things around, who knows where it is now."

"Find it!" Sheldon insisted. "I have to have it tomorrow."

Natalie sighed and began digging through Sheldon's stuff. She picked up a CD. "This isn't yours, is it?"

Sheldon shook his head. "It's Tony's. I keep forgetting to return it."

Natalie dug a bit deeper. "Where did you get this book?"

"Oh, that's Mark's," replied her brother. "He loaned it to me a while back."

"Hey!" Natalie exclaimed. "Here's the pen you borrowed from me last month! You said you lost it!" She looked up as Mother stuck her head in the door to see what was going on. "Half the stuff in here is borrowed. And to not return it is like stealing it."

Mother frowned. "Natalie's right," she told Sheldon as she stuck her head into the room.

"Here's your book—I told you I had returned it," Natalie announced as she held up a book. Sheldon quickly snatched it.

"Just as you want what you loaned returned, you should return what you have borrowed," Mother said. "Now clean this room and make a pile of all the things you've borrowed. Looks like you'll be busy for a while, returning everything." *BJW*

HOW ABOUT YOU?

Have you borrowed a pencil, a game, or a book that you've neglected to return? Maybe you wouldn't deliberately lie or steal, but it's easy to do both by not returning borrowed items. Check your belongings. Collect all the borrowed items and return them today.

Return What You Borrow

MEMORIZE:
"The wicked borrow and never repay,
but the godly are generous givers."
Psalm 37:21

Folding Up the Tent

(Read 2 Corinthians 5:1-10)

"I sure enjoyed this camping trip," said Jeff, as he helped Dad pull out the stakes that held their tent in place. "But I miss Grandpa," he added soberly.

Dad stretched out an arm and drew Jeff close. "I know, Jeff," he said gently. "I miss him, too. But we know he's with God now."

Jeff nodded. "I know, but it's hard to understand why he had to die."

Dad was silent as they folded up the tent. Jeff patted it affectionately. "Jeff," said Dad suddenly, "I know you're a little sad to fold up our tent and leave here, but aren't you looking forward to being home again?"

"Sure," said Jeff readily. "I kind of miss Mom." He gave an impish grin. "Believe it or not, I even miss Timothy!"

Dad laughed. "Yeah, you miss teasing him!" Then he grew serious. "Jeff, this camping trip may help us understand something about dying."

Jeff raised his eyebrows and waited for Dad to explain.

"We had a fun week of living in a tent and cooking outdoors, right?" Jeff nodded. His eyes sparkled as he remembered their campfires and games and visits with the neighboring campers. "The tent was a temporary home, but now it's time to fold it up and go back to our real home—with Mom and Tim waiting to welcome us," continued Dad. He paused. "When Grandpa died, he 'folded up his tent.'"

"You mean he went to his real home, heaven. Right?" asked Jeff.

"Right," said Dad. "His body was like a temporary home for him while he was here on earth; now he's gone to his permanent home—to be with God and Grandma."

"And they've welcomed him, haven't they!" exclaimed Jeff. "And he's glad to be with them, even though he liked it here, too."

Dad nodded. "I think you've got the picture," he said. *MTF*

HOW ABOUT YOU?

Did someone you love die? Do you worry about your own death some day? If you know and love God, you need not worry, even though death does bring feelings of sadness. Your body is like a tent—once it has served its purpose here on earth, it is "folded away" and you go to your real home with God. That will be a permanent home which you will never have to leave.

MEMORIZE:

"For we know that when this earthly tent we live in is taken down—when we die and leave these bodies—we will have a home in heaven, an eternal body made for us by God himself and not by human hands."
2 Corinthians 5:1

**Heaven Is Our
Permanent Home**

The Worst Pain of All

(Read 1 John 3:21-24)

Eric savagely kicked a stone, sending it flying along the sidewalk. He heard someone coming up behind him and turned. It was Doug, one of the few people in his class at school who didn't make fun of Eric's bald head. "What's wrong?" Doug asked when he saw how upset Eric looked.

"Oh, not much," mumbled Eric. "It's just that the kids have been making fun of me again."

"Does having leukemia make your hair fall out?" Doug asked cautiously.

Eric shook his head. "That's caused by the treatments I have to take," he explained. He bit his lip, struggling not to show how much the teasing hurt. "Thanks for never teasing me, Doug," he added.

"Oh, that's all right," smiled Doug. "Want to come over and play with my race car set? You can call your mom from my house."

After getting permission from his mother, Eric followed Doug to the basement. As his little car sped around the track, Doug asked, "Does it hurt to have leukemia?"

"Some of the tests hurt, and the treatment makes me feel sick to my stomach. But for me, the worst part is that my hair falls out," said Eric, stopping his car. "I feel so ugly, and the teasing just makes it worse. How come you don't tease like the others?"

"Because Jesus wouldn't want me to," Doug said.

"Wish the other kids knew more about Jesus then," said Eric. "I don't know much about him, either."

Doug smiled. "Let's go upstairs and have some cookies and milk, and I'll tell you more about him," he said. *CEY*

HOW ABOUT YOU?

Do you know someone who is teased because he or she looks different? You can make life easier for that person by refusing to join in the teasing. It's a powerful witness to Jesus in your life when you befriend someone who is teased by others.

Love Others for Jesus' Sake

MEMORIZE:
"And this is his commandment: We must believe in the name of his Son, Jesus Christ, and love one another, just as he commanded us."
1 John 3:23

Two Birthdays

(Read John 1:12-13; 3:1-7)

Jeremy was at Sunday school for the very first time. He had come with his friend Tony, and he was enjoying it. He liked being with other kids his age, and he even liked the singing. Then a man in a dark suit got up. "He's the superintendent," whispered Tony. "You know—the guy in charge of Sunday school."

"We want to sing 'Happy Birthday' to those who had a birthday this past week," announced the superintendent.

Jeremy felt Tony's elbow in his ribs. "Hey, that includes you, Jeremy! Go on up to the front, and you'll get a gift."

At first Jeremy was a bit embarrassed, but when he saw he wasn't the only one, he slipped out of his seat and headed down the aisle. The superintendent shook Jeremy's hand and gave him a neat leather bookmark. Then everyone sang "Happy Birthday"—two verses. Jeremy recognized the first verse, but he'd never heard the second verse before—"Happy birthday to you. Only one will not do. Born again means salvation. How many have you?"

"I hope each of you boys and girls has had two birthdays, not just one," said the superintendent.

After class Jeremy had several questions. "What in the world did that guy mean when he said he hoped we had two birthdays?" he asked. "I just had my tenth!"

"Nope, Jeremy," Tony replied, "you've only had one birth day . . . the day you were born. The rest of the time you were just remembering your birthday."

"OK," agreed Jeremy. "But what about that second birthday then? Why would I need two birthdays?"

"When you were born the first time, you became a child of your mom and dad," explained Tony, "and that gives you life on earth. But we all do bad things— we sin, and no sin is allowed in heaven. So the only way we can be forgiven and go to heaven is to be 'born again'—born into God's family. That happens when we ask him to save us—then we have two birthdays." *CVM*

HOW ABOUT YOU?

How many birthdays do you have? Have you been born into the family of God by asking Jesus to be your Savior? If you want to know more, talk to a trusted friend or adult.

MEMORIZE:

"So don't be surprised at my statement that you must be born again." John 3:7

You Need Two Birthdays

The Firefly

(Read Matthew 5:14-16; 6:22-23)

The evening air was cool. The earthy smell of the forest filled the air, and stars shone brightly through the trees. Kevin and Jimmy lingered around the dying fire at their church's camp retreat. "Look at those stars," Kevin said. "They're really bright tonight."

Jimmy looked up toward the sky. "They just look brighter because there are no other lights around. They stand out more against the darkness."

"Look," said Kevin, pointing to the ground a few feet from the fire. There the light of a firefly flickered on and off in a pattern. "Maybe he's sending a message in Morse code," joked Kevin. "Why don't you see if you can decipher it?" Jimmy laughed as they watched the firefly blinking.

Randy, their counselor, spoke from the darkness beyond the fire. "Fireflies are interesting, aren't they?" he said. "And they have a good lesson for Christians. Can you guess what it might be?"

The boys were silent for a moment. "Maybe it's that we need to let our light shine for God," suggested Jimmy.

"Yeah," agreed Kevin, "and we shouldn't let it flicker off and on like the firefly does."

"Good thinking," approved Randy. "Sometimes we're like that firefly. Our lights flicker off when we sin. And can you tell me what's bad about that?"

"Well . . ." Kevin hesitated, then said, "If my light is shining, someone might see it and want to be a Christian, too. But if my light flickers, it might not be on when that person is looking."

"You're right,"said Randy. *LJD*

HOW ABOUT YOU?

Are you a Christian whose light shines even when things go wrong? Or does your light flicker like a firefly's does? You never know when others are watching. Keep your light shining so other people will see it and want what you have.

Let Your Light Shine

MEMORIZE:
"In the same way, let your good deeds shine out for all to see, so that everyone will praise your heavenly Father." Matthew 5:16

The Computer

(Read Romans 3:19-23)

Dan liked to play quiz games on Uncle Tim's computer. "I made up a new quiz for you," his uncle said one afternoon. "The code name is 'Heaven.' Try it out while I run a few errands for Aunt Kristen."

A short time later, Dan punched a few keys, and the computer flashed this message on the screen: "Take this quiz to see if you will go to heaven. First question: Have you asked Jesus to be your Lord and Savior?"

Dan felt uncomfortable. He knew he hadn't accepted Jesus as his Savior, even though Uncle Tim had talked to him about it many times. After a moment's hesitation, he punched "No" into the computer. Then the computer asked a series of questions about his church attendance, his grades in school, community projects he had helped with, and how much he had given to charity. By the end of the quiz, he was well satisfied with himself. *I've done lots of good things,* he thought. *I ought to get a pretty high score.*

The computer displayed this message: "Look up 1 John 5:12."

Seeing a Bible on Uncle Tim's desk, Dan picked it up, found the verse, and read, "So whoever has God's Son has life; whoever does not have his Son does not have life." "How come it says that?" he said. "Don't the good things I do count for something?"

Just then, Uncle Tim walked in. "Hi, Dan," he said. "I heard what you said just now. And while doing good is important, it cannot get you into heaven. The first question was the only one that really mattered. If you had answered 'Yes,' this would have happened."

When Uncle Tim punched a few keys, the computer flashed this message: "Matthew 25:34. 'Come, you who are blessed by my Father, inherit the Kingdom prepared for you from the foundation of the world.'"

Dan looked thoughtful. "You mean, no matter how I answered the other questions, it wouldn't have made any difference when I got to the end?"

"None at all," said Uncle Tim. "Accepting Jesus is the only way to heaven."

After a moment, Dan grinned at his uncle. "I know you've told me that lots of times before," he said, "but this is the first time I've ever been witnessed to by a computer. I'll have to think about it." *SLK*

HOW ABOUT YOU?

What would you have thought if you took the quiz Dan took? Have you accepted Jesus as your Savior? If not, talk to a trusted friend or adult to find out more.

MEMORIZE:

"So whoever has God's Son has life; whoever does not have his Son does not have life." 1 John 5:12

You Must Accept Jesus

Birds of Fire

October 27

(Read 1 Peter 1:3-9)

"Well, Adam, what happened at school today?" asked Dad. "Did you learn anything new?"

Adam grinned because nearly every night Dad asked the same question at the supper table. Today he had an answer ready. "We learned about the 'birds of fire,'" he reported.

"Birds of fire?" asked Mom. "I've never heard of them!"

"The real name for them is Kirtland's warblers," Adam told her, "but they're called 'birds of fire' for a neat reason."

"And what is that?" asked Mom.

"Well," said Adam, "they nest in jack pine trees, but the jack pinecones will open and release their seeds only when it's very hot. So, in order for Kirtland's warblers to have trees to nest in, the forest rangers sometimes start fires near the jack pine trees."

"Really?" said Mother. "I thought forest rangers stopped fires."

"Yeah," Adam replied, "but the jack pine trees are getting scarce, so the rangers use controlled fires to make the forest grow. It's weird, isn't it?"

Later that evening, as they gathered in the den for devotions, Dad referred to the birds again. "I've been thinking about Adam's science lesson today—and the fire that is needed to make trees grow so those birds can have homes," he said. "We find it rather strange, but did you know that, in a way, God often allows 'fires' in our lives to make us grow spiritually?"

"Fires in our lives? What do you mean?" asked Adam.

"The Bible compares problems, or trials, to fire," said Dad, "and as much as we dislike them, they do help us grow. Let's pray that we'll be willing to grow, even if it takes 'fire'—or problems—in our life!" *REP*

HOW ABOUT YOU?

Have you ever wondered how trials or problems could be helpful? While we won't ever understand why God allows certain things to happen in our life, we can know that he will use those things for good. Ask him to show you what you could learn through your problems.

Grow through Trials

MEMORIZE:

"Dear brothers and sisters, whenever trouble comes your way, let it be an opportunity for joy. For when your faith is tested, your endurance has a chance to grow." James 1:2-3

October

28

Who Needs Help?

(Read Deuteronomy 15:7-11)

Jason tossed his basketball at the hoop. It sailed through the net. "Hi, Son," Dad called from the garage. "Are you ready to go with me to serve the evening meal at the homeless shelter?" Every third Tuesday Jason's father went to help serve a meal and tell people about Jesus.

"I decided not to go, Dad," Jason said. He threw the ball again.

Dad was surprised. "I thought you were looking forward to it," he said. "What made you change your mind?"

"Well . . . Brett Thompson says it's a waste of time because those people could help themselves if they really wanted to," replied Jason. "Then they wouldn't be poor and homeless anymore."

"I see," said Dad. "But is it up to us to decide who needs help and who doesn't? Or is serving others a way to serve God?" Dad looked at the basketball Jason dribbled on the driveway. Then he added, "You've sure improved in basketball skills! It was nice of Coach Perkins to spend so much time helping you."

"Yeah!" agreed Jason. "I didn't know what I was doing wrong. Some of the guys wanted me off the team. They even told the coach to dump me."

"I'm glad Coach Perkins didn't listen to them," said Dad, "or let them decide who deserved his help and who didn't."

Jason nodded. "If he hadn't helped, I would still be struggling. . . ." Jason froze, and the ball rolled down the concrete driveway. *When I needed help, Coach Perkins gave it to me,* he thought. *He didn't listen to the guys who thought I'd never learn.* Jason looked at his father. "I guess you're right, Dad," he admitted. "It's not up to me to decide who needs help and who doesn't. Can you wait until I put my basketball away so I can go to the shelter with you?"

"Sure, Son." Dad smiled as Jason ran after his ball. *SSA*

HOW ABOUT YOU?

In what ways can you help others? Can you baby-sit for a single mom, or do a "fix-up" job for an elderly person?

MEMORIZE:
"Blessed are those who help the poor." Proverbs 14:21

Serve without Judging

Get Smart

(Read Deuteronomy 10:12-13, 17-21)

"I'm going to climb the fence around the power station's transformer," Jon announced to his friend.

Michael's eyes widened. "Don't do it, Jon. Dad says it's dangerous. Why do you think the electric company put up that high fence with warning signs around it?"

"To keep out scaredy-cats like you," said Jon. "Well, have a good time playing with the girls."

I'd better stop him, Michael thought as he watched Jon leave. He jumped to his feet and ran toward the house. *I'll tell Mother.*

As soon as Michael's mother heard about it, she called the electric company. Minutes later, she and Michael ran into the front yard when they heard sirens approaching. "Stay here," Mother ordered as she ran down the street.

When Mother returned, her eyes were red. She gave Michael a watery smile. "We were almost too late. Jon touched a high voltage wire just as the emergency squad arrived. They think he'll live, but he's badly burned. It will be a long time before he recovers."

"Jon said he wasn't afraid of anything," Michael told his mother.

Mother sighed. "It's good to fear some things," she said. "For instance, the Bible says that the 'fear of the Lord is the beginning of wisdom.'"

"Does that mean we're supposed to be afraid of God?" asked Michael.

"We are to fear God in the sense that we respect and obey him," answered Mother.

"Like I respect and obey you?" Michael asked.

Mother nodded. *BJW*

HOW ABOUT YOU?

Are you afraid of God? You don't need to be afraid. But he does ask that we respect and obey him.

MEMORIZE:
"Reverence for the Lord is the foundation of true wisdom."
Psalm 111:10

Fear God

Mixers and Music

(Read 1 Peter 4:7-11)

"How embarrassing!" exclaimed Caleb. "Mrs. Phillips wants me to sing a solo in church Sunday."

Mother smiled. "That's wonderful, honey," she said.

"Wonderful? I'm not doing it," declared Caleb. "What if I make a mistake? All my friends would laugh at me."

"It's your decision," said Mother. "But God gave you a beautiful voice. It's a shame not to use it."

"Well, I'm not going to do it," Caleb said stubbornly.

When Caleb came home from school the next day, his mother stood at the kitchen counter vigorously beating some batter with an old-fashioned eggbeater. "What are you making, Mom?" Caleb asked.

"Dad's birthday cake," replied Mother.

"Oh, good!" exclaimed Caleb. But he frowned as he peered into the bowl. "Where's the mixer we got you last week?" he asked. "Is it broken?" Mother shook her head as she added more flour. "Well, then," said Caleb, "I don't understand why you're not using it. I thought you liked it."

"Are you disappointed that I'm not using the gift you gave me?" asked Mother. Caleb shrugged. "A little, I guess."

"Hmmm," murmured Mother. "You and I each have a gift we're not using, don't we?" At Caleb's questioning look, Mother explained. "There's my mixer and your music—your voice."

"Oh!" Caleb was startled. "I never thought of it like that."

"The reason I'm not using my gift is that Mrs. Cooper next door asked if she could borrow it. Hers broke, and she had to make several cakes, so I loaned it to her." Mother paused. "Do you have a good reason for not using your gift?" *MS*

HOW ABOUT YOU?

What abilities has God given you? Do you use them? If you can sing, do that. If you can work in the nursery, do that. If you can play an instrument, play it for him. Use whatever abilities God has given you to bring honor to his name.

MEMORIZE:

"God has given gifts to each of you from his great variety of spiritual gifts. Manage them well so that God's generosity can flow through you."
1 Peter 4:10

Use Your Talents for God

Not Just a Disguise

(Read John 1:1-5, 14)

"I'm a beggar now! Look at me!" squealed Ben, prancing around the room in ragged brown pants, torn shirt, and shoes with holes in them.

"You certainly look like one," agreed Dad, looking in. "What's all this for? A costume party or something?"

Ben nodded. "Yeah, Tom and Sarah are having a costume party on Saturday—and there's a prize for the best costume. Don't you think I'm just like the real thing? I think I'll win that prize!" He winced and kicked off his shoes. "Ouch! These shoes hurt!"

"Well, if you want to be realistic, that's good," said Dad. "Beggars' shoes probably don't fit very well. And real beggars don't always have a roof over their heads, either. Nor do they have much food, and they have to beg for a living." Dad grinned. "If you really want to be realistic and win that prize, maybe you should go out and beg for your supper," he teased.

"No thanks!" said Ben firmly. "I'm quite happy to just pretend. I don't want the real thing."

"I thought not," said Dad. Then his face grew serious. "But you know what? That's just what Jesus did!"

"What? Became a beggar?" asked Ben.

"No, not a beggar," said Dad, "but when he came to earth, he became human—the real thing, just like one of us. He didn't just put on a coat of flesh or wear some divine disguise and pretend to be a man. Although he was still God, he also really and truly became a person, just like any other person except that he had no sin."

"It'd be tough to have to go live on the streets and not have enough food," murmured Ben thoughtfully, "and I guess it must have been tough for Jesus to leave heaven and come to live on earth." *MTF*

HOW ABOUT YOU?

Do you sometimes think that because Jesus is God and never sinned, he cannot understand the difficulties and temptations you face? Remember that although Jesus is fully God, he also became fully human. So when you're tempted to lie or cheat, or when your friends make fun of you for obeying God, or when you feel foolish because you're not doing the things everyone else does, Jesus understands exactly how you feel.

MEMORIZE:

"This High Priest of ours understands our weaknesses, for he faced all of the same temptations we do, yet he did not sin." Hebrews 4:15

Jesus Understands You

Clean Chimneys

(Read Psalm 66:16-19)

"How come you have to work so much these days?" Eddie asked as he watched his dad load up the car.

"You know that winter is a busy time for chimney cleaning," Dad answered, "but I'll be home before dark. Aren't you and Mark going to play hockey this afternoon?"

"Not anymore," Eddie said angrily and kicked the car tires. "He called it off again!"

"Did he have a good reason?" asked Dad.

"I don't know," growled Eddie. "I'm not talking to him anymore."

"That can't feel very good," said Dad.

Eddie shrugged. "There are lots of other guys to play hockey with," he said.

"Do you know why I clean chimneys every winter?" Dad asked.

"Sure," said Eddie, glad to be talking about something else. "When it's cold, people build fires, and if the chimney is clogged and dirty, the smoke sometimes can't go up. Then it all comes back in the house. Sometimes dirty chimneys cause fires, too."

"Exactly," Dad said. "Keeping a chimney clean is hard work, but it needs to be done."

Eddie picked up one of Dad's brushes and raised it above his head. "These are heavy, but it's not hard for you, is it?" asked Eddie. "You're strong!"

Dad chuckled. "Thanks for your confidence," he said. "Yes, it's true that I don't find the work as hard as when I first started." He surprised Eddie with another question. "Do you know that our relationship with God is a little like a chimney?" Eddie looked at him curiously. "When we pray, God sometimes answers immediately," Dad continued, "but if sin is clogging our hearts, it may seem like our prayers aren't getting through—just like smoke can't get up a dirty chimney."

"Sin?" asked Eddie. "Like not forgiving those who hurt us?"

Dad nodded.

"Forgiving is hard," Eddie mumbled.

"The first time it will be," Dad agreed, "but it gets easier as you practice." *HMT*

HOW ABOUT YOU?

Is your heart clean? Or is some sin clogging it—a lie, a dishonest act, unwillingness to forgive . . . or something else? If you cling to sin in your life, you cannot expect God to hear your prayers. Examine your heart today, and be willing to clean out all the mess. Ask God to help you.

MEMORIZE:

"If I had not confessed the sin in my heart, my Lord would not have listened." Psalm 66:18

Keep Your Heart Clean

The Blender

(Read 1 Corinthians 12:4-11)

"Mom!" Victor yelled. "Tell Sally not to put all the little animals in the Noah's Ark until the big ones are in. That's how I do it. That works better. Why can't she do things like I do?"

"Because I'm different," said Sally, trailing into the room behind her brother. "You're always telling me how I should play games or put puzzles together or color or . . . or whatever I'm doing. You think everybody has to do things your way!" She saw that Mother was putting plates on the table. "Oh, yummy! Supper is ready," she added.

The children hurriedly sat down, and their mother put food on their plates. First, a big spoonful of rice, then a piece of chicken, and finally, some vegetables. Victor smacked his lips as he eyed the colorful array of food before him.

"Victor," said Mom, holding out her hand, "would you like me to put all this in the blender for you?"

Victor looked puzzled. "In the blender? Why?" he asked.

"I thought you liked for everything to be the same," said Mother. "If I put this in the blender, everything will come out looking and tasting the same."

"But I don't want it all the same," said Victor. "I like it the way it is now. It's nicer to have all the different stuff."

Mom smiled and nodded. "I agree, and that's true when it comes to people, too, isn't it, Victor?" she asked. "God has made each of us different. We all look different; we have hair and skin of different colors; we have different shapes; we have different characteristics and personalities with different jobs to do. Now why would we want everyone to be the same and do everything the same?"

"Yeah, Victor," said Sally quickly. "I'm me, and you're you!"

Victor frowned. "Well . . . all right. I guess it's OK if you're different from me," he admitted. Then he grinned. *MTF*

HOW ABOUT YOU?

Do you readily accept people who are different from you? Or do you try to get others to do things your way? Are you patient with people who are slower than you or not as talented as you? Remember that all Christians are part of the body of Christ. Each part of a body—the hand, the foot, the eye, and so on—is quite different in looks and in function from the others. But each part is important.

MEMORIZE:

"There are different kinds of gifts, but the same Spirit. There are different kinds of service, but the same Lord."
1 Corinthians 12:4-5, NIV

Allow Others to Be Different

No Greener Grass

(Read Psalm 100)

Ted was always dissatisfied. "If Jack Stark can go to the park alone, why can't I?" he would ask. Or, "Why do I have to eat carrots? None of my friends have to eat what they don't like!" Rules about TV also brought many complaints. "Other parents think those programs are OK, but you never let me watch anything!" declared Ted. And at bedtime, it was, "Can't I stay up longer? Nobody else has to go to bed so early."

When Ted complained one day because his father was out of town for a few days, Mother sighed. "Can't you just be thankful Dad has a job, even if it does take him away sometimes?" she asked. "Be glad for all the good things God has provided for you."

"Well, I am, but everybody else has it better," Ted murmured. "I wish I could live like Jack does."

It was only a day later that Mother fell and sprained her ankle. To help out, Jack's mother invited Ted to spend several days at their home.

When he returned home, Ted seemed as delighted to be back as his mother was to have him. "Well, how did you like eating only your favorite foods?" asked Mother. "And I do hope you didn't stay up too late every night, watching wild TV programs."

"Oh, no, Mom," Ted assured her. "Jack's whole family goes to bed early. And we had to eat all kinds of things—even carrots. His mother said she wanted me to look healthy when I came home." He paused, then added, "They're real nice, Mom, but I found out that it's not really nicer there than at home. I like it here."

Mother laughed. "They say the 'grass is always greener on the other side of the fence,' but when we finally manage to get there, we usually find it isn't really true," she said. "We need to learn to appreciate what God has given us, and be thankful for it." *AGL*

HOW ABOUT YOU?

Do things always look better to you somewhere else? Others probably think that what you have looks good. Learn to be thankful for what you have! And remember to thank God today, and every day, for all he has given you.

Be Thankful

MEMORIZE:
"Give thanks to him and bless his name." Psalm 100:4

Good-bye and Hello

(Read John 14:1-6)

"Tuffy is barking!" yelled Brian as he raced with his dog to the front door. "Maybe James is home!" Scooping the feisty terrier into his arms, Brian peered through the peephole, then shook his head in disappointment. "It's just the mailman."

"Your brother will be here soon," Mother called from the kitchen, where she was putting finishing touches on a chocolate cake. "Would you please go and get the mail?"

After Brian left, his sister, Jennie, set the last two plates on the dining-room table. "Mom," she said with a sigh, "I feel kind of strange. I'm excited about seeing James, but I'm sad because the reason he's coming home from college is to go to Grandma's funeral."

Mother came to put her arm around Jennie. Fresh tears glistened in her eyes. "I understand, honey," she said. "I loved her and will miss her so much! But I love James, too, and I'm so eager to see him walk through that door and say hello."

"'Hello' is a much happier word than 'good-bye,' isn't it," said Jennie.

Mother nodded. "Just think, Jennie, while we are saying good-bye to Grandma, she's saying hello to Jesus in heaven because she has put her trust in him for salvation. And she's saying hello to loved ones who've gone before her." She paused and wiped her eyes. "Whenever I'm missing Grandma terribly, I like to picture her in heaven celebrating with Jesus."

Jennie's face broke into a smile as she thought about that.

"Hey, Mom!" Brian burst through the door. "I didn't have to get the mail. James got it!" His grinning brother stepped into the room as Mother and Jennie rushed to give James a big hug. *LRS*

HOW ABOUT YOU?

It's sad for you when those you love die. But try to remember that, if they belong to Jesus, he will be welcoming them in heaven. You will miss them and feel sad at times, but you can be happy for them, too.

MEMORIZE:

"Precious in the sight of the Lord is the death of his saints." Psalm 116:15, NIV

Jesus Welcomes Us Home

Sin Splinters

(Read John 16:7-8, 13-15)

"Ouch!" exclaimed Seth. He held up his pinky finger and touched a sore spot. "Mom, it hurts right here," he cried.

"I can't see anything," Mom replied. "Maybe you've just bruised it. And don't eat any of the candies on the counter. I need them to bake cookies, and I have just enough."

"Uh-h-h . . . OK," Seth mumbled. He quickly wiped his mouth and slipped out the back door to play with his dog, Patches.

Later that morning, Seth went into the kitchen and saw the cup full of M&M candies. He picked out several red pieces. "Mmmm," he murmured. Then he picked out some yellow ones. *I don't think Mom will notice,* he thought.

When Mom noticed that the cup of candies was no longer full, she called to Seth. "Did you eat any candy?" she asked.

"No," Seth said, quickly turning back to play with Patches.

At supper, Seth was unusually quiet. He didn't even ask why Mom had not baked cookies. After he went to bed, he tossed and turned but couldn't sleep. Mom heard him rolling around and went to check on him. "What's the matter?" she asked.

"My finger hurts," complained Seth, holding up a puffy, red finger.

"Ah-h-h. It's infected. I can see a splinter now," Mom said as she went to get some tweezers. She carefully removed the splinter from Seth's finger and held it up. "I have a feeling that something else is infected, too," she said, looking at Seth. "Would you care to tell me about it?"

Tears escaped down Seth's cheeks. "I ate some of the candy you were going to use for cookies," he confessed. "I'm sorry I lied."

Mom nodded. "I see," she said. "Just like a little splinter can trouble your whole finger, one little splinter of sin can trouble your heart. Since you've trusted Jesus as your Savior, his Holy Spirit makes you feel guilty when you do something you know is wrong. He wants you to ask forgiveness and turn away from doing wrong things." *LJR*

HOW ABOUT YOU?

Is the Holy Spirit troubling you about something you've done wrong? Maybe you're trying to hide a lie. Maybe you've spoken angry words or cheated on a test. If so, listen to the prompting of the Holy Spirit and ask for forgiveness.

MEMORIZE:

"And when he comes, he will convince the world of its sin, and of God's righteousness, and of the coming judgment." John 16:8

Listen to the Holy Spirit

November

6

No Time to Eat

(Read 1 Peter 2:1-5)

Ron grabbed his school books and ran out the door. If he didn't hurry, he'd be late for class! It was that way every day—he'd sleep too long and then have to hurry to get ready on time. But no matter how late he was, he'd always take time for a big breakfast before rushing off to school.

One day a nutritionist, Mr. Pierson, came to speak to the youth group at church. He spoke about Ron's favorite subject—eating! "How many hours are there between breakfast and lunch?" Mr. Pierson asked one of the girls.

"About four or five," she replied.

"How many hours between lunch and supper?" he continued, turning to a boy.

"About the same," was the answer.

"And how many hours from suppertime until you eat again?" This time he pointed to Ron for an answer.

"Too many," moaned Ron as he rubbed his stomach. Everyone laughed.

"Now let's ask those same questions about our spiritual intake," Mr. Pierson continued. "How long does your spiritual life have to wait for food from the Bible?"

Ron was glad he did not have to answer that question out loud. Although he wouldn't think of missing meals, he hadn't been very faithful about having his spiritual food lately. Sometimes he'd go from one Sunday to the next without even opening his Bible.

"If you skip meals," the nutritionist was saying, "your physical body suffers. And if you do not regularly 'eat' from the Word of God, your spiritual life will suffer. Don't forget Peter's reminder to 'grow in grace and in the knowledge of our Lord and Savior Jesus Christ.' We can only grow when we eat."

As the youth meeting ended, Ron made a decision. He would get up early enough to have time for Bible reading and prayer to start the day with God. Then he would go down for breakfast. *RIJ*

HOW ABOUT YOU?

Did you eat food today? Did you also "eat" from God's Word? It's important to take care of both your physical and spiritual needs on a daily basis.

MEMORIZE:

"Blessed are those who hunger and thirst for righteousness, for they shall be filled." Matthew 5:6, NKJV

Eat Spiritual Food

Just a Starter

(Read 2 Timothy 4:7-8)

Zach and several other young people from his church gathered after school on Monday night to begin working on a special project. Packing clothes, toys, games, and literature for a downtown mission turned out to be more work than they had expected. They didn't get it finished in one night.

"I'm glad you're taking such an interest in helping with that project," said Zach's mother when he returned home after the second evening of work.

"Yeah," Zach replied, "but we're still not done. And only four of us showed up tonight. Well, only two, really—Mary Lane and me. The other two were Mr. and Mrs. Nolting."

After school the next day, Zach was shooting baskets with some of the boys in the neighborhood. "Zach," Mother called after a time, "are you going to help with the church project? It's getting late."

Zach grunted unhappily, then turned and shot a few more baskets. *I'm not going to the work session tonight,* he decided. *It's someone else's turn. I'll skip tonight and then go again tomorrow night—if they still need more help.*

After supper, Zach called Mary Lane to see how much work they had done on the project.

"I don't really know," Mary confessed. "I didn't go today, either." Her words bothered Zach just a little as he hung up the phone.

Minutes later Mary called back. "I just talked to Mrs. Nolting," she said. "She told me nobody showed up today. Mr. and Mrs. Nolting were the only ones there. I asked if we were going to work at it again tomorrow, but she said they planned to finish it by themselves because they don't think anybody else cares anymore." Mary paused, then added, "Oh, Zach, I felt so bad for them."

When they had finished talking, Zach slowly hung up the phone. He had been so enthusiastic about the project when it was first announced, but his interest had dwindled down to nothing. Now he felt miserable. *RIJ*

HOW ABOUT YOU?

Do you work hard on something for a little while and then leave it for someone else to finish? Be sure to finish what you start.

Finish What You Start

MEMORIZE:
"If only I may finish the race and complete the task." Acts 20:24, NIV

8

Backpacks and Burdens

(Read Romans 15:1-7)

Jason, Tom, and the rest of the youth group listened as Mr. Brown finished giving instructions for the day's hike. "Everyone carries his own backpack," Mr. Brown concluded as they got ready to head down the trail.

Soon they were on their way. They were having a great time as they hiked along, sometimes walking easily on the well-beaten trail; sometimes scrambling over fallen trees or making their way around them.

"This is cool!" exclaimed Jason. "Beat you to the next curve in the trail, Tom." But as Jason started off, he tripped on a tree root and down he went! "Ouch!" he cried, grabbing his ankle.

Mr. Brown hurried over just as Jason stood up. "I think I can walk OK," said Jason, gingerly testing his ankle.

"All right, but no racing for a while," said Mr. Brown. "I think it would be easier for you if you didn't have the extra weight of that backpack."

"I'll carry his backpack," offered Tom.

"Me, too," chimed in several other voices.

"Thank you, boys," said Mr. Brown. So for the rest of the hike, the boys took turns carrying Jason's backpack.

At the end of the hike, the boys built a campfire, and after lunch, Mr. Brown led in a short devotional time. "What you boys did today for Jason reminds me of what Jesus tells us to do," he said. "We each carry our own 'burden'—our own 'backpack' of responsibilities—but if any one of us has a load that is too heavy, we're to help him carry it until he's able to safely bear it alone again. You did that physically, and Jesus wants us to do that spiritually as well. Think of a few ways kids like you get burdened down and what you could do to help."

After a moment, Jason raised his hand. "Some kids have a lot of trouble with schoolwork," he said. "Sometimes we could help them."

"We could make friends with new kids at school," offered Tom.

Mr. Brown nodded. "Good suggestions," he said. *GJT*

HOW ABOUT YOU?

Are you taking responsibility for your own actions? Do you also offer help to those whose "backpacks" of responsibilities become too overwhelming for them?

MEMORIZE:

"Share each other's troubles and problems, and in this way obey the law of Christ." Galatians 6:2

Help One Another

Noah's Ark

(Read Psalm 133:1-3)

"George is such a pain," complained Ben as he placed the Noah's ark toy elephants side by side. "He's always talking about how he played soccer in the school he used to go to. Who cares?"

Katie picked up the pig. "He couldn't be worse than Anna," she said. "I don't think she ever takes a bath and her hair looks like a broom! I'm going to ask Mrs. James if I can change places next week." She set the pig down.

"Hey! You better not put your pig next to Mrs. Noah," said Ben. "I'm sure she wouldn't like the smell!"

Katie giggled. "I wouldn't have liked to be Mrs. Noah, living with a boat full of smelly, noisy animals! I bet they fought a lot, too."

"I like to think neither the Noah family or the animals had fights," said Mom. "I should think they would have been so thankful to be on the ark—their safe place from the storm and flood—that they would have put up with bad smells and loud noises."

"I guess so," agreed Katie. "I mean, what's a bad smell—even pigs—compared to being drowned?"

"But I guess you two would have grumbled and complained even inside the ark!" continued Mom.

"Mom!" cried Katie indignantly. "Why would you say that?"

"Well, listen to you grumble about your classmates," said Mom. "I understand that George and Anna's habits and manners may be pretty annoying sometimes, but from what you've told me before, I gather that they both come from homes where no one gives them much attention. Have you forgotten that you are blessed to be part of a Christian family and that you know Jesus? He provides a safe place from the storms of the world. Perhaps George and Anna don't have that." *MTF*

HOW ABOUT YOU?

Are you constantly annoyed with your brothers and sisters in Christ? Do you snap at those who are slow? Do you ridicule those who are clumsy? Do you ignore those you consider ugly? Christ's body, the church, is like Noah's ark—it carries all God's children, including those who look different, talk different, act different, even smell different! It's not always easy to like or understand others, but we are called to accept them and live in harmony with them.

Accept One Another

MEMORIZE:
"I plead with you to be of one mind, united in thought and purpose."
1 Corinthians 1:10

10

Don't Make Excuses

(Read James 1:12-15)

Barry felt grumpy. First he had to shut off the ball game on TV and do his home-work—just because he'd gotten an F on his last history test. It wasn't his fault he'd been too busy to study. After all, he'd been working on a Sunday school project, so you'd think the Lord could have helped him with the exam!

Next, Mom got after him for leaving his things all over the house. He tried to tell her he couldn't help being messy—that was just his personality. It was the way God made him. But Mom made him pick up his things anyway.

And now she was fussing about his friends. "Oh, Mom," he complained. "You get so upset about nothing! So what if the guys use a little rough language? I don't use it, and there's nobody else to hang around with after school."

"Well, you've been staying out much too late," Mother answered, "and I'm not sure what kinds of activities those boys might lead you into."

"Bring them home to play games," suggested Dad, "or invite them to your church activities."

"Hmph!" snorted Barry. "What for? I go, and I'm a Christian, but I wonder what difference it makes."

"I see," Dad mused. "You blame God for your bad grades and for the way you leave things lying around. Now it seems you hold him responsible for your bad companions. Your problems are all God's fault, right?"

Barry looked ashamed. "I didn't mean it that way," he mumbled. "I guess I just didn't want to take the blame myself." Soon he looked up and grinned. "You win. I know it's my fault. I'll ask the Lord to help me study and be neat. And I'll ask him to help me find new friends or change the old ones." *HWM*

HOW ABOUT YOU?

When you get into trouble, do you blame God? When you do something wrong, do you really feel it's God's fault—or at least, not your own? Never blame God. Instead, ask him to forgive and change you.

MEMORIZE:

"And remember, no one who wants to do wrong should ever say, 'God is tempting me.' God is never tempted to do wrong, and he never tempts anyone else either." James 1:13

Don't Blame God for Your Problems

The Pottery Lesson

(Read Jeremiah 18:1-6)

Joan and the others in her ceramics class watched as her mother poured a liquid into a mold. All the girls were interested in seeing how something so runny could get hard enough to become a lovely vase. Then Mother brought out a piece that had been molded a few days ago.

"Is that one done?" asked one of the girls.

"Oh, no," replied Joan's mother. "As soon as it's dry enough to handle, it needs to be rubbed and cleaned and scraped, and then it will be put into the fire."

The girls watched again as Joan's mother worked on the piece of pottery. With a knife, she scraped away the excess clay. Then, with a piece of sandpaper, she smoothed the pottery. Finally, she rubbed it with a soft sponge.

"All that work?" Joan said.

"That's just the beginning," Mother answered. "After it has gone through one firing, a colorful glaze will be applied. Then it will be put into the fire again. You know, girls, this reminds me of our life. God works on Christians, scraping off our bad habits, smoothing us out to become more like him, and finally making us beautiful and shiny by putting us through the fire."

"But I don't think I'd like to be put through all those things," remarked one girl.

"Neither would I," Joan agreed.

"If we're not willing to let God work in us—taking away bad habits, sinful thoughts, angry words, and stubborn attitudes—then our life will not shine for Jesus," Joan's mother replied. "It's part of his plan to make us more like him." *RIJ*

HOW ABOUT YOU?

Has God been scraping off the bad habits and sinful deeds in your life? Has he taught you patience through illness or through doing without something you really want? When he works in your life, do you get angry? Let him have his way. You'll be glad you did.

MEMORIZE:
"Does not the potter have the right to make out of the same lump of clay some pottery for noble purposes and some for common use?"
Romans 9:21, NIV

Let God Mold You

Danger!

(Read Ephesians 6:10-13)

Stefan glanced uneasily at the danger signs posted around the old mine shaft. "Come on," urged his older brother, John, as he climbed over the fence and dropped down inside the enclosure.

"What if someone finds out we came here?" protested Stefan. "We're supposed to be gathering wood for the fire."

John shrugged and walked away. Then a horrible, crashing sound filled Stefan's ears as John disappeared. "John!" cried Stefan. "Where are you?"

"Down here," came the muffled reply. "I can't . . . move."

Stefan gulped. "Hang on," he called. "I'll go get Grandpa." Frantically he ran to the site of the winter church retreat where the men were setting up camp while the boys collected firewood. "Help! John's trapped in an old mine!" he yelled.

The rest of the evening was a blur to Stefan. He dimly remembered Pastor Jack calling for help on his ham radio, the wait for the rangers to come in the helicopter, and the wait for his grandpa to return with news from the hospital. How Stefan wished he and John had obeyed the instructions to stay within sight of camp! How he wished they had paid attention to the danger signs!

When Grandpa returned, Stefan was relieved to hear that John would be all right. He told his grandpa how sorry he was that he had disobeyed. Grandpa nodded. "I hope you've learned a lesson," he said. "What did the signs at the mine say?"

"They said, 'Danger. Keep out!'" replied Stefan.

"Exactly," said Grandpa, "and when you and John didn't obey them, you had to pay the consequences. God's Word also says, 'Danger. Keep out of sin, or you will have to pay the consequences.' Don't ignore God's warnings." *JAB*

HOW ABOUT YOU?

Do you think you can disobey, cheat, or lie—"just once"—and it won't matter? Do you think nobody will ever find out? God already knows, and very often other people find out, too. Sin is dangerous and has serious consequences. Ask God to help you to do what is right.

MEMORIZE:

"Plant the good seeds of righteousness, and you will harvest a crop of my love." Hosea 10:12

Sin Is Dangerous

What Did You Promise?

(Read Ecclesiastes 5:1-7)

The church that Peter and Julie attended was going to collect a special offering for their missionaries in South America. As the family talked about it, Peter said, "I promised I'd put half of my allowance in the missionary offering next week."

"I will, too," nodded Julie.

But when the offering plate was passed the following week, Peter put in only a dime, and Julie put in a nickel. Mother noticed, but said nothing.

Later that day, Peter's friend Jack came over with his new book about space exploration. "I want to be an astronaut when I grow up," said Jack.

"Me, too," Peter agreed. Julie overheard them and commented, "Not me. I want to be a fashion model. They make lots of money."

After Jack left, Mother spoke. "I thought you both told your church teacher that you were going to be missionaries," she said.

"Well, uh, I guess we forgot," said Peter.

"What difference does it make?" asked Julie. "Is it wrong for a Christian to be an astronaut or a model?"

"Not necessarily. And it's not necessarily wrong to put a nickel or dime in the offering plate, either," said Mother. "But if you make a promise to God and then break it, that's wrong. You both promised God half of your allowance. If you're unable to keep a promise through no fault of your own, that's one thing. But if you keep changing your mind whenever you feel like it, that's wrong. It's better not to make a promise than to make one and not keep it."

Peter's face was red. "I think I'll have to be more careful about the promises I make—and about keeping them, too."

"Me, too," agreed his sister. "I'm gong to put the rest of the money I promised in the offering tonight." *SLK*

HOW ABOUT YOU?

Are you quick to make promises to God—or to others—but reluctant to carry them out? God always does what he says he will do. You should, too. If keeping your promise means doing something hard or inconvenient, do it anyway. Think before you promise!

Keep Your Promises

14

Just like Toothpaste

(Read James 3:1-8)

Jason was baby-sitting his little brother, Ben. The afternoon had started out fine, but then the phone rang. It was Jason's friend Hal, and the boys talked quite a while before Jason returned to the kitchen where he had left Ben. But his brother was no longer there. Suspicious noises were coming from the bathroom, so Jason hurried to see what Ben was up to. Ben was trying desperately to push toothpaste back into the tube.

"You dummy!" exclaimed Jason. "Why can't you leave things alone?" As he began to clean up the mess, he continued to scold his little brother.

"I'm sorry," whimpered Ben. "I'll put it back."

"You can't," growled Jason. "Once toothpaste is out, it stays out!"

Ben began to cry. "I guess I'm a dummy," he sobbed.

When Jason saw how upset his little brother was, he wished he hadn't been so harsh. "No, Ben," he said, "you aren't a dummy."

"But you said . . . ," began Ben.

Jason rumpled his little brother's hair. "Forget that. I shouldn't have said it in the first place, and I'm sorry."

When their parents arrived, they heard all about the toothpaste episode. "I'm a dummy," confessed Ben with trembling lips.

"I told you you're not," protested Jason, "and I said I was sorry."

"Ben, you were very wrong," said Mother, "and, Jason, you were too hasty with your tongue. I'm glad you apologized, but there's a lesson here. Just like you can't get toothpaste back in the tube, you can't take back words that come out of your mouth. Be careful of the words you say." *LMW*

HOW ABOUT YOU?

Do you sometimes say things in anger? Or do you sometimes say things jokingly, but you know they really hurt the one to whom you are talking? Words can never be unsaid. The Bible says your speech is to be always with grace. Is yours?

MEMORIZE:

"Don't use foul or abusive language. Let everything you say be good and helpful, so that your words will be an encouragement to those who hear them." Ephesians 4:29

Speak Kindly

It Could Be Worse (Part 1)

(Read Proverbs 15:13-15)

Football rated number one in Art's life. But one day, he found himself at the bottom of a pile of kicking, yelling players, and he received an injury that required surgery.

Ann, one of his neighbors, visited him at the hospital. "Hi, Art," she said, shoving a bunch of flowers at him. "See what I brought you. These will brighten your room."

"A-a-choo! Thanks, Ann. A-a-choo!" Art sneezed again. "But would you take them away, please?" he begged. "I'm allergic to them."

"Oh, my!" gasped Ann. "Well, I'm glad it's only the flowers making you sneeze. I was afraid you had a cold. My mother knew a lady who caught a cold in the hospital, and she died of pneumonia. After all, there's all kinds of germs in a hospital, you know. You're liable to catch most anything. You don't feel very good, do you?"

"Oh, I'm fine," Art replied. "Most of the pain is gone."

"That's because the doctor gives you pills," Ann told him. "That's what my mother says. You could be dying for all you know. Doctors never tell you anything. Too bad you won't be able to play football anymore this year. You'll just have to watch the other kids play." She shook her head. "Did you know . . ." She clapped her hand over her mouth.

"Know what?" asked Art.

"Well, I wasn't supposed to tell you, but since it almost slipped out . . . well . . . your dog got run over," Ann said sadly.

"Spot?" gasped Art. "Is he . . . is he . . ."

"Uh-huh." Ann nodded. "He's dead. I'm sorry."

"Oh, that's awful," moaned Art.

"Well, don't worry," Ann advised sympathetically. She glanced at her watch. "I've gotta get going, but I did want to drop in and cheer you up a bit. Take care now." *HCT*

HOW ABOUT YOU?

Do you know someone who is sick? You should go to visit, but do talk about cheerful things. (Don't be like Ann.) If the sick person is feeling bad because of some unhappy news, allow him or her to talk about it, but don't pry. Be sympathetic and pray for the person. If you wish to take a small gift, be sure it's something the patient is allowed to have.

Cheer the Sick

MEMORIZE:
"A cheerful heart is good medicine."
Proverbs 17:22, NIV

16

It Could Be Worse (Part 2)

(Read Psalm 16:5-8)

When Dr. Baker entered the hospital room, he found Art in tears, and he heard about Ann's visit. "Why does everything happen to me?" asked Art with a sob.

Dr. Baker shook his head sympathetically. "Tell you what," he said, "whenever you think you're bad off, look around, and you'll find you have a lot to be thankful for." He pushed Art's bed close to the window. "Look down to that corner window in the next building," he said. "In that room there's a boy who may never walk again. In view of that, your situation doesn't seem so bad, does it—even though you won't be able to play football?" Looking ashamed, Art shook his head, and Dr. Baker continued. "On the top floor, right above you, is a lady who's been flat on her back for 20 years." As he was speaking, their attention was drawn to the hall where a young couple and a little girl were passing. The little girl was sobbing, and the lady was trying to comfort her.

Art looked at Dr. Baker. "Something terrible must have happened," he said.

Dr. Baker nodded. "The little girl's mother is very sick."

"I-I guess I'm not as bad off as I thought," Art decided. *HCT*

HOW ABOUT YOU?

Do you sometimes think everything is going wrong? Whenever you start feeling sorry for yourself, just look around. There's always someone with a bigger problem than your problem. But no matter how bad the problem, remember Jesus' promise to always be with you.

MEMORIZE:

"Stay away from the love of money, be satisfied with what you have. For God has said, 'I will never fail you, I will never forsake you.'" Hebrews 13:5

Thank God for Blessings

When the Flag Flies

(Read John 13:34-35; 1 John 4:7-11)

Barry settled down to listen as Mr. Jensen, his Sunday school teacher, began to speak. "I want to tell you about an article I read this week that told of some traditions in England," said Mr. Jensen. "It said that the Queen of England has several castles, or homes. Sometimes she lives in one, and sometimes in another. Whenever she's in one of her homes, her flag flies on top of that roof. It lets her subjects know their queen is inside." Mr. Jensen paused as he looked at the boys. "You know, as Christians, the King of kings lives within each of us," he added. "What are some things we could use as a banner—things that would show that we have Jesus in our life?"

Josh raised his hand. "We could read Christian books," he suggested when the teacher called on him.

Mr. Jensen nodded. "Who else can suggest something to use as a banner?"

Barry had a suggestion. "We should obey our parents," he said.

Mr. Jensen nodded. "And why should you obey them?" he asked.

"God says we should," replied Barry.

"That's right. In other words, we should obey God, shouldn't we? We should do what he says—we should keep his commandments. Where do we find them?"

"The Bible gives the Ten Commandments," said one of the boys.

Mr. Jensen nodded. "Right, and they're very important," he agreed. He held up his Bible as he added, "But our lesson today talks about a new commandment Jesus gave his disciples—including us. Perhaps this is the best banner we could show others. It's the one that Jesus says will show them that we belong to him. Turn in your Bibles to John 13:35 and tell me what that new commandment is." *MRP*

HOW ABOUT YOU?

Did you find the new commandment—that you show love to one another—as you read today's Scripture? Do others see that you belong to Jesus? He says they will if you show love. By doing this, you are holding high the "banner of love" and indicating to others that Jesus lives within your heart.

Love One Another

MEMORIZE:
"Your love for one another will prove to the world that you are my disciples." John 13:35

18

All Roads Lead to Rome (Part 1)

(Read Matthew 7:13-20)

"This picnic is fun!" Kara told Aunt Sue and Uncle Don. "I love it here. Don't you wish we could live here in the Rockies, Peter?" she asked her brother.

"It sure is nice," agreed Peter as he glanced around him. "Look—there are at least a dozen different paths, all leading to this picnic area. It's just like the city of Rome." He laughed at the puzzled expression on his aunt's face. "Last week our preacher said that in the days of the Roman Empire, you could follow any road, and it would lead you to Rome," he explained. "He said that's like going to heaven, too. No matter what religion we follow, it will lead us to heaven if we are sincere and do our best."

"Perhaps all roads did lead to Rome, but all roads certainly do not lead to heaven," declared Uncle Don. "The Bible has something to say about that."

Aunt Sue nodded. "In the Bible, Jesus said that he is the way. He is the road or path that leads to heaven. He said no one can come to the Father except through him."

Kara looked doubtful. "I never heard our minister say that," she murmured. "Wouldn't you think he'd know?"

"If we want to know what is right or wrong, we can't accept the word of any person—no matter who he is or how nice he may be," explained Uncle Don, "unless what he says agrees with what we read in the Bible."

"I never thought about that," said Peter. "I always thought whatever our preacher said was true, but I suppose he could be wrong sometimes. I guess I should check out what he says more often." *HCT*

HOW ABOUT YOU?

Do you attend church and Sunday school? Do you read good books? Do you listen to Christian broadcasts and TV programs? That's great. But no matter how nice your teachers may be, or where you hear things, it's important to make sure that what you are learning agrees with the Bible. As some of the early Christians did, you should search the Scriptures daily to see if what you are taught is true.

MEMORIZE:

"They searched the Scriptures day after day . . . to see if they were really teaching the truth." Acts 17:11

Study the Bible

All Roads Lead to Rome (Part 2)

(Read Matthew 7:21-27)

Uncle Don pointed toward the many paths that led from the picnic area. "Do you remember which path we took to get here?" he asked.

"Uh . . . I think the one by the swings," said Kara.

"No," disagreed Peter, "the one by that flowering bush."

"Uh-uh! I remember seeing the swings right away," insisted Kara, "and I . . ."

"But there's some ivy on the other side of that bush," interrupted Peter. "I remember looking at the leaves to see if it's the poisonous kind."

Uncle Don laughed. "Well," he said, "you two don't agree, so let's try an experiment. You each sincerely believe you're right, don't you?"

"Yes!" shouted both of the children.

"All right. Suppose you each try your path, and we'll see who's right," suggested Uncle Don. "Let's see. It took about three minutes for us to walk here from the car. So if you walk for . . . let's say five minutes . . . and haven't reached the car, come back. Or, if you do find the car, bring back the little flag that's attached to the mirror. The loser has to wash the dishes when we get home, OK?"

"You bet!" the children agreed, and off they went. Fifteen minutes later, they were back at the picnic spot, but neither one had the flag. "I can't believe neither one of us found the car!" exclaimed Peter. "Uncle Don, do you know where it is?"

Uncle Don laughed. "The only path leading to the car is the one over there by those wildflowers," he told them. "Come on. I'll show you." Away they trooped, and a few minutes later, sure enough, there was the car. "You see," said Uncle Don, "you were very sincere in believing that the path you chose would lead to the car, but your sincerity didn't help you. You can also be very sincere about the path you choose to go to heaven. But unless you choose the one path that leads there—the Lord Jesus—your sincerity won't help you get there, either." *HCT*

HOW ABOUT YOU?

Are you taking the only path that leads to heaven? You may think such things as being good, going to church, saying prayers, or being kind are the right way, but the Bible says Jesus is the only way to heaven. Doing good is important, but it will not get you into heaven.

**Jesus Is the
Way to Heaven**

MEMORIZE:
"There is a path before each person that seems right, but it ends in death." Proverbs 14:12

Justin's Illustration

(Read Proverbs 3:1-8)

"So what you're saying, Justin, is that living your life is something like driving a car?" asked Mrs. Felten. The children in the Sunday school class all laughed, and Justin shifted his position on the chair. "Wait a minute, class. Justin may be on to something here. Let's talk about it and see how far we can go with this illustration. Let's picture each of us in a car—a 'life-car'—going down the highway of life. Who's driving the car?"

"We are," the class called out.

"OK," said Mrs. Felten. "Now as we go along, at some point we're asked if we want to trust Christ as Savior and be assured of eternal life."

"And if we accept Jesus, it's like we're asking him to be a passenger in our car," Tracy suggested.

"You've got the idea, Tracy," said Mrs. Felten, "but should he be a passenger? After you invite him in, should you still be steering and deciding where to go?"

Christy raised her hand. "We should let Jesus be in control of our life," she said. "He should be the one driving."

"Right!" agreed Mrs. Felten. "Now . . . is there anything else we can use in our picture? How about road signs and stoplights?" She looked at her class. "Justin, you began this idea. What do you think?"

Justin sat up straighter. "Well, I guess following road signs would be like reading the Bible," he suggested. "It gives us directions for how to live. And the stoplights could be when God says no to something we want."

"That's a good thought." Mrs. Felten nodded. "What happens in real life if you go through a red light?"

"You might get hit by other cars," Justin said, "and you might get hurt."

"Right," said Mrs. Felten, "but when you let Jesus drive, you can be sure he'll follow the road signs and never run a stoplight. You all ride in cars often, and when you climb into one from now on, I hope you'll be reminded that you need Jesus in your 'life-car' and that you need to let him drive. Thank you, Justin, for a good illustration." *VLC*

HOW ABOUT YOU?

Have you asked Jesus to get into your "life-car"? Is he in the driver's seat, or are you? If you allow Jesus to "drive," you'll avoid many "accidents"—many heartaches and troubles.

MEMORIZE:

"Seek his will in all you do, and he will direct your paths." Proverbs 3:6

Let Jesus Steer Your Life

The Christian Thing to Do

(Read Luke 17:11-19)

Blake had just received a birthday present from his grandmother—a large Lego set. "Wow! Just what I wanted!" he exclaimed in delight. Dumping the blocks on the floor, he began building a space station like the picture on the box cover.

"Before you get too busy, why not write Grandma a thank-you note?" his mother suggested. "Let her know how much you appreciate her gift."

"Aw, Mom, do I have to?" objected Blake. "I want to play with this now. Besides, I can thank her when she comes to visit us next month."

"Blake, your grandmother loves you very much," Mother answered. "She went to a lot of trouble to find the exact blocks you wanted. I happen to know she had to spend an entire afternoon going from store to store before she found the right ones. The least you can do is spend 15 minutes writing her a thank-you note."

Blake knew his mother was right. He knew that, as a Christian, he should be thankful for things, and he should also be courteous. In this case, he needed to let his grandmother know that he thought she was a very special lady and that he loved her very much. He pushed the blocks aside. They could wait. Right now he had a job to do! *LMW*

HOW ABOUT YOU?

Do you think writing thank-you notes is a boring job? Do you sometimes forget to write them? When Jesus was here on earth, he noticed who said thank you and who didn't. Don't assume that everyone knows how thankful you are. Say it. Write it when necessary. Express it to other people, and to God as well.

MEMORIZE:

"And let the peace that comes from Christ rule in your hearts. For as members of one body you are all called to live in peace. And always be thankful." Colossians 3:15

Express Thanks to Others

Grandma's Trophies

(Read Matthew 6:19-21)

One Saturday, everyone in the Baker family was enlisted to help clean the attic. "Look!" exclaimed Penny as she pulled a small book out of an old trunk that had belonged to their great-grandmother. On the cover of the book were printed the words "My Trophies."

"Wow," said Mike, "I wonder what kinds of trophies Grandma Baker won."

"Not long-distance running, like you're hoping for, I bet," said Penny with a grin. "Maybe she entered a reading contest and won a trophy like the one I'm trying to win."

Opening the book, Mike read, "May 10. Thank you, Lord, for letting me talk to Sarah today. She accepted you as Savior." Turning some pages he found, "July 16. Today William left for India as a missionary. William was such a trouble-maker before he became a Christian."

"Who were Sarah and William?" asked Penny.

"I think they were children Grandma Baker led to the Lord," Dad replied. "She worked as a missionary for many years. These children became living trophies of God's grace as they became Christians."

"Yes," agreed Mother. "She didn't have much earthly treasure, but she was rich in heavenly treasures. There are some verses in Matthew that tell us it's important to lay up treasure in heaven."

"There's a good lesson here for all of us," added Dad. "Each of us should ask ourselves, 'What kind of treasure am I storing up?'"

"But do we get treasure in heaven just by leading somebody to Jesus?" asked Penny.

"Actually, I believe we lay up treasure in heaven whenever we do something for Jesus—whether it's witnessing to someone, being kind, or maybe just willingly helping at home. If we do it for the Lord, he'll reward us." *JLH*

HOW ABOUT YOU?

Where is your treasure? Are you concerned only about the things you can gain for yourself on this earth? As a Christian, you need to lay up, or store, treasure in heaven by witnessing, helping others, and being obedient to parents and to God.

MEMORIZE:

"Store your treasures in heaven, where they will never become moth-eaten or rusty and where they will be safe from thieves." Matthew 6:20

Lay Up Treasure in Heaven

Ups and Downs

(Read Psalm 37:3-5)

"That water log ride was fun!" exclaimed Jim. "Let's go on the roller coaster next, OK?"

"The roller coaster!" Dad groaned. "You're sure we want to go on that? All those ups and downs and curves. I never know what to expect next."

Jim laughed. "That's what makes it fun," he said. "C'mon!" So they headed for the roller coaster.

"Just like life," murmured Dad as they walked along.

"Like life?" Jim looked at Dad curiously. "What's like life?"

"The roller coaster," said Dad. "Like the roller coaster, life is full of ups and downs. You never know what's around the next curve." They bought their tickets and waited for their turn to ride. "Life can have a lot of unexpected events," continued Dad. "Some good; some bad."

Jim frowned. "Yeah . . . but at least all the ups and downs on the roller coaster are fun," he said. "The downs in life sure aren't."

Dad patted Jim on the shoulder. "It's a good thing we have Jesus in our life, isn't it?" he said. "He's always there to help us, comfort us, and protect us whenever we need him. He'll never leave us to face the ups and downs of life alone."

"That makes it easier to get through the down times, doesn't it?" said Jim.

"It sure does," agreed Dad. "Knowing the Lord is there to pull us back up—like the chain on that roller coaster—helps. We just need to keep trusting him." Dad smiled. "Well, looks like we get to go on next," he said. "Are you sure you're ready for this?"

"Sure thing!" said Jim. "Let's go!" *GJT*

HOW ABOUT YOU?

Are you going through a "down" time in your life? Does it seem like the curves are too scary? Are you afraid of what is around the next bend? The things that are happening in your life are no surprise to God. Talk to him about your feelings and your fears.

Trust God

MEMORIZE:
"Trust in the Lord with all your heart;
do not depend on your own
understanding." Proverbs 3:5

How's Your Appetite?

(Read 1 Peter 2:2-3; 1 John 2:15-17)

"What's for dinner?" asked David. "I'm starved!"

"Beef and vegetable casserole," replied Mother as she passed the dish. She smiled at his enthusiastic response. "I remember when you didn't like it," she added. "In fact, you used to like very few vegetables. I'm glad that's changed."

"Me, too," agreed David as he took a big helping. "I used to want to eat cookies and candy and pop all the time. I never told you, but sometimes when I ate too much junk food, I didn't feel real good."

"I'm not surprised," said Dad. "And I'm not surprised to see how strong and healthy you are now that you've learned to eat the things that are good for you."

After dinner, Dad took the family Bible from a kitchen shelf. David glanced at his watch. "Couldn't we skip devotions just this once?" he asked. "The football game will be on TV in just a couple of minutes."

"But this is more important," said Dad. "We talked earlier about how everything we feel like eating isn't always best for us, remember? When you train yourself to eat what is good for you, you'll reap healthy benefits. But if you choose to fill up on junk food . . ."

"You'll probably get a stomachache," interrupted David.

"That's right," agreed Dad. "That goes for your spiritual appetite, as well. When you feed your soul the best food every day—God's Word—you'll soon be reaping the benefits of a stronger, healthier Christian life."

Mother nodded. "Do you remember how you learned to like vegetables?" she asked.

"You made me eat a little every time we had them," replied David.

"Yes," said Dad as he opened the Bible. "By eating them, even if you didn't feel like it, you developed an appetite for them. That happens with spiritual things, too. You may not always feel like reading and obeying God's Word or like attending church or participating in other church activities, but doing so helps develop your appetite for those things." *PLF*

HOW ABOUT YOU?

What are you feeding your soul? Are you filling your heart and mind with the world's music, fashions, and literature? Retrain your spiritual appetite by feasting on the riches of God's Word, listening to Christian music, and reading good literature. Then exercise—be a doer of the Word. Soon you'll be in great spiritual shape.

MEMORIZE:

"You must crave pure spiritual milk so that you can grow into the fullness of your salvation." 1 Peter 2:2

Develop Your Spiritual Appetite

A Handful of Rice

(Read John 6:5-14)

"I know Pastor said we're supposed to witness wherever we are," Anthony told his mother, "but he doesn't know what it's like in my class."

"What is it like in your class?" asked Mom, scooping up some rice.

"Oh, Mom, there are 30 kids in my class, and as far as I know only Jeff and I are Christians. . . ." Anthony broke off and sniffed appreciatively. "What's cooking?"

"Chicken curry," said Mom. "Aunt Alicia and Uncle Tom are coming over for lunch, and we're having chicken curry and rice," went on Mom, pouring the rice into a pan and holding it under the tap. "And I'm thinking that you and Jeff can be like rice."

"Like rice!" exclaimed Anthony. "What do you mean?" He looked at the layer of small grains that lay at the bottom of the pan. "That won't be enough rice," he observed.

"It should be plenty," Mom assured him, smiling as she set the pan on the burner.

"But Uncle Tom eats lots," said Anthony anxiously.

But Mom only shook her head. "Wait and see," she told Anthony.

A little while later Mom called Anthony to come and wash up for lunch. As he started through the kitchen, he decided to check the rice. He lifted the lid of the pan and peeked anxiously inside. He gasped. "Why, there's enough rice to feed lots of people," he said in surprise. "I knew rice swelled when it was cooked, but I didn't think it would make that much!"

"A small amount goes a long way," said Mom.

"I'll say it does!" exclaimed Anthony. "The pan is full."

"Remember that I said you and Jeff could be like rice?" asked Mom. Anthony nodded, still wondering what she meant. "A small amount of rice, after it's boiled, fills a whole pan. Don't you think a couple of Christians could reach out to a whole classroom?"

"Yeah, I guess they could," said Anthony. *MTF*

HOW ABOUT YOU?

Do you sometimes feel you're so badly outnumbered that there's nothing you can do? Do you feel like you're too small, too young, too shy, too dumb—too whatever—to make a difference? Remember, Jesus fed more than five thousand people with just five loaves and two small fish. And he can certainly use even one little you to reach out to more people than you can even count.

God Can Use You

MEMORIZE:
"For I can do everything with the help
of Christ who gives me the strength
I need." Philippians 4:13

November
26

As I See It

(Read Luke 6:31-38)

"Guess where Cal Gordon thinks our gym class should go for a field trip," remarked George. He was sitting on the back porch steps with his friend Frank, watching the clouds float lazily by. "To see a high school football game," continued George, sounding very disgusted at the idea.

"Oh no!" groaned Frank. "It would be lots more fun to go to Sportland, U.S.A. I suppose he'll go around trying to get everybody to vote for the football game. I can't stand that guy!"

"Me, neither," agreed George. He pointed up at one of the clouds. "Speaking of footballs, that big cloud up there looks just like a foot kicking a football."

Frank looked where George was pointing. "I don't see a football. I see a dog with a bone."

"How about that one?" George pointed again. "That's a dragon with big teeth and a long tail."

"No, that's an alligator," said Frank with a grin. "You'd better get glasses." The boys spent the next few minutes pointing out various pictures they saw in the cloud formations. Sometimes they agreed on what the clouds looked like; sometimes they didn't.

"You know, it doesn't bother us that we see different things in the clouds," George said thoughtfully. "It doesn't make us mad that we don't look at them in the same way. Maybe it shouldn't make us mad if people look at other things differently from the way we do, either."

Frank looked at his friend. "You mean Cal, don't you?" he asked. He sighed. "I suppose you're right. I guess there's no law that says he has to like the same things we like. But I'm still going to try to get kids to vote for Sportland!" *HWM*

HOW ABOUT YOU?

Do you get angry if people disagree with you? You need to be tolerant of the opinions of others as long as they're not in opposition to the Scriptures. (For example, the Bible teaches that certain things—such as stealing, murder, homosexuality—are wrong.) People look at many things in different ways. Sometimes there is no definite right or wrong, and you need to agree to disagree. Love people and accept them even if they don't see things exactly as you do.

MEMORIZE:

"Do for others as you would like them to do for you." Luke 6:31

Understand Others' Views

The Cat and the Hamster

(Read Psalm 145:17-21)

Robert was carrying the cat out of his bedroom when he met his mother in the hall. She frowned. "What are you doing up?" she asked. "You're supposed to stay in bed. Do you feel better?"

"No," said Robert, "but Lucky wandered into the house and jumped on top of the hamster cage. And look at my silly hamster. He's climbing the cage like he wants to get out. He doesn't even know there's a cat out here waiting to catch him."

Mom nodded. "He doesn't always know what's best for him," she said. "Now put Lucky out and go back to bed. I'll bring you some juice."

When Mom came back, Robert was lying in bed staring glumly at the wall. "I don't see why I had to get so sick today. We have our class basketball play-offs after school this afternoon, and I prayed all morning that I'd get well enough to go. Instead, I'm still running a fever. I don't think God is very fair," he grumbled.

Mom put the juice on the bedside table and sat on the edge of the bed. "Your hamster seemed to want to get out of his cage a few minutes ago, but you didn't let him out, did you?" she asked. "Do you think he understood why you wouldn't let him out?"

Robert smiled. "Of course not," he said.

"Right. Being inside the cage kept him safe," agreed Mom. "And like your hamster, we don't always understand why God lets certain things happen in our life."

Robert thought about Mom's words. He shrugged. "Yeah, I guess so," he said.

Mom smiled. "Letting you be sick today might be God's way of teaching you to be patient or to trust him. I don't know . . . but I do know that he loves you."

Robert sighed, but he nodded. "I'll try to remember that," he said. *KEC*

HOW ABOUT YOU?

Do you blame God when he doesn't answer your prayers the way you want? Do you think he's not fair when he lets you go through hard things? Remember that God wants what is best for you, and that he will walk with you through any suffering he allows you to face.

MEMORIZE:
"And we know that God causes everything to work together for the good of those who love God and are called according to his purpose for them." Romans 8:28

Trust God

Filled Up

(Read Hebrews 10:19-25)

"Don and Jack asked me to go to Ski Valley with them tomorrow, Uncle Tim," said Mike. "The snow is just right!" Uncle Tim didn't say anything as he put down a can of oil, but Mike knew what he was thinking—tomorrow was Sunday. "I'd miss Sunday school just this once!" Mike added. "That wouldn't hurt, would it?"

"You've already missed more than once." Uncle Tim spoke kindly to his nephew. The two were especially close since Mike's parents didn't have much interest in church.

Mike's face fell. "Yeah, I guess," he muttered. "There were a few times when my parents had special plans. But what can it hurt to miss once more? There haven't been many good ski days this winter, and I'd sure like to go!"

"What can it hurt?" repeated Uncle Tim. "It might hurt you, Mike."

"Me?" Mike shrugged. "I don't think it would hurt me," he said.

Turning toward his car, Uncle Tim pulled out the dipstick to measure the oil. He whistled. "It's pretty low," he said, picking up the oil can. Then he put the can down again. He shrugged and scratched his head. "Oh, well," he said. "At least it will still run." He closed the hood.

"Uncle Tim!" exclaimed Mike. "If you run it without oil, you could ruin the motor!" He was a little proud of his knowledge of cars.

"Hmmmm, that's true. A car without oil can't go far," Uncle Tim agreed. Then he returned to the previous subject. "And a Christian who is low on spiritual food can't go very far, either. One of the best places to get that food is in church."

"Oh . . . right." Mike was startled, but he grinned good-naturedly. "You got me, Uncle Tim. I'll be in church tomorrow," he promised. *VJL*

HOW ABOUT YOU?

When you or your parents are sick, you may not be able to get to church or Sunday school. Occasionally, the weather makes it too dangerous to drive or walk. Sometimes there are unusual circumstances that make it impossible to go. But go as often as you can. You need church. You must not let your "spiritual oil" get low.

MEMORIZE:

"May you experience the love of Christ, though it is so great you will never fully understand it. Then you will be filled with the fullness of life and power that comes from God."
Ephesians 3:19

Don't Skip Church

The Hitchhiker

(Read 1 Thessalonians 4:9-12)

"Oh, no!" exclaimed Mother. "Look where they stacked the firewood! I told them to put it on the patio."

"Looks like you get to move the firewood, Son," said Dad as they pulled into the driveway.

"Why me?" demanded Justin. "Why do I get all the dirty jobs around here?"

"I work on the car and cook the dinners. Mother cleans the house and chauffeurs you around, and I hardly think Jennifer can move all that wood." Dad grinned at his small daughter.

"Can too!" argued four-year-old Jennifer. And later, as Justin loaded Jennifer's little red wagon with wood, she announced, "I'm gonna help you."

"Great!" answered Justin sarcastically as he started off with a load.

Jennifer got behind the wagon and started pushing. "See, Justin, I can help."

"Yeah," agreed Justin reluctantly. "That does help." For several loads they worked together. Then Justin noticed that the loads were heavier. "Either I'm getting tired or the wood is gaining weight," he complained.

Dad looked up from his work and grinned. "Look behind you, Son," he suggested. When Justin turned around, he saw Jennifer sitting on top of the wood. "No wonder it's heavier," laughed Dad. "You have a hitchhiker!"

"You get off right now, Jennifer!" ordered Justin.

"Now you can understand how much easier things are when everyone does his share," said Dad as he helped Jennifer get down. "God's plan for the family is for them to work together. When someone sits down on the job, it's harder for everyone else. Jennifer is small, but when she pushed, your job was easier. When she hitchhiked, it made your job harder."

"Sure did," agreed Justin. "Now, little hitchhiker, start pushing again!" *BJW*

HOW ABOUT YOU?

Do you grumble and complain about doing your share of the work? Perhaps you do have more responsibility than your little brother or sister. That's because you're able to pull a heavier load. Be a good worker, not a hitchhiker.

Do Your Share

MEMORIZE:
"This should be your ambition: to live a quiet life, minding your own business and working with your hands, just as we commanded you before." 1 Thessalonians 4:11

The Hike

(Read Psalm 119:33-40)

"Let's go for a hike," Mandy suggested after the big meal at the family reunion. "Let's take one of those nature trails." Soon several of the children found their way to the trail where a large map was posted beside the path. Though some glanced at it, no one stopped to study it.

After walking awhile, they came to a place where the trail divided. "Let's take the path to the left," said Mandy. "It doesn't look as steep as the other one."

"Sissy! I'm going to take the trail that goes up the mountain and around the lake," declared George.

The girls hesitated. "How long is it?" asked Carolyn.

"And where does it end?" asked Mandy.

Len shrugged. "I'd guess it circles back to the road. C'mon. Let's go." He led the way.

It was fun at first, but after nearly an hour, many were getting tired. "How much farther?" asked Joyce.

"How should we know?" George snapped.

"Didn't you read the map?"

"Sorta," he replied. "Didn't you?"

Joyce shook her head. "I thought you guys did."

"We only glanced at it," Len told her. "But this trail is bound to lead back to the road—sooner or later."

Mandy stood still. "Well, I'm exhausted," she said. "I'm going back the way we came." The others agreed.

Although there was some grumbling, soon everyone was heading back down the trail. When they came to the map much later, they stopped to look at it. Len laughed. "I can just hear what Granny Williams will say when she hears about this."

Mandy shook her finger at the group. "You're just like all those people who try to get through life without reading the Bible," she said in her best "Granny" voice. *BJW*

HOW ABOUT YOU?

Are you studying God's "map"—the Bible—or are you depending on someone else to tell you what God says? Good teachers who love the Lord can be a great help, but you need to read the Bible for yourself, too.

MEMORIZE:

"Show me the path where I should walk, O Lord; point out the right road for me to follow." Psalm 25:4

Read Your Bible

Keep in Practice

(Read Philippians 3:12-16)

Jeff dribbled the ball past Eric and shot it toward the basket. He winced as it hit the rim and bounced off. "Missed it again!" he exclaimed. "I've made that shot a million times before."

"Maybe your two-week vacation got you out of practice," said Eric.

When Jeff arrived home from basketball practice, he grabbed some milk and cookies. As Mom worked in the kitchen, he told her about the problem he was having making baskets. "I guess I'm out of practice," he said. "I meant to practice while we were gone, but you don't find many basketball courts at motels."

Mom smiled. "I'm sure you'll make time to work on your shots now," she said.

"I sure will," agreed Jeff. "I found out what happens when I let up. I think I'll see if Eric will go to the gym with me for a while after supper."

Mom frowned. "Don't you have youth group tonight?"

Jeff sighed. "I've missed two weeks. It won't hurt if I miss one more time."

Mom wiped up a spill of milk. "Remember what happened when you let up on basketball practice? You lost some of your skill." Jeff looked puzzled. "We can get 'out of practice' when it comes to spiritual things, too," continued Mom. "One way to keep 'in practice' spiritually is to study God's Word—and then, of course, practice the things we learn from it. If we don't do that, we may find ourselves doing and saying things that we know are wrong. It takes dedication and practice to be a strong Christian."

Jeff nodded. "Yeah, but can't I practice spiritual things without going to youth group tonight?" he asked. "I'll go to church and we have devotions every day, so why would it hurt to skip youth group just one more time?"

"One more time might not hurt so much," Mom said, "but then again, it might be the beginning of a bad habit." *KEC*

HOW ABOUT YOU?

Do you work hard at things like schoolwork, music, or sports? It's good to work on these things. But it's also important to remember that just like it takes practice to become good at sports, it takes practice to become a strong Christian. Be faithful in the things that build your faith. These would include Bible study, spending time with other Christians, and prayer.

Practice Christianity

MEMORIZE:
"Jesus replied, 'My mother and my brothers are all those who hear the message of God and obey it.'"
Luke 8:21

Flying Too High

(Read Proverbs 16:17-20)

"Mr. Hillis read us another story from Greek mythology today," announced David.

"Really? Tell me what it was," begged Johnny at once.

David grinned. He knew his little brother loved stories. "Well, OK," he agreed. "These stories aren't true, you know. But this one says that once there was a father and son called Daedalus and Icarus, who were imprisoned by the king. One day, Daedalus took some feathers and made two pairs of wings so they could fly away. As he fastened the wings onto his son's back with wax, he warned Icarus not to fly too near the sun because the heat would melt the wax and the wings would fall off."

"Did they fly?" asked Johnny impatiently. "Did they get away?"

David nodded. "Yep, they both flew away. But as Icarus flew higher and higher, he began to feel so powerful and so proud about actually flying that he forgot what his father had said and flew too near to the sun. And sure enough—the wax melted, just like his father had warned him, and the wings fell off. Poor Icarus fell into the sea and drowned."

"That's terrible!" cried Johnny. Then he thought of something scary. "Hey, David, do you think that might happen when we take that plane trip next month?" he asked anxiously.

"Of course not," said David. "The plane's wings aren't fastened on with wax."

Dad, who was also listening, shook his head. "Don't worry about the plane, Johnny," he said. "But that story does remind me of what can happen to people—what might even happen to us if we're not careful."

David frowned. "What do you mean?" he asked.

"Sometimes, especially when everything is going well in our life, we start boasting and acting real proud of ourselves and think we can get along without God," explained Dad. "If that happens, sooner or later, we will fall. We need to recognize that we are dependent on him." *MTF*

HOW ABOUT YOU?

When you accomplish something—such as doing well in your exams or winning a prize in a contest—do you boast about it, or do you acknowledge that you did it with God's help? When faced with a challenge or difficulty, do you feel proud that you can "handle things," or do you turn to God for wisdom and strength?

MEMORIZE:

"His mighty arm does tremendous things! How he scatters the proud and haughty ones!" Luke 1:51

Don't Be Proud

You Are My Witnesses

(Read Acts 1:1-8)

"Tell me, boys . . . if you received a new watch, would you hide it?" Mr. Mull asked his Sunday school class. "Well, having Jesus is even more wonderful than having a new watch. Why keep it a secret? Do you love him, boys? Then talk about him! As we bow our heads, ask the Lord to give you the name of someone for whom you will pray and to whom you will witness."

As the boys sat quietly, a name did come to Brent's mind. *Oh, no!* he thought. *Not Ted! He's just about the toughest kid in school. How can I witness to him?*

After class, Brent talked with Mr. Mull about it. "Look out the window here," said Mr. Mull. "See those huge rocks on the hillside over there, with a tree growing in the middle of them? How do you suppose the tree got there?"

Brent was puzzled. "I guess a seed from another tree fell there and found a soft spot and took root," he answered.

"Do you think the parent tree worried about how hard the rocks looked when it let the seed drop?" asked Mr. Mull. Brent shook his head. "The tree just let the seed fall, didn't it," continued Mr. Mull, "and God did the rest. That's what we need to do, too. Let the Word of God fall. Don't worry about how it takes root. That's God's work."

"But to talk to Ted!" exclaimed Brent. "He's so tough! I know he'll just laugh and poke fun at me."

"That won't hurt you, Brent," answered Mr. Mull. "And remember—the Word of God can soften hearts. Don't let Ted scare you. You do your part, and God will do his. I'll be praying for both you and Ted, OK?" Slowly Brent nodded, as he walked to the door. *I will witness to Ted,* he thought with determination. *AGL*

HOW ABOUT YOU?
Are you afraid of being laughed at if you witness for Jesus? Do you feel the kids just won't listen anyway? Remember that your job is to spread the seed of God's Word. The rest is up to him. Why not bow your head right now and ask the Lord to give you the name of someone to whom you will witness.

Witness for Jesus

MEMORIZE:
"'You are my witnesses,' declares the Lord." Isaiah 43:10, NIV

December
4

Double Pay

(Read 1 Thessalonians 4:7-12)

With only two weeks left before his class trip to Funland, Brandon was worried. He knew his parents didn't have money for the trip. But when he came in from school one day, Mother met him with a smile. "Mr. Walsh, next door, wants you to take care of his dogs," she said. "He's going to the hospital for surgery." She handed Brandon some money. "He's paying in advance." When Brandon counted the money, he let out a whoop of delight. He was halfway to Funland!

A week later, Brandon's family learned that Mr. Walsh had died. His son picked up the dogs and took them to his farm.

Brandon tried to find another job to earn the rest of the money he needed for the class trip, but he was unable to do so. Then, just a couple of days before they were to leave for Funland, a letter came for Brandon. "Look, Mom!" he squealed as a check fell out of the envelope. "It's from Mr. Walsh's son. He says he's sorry he forgot to pay me when he picked up the dogs."

"But Mr. Walsh had already paid you," Mother reminded him.

"I guess his son didn't know that," Brandon replied.

"Do you plan to keep that money?" Mother asked softly.

Brandon looked at the floor. "Well, I asked the Lord to give me the money so I could go," he said, "and here it is!"

"Do you honestly think the Lord sent it to you, Brandon?" asked Mother.

Tears filled Brandon's eyes. "No," he admitted.

Mother hugged him. "I know it's hard to give the money back, Son," she said. "But being honest is the right thing to do."

Brandon felt a little sad when he woke up on the morning his class left on their trip. But as the day passed, he was surprised at the peace in his heart in spite of his disappointment. There would be other trips to Funland, he realized. And when he went he would enjoy himself with a clear conscience. And a clear conscience is a priceless treasure! *BJW*

HOW ABOUT YOU?

Do you sometimes want to keep things that don't belong to you? One wrong choice, one lie, one instance of shoplifting can start you on the wrong road. On the other hand, a right choice results in peace. Always be honest.

MEMORIZE:
"Do things in such a way that everyone can see you are honorable."
Romans 12:17b

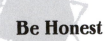

Be Honest

The Copycat

(Read 1 Peter 2:21-25)

At supper, Clay picked the peas out of his mixed vegetables and pushed them off to the side of his plate. Two-year-old Erin did the same thing. "Why aren't you eating your peas?" asked Mom.

"I don't like them," Clay answered, twisting his "WWJD" bracelet.

"I don't like 'em," Erin mimicked.

"Yes you do, Erin," Mom said, scooping some peas into Erin's spoon and holding them up to her mouth.

"Yum," Erin said. "More."

Clay picked up his glass of milk and blew bubbles in it. Erin picked up her glass of milk and blew bubbles in it, spilling milk all over the table. "Clay! Get a towel and help clean up your sister's mess," scolded Mom.

Clay obediently got the towel and began wiping the table. Erin grabbed it. "Me, too," she said, trying to wipe the table.

"You little copycat," grumbled Clay. "Mom, make her stop copying me."

"She copies you because she wants to be just like you. That's quite a compliment," said Mom. She frowned. "But you sure haven't been a very good example this evening—not eating your peas and blowing bubbles into your milk," she added.

"Sorry," mumbled Clay.

"Others are always watching you," said Mom. "You never know when someone will copy you, so you should try to be a good example. The best way to be a good example is to be a copycat yourself." She pointed to his wrist. "Don't just wear that bracelet," she said. "Think about what 'WWJD' means . . .'What Would Jesus Do?'" *LJR*

HOW ABOUT YOU?

What do you do when someone cuts in line in front of you? What do you do when someone teases or calls you names? Do you copy what Jesus would do? He would not shove the person back out of line. He would not call others names or tease them. What would Jesus do if a new person came to class? What would Jesus do if someone dropped his pens and pencils all over the floor? WWJD is not just four letters to wear around your wrist. It's a reminder that you should copy Jesus.

Be a "Copycat" of Jesus

MEMORIZE:
"To this you were called, because Christ suffered for you, leaving you an example, that you should follow in his steps." 1 Peter 2:21, NIV

Let It Heal

(Read Leviticus 19:16-18)

"My finger's bleedin' again, Mama!" Jason cried as he ran into the kitchen.

Mother sighed and handed a paper towel to her four-year-old. Jason wrapped it around his finger and watched, fascinated, as the red stain grew. "Jason, if you don't leave that cut alone it will take even longer to heal, and it will leave a scar," Mother scolded. "I wish . . ." The front door slammed, drowning out the rest of her words. Stacy stomped into the room and threw her books on the table.

"Look, Stacy!" Jason held his finger in front of his big sister's face. "My finger's bleedin' again."

"You're not going to get any sympathy from me," Stacy yelled. "Stop picking it!"

"How was school today, Stacy?" Mother asked.

"Terrible!" complained Stacy. "Jodi ignored me last week. This week she wants me to be her friend."

Mother frowned. "I thought Jodi apologized for not inviting you to her slumber party," she said.

"Oh, she did," Stacy said. "Since I had mentioned earlier that we were going to Grandma's, she thought I couldn't come anyway. If she had asked, I would have told her Dad had changed our plans. But did she ask? Oh no! She really didn't want me to come."

"Now, Stacy, that's not fair." Mother looked straight into her daughter's eyes. "You need to stop picking the sore, Stacy, or it will leave a scar."

Stacy stammered, "But I don't know what you . . ." She paused. "I do see what you mean, Mom," she finally admitted. "I've been acting just like Jason."

"You cut your finger, Stacy?" Jason asked.

Stacy grinned. "No, but my feelings were hurt."

Jason unwrapped the paper towel from his finger. "Look, Mama. It's stopped bleedin'. Has your sore feelings stopped bleedin', Stacy?"

Mother and Stacy laughed as Stacy gave her answer. "Yes. Everything will be all right now." *BJW*

HOW ABOUT YOU?

Has someone wounded your feelings or hurt your pride? Are you picking the sore, refusing to forgive and forget? Promise yourself right now to stop thinking about your hurt, and let it heal.

MEMORIZE:

"You must make allowance for each other's faults and forgive the person who offends you. Remember, the Lord forgave you, so you must forgive others." Colossians 3:13

Let Hurt Feelings Heal

A Low Score

(Read Psalm 103:8-14)

"Promise you won't tell," said Kip as he and his sister stepped off the school bus. He looked at his science report before putting it back in his pocket. "I didn't expect to get a very high grade on this, but I sure didn't think it would be this bad."

Sally shrugged. "I won't tell," she agreed. "But Mom and Dad will find out anyway."

When he got home, Kip disappeared into his room. He stayed there until he was called for dinner. "Your science teacher called a few minutes ago," said Mother when Kip came to the table. "He was checking his records, and he said he thinks he put the wrong grade on your science report. He said you've been doing much better in science."

Kip jumped out of his chair and pulled his science report from his pocket. "I knew it!" he said. "I knew I did better than what he marked on this paper!"

Dad reached for the paper and looked it over. "Well, I'm glad to hear that this isn't the correct grade," he said. "But how is it that you didn't show us this before?"

"I was afraid you'd be really mad at me for getting such a low grade," said Kip.

"Mad at you?" said Mother. "Oh, Kip, we would have been concerned, but not mad. We know how hard you've been working."

"Grades are a measure of the progress you're making," said Dad, "but they are not a measure of our love. You're our son, and we will always love you."

Sally grinned at her brother. "My Sunday school teacher says God is like that, too—he loves us even when we fail." *GLJ*

HOW ABOUT YOU?

Are you afraid God loves you less when you don't "score high" in your Christian life? Remember that he died for you while you were still in your sin, and he loves you now, too. If you need forgiveness, ask him for it. Seek his help in obeying him and living as he wants you to live. He delights in those who put their trust in him.

MEMORIZE:
"For he understands how weak we are; he knows we are only dust."
Psalm 103:14

God Loves You Always

Raging Waves

(Read Jude1: 3-4, 12-13, 16-17)

Greg was visiting his grandparents in Florida. It was fun being outdoors in the sunshine, especially when he thought about the cold and snow at home in Minnesota. The neatest thing about visiting his grandparents was that they lived so close to the Atlantic Ocean. In fact, they could walk to the beach from their house.

One evening, Greg and his grandfather were playing catch. It was windy, and they could hear the waves beating against the rocks even though they were a couple of blocks away. "I've never heard the waves sound so loud," Greg said.

"They do get wild and noisy sometimes," Grandpa agreed. "Would you like to walk down and see them?"

"Sure." After Greg put his ball and glove in the house, he and his grandfather walked to the ocean. "Wow! Look at those waves!" Greg exclaimed. The water was crashing against the shoreline, sending spray high into the air.

"They're fun to watch," agreed Grandpa, "but the people who live in the houses along here are concerned because the water level is high, and it's washing away some of the soil from their yards. The waves are fascinating, but they're also quite destructive. Many homeowners have had to build stronger breakwaters to try to stop the erosion."

"And that probably costs a lot of money," said Greg.

"Right." Grandpa nodded. "By the way, Greg, did you know that the Letter of Jude uses waves to describe people who teach wrong things about God? Jude says that those who twist and change what is written in the Bible are like raging waves of the sea, destroying the people who believe what they say."

"I'm glad I believe in Jesus," Greg said quietly, "and I'm glad I go to a church where the truth is preached." *LMW*

HOW ABOUT YOU?

Have you ever watched waves beat against the shore? They're interesting, but they can do a lot of damage. Remember, raging waves are a picture of people who sometimes use words that sound as if they come from the Bible. They may be interesting, but they're preaching their own words, not God's. Learn what God's Word says so you will not be fooled by these "raging waves."

MEMORIZE:
"But you, my dear friends, must remember what the apostles of our Lord Jesus Christ told you." Jude 1:17

Learn What the Bible Says

A Bird Named "Witness"

(Read Matthew 28:16-20)

Joel watched as his mother took a bag of birdseed out to the patio and emptied the contents into the feeder. When she came back into the house, she stood by the glass doors for several minutes, all the time staring at the bird feeder.

"Are you looking for the birds to show up?" Joel asked, leaving his chair and joining his mother at the door.

"Well, yes," replied Mother. "Actually, I'm just looking for one bird right now."

Joel laughed. "One bird? For all that food?"

"Oh, no," answered Mother quickly. "I'm hoping for lots of birds. But right now, I'm just watching for my little witness to arrive."

"Witness?" asked Joel. "A sparrow named 'Witness'? What a funny name!"

His mother laughed. "That's just what I call him," she said. "The last few days, I've noticed that only one bird shows up when I first fill the feeder. He eats a little and then flies away. In just a short time, a whole flock of birds shows up. So I let my imagination work, and I see this little witness going back to his family and telling them there is food at our house."

"That's why you named him 'Witness'!" Joel said knowingly.

Mother nodded. "This little bird reminds me that I should be a witness, too. We have the good news of Jesus, Joel, and we need to share that news with others."

"How do you know it's the same bird every day?" Joel wanted to know.

Mother laughed. "Oh dear! I don't, but I never thought of that," she said. "I don't know one sparrow from another, so there actually could be several little bird-witnesses."

"Just like us," Joel added. *RIJ*

HOW ABOUT YOU?

If birds can share the good news of food with other birds, shouldn't you be willing to share the good news of eternal life with those around you? Be God's witness by telling others about him.

MEMORIZE:
"You will receive power and will tell people about me everywhere."
Acts 1:8

Be God's Witness

December 10

Different Gifts

(Read 1 Corinthians 12:4-11)

When the Martin twins came in from school, Mark bounded into the kitchen and Matt went to his room. "I made all A's on my report card," announced Mark proudly.

Mother hugged him. "Good for you! That makes me very happy. Where's Matt?"

Mark shrugged. "Gone to his room, I guess."

Mother went down the hall. "May I come in, Matt?"

"I guess so," came the muffled reply. "I suppose you want to see my report card." Without looking at Mother, Matt handed it to her.

"Hmmm . . . not too bad," Mother said with a smile.

"And not too *good* either," Matt added angrily. "Mark got all A's. I didn't even make the honor roll."

"Making the honor roll isn't the most important thing in life." Mother sat down beside Matt. "I'm proud of both you and Mark. You're twins, but you're very different, and that's good. Mark loves to read and study. You—"

"Are stupid," Matt interrupted.

"Matt, don't say that!" Mother scolded. "You're smart, too, but in a different way from Mark. For instance, when his bike was broken, who fixed it?"

"I did, but there wasn't much wrong with it," Matt said with a shrug.

"You have mechanical abilities that Mark doesn't have. Last year we gave Mark a chess game, and we gave you a set of tools, remember? Did it make you mad because we gave you different birthday gifts?" Mother asked.

"Of course not," Matt exclaimed.

"God gives each Christian different gifts, too," Mother explained. "Remember the verses we read from Corinthians this morning?" Matt nodded, and Mother continued. "Don't think less of your abilities just because they're not like Mark's. Thank God for the talents you have, and use them." *BJW*

HOW ABOUT YOU?

Do you compare your abilities with those others have? You shouldn't do that because God has not given you the same gifts he gave others. Don't try to be anyone else. Be yourself.

MEMORIZE:

"Each one should use whatever gift he has received to serve others."
1 Peter 4:10, NIV

Be Yourself

The Best Path

(Read Psalm 16:5-8, 11)

Bruce and his dad decided to go cross-country skiing one morning, accompanied by their two dogs, Ebony and Blackie. "See how Blackie's playing!" Bruce called as the dog bounded through the three-foot snow drifts. "Ebony just stays on the trail and hardly ever breaks through the packed crust on the snow. I don't think she's having much fun."

"I'm not so sure," said Dad. "I think she's just enjoying her walk."

When they returned home, they let the dogs come into the house with them. "Look at Blackie," said Dad as they sat down with some popcorn in the family room. "He's exhausted." Blackie was stretched out in front of the fireplace.

"Yeah. But Ebony isn't. She looks like she's ready to play," said Bruce.

Dad nodded. "I guess that's because Ebony stayed on the path most of the time, but Blackie didn't," he said. "Those dogs remind me of God's path for us. Sometimes we see others doing whatever they want, and even though they're doing wrong things, they're having a great time! At least it looks that way. But in the end, we find that God's path is the best path for us." Dad grinned at Bruce. "Can you think of some of the advantages of following God's path?"

"Having a clear conscience," Bruce said thoughtfully. "And I won't have to worry about messing up my brain with drugs or alcohol. Because I won't use them." *HLA*

HOW ABOUT YOU?

Does it seem like life would be more fun if you could do things your own way instead of God's way? You can be sure it isn't worth the consequences and worries that would follow. Following God's path is the best way to live your life.

MEMORIZE:
"You will show me the way of life,
granting me the joy of your presence."
Psalm 16:11

Follow God's Path

December
12

Surprises

(Read James 4:13-15)

Kyle looked out the car window at the houses, trees, and fence posts they were passing. A vacant lot where scrubby, frost-tipped branches poked out of the brown grass looked familiar. "Mom," he said, pointing out the window, "isn't that the field where we picked blackberries this summer?"

Mom glanced over. "Sure enough," she said.

"You know what else?" said Kyle. "Driving home from picking berries that day was the last time I rode in the blue car."

"The day before the accident," Mom said thoughtfully.

Kyle remembered the day of the accident. The phone had rung as he was eating breakfast. After answering it, Mom had looked stunned. "Dad's been in an accident," she had said. "Thank God he's not badly hurt. He says the car looks like a crushed tin can!"

Now Kyle looked from the field back to Mom. "That day we drove home from picking berries," he said, "I never thought that the next day Dad would be in an accident and the car would be smashed."

"None of us did," said Mom. "The book of James reminds us that we never know what will happen from one day to the next. And that could include good things as well as bad." She smiled at Kyle. "It reminds me, too, that when Jesus comes again it will be an ordinary day—we'll just be doing ordinary, everyday things, expecting life to go on as it always has, and suddenly—" she snapped her fingers—"Jesus will come back to take us to heaven with him. Just like the car accident was a surprise to us, Jesus' return to earth will be a surprise. But it will be a good surprise." *VEN*

HOW ABOUT YOU?

Do you know Jesus as your Savior? If not, talk to a trusted friend or adult to find out more.

MEMORIZE:

"You also must be ready all the time. For the Son of Man will come when least expected." Matthew 24:44

Be Ready When Jesus Returns

Seek and Find

(Read Proverbs 6:20-23)

"Dad, where are my skates?" Ken called from his room. "I need them right away. Carl and Peter are waiting for me. Their mom will drop us off at the rink."

"I'm sorry, but I'm stirring something on the stove right now. I can't stop until it's done, or it will scorch," Dad called back. "Just go ahead and look. Check all the closets."

"I don't have time. Come help me!" Ken hollered.

"I'll be with you in a few minutes," Dad said. When he got there, Ken was sitting on the bed looking at his baseball cards. "Find the skates?" asked Dad.

"No," Ken said. "I was waiting for you."

"Well, here I am. Where did you already look?" Dad asked as he glanced at the closet.

Ken blushed. "I didn't look yet," he admitted.

Dad reached up to the closet shelf and soon found the skates under Ken's sleeping bag. Ken took them and hurried out the front door, but he soon returned with a scowl. "What's wrong now?" Dad asked as Ken slammed the door.

"They left without me! Fine friends they turned out to be!" grumbled Ken.

"Well, you did keep them waiting a long time," said Dad.

"It's not my fault I couldn't find my skates," Ken protested.

"It is," Dad said. "You couldn't find them because you didn't look for them."

"Well, what am I gonna do now?" whined Ken.

"Study your youth group lesson," suggested Dad. "Get that all ready—learn your verse, too."

"Aw, Dad," objected Ken. "That's no fun. Besides, I don't get much out of it when I do it by myself. Why can't I just go to youth group and listen? That helps me more."

Dad sighed. "Ken," he said, "don't treat Jesus the way you treated your skates."

"Huh?" grunted Ken, looking puzzled.

"You wanted the pleasure of using the skates, but you didn't want to bother to look for them," said Dad. "That's a bit like wanting help from God to solve problems, but not taking the time to read his Word or to pray. I hope you won't be like that!" *JLH*

HOW ABOUT YOU?

How well do you know your Jesus? Do you ignore him most of the time, but want to be able to call on him when you need help? Do you read and study the Bible to get to know God better? Or do you want somebody else to study it and tell you about it?

Search the Scriptures

MEMORIZE:
"You search the Scriptures." John 5:39

Two Kinds of Food

(Read Psalm 119:97-104)

Mealtime was Mitch's favorite time of the day! He loved to eat, and his mom was a good cook! Mitch was also a "nibbler," eating between meals.

"Boy, Mom, that was a good supper," Mitch said one evening.

"I'm glad you like my cooking and have a good appetite, honey, but how about your appetite for spiritual food?" Mom asked, knowing that Mitch often skipped his "quiet time" of personal devotions. "Have you been memorizing the verses you're supposed to learn for church? And don't forget that it's important to spend some time with the Lord each day—'feeding' your soul."

"But, Mom," Mitch protested, "I just don't have time for all that."

"You have time to play and watch TV, don't you?" asked Mother. "And you certainly have time to eat. We all seem to have time for everything we really want to do. It's simply a matter of taking the time to do it." Mitch tried to interrupt, but his mother went on. "What would happen if you didn't eat food for a whole week?"

"I'd probably get sick!" Mitch exclaimed.

"Probably," agreed Mother. "And when you neglect the Lord and his Word, you get spiritually sick. Think about it." *GM*

HOW ABOUT YOU?
Are you interested in spiritual as well as physical food? Do you take time to read your Bible and to pray? Don't let anything in your busy schedule keep you from getting the spiritual food you need to live the kind of life God wants you to live!

MEMORIZE:
"Your words are what sustain me. They bring me great joy and are my heart's delight, for I bear your name, O Lord God Almighty." Jeremiah 15:16

God's Word Is Spiritual Food

What Really Counts

(Read Luke 18:9-14)

The children in Paul's class were stunned. A classmate had been killed in a car accident. "Sometimes it makes us feel better to remember happy things about a person who has died," Miss Kendall said. "Would anyone like to mention something special about Jonathan?" So one by one the students shared things they liked about their friend.

Allison was first. "Jonathan played his horn really well," she said.

"Jonathan was smart," offered Jason. "He could figure things out real quick."

"He was a good-looking boy," said Marcy.

"He was a good person," said Todd. "He always went to church."

Paul fidgeted in his seat. The things the kids said were true, but nobody had mentioned the most important thing of all. *Do I dare tell them?* he wondered. He hesitated a few minutes longer, then slowly raised his hand.

"Paul?" His teacher smiled at him.

"My dad always says people are like cars," began Paul nervously. He gained more confidence as he went on. "He says it's what's under the hood—what's inside—that really counts. When my brother, Steven, wanted to buy a car, he brought it home to show my dad. He pointed out the nice appearance, the tape player, and the speakers and stuff. But Dad wasn't impressed. He kept saying, 'What about the engine? It's what's under the hood that's important.' But Steven didn't listen, and now his car won't run half the time."

Paul paused, surprised at the long speech he was making. "I'm gonna miss Jonathan," he finished. "We've heard a lot of good things about him, but I'm glad I can tell you he's not like Steven's car—he didn't just look good. A couple of months ago he told me he had accepted Jesus as his Savior. That's what really counts."

"Thank you, Paul," said Miss Kendall with a smile. *HWM*

HOW ABOUT YOU?

Has anyone in your family been fooled by a good-looking car? It's bad enough when that happens with a car. It's much worse when it happens with a life. Check your own life. Are you helpful and kind? Do you attend church? That's fine, but it won't get you to heaven.

Trust in Jesus

MEMORIZE:
"But people are declared righteous because of their faith, not because of their work." Romans 4:5

Blurry Images

(Read 1 Corinthians 13:9-12)

Justin leaned forward, peering out the van window. Rain streamed down the glass, blurring the view of the trees. The windshield wipers swished at top speed. "Mom, when will it stop raining? We haven't seen the sun in two weeks!" complained Justin.

"I know, honey," said Mom. "The rain is sure coming down fast today. I can hardly see through these windows." She turned in at the grocery store entrance and parked near the door.

As Justin got out of the car, a blind man shuffled by. He gripped the harness of a golden retriever who led him through the doorway. As Justin watched the blind man, he bit his lower lip. He thought of the paralyzed girl in his class who got around in a wheelchair.

"Mom, I've got some questions," said Justin when they were on their way home again. "There are some things about God that I just don't understand. Like . . . why are there blind and handicapped people? And why does God allow all this rain? It's causing big problems for a lot of people."

Justin's mom nodded. "I've asked those same questions myself," she said. "I can only tell you that such things occur due to the fact that there's sin in the world. But God can take even the worst circumstances and turn them around for good."

Justin sighed. "I don't see how," he said. "I wish I could understand things about God better."

Mom nodded. "I do, too," she agreed, "but . . ." She pointed to the rain still streaming down the windshield. "See how blurry everything looks through the rain?" Justin nodded. "Well, our understanding of God is like looking through that blurry windshield," said Mom, "but in heaven we will see God clearly and understand his greatness. For now, we just need to trust that God loves us and has a purpose for all things." *LEC*

HOW ABOUT YOU?

Do you wonder what God looks like? Do you wonder why he allows sickness and poverty? These are things that we cannot understand perfectly now, but if you know Jesus, someday you'll see him clearly and no longer wonder about such things. In the meantime, trust that he has a good plan for you.

MEMORIZE:

"Now we see things imperfectly as in a poor mirror, but then we will see everything with perfect clarity."
1 Corinthians 13:12

Trust God

The Treasure Hunt

(Read Ecclesiastes 5:18-20)

Samantha was enjoying the party for her friend Bill. His mom had handed out brightly colored paper hats for them to wear. They had played musical chairs and pass-the-cushion. Now it was time for a treasure hunt. "The treasure is a golden star," said Bill's mother. "Let's see who can find it first."

The kids ran all around the house, looking for the golden star, but no one found it. They checked out the garden. Sam looked up at all the trees, poked around the flower beds, and searched every inch of the lawn. Still no one found the treasure. They looked at each other, wondering what to do next. Suddenly, Sam's friend Annie squealed in delight. "I see it!" she cried. "I see the golden star!"

"Where? Where?" cried the children, looking all around.

"I see it, too!" yelled Darrin, jumping up and down in excitement.

Sam looked all around. She looked hard at Annie and Darrin, trying to figure out where their eyes were focused. They seemed to be looking in her direction, but she couldn't figure out where the treasure was. One by one, the kids said they could see the golden star . . . all except Sam.

At last, Annie walked up to Sam. She pulled off the paper hat that had been perched on Sam's curly, yellow hair, and handed it to Sam. Sam's eyes widened in surprise. There on her bright blue cap shone a single golden star. She had the treasure, and she hadn't even known it!

"OK," said Bill's mother, "Annie was the first to find the star, so she wins the prize." She smiled at Sam as she added, "And Samantha gets one, too, since it wasn't possible for her to see the star on her own head!" *MTF*

HOW ABOUT YOU?

Do you have a treasure that you have failed to see? Perhaps you have an undiscovered talent. Or maybe you take for granted someone in your life who is really a "treasure"—perhaps a family member, a pastor, or a teacher. Has God blessed you with a home, clothes, and food to eat? Ask God to help you see and enjoy all the treasures he has given you.

MEMORIZE:
"The living God . . . richly gives us all we need for our enjoyment."
1 Timothy 6:17

Enjoy Your Treasures

Aliens!

(Read 1 Peter 2:9-12)

"Mom!" called Brett as he came running into the house. "Miss Robbins says we're going to have a visitor next week! An alien!"

"From outer space?" asked sister Vicky, her eyes wide as saucers.

Mom laughed. "Aliens are everywhere. In fact," she whispered, looking around cautiously, "I'm an alien. And you are, too!"

"No, we're not!" protested Brett and Vicky together.

"What do you think an alien is?" asked Mom.

"Someone who doesn't belong here," Vicky answered.

"Someone who looks and acts different than we do," Brett added.

"And talks funny," said Vicky. "Someone from another country."

"Like Mr. and Mrs. Yoshida?" asked Mom. "Mr. Yoshida is here studying, but Mrs. Yoshida is very homesick for her family and their home in Japan."

"Yeah, like that," agreed Vicky. "But *we're* not aliens!"

"Think about this," Mom answered. "Is this earth our real home?"

"Ah . . . well . . . no," replied Brett. "When we accept Jesus as Savior, we have a home in heaven, right?"

"Right. And this isn't the real you," said Mom, playfully pinching Vicky's arm. "When we die these bodies will be buried, but if we've trusted in Jesus, the real you and me living inside these bodies will go to heaven to live with him."

"I get it!" Vicky said. "We're aliens on earth because our real home is in heaven. And we need to look and act different than people who aren't Christians."

"Yes, we do," said Brett. "We're supposed to live like Jesus would—like be kind and helpful to others and treat them nice even if they're mean to us and not be selfish and love everybody . . . stuff like that. Yep, we're aliens all right," he said, "and that explains it."

"That explains what?" asked Vicky.

"Why you're so goofy," teased Brett, laughing as he ran out of the room before Vicky could catch him. *LJR*

HOW ABOUT YOU?

Can your friends tell that there's something "different" about you because you are a Christian? Are you truthful when others lie? Are you cheerful even when things go wrong? Do you obey your parents? Do you enjoy helping others?

MEMORIZE:

"He gave his life to free us from every kind of sin, to cleanse us, and to make us his very own people, totally committed to doing what is right."
Titus 2:14

Dare to Be Different for Jesus

Sarah's List

(Read Romans 12:9-18)

Sarah stared at the bulky cast on her right leg. "Christmas vacation is just start-ing, and I break my leg!" she moaned. "What am I going to do now? I'm bored already!"

Mother sat down beside Sarah on the sofa and gave her a quick hug. "I'm so sorry this happened to you," she sympathized. "Looks like you're going to have to develop some patience."

"But what am I going to do, Mom?" asked Sarah. "I can't go sledding. I can't skate. I can't play basketball. Right now I can't even go shopping."

"Instead of thinking about all the things you can't do, why don't we make a list of things you *can* do," suggested Mother. "Let me get paper and a pencil."

Soon ideas were popping like popcorn, and they wrote: (1) Write a letter to Grandma. (2) Have devotions each day and pray. (3) Make cards for people in a nearby nursing home or for friends who are sick. (4) Write a thank-you note to someone who has helped me in the past. (5) Read a book. (6) Make cookies for someone special—and for myself. (7) Work a puzzle. (8) Make a prayer-list book-let, listing names of people and their needs. (9) Invite a friend over to play a game. (10) Phone some school friends. (11) Keep a diary of the ideas I use.

The list grew and grew. "This is enough!" Sarah exclaimed at last. "This should keep me busy way past vacation time."

When Sarah's cast finally came off, the doctor said her leg had healed well. "Not only did your bone grow together properly," said Mother that evening, "but you also grew spiritually these past weeks."

"By doing things for other people, I quit feeling sorry for myself," agreed Sarah. "It was fun." *GLS*

HOW ABOUT YOU?

Are you bored? When we take our mind off ourselves and think of others, we can usually find lots to do. Add your own ideas to Sarah's list. Put them into practice this coming year. In other words, don't just think about what good ideas they are; do them. Grow in the Lord and have fun at the same time.

Grow in the Lord

MEMORIZE:
"But grow in the special favor and knowledge of our Lord and Savior Jesus Christ." 2 Peter 3:18

December

20

Pilot in Control

(Read Psalm 121)

Jan clasped her hands together nervously as the plane taxied down the runway. She had always wanted to fly, and here she was—flying with her brother, Don, to visit their grandmother. But now she was nervous.

After they were airborne, Jan didn't relax at all. "Do the engines sound funny?" she asked several times. "Should we be flying so high? We're not going to go through clouds again, are we? What if there's another plane in the clouds? Won't we crash?"

"Why don't you go up to the cockpit and take over at the controls?" Don finally asked. "The pilot knows what he's doing. I'm having fun."

"Me, too," said Jan, but she was glad when they were finally back on solid ground.

"Did you have a good flight?" asked Grandma.

Don nodded. "I did. But Jan was as nervous as a cat. I told her she should take over for the pilot. I'm glad she didn't, though, because then I'd have been nervous."

"I guess so!" exclaimed Grandma, putting an arm around Jan's shoulders. "I'm afraid we all lack trust in our Pilot from time to time."

Jan looked at Grandma in surprise. "Are you afraid of flying, too, Grandma?"

Grandma smiled. "Not really," she said. "I was thinking of how we sometimes fail to trust our Pilot through life. Do you know who I mean?"

Jan nodded. "God," she said.

"Yes," said Grandma. "Of course, the airplane pilot wouldn't have let you take over that flight, because it would have meant disaster. I'm glad God keeps control of our life, too—it's foolish for us to try to take over." *HWM*

HOW ABOUT YOU?

Are you enjoying your "trip through life"? Or do you fret about things that happen over which you have no control? Trust God. Remember that he loves you and will walk with you through whatever comes your way.

MEMORIZE:

"You will keep in perfect peace all who trust in you, whose thoughts are fixed on you!" Isaiah 26:3

Trust God with Your Life

Hot or Cold?

(Read 1 Timothy 6:6-12)

"It's so cold! I can't stand it a minute longer." Jess pulled his coat tightly around him.

"Oh, Jess," said Mom, "you were just as excited about coming downtown to see the Christmas lights as the rest of us! Now you're complaining, and we've only been here ten minutes."

"But I'll freeze to death!" chattered Jess.

"You will not freeze to death," replied Mother. "I can guarantee that!" She laughed. "Seems to me, I remember a day last July when you complained for an entire morning about the heat. You wished for winter, remember? You put Christmas music on the stereo. Now it's cold for real, and you're wishing for hot weather! Aren't you ever satisfied?"

"But, Mom . . . ," Jess protested.

"It's not that cold, honey," said Mother firmly. "I think you should listen to yourself sometimes. You never seem to be happy. If it's hot, you want it cold. If it's cold, you want it hot."

Jess did remember that day in July when he had complained about the heat! In fact, there had been more than one summer day when he had wished for winter. Suddenly he smiled. "Come on! Let's go see the rest of the Christmas lights." *LMW*

HOW ABOUT YOU?

Do you often wish for something you don't have? Or wish you could be doing something that you can't do? In his letter to Timothy, the apostle Paul wrote that Christians should be content no matter what their circumstances. So, instead of wishing for what you don't have, be thankful for what you do have. Listen to yourself talk. Are you a complainer, or are you content?

Be Content

MEMORIZE:
"Yet true religion with contentment is great wealth." 1 Timothy 6:6

Wishes

(Read Matthew 7:7-11)

Judy and Jack were playing in the attic when they found an old brass lamp. "Hey, this reminds me of the story of Aladdin's lamp," said Jack. "You know—the one where a magic genie told Aladdin he could have any three things he wanted. Wouldn't it be neat if we could have three wishes by rubbing this lamp?" Jack polished it on his sleeve.

"Yeah!" Judy exclaimed. "We could wish for a new video game and a million dollars."

"I heard that!" Mother smiled as she walked into the attic. "Suppose you could really have anything you wished for—as long as it wasn't a selfish wish. What would it be?" she asked.

"Hmmm. I guess it would be selfish to wish for a million dollars," said Judy thoughtfully. "I know—my wish would be that Grandma and Grandpa Wyler would come to know Jesus."

"That's a good wish." Mother nodded. "Anything else?"

"Well, I suppose a video game would be selfish, too," said Jack reluctantly. "How about if I'd wish to do lots of things to help others. Would that be OK?"

"Sounds fine," said Mother. "And you know, kids, there is a way to have your wishes granted—if they're proper wishes."

"How?" asked Judy. "This isn't really a magic lamp."

Mother laughed. "Of course not!" she said. "But God has promised to answer the prayers of his children."

"He doesn't give us everything we ask for, though," said Judy. "Sometimes he doesn't give us what we want because he knows it isn't good for us, right?"

"Right," agreed Mother.

"We also need to pray in Jesus' name," offered Jack, "and ask for his will to be done—not make selfish requests."

Mother nodded. "Good. Let's remember those things, and then let's boldly take our requests to God. And let's never forget to thank him for all his goodness to us." *SLK*

HOW ABOUT YOU?

Do you ever wish that you could find a "magic lamp"? Prayer is better. There are many, many things that Christians can have simply by asking God for them and trusting him for the answer.

MEMORIZE:

"Ask, using my name, and you will receive, and you will have abundant joy." John 16:24

God Answers Prayer

Scars

(Read John 20:24-29)

For as long as Peter could remember, his mother had had ugly, red scars on her face and hands. Although he loved her, he was embarrassed to be seen in public with her. Sometimes he even failed to tell her about school programs or picnics because he really didn't want her to go.

Mother knew how Peter felt, and one day she decided to talk to him about it. "Peter, you're ashamed of these scars, aren't you?" she asked gently.

Peter looked at the floor. "I . . . I guess so," he admitted. "But why will you never tell me how you got them?"

"I thought I was doing the right thing not to tell you," answered Mother, "but perhaps I was wrong. You see, you were just a little baby when I got these scars. We had a fire in the house one day, and the whole area where you were was ablaze. I ran in and grabbed you and wrapped you up in some blankets. I was able to shelter you as I ran out of the house. We both were all right, but as you can see, my hands and face never lost their ugly scars."

Tears came to Peter's eyes. "Oh, Mom," he cried, "you got them saving me! I didn't know! Can you ever forgive me?" Mother put her arms around Peter and squeezed him tight. Peter hugged her back. "Knowing what you did for me . . . it makes me love you more than ever!" he told her.

Mother smiled. "You know, Peter," she said, "you've had a lot of questions about what Jesus did for you on the cross. Maybe my scars can help you understand. You see, Jesus saw us in our sins—as helpless as a baby. So he gave himself—he bore the pain and suffering and died that we might have eternal life. His body was scarred, too. Can you understand that, Peter?" Slowly, Peter nodded. *HCT*

HOW ABOUT YOU?

Are you aware that Jesus gave his life for you? If you would like to know more, talk to a trusted friend or adult.

Jesus Died for You

MEMORIZE:
"For God so loved the world that he gave his only Son, so that everyone who believes in him will not perish but have eternal life." John 3:16

The Empty Box

(Read Luke 2:8-14)

"Oh, Mom! I'm so excited about my Christmas birthday party!" exclaimed Roger.

The Saturday before Christmas dawned bright and clear. Soon Roger's party was in progress, and it was a smashing success. Finally it was time to open gifts, and Roger was thrilled with each one. Then one of the boys said, "Here! There's one more gift."

"Who is it from?" Roger asked. "There's no card."

"Maybe it's on the inside," someone suggested.

Roger smiled and quickly removed the wrapping. "There's a note inside! It says, 'You share a birthday with someone who gives us gifts. Do you know who?'"

Chris answered, "I think I know."

"Who?" asked Roger.

"Jesus!" he explained.

"You're right," said Roger. "I wonder what kind of gifts we can give him for his birthday?"

"How about our praise?" asked John

"And our time and money?" added Brett.

"And our hearts," finished Roger.

Just then Mother entered the room carrying a beautiful cake that said, "Happy Birthday Roger and Jesus!" She told the kids that she was very proud of them for all the gifts they had talked about giving to Jesus. What about you? What gift will you give him this Christmas? *REP*

HOW ABOUT YOU?

Do you remember Jesus on Christmas Day? Do you get impatient when Mom and Dad take time to read the Christmas story before you're allowed to open your gifts? This year, give him a place of honor in your thoughts, words, and actions.

MEMORIZE:

"The Savior—yes, the Messiah, the Lord—has been born tonight in Bethlehem, the city of David!"
Luke 2:11

Remember Jesus on His Day

The Go-Between

(Read John 14:1-6)

Tonya, Mark, and Jon listened intently as Dad read the story of Rodney, a very poor boy who lived long ago in a faraway country. According to the story, Rodney had been told that the king of his country was very kind, so he decided to go see him and ask for help.

Arriving at the palace, Rodney was stopped at the gate. He explained that he wanted to see the king, but he was refused admission. *Now what shall I do?* wondered Rodney. *I know! I'll just climb over the wall way back over there.* He looked around carefully before he tried it. *Hey! This is pretty easy,* he decided, but at that very moment several fierce dogs inside the fence rushed up, and Rodney dropped back. *This won't work after all,* he thought. *The only way in is through the gate.* So he walked back to the gate, where, discouraged, he sat down at the side of the road.

Soon a carriage drove up, and a young man stepped out. "What's the matter?" asked the young man. Rodney explained his problem, and the young man nodded. "Come with me," he said. Then he gave orders, and the gates were opened. They went inside, and Rodney cringed when he heard the dogs barking. He could see them out of the corner of his eye. But again the young man gave orders, and the dogs were restrained.

Rodney was wide-eyed. "Why does everyone obey you?" he asked in wonder.

The young man smiled. "Because I am the prince," he replied. "And now we'll go see my father—King John." And so it was that Rodney was able to meet the king and ask for the help he needed. *HCT*

HOW ABOUT YOU?

Are you something like Rodney? Are you hoping someday to see God—the King of kings—and live with him in heaven? The prince was the "go-between" for Rodney. Because Rodney made his acquaintance, he gained admittance into the palace and into the presence of the king. So it is with you—you cannot get into heaven by yourself. You need a "go-between." The Bible says that Jesus is the only one who can be your mediator, or your "go-between."

Jesus Is Our "Go-Between"

MEMORIZE:
"For there is only one God and one Mediator who can reconcile God and people. He is the man Christ Jesus."
1 Timothy 2:5

The Chicken and the Eagle

(Read Romans 8:1-4, 12-13)

Matt curled up on the couch with his new animal storybook.

"Enjoying the story?" asked Mom.

"Yes," said Matt. "I've just finished it. It's about a baby eagle who thought he was a chick."

"How come?" asked his brother Brian, curiously.

"Well, when he was still inside an egg, the egg was stolen and taken to the henhouse," Matt informed Brian. "The hen didn't know that it was an eagle egg so she sat on it with the rest of her eggs. And after the eggs hatched, she brought him up exactly like one of her chicks."

"Someone should have told him he was an eagle," said Brian.

"Someone did!" said Matt quickly. "The wise old owl who lived near the farm told him he was an eaglet—and that he could fly high in the sky like the great eagle—but he didn't believe it. He lived like a chicken his whole life."

"Dumb!" pronounced Brian. "He could have soared in the skies and all he did was scratch the sand."

"We do that sometimes, too," remarked Mom.

"We do?" responded Matt. "We don't scratch in the sand."

"Well, not literally," said Mom. "But the Bible tells us that we were once slaves of sin, but Jesus came to set us free."

"In other words, sin used to be our boss, but when we become Christians, Jesus is our boss," said Matt.

"That's right," said Mom. "And like that eaglet who chose to live like a chicken, some Christians live like sin is the boss instead of Jesus." *MTF*

HOW ABOUT YOU?

Have you become a Christian yet? If so, Jesus is your new boss, not sin. And he has given you the power to soar above wrongdoing.

MEMORIZE:

"So Christ has really set us free. Now make sure that you stay free, and don't get tied up again in slavery to the law." Galatians 5:1

Don't Be a Slave to Sin

Just Different

(Read Romans 12:4-11)

"Four more days," said Jerry, "and we can watch the best ball game of the year." He picked up the football he had received for Christmas. "The next best thing to playing football," he declared, "is watching the Rose Bowl game."

"Football!" scoffed his sister Beth. "Best thing about football is that the season's almost over." She picked up the sports equipment she had received—a tennis racket and some bright yellow balls. "Now these are pretty," she declared.

Mother looked up. "Well, I might as well get into this discussion, too," she said. "Now, I think the best ball of all is my new bowling ball. It's big and beautiful. And it's going to help my bowling average—I just know it is."

Dad spoke up. "It's big all right," he agreed, "but if you want to see beauty, you need to take a look at my golf balls." Dad grinned. "Whoever would have thought that buying everybody sports equipment for Christmas would start a family feud?"

Jerry laughed. "As Mother is always saying, we'll just have to agree to disagree."

"Better yet," said Mother, "let's agree that everybody's sport is great. Not one of these various balls is better than the others—they're just all different. Each has its own special purpose."

"That's true," agreed Dad. "And that's the way it is with people, too. Some of us are skilled in one area and some in another. Some can sing. Others can speak well. Still others do a good job taking care of little children or building homes. Some are good in science, sports, or math. Just as it's unfair to compare a tennis ball and a bowling ball, it's unfair to compare people to each other. God made each one different and special." *HWM*

HOW ABOUT YOU?

Do you think someone is better than you because he has skills you'd like? Or do you think you're better than someone else because you can do something he can't? Don't compare people. God wants you to be yourself. Develop the skills he gave you.

God Made Each One Special

MEMORIZE:
"Having then gifts differing according to the grace that is given to us, let us use them." Romans 12:6, NKJV

Throw Out the Junk

(Read 2 Corinthians 5:16-21)

"Just think, Dad—we get to stay up till two o'clock!" Steve exclaimed as he told his dad about the New Year's Eve party his Sunday school class would be having.

"Sounds great," Dad said. Then, with a twinkle in his eye, he added, "Have I ever told you about the New Year's Eve celebrations we had when I was a boy back in Italy?"

"Did you have a parade or something?" Steve asked.

"Yes, and fireworks, too," Dad said. "But what happened that night was the most interesting part of the whole celebration. As midnight approached, people gathered up all their trash, old clothing, boxes, and whatever else they wanted to get rid of. There was a New Year's Eve custom of 'throwing out the old to make way for the new,' so they simply tossed it all out the windows."

"I'd sure hate to be the street cleaner the next day," Steve said, laughing.

Dad agreed. Then he said, "I think that we, as Christians, could learn a lesson from that strange custom," he said. "The Bible says, 'If anyone is in Christ, he is a new creation; the old has gone, the new has come!' But we sometimes try to 'put on' Christian habits—prayer, attending church, witnessing—without 'putting off' our sinful habits. God cannot bless us and help us to grow until we get rid of the 'old junk' in our life. Let's both make a list of some of the 'junk' we need to get rid of." *SLK*

HOW ABOUT YOU?

Do you sometimes wonder why it's so hard to do the right things, to form good habits, or to grow as a Christian? Perhaps there's some "junk" in your life that needs to be thrown out. It might be a record collection, immodest clothing, or questionable books and magazines. It might be cigarettes or drugs. Or maybe it's a sin like anger or envy. Whatever it is, get rid of it. God will give you something new and much better to take its place!

MEMORIZE:

"If anyone is in Christ, he is a new creation; the old has gone, the new has come!" 2 Corinthians 5:17, NIV

Throw Out Sinful Habits

A Good Police Officer

(Read Revelation 21:4-8)

"If God is so loving, I don't think he would keep people out of heaven," said Trevor firmly.

"Well," his friend Don began, praying for the right words to say, "the Bible—" A loud outburst of yelps from his dog interrupted the discussion. The boys rushed to the door just in time to see a boy ride off on Trevor's new bike. They ran after him, but soon realized it would do no good.

Trevor moaned. "Call your dad." Don's father was a police officer.

Don ran to the phone, and soon a squad car pulled up to the curb. Don's father emerged and led a young boy up to the house. Another officer lifted a mangled bike from the trunk. Trevor's jaw sagged as he recognized the bent frame, and he started shouting at the boy. Don's father held up his hand. "Calm down, Trevor," he said. "If that's your bike, this boy will have to pay for the damage."

Later that day, the boys resumed their discussion about whether God would send anyone to hell. When Trevor continued to insist that a loving God wouldn't do that, Don had an idea. "Hey, Trevor," he said, "why should the kid who took your bike today have to be punished for it?"

Trevor stared at him. "Because he stole it and ruined it!"

"But aren't you a loving person?" Don asked.

"Well, sure, but—" Trevor stopped. He saw where this conversation was going.

"What if my dad had seen that boy commit a crime but refused to do anything about it?" Don continued.

"He wouldn't refuse," replied Trevor. "He's a police officer!"

Don nodded. "It would be wrong for him to ignore crime," he agreed. Then he made his point. "God is holy and he can't ignore crime, either—the crime of sin. That's why he can't let sinners into heaven. But if we believe that Jesus took the punishment for our sins, then we can go to heaven."

"I guess you're right," Trevor said. He would give this matter more thought. *JAB*

HOW ABOUT YOU?

Because God is holy, he cannot allow sin to enter heaven. Because God is loving, he provided a way to heaven through Jesus. Do you know him personally? If not, talk to a trusted friend or adult to find out more.

MEMORIZE:
"The wicked will go down to the grave. This is the fate of all the nations who ignore God."
Psalm 9:17

God Is Holy

Meeting Father Time

(Read Philippians 4:11-13)

When John's mother made him shut off a violent program on TV, he headed for his room, muttering angrily to himself. "I hate being a kid," he growled as he climbed into bed. "I wish I was grown-up so I could do as I please!" It seemed only a moment later when he heard footsteps. "Is that you, Mom?" he asked.

A shaky voice answered. "No. My name is Father Time, and I understand you want to be older. I can make you any age you want to be."

John couldn't believe his ears! "What luck!" he murmured. "I think I'll be 21." Immediately he found himself in the middle of a battlefield! Bullets whizzed around him as he begged to move on to a different age.

Father Time agreed that John could move on if he wished. So he tried being 40. That was even worse! He found himself at his mother's funeral! After again begging to go on, John saw that at 50, he was a cross, worried businessman with no time for pleasure. "This is awful," grumbled John. "Can I be 65? I should be retired then, so I can take it easy."

Father Time again granted his wish, but, alas! Instead of enjoying his retirement, John found himself sick and dying. "I don't want to be here!" he cried. "I want to go back. I want my mother! Mother! Mother!"

The next thing John knew, Mother was beside him. "I'm here," she comforted. "You must have had a nightmare."

John was shaking, but he was so relieved! "I did," he said, "and you know what? I found out how good I've got it. I'm glad I'm a kid." *HCT*

HOW ABOUT YOU?

Are you eager to grow up? Don't be in such a hurry. Remember that every age has both advantages and handicaps. With God's help, let Jesus be the Lord of your life. Then you'll be content, and you'll get the very best out of life, no matter what age you are.

MEMORIZE:

"Be satisfied with what you have."
Hebrews 13:5

Enjoy Each Day

The Weight Lifter

(Read 1 Timothy 4:6-13)

Ryan dropped the weight he was holding. His face was covered with beads of sweat. "Mother has dinner ready, Champ," Dad said. "You need food as well as exercise, you know."

When Ryan finished his meal, he announced his plans for the evening—more weight lifting and exercise. Dad frowned. "You've been spending more than enough time working out," he said. "As a matter of fact, Son, you've been neglecting your chores. And what about homework?"

"Yes," added Mother, "and what about your devotional life? When you came back from the youth retreat, you told me God had shown you that you should spend some time each day with him. Have you been doing that?"

Ryan looked down at the floor in embarrassment. "There's nothing wrong with wanting to have a strong body, is there?" he asked.

"Not at all," replied Dad, "but a well-exercised body is only part of a complete person. The apostle Paul knew about exercise and training. He spoke often of running races and disciplining our bodies."

"He did?" Ryan's eyes widened in interest.

"Yes. He wrote to Timothy that bodily discipline or exercise could not compare with the benefits he obtained from spiritual exercise," replied Dad. "Just as you work hard to build up your muscles, so you must work at living God's way to build up your Christian life."

"You mean practicing things like Bible reading and prayer and sharing Christ with others. OK, Dad," he said. "I'll try to keep a balance between my physical and spiritual exercise." *LSR*

HOW ABOUT YOU?

Is there a special activity that takes too much of your time? Perhaps you play sports or have a pet with which you spend your free time. Maybe you spend a lot of time with your best friend. These things are fine, but be sure you don't neglect your time with God. As you begin a new year, remember that you need to take time each day for your spiritual exercise!

MEMORIZE:
"Physical exercise has some value, but spiritual exercise is much more important, for it promises a reward in both this life and the next."
1 Timothy 4:8

Get Spiritual Exercise

Index of Topics

Index of Scripture Readings

Index of Memory Verses

John 14:6 *March 19, August 24*
John 15:4 *September 27*
John 15:5 *June 23, September 15*
John 16:8 *November 5*
John 16:24 *December 22*
John 20:29 *March 28*
John 21:22 *April 30*
Acts 1:8 *February 9, December 9*
Acts 3:19 *August 19*
Acts 8:4 *July 16*
Acts 16:31 *May 7*
Acts 17:11 *November 18*
Acts 17:26 *September 22*
Acts 20:24 *November 7*
Acts 20:26-27 *August 10*
Romans 2:11 *March 30*
Romans 4:5 *December 15*
Romans 5:6 *June 29*
Romans 5:8 *January 21, March 29,*
   April 4
Romans 6:23 *August 12*
Romans 8:16 *April 9*
Romans 8:28 *March 24, November 27*
Romans 8:29 *March 27*
Romans 8:31 *February 18*
Romans 9:21 *November 11*
Romans 10:13 *February 23, May 6*
Romans 10:17 *April 5*
Romans 12:6 *September 24,*
   December 27
Romans 12:11 *May 13*
Romans 12:17b *December 4*
Romans 12:21 *September 23*
Romans 13:1 *February 13*
Romans 14:12 *February 10*
Romans 14:19 *May 20*
1 Corinthians 1:10 *November 9*
1 Corinthians 3:9 *June 26*
1 Corinthians 4:7 *October 7*
1 Corinthians 6:20 *June 2*
1 Corinthians 9:22 *September 20*

1 Corinthians 12:4-5 *November 2*
1 Corinthians 12:26 *August 4*
1 Corinthians 12:27 *April 21*
1 Corinthians 13:12 *December 16*
1 Corinthians 15:51 *May 2*
1 Corinthians 15:58 *June 6*
2 Corinthians 4:2 *October 10*
2 Corinthians 4:7 *September 25*
2 Corinthians 4:8 *September 13*
2 Corinthians 5:1 *October 22*
2 Corinthians 5:7 *June 7*
2 Corinthians 5:8 *July 24*
2 Corinthians 5:17 *September 11,*
   October 8, December 28
2 Corinthians 5:21 *March 26*
2 Corinthians 6:2 *March 2, May 23*
2 Corinthians 9:6 *February 6*
2 Corinthians 9:8 *May 8*
2 Corinthians 11:14 *July 6*
2 Corinthians 12:10 *September 9*
Galatians 2:20 *February 11, July 4*
Galatians 5:1 *December 26*
Galatians 5:9 *September 17*
Galatians 5:22 *May 22*
Galatians 5:22-23 *July 26*
Galatians 6:2 *October 2, November 8*
Galatians 6:9 *July 7*
Ephesians 2:8-9 *March 7*
Ephesians 2:10 *August 13*
Ephesians 3:19 *November 28*
Ephesians 4:14 *July 31*
Ephesians 4:24 *June 8*
Ephesians 4:27 *March 12*
Ephesians 4:29 *January 24,*
   November 14
Ephesians 4:32 *March 5*
Ephesians 6:2 *April 15*
Ephesians 6:2-3 *June 9*
Ephesians 6:10 *March 15*
Ephesians 6:11 *July 19, October 17*
Philippians 2:14 *March 11*

Philippians 3:21 *October 18*
Philippians 4:7 *April 26*
Philippians 4:8 *January 11*
Philippians 4:9 *October 3*
Philippians 4:13 *September 29, November 25*
Colossians 3:8 *July 13*
Colossians 3:8, 10 *January 12*
Colossians 3:12 *March 4*
Colossians 3:13 *December 6*
Colossians 3:15 *November 21*
Colossians 4:6 *May 31*
1 Thessalonians 2:12 *March 22*
1 Thessalonians 4:11 *November 29*
1 Thessalonians 5:17 *February 14*
1 Thessalonians 5:18 *August 5, 26*
2 Thessalonians 1:9 *February 27*
1 Timothy 2:5 *December 25*
1 Timothy 2:9-10 *October 11*
1 Timothy 4:8 *December 31*
1 Timothy 4:12 *April 2*
1 Timothy 6:6 *December 21*
1 Timothy 6:17 *September 16, December 17*
2 Timothy 1:12 *April 16*
2 Timothy 2:15 *April 25, June 22*
2 Timothy 2:19 *April 27*
2 Timothy 2:22 *July 11*
2 Timothy 3:4-5 *June 18*
Titus 2:14 *December 18*
Hebrews 1:9 *January 16*
Hebrews 4:15 *October 31*
Hebrews 10:24 *July 2*
Hebrews 10:24-25 *January 4*
Hebrews 10:25 *April 28, June 21, October 4*
Hebrews 13:5 *November 16, December 30*
Hebrews 13:17 *January 19*
James 1:2-3 *October 27*
James 1:4 *August 31*

James 1:13 *November 10*
James 1:15 *February 19, May 27*
James 1:22 *January 14, August 14*
James 2:9 *October 15*
James 2:10 *May 9, 18, October 1*
James 2:17 *June 11*
James 3:10 *June 25*
James 3:17 *February 21*
James 4:7 *January 31, April 1, August 6, October 12*
James 4:8 *August 22*
James 4:15 *June 27*
James 4:17 *May 29*
James 5:8 *July 10*
1 Peter 1:3 *April 8*
1 Peter 1:8 *October 6*
1 Peter 2:2 *April 10, May 4, November 24*
1 Peter 2:13 *October 14*
1 Peter 2:21 *December 5*
1 Peter 3:8 *March 23*
1 Peter 3:10 *January 20*
1 Peter 4:10 *October 30, December 10*
1 Peter 5:7 *January 17*
1 Peter 5:8 *January 10, August 15*
2 Peter 3:11 *March 20*
2 Peter 3:16 *June 16*
2 Peter 3:18 *February 5, June 28, December 19*
1 John 1:7 *May 28*
1 John 3:18 *September 30*
1 John 3:23 *October 23*
1 John 4:11 *February 28*
1 John 4:19 *June 30*
1 John 4:21 *February 25*
1 John 5:3 *February 1*
1 John 5:12 *October 26*
1 John 5:21 *April 3*
Jude 1:17 *December 8*
Revelation 3:20 *August 17*